# IN THE
# LIKENESS OF GOD

**Books by Philip Yancey and Dr. Paul Brand**

*Fearfully and Wonderfully Made*
*In His Image*
*The Gift of Pain*

**Books by Dr. Paul Brand**

*God's Forever Feast*
*Clinical Mechanics of the Hand*

**Books by Philip Yancey**

*The Bible Jesus Read*
*Church: Why Bother?*
*Disappointment with God*
*Finding God in Unexpected Places*
*I Was Just Wondering*
*The Jesus I Never Knew*
*Meet the Bible (with Brenda Quinn)*
*Prayer: Does It Make Any Difference?*
*Reaching for the Invisible God*
*A Skeptic's Guide to Faith*
*Soul Survivor*
*The Student Bible (with Tim Stafford)*
*What's So Amazing About Grace?*
*Where Is God When It Hurts?*

# IN THE
# LIKENESS OF GOD

THE DR. PAUL BRAND TRIBUTE EDITION OF
*FEARFULLY AND WONDERFULLY MADE*
AND *IN HIS IMAGE*

# DR. PAUL BRAND
# PHILIP YANCEY

**ZONDERVAN**®

**ZONDERVAN**.com/
**AUTHORTRACKER**
*follow your favorite authors*

We want to hear from you. Please send your comments about this book to us in care of zreview@zondervan.com. Thank you.

ZONDERVAN

*In the Likeness of God*
Copyright © 2004 by Philip Yancey

*Fearfully and Wonderfully Made*
Copyright © 1980 by Paul Brand and Philip Yancey

*In His Image*
Copyright © 1984 by Paul Brand and Philip Yancey

Requests for information should be addressed to:

Zondervan, *Grand Rapids, Michigan 49530*

Library of Congress Cataloging-in-Publication Data

Yancey, Philip.
    In the likeness of God : the Dr. Paul Brand tribute edition of Fearfully and wonderfully made and In His image / Philip Yancey and Paul Brand.
        p.  cm.
    Previous editions entered under Brand, Paul W.
    Rev. ed. of the authors Fearfully and wonderfully made. © 1980, and In His image. © 1984.
    Includes bibliographical references and index.
    ISBN 978-0-310-25742-4
    1. Church.    2. Body, Human—Religious aspects—Christianity.    I. Brand, Paul W.    II. Brand, Paul W. Fearfully and wonderfully made.    III. Brand, Paul W. In his image.    IV. Title.
BV600.5.Y36  2004
233'.5—dc22

                                                                2004005670

*Interior design by Michelle Espinoza*

*Printed in the United States of America*

10  11  12  13  14  •  23  22  21  20  19  18  17  16  15  14  13  12  11  10  9  8  7  6  5  4  3

*Sometimes when uncertain of a voice from its very loudness, we catch the missing syllable in the echo. In God and Nature we have Voice and Echo.*

Henry Drummond

# CONTENTS

# PREFACE

I first learned about Dr. Paul Brand in 1976 while writing my book *Where Is God When It Hurts?* As I was ensconced in libraries researching the problem of pain, my wife cleaned out the closet of a medical-supply house and in the process stumbled across an intriguing essay he had written on "The Gift of Pain." The author had a unique point of view. Whereas I had interviewed scores of people who wanted desperately to escape pain, Brand told of spending several million dollars trying to *create* a pain system for his patients. "Thank God for pain!" he said. "I cannot think of a more valuable gift for my leprosy patients."

An orthopedic surgeon, Dr. Brand had spent most of his medical career in India, where he made a dramatic discovery about leprosy, one of the oldest and most feared diseases. Careful research convinced him that the terrible manifestations of that cruel disease — missing toes and fingers, blindness, ulcers, facial deformities — all trace back to the single cause of painlessness. Leprosy silences nerve cells, and as a result its victims unwittingly destroy themselves, bit by bit, because they cannot feel pain. When he moved to a high-tech laboratory in the United States, he applied what he had learned about painlessness to other diseases, such as diabetes, thus helping to prevent tens of thousands of amputations each year.

Brand's ideas so captivated me that I called him out of the blue from Chicago and arranged an interview. We met on the grounds of the only leprosarium in the continental United States (later closed due to budget cuts). Louisiana authorities who founded the hospital in the nineteenth century situated it well away from population centers, and I drove along the Mississippi River for several hours from New Orleans to reach the tiny town of Carville. Laid out in sprawling, colonial style under massive live oak trees, the leprosarium resembled a movie set of a tropical plantation; it had, in fact, been built on the site of an antebellum plantation. Patients on crutches and in wheelchairs moved slowly along double-decker arched walkways that connected the major buildings.

I knew of Dr. Brand's stature in the world medical community in advance of my visit: offers to head up major medical centers in England and the U.S., distinguished lectureships all over the world, the hand-surgery procedures named in his honor, the prestigious Albert Lasker Award, his appointment as Commander of the Order of the British Empire by Queen Elizabeth II, his selection as the only Westerner to serve on the Mahatma Gandhi Foundation, his service as an expert consultant to the World Health Organization. His face appeared in the most unlikely places: alongside an article extolling the virtues of bare feet in the consumer magazine *Seventeen*, as a guest of Johnny Carson on *The Tonight Show*.

A slight man of less-than-average height and stiff posture entered the room where we had agreed to meet. He had graying hair, bushy eyebrows, and a face that creased deeply when he smiled. In a British accent — a striking contrast to the bayou tones heard in hospital corridors — he apologized for the flecks of blood on his lab coat, explaining that he had just been dissecting armadillos, the only nonhuman species known to harbor leprosy bacilli. He wore outdated clothes, lived in a rented bungalow on the hospital grounds, and drove an economical, run-down automobile. At heart, Paul Brand was still a missionary, unimpressed by and unaccustomed to relative prosperity and fame.

That first visit lasted a week. I accompanied Brand on his rounds, sitting beside him as he studied the ulcerated feet and hands of patients and visiting the labs that whirred with the sounds of early-generation VAX computers. At night in their wooden house on the hospital grounds, I would share a rice-and-curry meal with him and his wife, Margaret, a respected ophthalmologist. Then Paul would prop up his bare feet, and I would turn on the tape recorder for discussions that ranged from leprology and theology to world hunger and soil conservation. Every topic I brought up, he had already thought about in some depth. He quoted Shakespeare and discussed the derivation of Greek, Hebrew, and Latin words. During breaks he taught me such things as how to select a ripe fig (watch the ones butterflies light on several times, testing, before flitting on to their preferred overripe fruit) and how African weaver birds build their elaborate nests using only one foot and a beak.

The conversations that stand out sharpest to me now are those in which he recalled individual patients, "nobodies" on whom he had lavished medical attention. When he began his pioneering work, he was the only orthopedic surgeon in the world working among fifteen million victims of leprosy. He and Margaret performed several dozen surgical procedures on some of these patients, restoring rigid claws into usable hands through innovative tendon transfers, remaking feet, forestalling blindness, transplanting eyebrows, fashioning new noses.

He told me of his patients' family histories, the awful rejection they had experienced as the disease presented itself, the trial-and-error treatments of doctor and patient experimenting together. Almost always his eyes would moisten and he would wipe away tears as he remembered their suffering. To him these, among the most neglected people on earth, were not nobodies, but people made in the image of God, and he devoted his life to try to honor that image.

(Later, as I began working with Brand and following him around the world, I met many other dedicated Christians who devote their lives to healing the wounds of humanity. In India, for example, where less than 3 percent of the population claims to be Christian, nearly a fifth of all medical work is performed by Christian doctors and nurses, many of them trained at Brand's old hospital in Vellore. If you say the word "Christian" to an Indian peasant — who may never have heard of Jesus Christ — the first image to pop into her mind may well be that of a hospital, or of a medical van that stops by her village once a month to provide free, personal care. And most of the medical advances in the treatment of leprosy came from Christian missionaries, not always the best-trained in the field, but often the only ones willing to work with people suffering from that feared disease.)

We made an odd couple, Dr. Brand and I. He was a silver-haired surgeon characterized by proper British reserve, and I an eager young journalist in my mid-twenties with bushy Art Garfunkel–style hair. I had interviewed many subjects: actors and musicians, politicians, successful business executives, Olympic athletes, Nobel laureates, and Pulitzer Prize winners. Something attracted me to Brand at a deeper level than I had felt with any other interview subject. My father died just after my first birthday, and in many ways Dr. Brand became a father-figure to me. Already an adult when I met him, I didn't have to go through teenage rebellion and the agony of individuation. I sat at his feet from the first day we met.

For perhaps the first time, I encountered genuine humility. The apostle Paul pointed to Jesus as an example of humility: "Your attitude should be the same as that of Christ Jesus: Who, being in very nature God, did not consider equality with God something to be grasped, but made himself nothing, taking the very nature of a servant, being made in human likeness." Meeting Dr. Brand, I realized that I had misconstrued humility as a negative self-image. Paul Brand obviously knew his gifts: he had finished first throughout his academic career and had attended many awards banquets honoring his accomplishments. Yet he recognized his gifts as just that, *gifts* from a loving Creator, and used them in a Christlike way of service.

When I first met him, Brand was still adjusting to life in the United States. Everyday luxuries made him nervous, and he longed for a simple life close to the soil. He knew presidents, kings, and celebrities, yet he rarely mentioned them. He talked openly about his failures and always tried to deflect credit for his successes to his associates. Most impressive to me, the wisest and most brilliant man I have ever met devoted much of his life to some of the lowest people on the planet: members of the Untouchable caste in India afflicted with leprosy.

After I had spent a few days at Carville and earned his trust, Dr. Brand admitted to me somewhat shyly that he had once attempted a book. Some years before, after he had delivered a series of talks to the Christian Medical College in Vellore, India, other faculty members encouraged him to write them down for publication. He made the effort, but the material filled only ninety pages, not enough for a book. Twenty years had passed, and he had not touched the manuscript since.

I persuaded him to dig through closets and bureau drawers until he located the badly smudged third carbon copy of those chapel talks, and that night I sat up long past midnight reading his remarkable meditations on the human body. I was staying in the hospital's vaulted antebellum guest room, and a ceiling fan periodically scattered the onionskin pages around the room. I kept gathering them up and resorting them, though, for I knew I had struck gold.

Brand wrote, "I have come to realize that every patient of mine, every newborn baby, in every cell of its body, has a basic knowledge of how to survive and how to heal, that exceeds anything that I shall ever know. That knowledge is the gift of God, who has made our bodies more perfectly than we could ever have devised." In ninety pages, he expressed that sense of wonder about the human body.

The next day I asked Brand if he would allow me to collaborate with him, expanding his medical and spiritual insights and adding more stories from his life. "It will be a very different book than this," I warned him. "But I sense something unique in these pages, and I would like to bring it to light." Eventually our collaboration led to two full-length books, combined now after his death in this tribute edition.*

As Brand saw it, studying the human body, a worthy endeavor in itself, yields an unexpected bonus. It sheds light on a metaphor used more than thirty times in the New Testament: the Body of Christ, in which the church is presented as a universal Body comprising individual members joined to Jesus Christ as Head. A likeness exists between the human body and spiritual Body, a likeness that derives from their common Source.

---

*In this edition, we have updated the relevant statistics and made slight revisions. We have, however, retained the present-tense voice of Dr. Brand in such phrases as "Now I have my own laboratory" and "Today when I visit India," as expressed in the original.

Dr. Brand described his writing journey this way: "In a sense we doctors are like employees at the complaint desk of a large department store. We tend to get a biased view of the quality of the product when we hear about its aches and pains all day. In this little manuscript, which I set aside long ago, I tried instead to pause and wonder at what God made, the human body. Then I lifted an analogy from the New Testament and updated it with the expanded knowledge we've gained from modern science. Curiously, every medical discovery seems to make the body analogy fit even better; not one has weakened the original meanings the apostle Paul set forth."

The idea of a book based on analogy attracted me because I too appreciate the harmony between the natural and spiritual worlds. Christians have largely abandoned the natural world to physics, geology, biology, and chemistry. In contrast, Brand strove to bring the two worlds, natural and spiritual, back together.

As I worked on this material, I had the sense of wrestling with several different books at once. I wanted to capture the essence of Dr. Brand's remarkable life practicing medicine on three different continents. In addition, I hoped to convey an appreciation for the human body by rendering medical facts in an appealing style. And, of course, the real core of the book lay in its spiritual application, drawn from analogy, that sometimes expressed reverence, sometimes praise, and sometimes prophetic challenge.

In every chapter, on almost every page, I strained to keep these three disparate kinds of material in balance. I often felt as if one or another of the three books was taking over, and I struggled to shape a unified book out of the three approaches. I persevered because I recognized that Dr. Brand offered a unique blend of gifts. Even after fifty years of medical practice, he retained a boyish enthusiasm for the grandeur of the human body. In two decades of missionary service in India he had gained fresh and profound insights into Christian truth. And, along the way, he experienced adventures and personal encounters with patients that were as dramatic and poignant as any I had come across.

The book got off to a rough start. The first publisher we approached turned it down. Then I accidentally left the first and only draft in a motel room (a substantial reward helped the motel staff remember that the sheaf of papers had not been thrown away after all). When *Fearfully and Wonderfully Made* finally went to press in 1980, Dr. Brand and I, as well as our publisher, awaited results with some trepidation. It was a difficult book to describe and present. Few books of analogies exist, and we could not predict how the public would respond.

More than two decades have passed, and some 700,000 readers have bought copies of *Fearfully and Wonderfully Made* or its sequel *In His Image*. We have heard from many of them: pregnant women thanking us for helping them appreciate the miracle of life and birth, medical students crediting these books for helping push them toward a career in medicine, high school and college biology teachers who use excerpts in their classes, and many other readers simply grateful for an opportunity to pause and reflect on the multiple wonders of the human body.

Sometime later Dr. Brand and I worked on a third volume, *The Gift of Pain*, a more biographical treatment, which focuses on his theories of pain. In all I have spent almost ten years following the threads of Dr. Brand's life. The more I questioned him, the more I seemed to be unraveling a giant skein. I would tug at one thread, and out would come a story from India I had not heard before, which would lead to a digression on why blue jeans feel cool to the touch while flannel feels warm. Somehow that conversation would lead to a spiritual point, perhaps a dissertation on Job or one of Jesus' parables.

My own writing took a different tack after these three books with Dr. Brand, turning more personal and meditative. Now I look back with nostalgia on the decade we spent working together. I had grand subjects to work with: the entire world of creation and specifically the magnificent human body; the exotic life of a surgeon who brought healing to people who knew no physical pain and therefore much suffering; and the mystery of Christ's Body, surely the most precarious venture ever made by God, entrusting the divine reputation to the likes of us his fickle followers.

Paul Brand was both a good and a great man, and I am forever grateful for the time we spent together. My faith grew as I observed with a journalist's critical eye a person enhanced in every way by his relationship with God.

Dr. Brand and I used to joke about the collaborative process. He said he felt guilty because he merely answered my questions and a few years later a book would emerge. I responded that all I did was ask questions, research, and write up the answers, whereas he had spent a lifetime serving leprosy patients in desolate places.

There was another exchange at work too, I now see — a trade with eternal significance. Wounded by the church, plagued by doubts, I had neither the maturity nor the ability to express much of my own fledgling faith. Yet I could write with utter integrity about Dr. Brand's faith, and through that process his words and thoughts became mine too. I now view the ten years I spent working with him as an important chrysalis stage. As a journalist, I gave words to his faith. In exchange, he gave faith to my words.

True friends get their measure, over time, in their effect on you. As I compare the person I was on our first meeting and the person I am now, I realize that large changes have occurred within me, with Paul Brand responsible for many of them.

I have written honestly about my early struggles, due in large part to lengthy exposure to toxic churches. I can imagine God taking great delight in steering me to Dr. Brand (through my wife's serendipitous discovery of his essay in a closet, of course) at a critical time in my spiritual journey. *Okay, Philip, you've seen some of the worst the church has to offer. Now I'll show you one of the best.*

In the movie *Manhattan*, Woody Allen turns to a woman he's courting and says, "You're God's answer to Job." He explains that when Job whines about how awful the world is, God could at least point and say, "but I can still make one of these." Similarly, as I grappled with the injustices of this world, the problem of pain, and other imponderables of theology, I could look to Paul Brand as a shining example of what God had in mind with the human experiment.

As much as anyone, he has helped set my course in outlook, spirit, and ideals. I look at the natural world, and environmental issues, largely through his eyes. From him I also have gained assurance that the Christian life I had heard in theory can actually work out in practice. It is indeed possible to live in modern society, achieve success without forfeiting humility, serve others sacrificially, and yet emerge with joy and contentment. To this day, whenever I doubt that, I look back on my time with Paul Brand.

As the years passed, our roles inevitably reversed. He started calling me for advice on such matters as which word processing software to use, how to organize research notes, and how to deal with publishers. After retiring from medical practice, the Brands moved to a small cottage overlooking Puget Sound in Seattle, the only home they ever owned. Paul served a few terms as president of the International Christian Medical and Dental Society, consulted with the World Health Organization, and into his eighties continued to lecture throughout the world. In 2001 he announced with pride that he and Margaret had become U.S. citizens.

Inevitably, health problems set in with age. Brand suffered a stroke on a trip to Turkey and a mild heart attack in London. For a time his speech slurred noticeably and his ability to recall names and events faded. Our conversation moved to issues of aging and mortality.

I got a call in June 2003 informing me that Dr. Brand had fallen while carrying a box of books to the second-floor office in his cottage. He had hit his head on the banister, and was now lying in a coma in a Seattle hospital. My wife and I were due to leave in a few days for a trip to New Zealand, and after some persistent calls United Airlines allowed us to reroute the trip through Seattle.

We spent five hours in an intensive-care room with the Brands' immediate family. Their five daughters and one son had gathered from scattered homes in England, Hawaii, Minnesota, and Washington. Paul was receiving expert medical attention (one daughter is a doctor, two are nurses, and two of their husbands are doctors), but it was clear to everyone that he would not recover. Dr. Brand had always insisted on no extraordinary measures should he ever reach a brain-damaged state, and an emotional family council had honored his wishes. He was receiving hydration, but no ventilator assistance with his breathing.

The fall itself had not caused the main damage. Only later that day, after he had complained of headaches, had his wife driven him to the emergency room. After the fall, a blood clot developed in the brain, and subsequent surgery, combined with blood-thinning medication that he took for strokes, led to further bleeding that destroyed most of his higher brain functions. First he became uncharacteristically combative, then lost speech, then slipped into the coma from which he never awoke.

Now he lay curled almost in a fetal position, his breathing heavy and raspy, his body moving restlessly from side to side. A long S-shaped scar creased his shaved head, blotched here and there with purple bruises, a mark of the surgery. Monitors flashed digital readouts of his pulse, blood pressure, and respiration, and a tube drained excess brain fluid into a plastic container. The hospital room overlooked beautiful Seattle and the mountain ranges that Dr. Brand so loved, but his eyes were vacant, uncomprehending.

In an email I had read on the plane, his daughter Pauline had recalled a scene from *The Lion, the Witch and the Wardrobe*: "It's when the two girls find Aslan's body shaved and bound up, and see that although such things had been done in order to strip the lion of his dignity they have only succeeded in emphasizing it. That's how it is with Dad's poor half-shaved head, and the ugly semi-circle of staples from the surgery, and the multitude of tubes taped to his face, neck and chest. Within it all, there is his grand old face. . . ."

By his bedside, suddenly I was overcome with emotion and could not speak. For nearly thirty years Paul Brand had been the towering giant in my life, the one to whom I turned for guidance, wisdom, inspiration, and faith. Now only a shell was left, the physical body we had written about. I bent over and kissed the smooth, baby-like skin on his shaven head.

His left hand grasped out for something to hold, and I put my hand in his. Incredibly, almost eerily, he began examining it with his fingers, running his own fingers up and down mine, squeezing, testing, analyzing. As I stood there, he did the same thing with his own right hand, which lay useless at his side. The instincts of fifty years of hand surgery had so imprinted on the synapses of his brain that even with much of it destroyed, this remained. Often he had told me that he could remember his patients' hands better than their faces. Now he could not speak, probably could not think, could barely breath, but still he reached out with the hands that had brought healing to so many.

A few days later, from an email received halfway around the world, I learned he had taken his last breath on July 8, a week before his eighty-ninth birthday. All that week, at unexpected times — waking up, in the shower, while praying — I would find myself sobbing. "What's wrong?" my wife asked the first few times. "I miss Dr. Brand," was my only answer. A phrase kept going through my mind: *I am not ready to walk alone.*

We returned to Seattle a month later for a public memorial service on the campus of CRISTA, a Christian relief organization, which both of the Brands served as board members. "A celebration of the life of Paul Brand," the service was billed, and indeed it was. Representatives from the hand-surgery society and leprosy missions, a delegate from the hospital in Vellore, India, as well as medical residents and ordinary citizens of Seattle and elsewhere who had been touched by his life gathered to pay tribute.

When it came my turn to speak, first I removed my shoes and socks and stood barefoot. It seemed somehow appropriate to honor in this small way a man who slipped off his own shoes at any opportunity, who lobbied against "No shoes, no shirt, no service" policies, and who had spent thousands of hours investigating how best to protect the insensitive feet of his leprosy patients, for whom tight shoes or rough sandals represented danger.

I also borrowed an object lesson from Dr. Brand himself, one I had seen him give in the stately chapel of Wheaton College in Illinois. In the middle of his address, he had reached in his pocket and pulled out a cluster of grapes. He stopped talking, took a plump, juicy grape, chewed it, then spat out the seeds on the plush carpet. After the audience laughter died down, he went on to make a serious point. He was speaking on the fruit of the Spirit described by Paul in Galatians 5: love, joy, peace, patience, kindness, goodness, faithfulness, gentleness, and self-control.

"These qualities are good for you in every way," he went on to explain. "They are qualities of God, and God's Spirit wants to grow them inside you. Yet as someone who has grown fruit trees, I also know that from the fruit's perspective, the ultimate goal is reproduction. The fruit is attractive and beautiful so that a bird or perhaps a person will find that grape, or apple, or blackberry, pick it, and do just what I have done: spit out the seed on the ground. If we were meeting outside, rather than in this beautiful chapel, I could come back in ten years or so and find a grape vine growing as a result of my sermon illustration this morning."

Later, in private conversation, I got a fuller version. Brand described how an apple or pear is weighted so that when it falls to the ground, it makes a slight indentation in the soil, and contains just enough meat to nourish the seeds inside. He observed, somewhat presciently, "My active life is mostly behind me. But I pray that my life and the principles that God has helped me to live by will continue to influence young lives. When we die we not only leave seed, but we also leave an effect on the soil in which future children grow and future spiritual seed will be nourished."

The morning of the memorial service, despite visits to several Seattle supermarkets, my wife and I could find only seedless grapes. I resorted to cherries, liberally spraying the seeds around the carpeted platform as I explained the object lesson. I then switched analogies, for in the hospital room where Dr. Brand lay dying I had remembered a trip we took to the Quinalt rain forest on the Olympic peninsula. In that moss-covered forest, which supports the greatest biomass of vegetation on earth, he pointed out to me a feature known as a "colonnade."

When one of the giant evergreen trees falls to the ground, seeds from the cones sprout and send out roots in search of soil. They find instead the dead bark and meat of the mother tree, which becomes a "nurse log" providing the nutrients needed for growth. After many years pass, you can return to the site of the fallen tree, which has now disintegrated, and see its very shape from the long colonnade of young trees whose roots form a series of arches over where the mother tree once lay.

I still am not ready to walk alone. But that I walk at all on this perilous journey of faith depends in large part on the strength I received from a giant of faith against whom I leaned for thirty years as one leans against a towering tree of the forest. As we heard in that memorial service, the colonnade left by Paul Brand stretches long and far, spanning continents, affecting not just fellow surgeons, but nurses, leprosy patients, neighbors, and ordinary people whose lives he touched.

I know no one who better illustrates Jesus' most-quoted statement, that "whoever loses his life for my sake will find it." From the perspective of a success-obsessed culture, an orthopedic surgeon spending his professional life among some of the poorest and most oppressed people on the planet is an example of "losing his life." Yet Dr. Brand lived as full and rich a life as anyone I know, combining humility, gratitude, and a grand sense of adventure.

Simone Weil once said, "Imaginary evil [such as that portrayed in books and movies] is romantic and varied; real evil is gloomy, monotonous, barren, boring. Imaginary good is boring; real good is always new, marvelous, intoxicating." I saw real goodness in Paul Brand, and found it new, marvelous, and intoxicating. I feel privileged, as his coauthor, to have had some role in shining a light on his life. You need only meet one saint to believe, to silence the noisy arguments of the world, and I had the inestimable privilege of spending leisurely hours getting to know a distinguished and faithful follower of Jesus. For that, Paul Brand, I thank you.

*Philip Yancey*

# FEARFULLY AND WONDERFULLY MADE

*Men go abroad to wonder at the height of mountains, at the huge waves of the sea, at the long courses of the rivers, at the vast compass of the ocean, at the circular motion of the stars; and they pass by themselves without wondering.*

Saint Augustine

*You created my inmost being; you knit me together in my mother's womb. I praise you because I am fearfully and wonderfully made.*

Psalm 139:13–14

# CELLS

# Chapter 1

# MEMBERS

*I have been trying to think of the earth as a kind of organism, but it is no go. I cannot think of it this way. . . . The other night, driving through a hilly, wooded part of southern New England, I wondered about this. If not like an organism, what is it like, what is it most like? Then, satisfactorily for that moment, it came to me: it is most like a single cell.*

Lewis Thomas

I remember the first time I saw a living cell under a microscope. I was twenty-one years old and taking a short course in tropical hygiene at Livingstone College in England. We had been studying parasites, but our specimens were dead; I wanted to see a living amoeba. Early one morning, before the laboratory was cluttered with students, I sneaked into the old science building. The imposing red brick structure stood next to a pond from which I had just scooped some water in a teacup. Bits of decomposing leaves floated in the turbid water, smelling of decay and death.

But when I touched one drop of that water to a microscope slide, a universe sprang to life. Hundreds of organisms crowded into view: delicate, single-celled globes of crystal, breathing, unfurling, flitting sideways, excited by the warmth of my microscope light. I edged the slide a bit, glancing past the faster organisms. Ah, there it was. An amoeba. A mere chip of translucent blue, it was barely visible to my naked eye, but the microscope revealed even its inner workings.

Something about the amoeba murmurs that it is one of the most basic and primordial of all creatures. Somehow it has enlisted the everyday forces of millions of spinning atoms so that they now serve life, which differs profoundly from mere matter. Just an oozing bit of gel, the amoeba performs all the basic functions that my body does. It breathes, digests, excretes, reproduces. In its own peculiar way it even moves, plumping a hummock of itself forward and following with a motion as effortless as a drop of oil spreading on a table. After one or two hours of such activity, the grainy, watery blob will have traveled a third of an inch.

That busy, throbbing drop gave me my first graphic image of the jungle of life and death we share. I saw the amoeba as an autonomous unit with a fierce urge to live and a stronger urge to propagate itself. It beckoned me on to explore the living cell.

—

Years later I am still observing cells, but as a physician I focus on how they cooperate within the body.

Now I have my own laboratory, at a leprosy hospital on swampy ground by the Mississippi River in Carville, Louisiana. Again I enter the lab early before anyone is stirring, this time on a chilly winter morning. Only the soft buzz of fluorescent lights overhead breaks the quietness.

But I have not come to study amoebae. This morning I will examine a hibernating albino bat who sleeps in a box in my refrigerator. I rely on him to study how the body responds to injury and infection. I lift him carefully, lay him on his back, and spread his wings in a cruciform posture. His face is weirdly human, like the shrunken heads in museums. I keep expecting him to open an eye and shriek at me, but he doesn't. He sleeps.

As I place his wing under the microscope lens, again a new universe unfolds. I have found a keyhole. The albinic skin under his wing is so pale that I can see directly through his skin cells into the pulsing capillaries which carry his blood. I focus the microscope on one bluish capillary until I can see individual blood cells pushing, blocking, thrusting through it. Red blood cells are by far the most numerous: smooth, shiny discs with centers indented like jelly doughnuts. Uniform size and shape make them seem machine-stamped and impersonal.

More interesting are the white blood cells, the armed forces of the body which guard against invaders. They look exactly like the amoebae: amorphous blobs of turgid liquid with darkened nuclei, they roam through the bat's body by extending a finger-like projection and humping along to follow it. Sometimes they creep along the walls of the veins; sometimes they let go and free-float in the bloodstream. To navigate the smaller capillaries, bulky white cells must elongate their shapes, while impatient red blood cells jostle in line behind them.

Watching the white cells, one can't help thinking them sluggish and ineffective at patrolling territory, much less repelling an attack. Until the attack occurs, that is. I take a steel needle and, without waking the bat, prick through its wing, puncturing a fine capillary. An alarm seems to sound. Muscle cells contract around the damaged capillary wall, damming up the loss of precious blood. Clotting agents halt the flow at the skin's surface. Before long, scavenger cells appear to clean up debris, and fibroblasts, the body's reweaving cells, gather around the injury site. But the most dramatic change involves the listless white cells. As if they have a sense of smell (we still don't know how they "sense" danger), nearby white cells abruptly halt their aimless wandering. Like beagles on the scent of a rabbit, they home in from all directions to the point of attack. Using their unique shape-changing qualities, they ooze between overlapping cells of capillary walls and hurry through tissue via the most direct route. When they arrive, the battle begins.

Lennart Nilsson, the Swedish photographer famous for his remarkable closeups of activity inside the body, has captured the battle on film as seen through an electron microscope. In the distance, a shapeless white cell, resembling science fiction's creature "The Blob," lumbers toward a cluster of luminous green bacterial spheres. Like a blanket pulled over a corpse, the cell assumes their shape; for awhile they still glow eerily inside the white cell. But the white cell contains granules of chemical explosives, and as soon as the bacteria are absorbed the granules detonate, destroying the invaders. In thirty seconds to a minute only the bloated white cell remains. Often its task is a kamikaze one, resulting in the white cell's own death.

In the body's economy, the death of a single white cell is of little consequence. Most only live several days or several weeks, and besides the fifty billion active ones prowling the adult human, a backup force one hundred times as large lies in reserve in the bone marrow. At the cellular level, massive warfare is a daily fact of life. Fifty thousand invaders may lurk on the rim of a drinking glass, and a billion can be found in a half-teaspoon of saliva. Bacteria enshroud my body — every time I wash my hands I sluice five million of them from the folds of my skin.*

---

*The quantities of bacteria viewed through the first effective microscopes so overwhelmed scientists that subsequent generations have lived in vivid awareness of "germs." Astute promoters market disinfectants to sterilize our environment, but too often the germ-killer, merely a cell-killer, also destroys the body's good cells. Today we need better publicity

To combat these threats, some of the blood's white cells are specifically targeted to one type of invader. If the body has experienced contact with a severe danger, as in a smallpox vaccination, it imprints certain white cells with a death-wish to combat that single danger. These cells spend their lives coursing through the bloodstream, waiting, scouting. Often they are never called upon to give battle. But if they are, they hold within them the power to disarm a foreign agent that could cause the destruction of every cell in the body.

⟞

Often I have reflected on the paradox of the amoeba and its mirror image, the white cell. The amoeba, a self-contained organism, alone performs all the basic functions of life, depending on other cells only when it ingests them as food. The white cell, though similar in construction and makeup, in a sense is far less free. A larger organism determines its duties, and it must sometimes sacrifice its life for the sake of that organism. Although more limited in self-expression, the white cell performs a singularly vital function. The amoeba flees danger; the white cell moves toward it. A white cell can keep alive a person like Beethoven or Newton or Einstein ... or you and me.

I sometimes think of the human body as a community, and then of its individual cells such as the white cell. The cell is the basic unit of an organism; it can live for itself, or it can help form and sustain the larger organism. I recall the apostle Paul's use of analogy in 1 Corinthians 12 where he compares the church of Christ to the human body. That inspired analogy takes on even more meaning to

---

for our bodies' able defenses and perhaps less fear of germs — the average American household is in more danger from chemical germ-killers than from germs. I prefer to leave the battle to my own cells.

me because of the expanded vistas allowed by the invention of microscopes. Since Paul's analogy renders a basic principle of God's creation, I can augment it like this:

> The body is one unit, though it is made up of many cells, and though all its cells are many, they form one body.... If the white cell should say, because I am not a brain cell, I do not belong to the body, it would not for that reason cease to be part of the body. And if the muscle cell should say to the optic nerve cell, because I am not an optic nerve, I do not belong to the body, it would not for that reason cease to be part of the body. If the whole body were an optic nerve cell, where would be the ability to walk? If the whole body were an auditory nerve, where would be the sense of sight? But in fact God has arranged the cells in the body, every one of them, just as he wanted them to be. If all cells were the same, where would the body be? As it is, there are many cells, but one body.

That analogy conveys a more precise meaning to me because though a hand or foot or ear cannot have a life separate from the body, a cell does have that potential. It can be part of the body as a loyalist, or it can cling to its own life. Some cells do choose to live in the body, sharing its benefits while maintaining complete independence — they become parasites or cancer cells.

# Chapter 2

# SPECIALIZATION

*To be a member is to have neither life, being, nor movement,*
*except through the spirit of the body, and for the body.*

Blaise Pascal

The scientist who collects and catalogs and the child who wanders barefoot through the woods are equally awestruck by the sheer profusion of creatures that populate this planet. The child marvels at the psychedelic design of a butterfly; she chases darting "skeeter hawks" (dragonflies), yelps at the spastic leap of a click beetle, breathlessly fondles a baby rabbit. The scientist looks closer. He takes a simple block of forest soil, one foot square and one inch deep, and begins counting. In this loamy world that we so thoughtlessly tread upon he finds "an average of 1,356 living creatures, including 865 mites, 265 springtails, 22 millipedes, 19 adult beetles, and various numbers of 12 other forms."[1] Without an electron microscope and infinite patience he cannot bother with the two billion bacteria and the millions of fungi and algae.

In his laboratory, the scientist begins with our friend the amoeba and works up, classifying from the "lower" to the "higher." What is this term "lower"? How can we trample a million creatures on a hike and return home guiltless? A devout vegetarian who gulps cold spring water imbibes a horde of creatures — animals! — without flinching. Why do we wince at a bloodied cat along the roadside but take no notice of the billions of tiny animals pulverized by the bulldozer scraping out a roadbed?

The key to our ranking of worth is specialization: the process of cells taking turns, dividing up labor, limiting their responses to a single task. We recognize a more meaningful life in the cat, a higher animal consisting of lower cells working together. The amoeba on my microscope slide is the animal at the bottom of the zoological ladder. It moves, yes, but barely an inch a day. It may spend its lifetime confined to a tin can or the hollowed part of an old tire. Unlike some humans, it will never tour Europe, visit the Taj Mahal, climb the Rockies. To do that one needs specialized muscle cells, rows and rows of them, aligned like stalks of wheat. The lower animals skitter, creep, or worm along, covering mere yards of turf. The higher ones hop and leap and gallop. Others, winged creatures, vault and soar and dive. It is a matter of specialization.

Consider the organ of sight. An amoeba has some crude visual awareness: it moves toward light — and that is all. Specialization gives the human the ability to be on the viewing end of the microscope, eyeing the subtleties of color in the near-senseless amoeba. The amoeba has one cell. Inside my human eye, peering at him, are 107,000,000 cells. Seven million are cones, each loaded to fire off a message to the brain when a few photons of light cross them. Cones give me the full band of color awareness, and because of them I can easily distinguish a thousand shades of color. The other hundred million cells are rods, backup cells for use in low light. When only rods are operating, I do not see color (as on a moonlit night when everything looms in shades of gray), but I can distinguish a spectrum of light so broad that the brightest light I perceive is a billion times brighter than the dimmest.

Between the amoeba and my eye exists a boggling range of specialization. The Copilia, a species of animal living in the Bay of Naples, has only one visual receiver, a cone cell attached to a muscular stalk which scans like a roving television camera. Although the Copilia can absorb only one light message at a time, presumably its brain can merge many messages into a crude picture of its environment.

The human brain receives millions of simultaneous reports from eye cells. If its designated wavelength of light is present, each rod or cone triggers an electrical response to the brain. The brain then absorbs a composite set of yes or no messages from all the rods and cones. It sorts and organizes them all and gives me an image of an amoeba swimming on my microscope slide. Compared to the amoeba's one-celled independence, the stationary lives of my rods and cones appear drab indeed. But who among us would trade ends of the eyepiece?

For specialization to work, the individual cell must lose all but one or two of its abilities. A rod or cone cell cannot locomote, while an amoeba can perform a whole array of minuscule activities. But the human cell can, through its limited role, make possible much "higher," more meaningful achievement. A single rod can provide me with the wavelength of light that completes my appreciation of a rainbow, a kingfisher plunging into a stream, or a subtle change of expression in the face of a dear friend. Or it may protect me from disaster by firing off a message to the brain when a rock is hurled from an expressway bridge at my approaching car.

—7.

In exchange for its self-sacrifice, the individual cell can share in what I call the ecstasy of community. No scientist can yet measure how a sense of security or pleasure is communicated to the cells of the body, but individual cells certainly participate in our emotional reactions. Hormones and enzymes bathe them, bringing on a quickened breathing, a trembling of muscles, a flapping in the stomach. If you look for a pleasure nerve in the human body, you will come away disappointed; there is none. There are nerves for pain and cold and heat and touch, but no nerve gives a sensation of pleasure. Pleasure appears as a by-product of cooperation by many cells.

What about sexual pleasure? Even that is not as specific and localized as you may think. Erogenous zones have no specialized pleasure nerves; the cells concentrated there also sense touch and pain. Besides the touch stimulation of skin against skin, sex includes a sense of need and visual delight, memories, and perhaps the auditory stimulus of background music. We also bring to sex that compulsion of romance that loves oneself and another at the same moment. At a still deeper, cellular level lies an urge to propagate life, to ensure survival, which is programmed into every cell. All these factors work together to produce sexual pleasure.

I greatly enjoy another human pleasure: listening to a symphony orchestra. When I do, the chief source of what I interpret as pleasure is located inside my ear. There I can detect sound frequencies that flutter my eardrums as faintly as one billionth of a centimeter (a distance one tenth the diameter of a hydrogen atom). This vibration is transmitted into my inner ear by three bones familiarly known as the hammer, anvil, and stirrup. When the frequency of middle C is struck on a piano, the piston of bones in my inner ear vibrates 256 times a second. Further in are individual cilia, comparable to the rods and cones of the eye, that transmit specific messages of sound to the brain. My brain combines these messages with other factors — how well I like classical music, how familiar I am with the piece being played, the state of my digestion, the friends I am with — and offers the combination of impulses in a form I perceive as pleasure.

Nature includes some organisms who cooperate but cannot quite pull off this ecstasy of community. For example, certain strains of amoebae come together for the purpose of reproduction. These "social amoebae," as few as ten and as many as five hundred thousand, join in a short-lived phenomenon called a slime mold. They group in an orderly fashion, forming a tiny, lustrous, bullet-shaped slug. As the slug inches forward, it leaves a trail of slime, hence the name. The cells in front cooperate until a tower of them reaches into the air. At the top forms an orbic spore full of amoebae, giving the slug a new shape, almost like a toadstool. Suddenly the spore explodes, scattering new amoebae into the environment. The whole phenomenon takes eight hours and demonstrates a simple form of cooperation among cells. Yet in the slime-mold amoebae something is lacking. At no point is there only one organism imprinted with the same genes and the same loyalties. Many slime-mold cells cooperate for the single event of reproduction, then break off and go their own way.

In contrast, the human body grows from the fertilization of a single egg. In *The Medusa and the Snail*, Lewis Thomas muses about why people made such a fuss over the first test-tube baby in England. The true miracle, he affirms, is the common union of a sperm and egg in a process that ultimately produces a human being. "The mere existence of that cell," he wrote before his death in 1993, "should be one of the greatest astonishments of the earth. People ought to be walking around all day, all through their waking hours, calling to each other in endless wonderment, talking of nothing except that cell.... If anyone does succeed in explaining it, within my lifetime, I will charter a skywriting airplane, maybe a whole fleet of them, and send them aloft to write one great exclamation point after another, around the whole sky, until all my money runs out."[2]

Over nine months these cells divide up functions in exquisite ways. Billions of blood cells appear, millions of rods and cones — in all, up to one hundred million million cells form from a single fertilized ovum. And finally a baby is born, glistening with liquid. Already his cells are cooperating. His muscles limber up in jerky, awkward movements; his face recoils from the harsh lights and dry air of the new environment; his lungs and vocal chords join in a first air-gulping yell.

Within that clay-colored, wrinkled package of cells lies the miracle of the ecstasy of community. His life will include the joy of seeing his mother's approval at his first clumsy words, the discovery of his own unique talents and gifts, the fulfillment of sharing with other humans. He is many cells, but he is one organism. All of his hundred trillion cells know that.

⟵.

I have closed my eyes. My shoes are kicked off, and I am wiggling the small bones in my right foot. Exposed, they are half the width of a pencil, and yet they support my weight in walking. I cup my hand over my ear and hear the familiar "seashell" phenomenon, actually the sound of blood cells rushing through the capillaries in my head. I stretch out my left arm and try to imagine the millions of muscle cells eagerly expanding and contracting in concert. I rub my finger across my arm and feel the stimulation of touch cells, 450 of them in each one-inch-square patch of skin.

Inside, my stomach, spleen, liver, pancreas, and kidneys, each packed with millions of loyal cells, are working so efficiently I have no way of perceiving their presence. Fine hairs in my inner ear are monitoring a swishing fluid, ready to alert me if I suddenly tilt off balance.

When my cells work well, I'm hardly conscious of their individual presences. What I feel is the composite of their activity known as Paul Brand. My body, composed of many parts, is one. And that is the root of the analogy we shall explore.

# Chapter 3

# DIVERSITY

*We often think that when we have completed our study on one, we know all about two, because "two is one and one." We forget that we have still to make a study of "and."*

Sir Arthur Eddington

More than amoebae and bats skulk in my medical laboratory. One drawer contains neatly filed specimens of an array of cells from the human body. Separated from the body, lifeless, stained with dyes and mounted in epoxy, they hardly express the churn of living cells at work inside me at this moment. But if I parade them under the microscope, certain impressions about the body take shape.

I am first struck by their variety. Chemically my cells are almost alike, but visually and functionally they are as different as the animals in a zoo. Red blood cells, discs resembling Life Saver candies, voyage through my blood loaded with oxygen to feed the other cells. Muscle cells, which absorb so much of that nourishment, are sleek and supple, full of coiled energy. Cartilage cells with shiny black nuclei look like bunches of black-eyed peas glued tightly together for strength. Fat cells seem lazy and leaden, like bulging white plastic garbage bags jammed together.

Bone cells live in rigid structures that exude strength. Cut in cross section, bones resemble tree rings, overlapping strength with strength, offering impliability and sturdiness. In contrast, skin cells form undulating patterns of softness and texture that rise and dip, giving shape and beauty to our bodies. They curve and jut at unpredictable angles so that every person's fingerprint — not to mention his or her face — is unique.

The aristocrats of the cellular world are the sex cells and nerve cells. A woman's contribution, the egg, is one of the largest cells in the human body, its ovoid shape just visible to the unaided eye. It seems fitting that all the other cells in the body should derive from this elegant and primordial structure. In great contrast to the egg's quiet repose, the male's tiny sperm cells are furiously flagellating tadpoles with distended heads and skinny tails. They scramble for position as if competitively aware that only one of billions will gain the honor of fertilization.

The king of cells, the one I have devoted much of my life to studying, is the nerve cell. It has an aura of wisdom and complexity about it. Spider-like, it branches out and unites the body with a computer network of dazzling sophistication. Its axons, "wires" carrying distant messages to and from the human brain, can reach a yard in length.

I never tire of viewing these varied specimens or thumbing through books which render cells. Individually they seem puny and oddly designed, but I know these invisible parts cooperate to lavish me with the phenomenon of life. Every second my smooth muscle cells modulate the width of my blood vessels, gently push matter through my intestines, open and close the plumbing in my kidneys. When things are going well — my heart contracting rhythmically, my brain humming with knowledge, my lymph laving tired cells — I rarely give these cells a passing thought.

But I believe these cells in my body can also teach me about larger organisms: families, groups, communities, villages, nations — and especially about one specific community of people that is likened to a body more than thirty times in the New Testament. I speak of the Body of Christ, that network of people scattered across the planet who have little in common other than their membership in the group that follows Jesus Christ.

My body employs a bewildering zoo of cells, none of which individually resembles the larger body. Just so, Christ's Body comprises an unlikely assortment of humans. Unlikely is precisely the right word, for we are decidedly unlike one another and the One we follow. From whose design come these comical human shapes which so faintly reflect the ideals of the Body as a whole?

⚊

Novelist Frederick Buechner playfully described the motley crew God selected in Bible times to accomplish his work:

> Who could have predicted that God would choose not Esau, the honest and reliable, but Jacob, the trickster and heel, that he would put the finger on Noah, who hit the bottle, or on Moses, who was trying to beat the rap in Midian for braining a man in Egypt and said if it weren't for the honor of the thing he'd just as soon let Aaron go back and face the music, or on the prophets, who were a ragged lot, mad as hatters most of them...?

> And of course, there is the comedy, the unforeseeableness, of the election itself. Of all the peoples he could have chosen to be his holy people, he chose the Jews, who as somebody has said are just like everybody else only more so — more religious

than anybody when they were religious and when they were secular, being secular as if they'd invented it. And the comedy of the covenant — God saying 'I will be your God and you shall be my people' (Exodus 6:7) to a people who before the words had stopped ringing in their ears were dancing around the golden calf like aborigines and carrying on with every agricultural deity and fertility god that came down the pike."[1]

The exception seems to be the rule. The first humans God created went out and did the only thing God asked them not to do. The man he chose to head a new nation known as "God's people" tried to pawn off his wife on an unsuspecting Pharaoh. And the wife herself, when told at the ripe old age of ninety-one that God was ready to deliver the son he had promised her, broke into rasping laughter in the face of God. Rahab, a harlot, became revered for her great faith. And Solomon, the wisest man who ever lived, went out of his way to break every proverb he so astutely composed.

Even after Jesus came the pattern continued. The two disciples who did most to spread the word after his departure, John and Peter, were the two he had rebuked most often for petty squabbling and muddleheadedness. And the apostle Paul, who wrote more books than any other Bible writer, was selected for the task while kicking up dust whirls from town to town sniffing out Christians to torture. Jesus had nerve, entrusting the high-minded ideals of love and unity and fellowship to this group. No wonder cynics have looked at the church and sighed, "If that group of people is supposed to represent God, I'll quickly vote against God." Or, as Nietzsche expressed it, "His disciples will have to look more saved if I am to believe in their savior."

Yet our study of the Body of Christ must allow for this impossible dream, for all we are is a collection of people as diverse as the cells in the human body. I think of the churches I have known: Is there another institution in town with such a mosaic assortment of unlikes? Young idealists, uniformed in jeans, share the pews with Republican bankers in three-piece suits. Bored teenagers tune out the sermon even as their eager grandparents turn up their hearing aids. Some members gather as methodically as a school of fish, then quickly break apart to return to their jobs and homes. Others want close communities and migrate together like social amoebae.

I could easily cluck my tongue at the absurdity of the whole enterprise, seemingly doomed to fail. Jesus prayed that we "may be one" as he and God the Father are one (John 17:11). How can any organism composed of such diversity attain even a semblance of unity?

As the doubts rumble inside me, a sober and quieting voice replies, "You did not choose me but I chose you." The chuckle at Christ's Body is caught in my throat like cotton. For if anything is to be believed about the collection of people who follow Jesus, it is that we were called by him. The word church, *ekklēsia*, means "the called-out ones." Our crew of comedians from central casting is the group God wants.

During my life as a missionary surgeon in India and now as a member of the tiny chapel on the grounds of the Carville leprosy hospital, I have seen my share of unlikely seekers after God. And I must admit that most of my worship in the last thirty years has not taken place among people who have shared my tastes in music, speech, or even thought. But over those years I have been profoundly — and humbly — impressed that I find God in the faces of my fellow worshipers by sharing with people who are shockingly different from each other and from me.

C. S. Lewis recounts that when he first started going to church he disliked the hymns, which he considered to be fifth-rate poems set to sixth-rate music. But as he continued, he said, "I realized that the hymns (which were just sixth-rate music) were, nevertheless, being sung with devotion and benefit by an old saint in elastic-side boots in the opposite pew, and then you realize that you aren't fit to clean those boots. It gets you out of your solitary conceit."[2]

A color on a canvas can be beautiful in itself. However, the artist excels not by slathering one color across the canvas but by positioning it between contrasting or complementary hues. The original color then derives richness and depth from its milieu of unlike colors.

The basis for our unity within Christ's Body begins not with our similarity but with our diversity.

It seems safe to assume that God enjoys variety, and not just at the cellular level. He didn't stop with a thousand insect species; he conjured up several hundred thousand species of beetles and weevils alone. In his famous speech in the Book of Job, God pointed with pride to such oddities of creation as the mountain goat, the wild ass, the ostrich, and the lightning bolt. He lavished color, design, and texture on the world, giving us Pygmies and Watusis, blond Scandinavians and swarthy Italians, big-boned Russians and petite Japanese.

People, created in God's image, have continued the process of individualization, grouping themselves according to distinct cultures. Consider the continent of Asia for a crazy salad. In China women often wear long pants and men wear gowns. In tropical Asia people drink hot tea and munch on blistering peppers to keep cool. Japanese fry ice cream. Indonesian men dance in public with other men to demonstrate that they are not homosexual. Westerners smile at the common Asian custom of marriages arranged by parents; Asians gasp at our entrusting such a decision to vague romantic love. Balinese men squat to urinate and women stand. Many Asians begin a meal with a sweet and finish it with a soup. And when the British introduced the violin to India a century ago, men started playing it while sitting on the floor, holding it between the shoulder and the sole of the foot. Why not?

Whenever I travel overseas, I am struck anew by the world's incredible diversity, and the churches overseas are now beginning to show that cultural self-expression. For too long they were bound up in Western ways (as the early church had been bound in Jewish ways) so that hymns, dress, architecture, and church names were the same around the world. Now indigenous churches are bursting out with their own spontaneous expressions of worship to God. I must guard against picturing the Body of Christ as composed only of American or British cells; it is far grander and more luxuriant than that.

I grew up in a denomination called the Strict and Particular Baptists, from which I learned faith and love for God and the Bible. Unfortunately, I also was taught how crucially better we were than every other church. We were not even allowed to have communion with other Baptist denominations. My great-grandparents, Huguenots, had escaped Catholic persecution in France, and as children we were taught that nuns and priests were akin to the Devil. My Christian growth since those days has required some abrupt adjustments.

I have learned that when God looks upon the Body that represents him on earth, spread like an archipelago throughout the world, God sees the whole thing. And I think God, understanding the cultural backgrounds and true intent of the worshipers, exults in the variety.

African-Americans in Murphy, North Carolina, shout their praises to God. Believers in Austria intone them, accompanied by magnificent organs and illuminated by stained glass. Some Africans dance their praise to God, following the beat of a skilled drummer. Sedate Japanese Christians express their gratitude by creating objects of beauty. Indians point their hands upward, palms together, in the *namaste* greeting of respect, that has its origin in the Hindu concept, "I worship the God I see in you," but gains new meaning as Christians use it to recognize the image of God in others.

The Body of Christ, like our own bodies, is composed of individuals, unlike cells that are knit together to form one Body. He is the whole thing, and the joy of the Body increases as individual cells realize they can be diverse without becoming isolated outposts.

# Chapter 4

# WORTH

*Whereas American mothers preserve, often in bronze, their
children's first shoes — celebrating freedom and independence — a
Japanese mother carefully preserves a small part of her child's
umbilical cord — celebrating dependence and loyalty.*

Stephen Franklin

—⇁

As a boy growing up in India, I idolized my missionary father
who responded to every human need he encountered. Only
once did I see him hesitate to help — when I was seven, and three
strange men trudged up the dirt path to our mountain home.

At first glance these three seemed like hundreds of other
strangers who streamed to our home for medical treatment. Each
was dressed in a breechcloth and turban, with a blanket draped
over one shoulder. But as they approached, I noticed differences: a
mottled quality to their skin, thick, swollen foreheads and ears, and
strips of blood-stained cloth bandaging their feet. As they came
closer, I noticed they also lacked fingers and one had no toes — his
limbs ended in rounded stumps.

My mother's reaction differed from her normal gracious hospitality. Her face took on a pale, tense appearance. "Run and get

Papa," she whispered to me. "Take your sister, and both of you stay in the house!"

My sister obeyed perfectly, but after calling my father I scrambled on hands and knees to a nearby vantage point. Something sinister was happening, and I didn't want to miss it. My heart pounded violently as I saw the same look of uncertainty, almost fear, pass across my father's face. He stood by the three nervously, awkwardly, as if he didn't know what to do. I had never seen my father like that.

The three men prostrated themselves on the ground, a common Indian action that my father disliked. "I am not God — he is the One you should worship," he would usually say, and lift the Indians to their feet. But not this time. He stood still. Finally, in a weak voice he said, "There's not much we can do. I'm sorry. But wait where you are; don't move. I'll do what I can."

He ran to the dispensary while the men squatted on the ground. Soon he returned with a roll of bandages, a can of salve, and a pair of surgical gloves he was struggling to put on. This was most unusual — how could he treat them wearing gloves?

Father washed the strangers' feet, applied ointment to their sores, and bandaged them. Strangely, they did not wince or cry out as he touched their sores.

While Father bandaged the men, Mother had been arranging a selection of fruit in a wicker basket. She set it on the ground beside them, suggesting they take the basket. They took the fruit but left the basket, and as they disappeared over the ridge I went to pick it up.

"No!" Mother insisted. "Don't touch it! And don't go near that place where they sat." Silently I watched Father take the basket and burn it, then scrub his hands with hot water and soap. Then

Mother bathed my sister and me, though we had had no direct contact with the visitors.

That incident was my first exposure to leprosy, the oldest recorded disease and probably the most dreaded disease throughout history. Although I might have recoiled from the suggestion as a boy of seven, I eventually felt called to spend my life working among leprosy patients. For the past thirty years I have been with them almost daily, forming many intimate and lasting friendships among these courageous people. During that time, many exaggerated fears and prejudices about leprosy have crumbled, at least in the medical profession. Partly because of effective drugs, leprosy is now viewed as a controllable, barely contagious disease.

However, in many parts of the world leprosy patients still lack adequate treatment. And even to those who are taking drugs, it remains a disease that can cause severe lesions, blindness, and loss of hands and feet. How does leprosy produce such terrible effects?

⚊

As I studied leprosy patients in India, several findings pushed me toward a rather simple theory: could it be that the horrible results of the disease came about because leprosy patients had lost the sense of pain? The disease was not at all like a flesh-devouring fungus; rather, it attacked mainly a single type of cell, the nerve cell. After years of testing and observation, I felt sure that the theory was sound.

The gradual loss of the sense of pain leads to misuse of those body parts most dependent on pain's protection. A person uses a hammer with a splintery handle, does not feel the pain, and an infection flares up. Another steps off a curb, spraining an ankle, and, oblivious, keeps walking. Another loses use of the nerve that triggers the eyelid to blink every few seconds for lubricating moisture; the eye dries out, and the person becomes blind.

The millions of cells in a hand or foot, or the living and alert rod and cone cells in the eye, can be rendered useless because of the breakdown of just a few nerve cells. Such is the tragedy of leprosy.

A similar pattern can be found in other diseases. In sickle cell anemia or leukemia the malfunction of a single type of cell can ultimately destroy a person. Or, if the cells that keep kidney filters in repair fail, a person may soon die of toxic poisoning.

This fact of the body — the worth of each of its parts — is graphically revealed by a disease such as leprosy. The failure of one type of cell can bring on tragic consequences. One who studies the vast quantity of cells and their startling diversity can come away with the sense that each cell is easily expendable and of little consequence. But the same body that impresses us with specialization and diversity also affirms that *each* of its many members is valuable and often essential for survival.

Interestingly, the worth of each member is also the aspect most often stressed in biblical imagery of the Body of Christ (see Romans 12:5, 1 Corinthians 12, and Ephesians 4:16). Listen to the mischievous way in which Paul expresses himself in 1 Corinthians 12: "Those parts of the body that seem to be weaker are indispensable, and the parts that we think are less honorable we treat with special honor. And the parts that are unpresentable are treated with special modesty, while our presentable parts need no special treatment. But God has combined the members of the body and has given greater honor to the parts that lacked it, so that there should be no division in the body, but that its parts should have equal concern for each other. If one part suffers, every part suffers with it; if one part is honored, every part rejoices with it" (vv. 22–26).

Paul's point is clear: Christ chose each member to make a unique contribution to his Body. Without that contribution, the Body could malfunction severely. Paul underscores that the less visible members (I think of organs like the pancreas, kidney, liver, and spleen) are perhaps the most valuable of all. Although I seldom feel consciously grateful for them, they perform daily functions that keep me alive.

I must keep coming back to the image of the body, because in our Western societies the worth of persons is determined by how much society is willing to pay for their services. Airplane pilots, for example, must endure rigorous education and testing procedures before they can fly for commercial airlines. They are then rewarded with luxurious lifestyles and societal respect. Within the corporate world, visible symbols such as office furnishings, bonuses, and salaries announce the worth of any given employee. As a person climbs, he or she will collect a sequence of important-sounding titles (the U.S. government once issued a book cataloging ten thousand of them).

In the military, the chain of command defines a person's worth. A soldier salutes superior officers, gives orders to those of lower rank, and the uniform and stripes alert everyone to his or her relative status. In civil service status is reflected in an individual's "GS grade," a numerical label.

Our culture is shot through with rating systems, beginning from the first grades of school when children receive marks defining relative performance. That, combined with factors such as physical appearance, popularity, and athletic prowess, may well determine how valuable people perceive themselves to be.

Living in such a society, my vision gets clouded. I begin viewing janitors as having less human worth than jet pilots. When that happens, I must turn back to the lesson from the body, which Paul draws against just such a background of incurable competition and value ranking. In human society, a janitor has little status because he is so replaceable. Thus, we pay the janitor less and tend to look down on him. But the body's division of labor is not based on status; status is, in fact, immaterial to the task being performed. The body's janitors are indispensable. If you doubt that, talk with someone who must go in for kidney dialysis twice a week.

The Bible directs harsh words to those who show favoritism. James spelled out a situation we can all identify with: "Suppose a man comes into your meeting wearing a gold ring and fine clothes, and a poor man in shabby clothes also comes in. If you show special attention to the man wearing fine clothes and say, 'Here's a good seat for you,' but say to the poor man, 'You stand there,' or 'Sit on the floor by my feet,' have you not discriminated among yourselves and become judges with evil thoughts?" He concludes, "If you show favoritism, you sin and are convicted by the law as lawbreakers. For whoever keeps the whole law and yet stumbles at just one point is guilty of breaking all of it" (James 2:2–4, 9–10).

Paul states the same truth positively, "Here there is no Greek or Jew, circumcised or uncircumcised, barbarian, Scythian, slave or free, but Christ is all, and is in all" (Colossians 3:11).

In our rating-conscious society that ranks everything from baseball teams to "the best chili in New York," an attitude of relative worth can easily seep into the church of Christ. But the design of the group of people who follow Jesus should not resemble a military machine or a corporate structure. The church Jesus founded is more like a family in which the son retarded from birth has as much worth as his brother the Rhodes scholar. It is like the body, composed of cells most striking in their diversity but most effective in their mutuality.

God requires only one thing of "cells": that each person be loyal to the Head. If each cell accepts the needs of the whole Body as the purpose of its life, then the Body will live in health. It is a brilliant stroke, the only pure egalitarianism I observe in all of society. God has endowed every person in the Body with the same capacity to respond. In Christ's Body a teacher of three-year-olds has the same value as a bishop, and that teacher's work may be just as significant. A widow's dollar can equal a millionaire's annuity. Shyness, beauty, eloquence, race, sophistication — none of these matter, only loyalty to the Head, and through the Head to each other.

—

Our little church at Carville includes one devout Christian named Lou, a Hawaiian by birth, who is marked with visible deformities caused by leprosy. With eyebrows and eyelashes missing, his face has a naked, unbalanced appearance, and paralyzed eyelids cause tears to overflow as if he is crying. He has become almost totally blind because of the failure of a few nerve cells on the surface of his eyes.

Lou struggles constantly with his growing sense of isolation from the world. His sense of touch has faded now, and that, combined with his near-blindness, makes him afraid and withdrawn. He most fears that his sense of hearing may also leave him, for Lou's main love in life is music. He can contribute only one "gift" to our church, other than his physical presence: singing hymns to God while he accompanies himself on an Autoharp. Our therapists designed a glove that permits Lou to continue playing his Autoharp without damaging his insensitive hand.

But here is the truth about the Body of Christ: not one person in Carville contributes more to the spiritual life of our church than

Lou playing his Autoharp. He has as much impact on us as does any member there by offering as praise to God the limited, frail tribute of his music. When Lou leaves, he will create a void in our church that no one else can fill — not even a professional harpist with nimble fingers and a degree from Julliard School of Music. Everyone in the church knows that Lou is a vital, contributing member, as important as any other member — and that is the secret of Christ's Body. If each of us can learn to glory in the fact that we matter little except in relation to the Body, and if each will acknowledge the worth in every other member, then perhaps the cells of Christ's Body will begin acting as Christ intended.

# Chapter 5

# UNITY

*We cannot live for ourselves alone. Our lives are connected by a thousand invisible threads, and along these sympathetic fibers, our actions run as causes and return to us as results.*

Herman Melville

The biologist takes from an incubator an egg containing a fully developed young chicken. Just fourteen days ago this egg was a single cell (the largest single cell in the world is an unfertilized ostrich egg). Now it is a mass of hundreds of millions of cells, a whirlpool of migrating protoplasm hurriedly dividing and arranging itself to prepare for life outside. The biologist cracks the shell and sacrifices the chick.

Though the embryo is now dead, some of its cells live on. Word travels fast through the body, but it may be days before the far outposts surrender. From the tiny heart the biologist extracts a few muscle cells and drops them in saline solution. Under the microscope the individual cells appear as long, spindly cylinders, crisscrossed like sections of railroad track. Their destiny is to throb, and they persist even in the anarchic world apart from the body. Each cell beats out an incessant rhythm — pitiful and useless palpitations when isolated from the chick. But if properly nourished, these lonely cells can be kept alive.

Unlinked by a pacemaker, the cells beat irregularly, spasmodically, each tapping out a rhythm approximate to the 350 beats a minute normal to a chick. But as the observer watches, over a period of hours an astonishing phenomenon occurs. Instead of five independent heart cells contracting at their own pace, first two, then three, and then all the cells pulse in unison. There are no longer five beats, but one. How is this sense of rhythm communicated in the saline, and why?

Some species of fireflies act similarly. A wanderer discovers a cluster of them in a jungle clearing, flickering haphazardly. As she watches, one by one the fireflies fall into synch until soon she sees not dozens of twinkling lights but one light, switched on and off, with fifty branch locations. The heart cells and the fireflies sense an innate rightness about playing the same note at the same time, even when no conductor is present.

Cooperation, a curious phenomenon of cells outside the body, is the essential regimen of life inside. There, every heart cell obeys in tempo or the animal dies. Each cell is flooded with communication about the rest of the body. How does the roaming white cell in the bat's wing know which cells to attack as invaders and which to welcome as friends? No one knows, but the body's cells have a nearly infallible sense of *belonging*.

All living matter is basically alike; a single atom differentiates animal blood from plant chlorophyll. Yet the body senses infinitesimal differences with an unfailing scent; it knows its hundred trillion cells by name. The first heart transplant recipients died, not because their new hearts failed, but because their bodies would not be fooled. Though the new heart cells looked in every respect like the old ones and beat at the correct rhythm, *they did not belong.* Nature's code of membership had been broken. The body screams "Foreigner!" at imported cells and mobilizes to destroy them. This persistence of the immune reaction continues to pose a challenge to organ transplant science.

To complicate the process of identity, the composite of Paul Brand today — bone cells, fat cells, blood cells, muscle cells — differs entirely from my components ten years ago. All cells have been replaced by new cells (except for nerve cells and brain cells, which are not replaced). Thus, my body is more like a fountain than a sculpture: maintaining its shape, but constantly being renewed. Somehow my body knows the new cells belong, and they are welcomed.

What moves cells to work together? What ushers in the higher specialized functions of movement, sight, and consciousness through the coordination of a hundred trillion cells?

—.

The secret to membership lies locked away inside each cell nucleus, chemically coiled in a strand of DNA. Once the egg and sperm share their inheritance, the DNA chemical ladder splits down the center of every gene much as the teeth of a zipper pull apart. DNA re-forms itself each time the cell divides: 2, 4, 8, 16, 32 cells, each with the identical DNA. Along the way cells specialize, but each carries the entire instruction book of one hundred thousand genes. DNA is estimated to contain instructions that, if written out, would fill a thousand six-hundred-page books. A nerve cell may operate according to instructions from volume four and a kidney cell from volume twenty-five, but both carry the whole compendium. It provides each cell's sealed credential of membership in the body. Every cell possesses a genetic code so complete that the entire body could be reassembled from information in any one of the body's cells, which forms the basis for cloning.

The Designer of DNA went on to challenge the human race to a new and higher purpose: membership in his own Body. And that membership begins with a stuff-exchange, analogous to an infusion of DNA, for each new cell in the Body. The community called Christ's Body differs from every other human group. Unlike a social or political body, membership in it entails something as radical as a new coded imprint inside each cell. In reality, I become genetically like Christ himself because I belong to his Body.

The more I ponder the implications of this analogy, the more it illuminates for me a spiritual truth which the Bible states often but in puzzling terms:

"Do you not realize that Christ Jesus is in you?" "I have been crucified with Christ and I no longer live, but Christ lives in me" — Paul. And, "I am in my Father, and you are in me, and I am in you." "I am the vine; you are the branches" — Jesus (2 Corinthians 13:5; Galatians 2:20; John 14:20; John 15:5).

I can only fathom the concept of being visited by the living Christ by considering its parallel in the physical world: the mystery of life in which DNA passes on an infallible identity to each new cell. Christ has infused us with spiritual life that is just as real as natural life. I may sometimes doubt my new identity or perhaps *feel* like my old self, but the Bible's statements are unequivocal. "Whoever believes in the Son has eternal life," said Jesus, "but whoever rejects the Son will not see life" (John 3:36). The difference between a person joined to Christ and one not joined to him is as striking as the difference between a dead tissue and my organic body. DNA has organized chemicals and minerals to form a living, growing body, all of whose parts possess its unique corporate identity. In a parallel way, God uses the materials and genes of natural man, splitting them apart and recombining them with his own spiritual life.

Jesus made the interchange possible: the virgin birth assumes that his DNA was fully God and fully human joined in one. And now, through union with him, I can carry within me the literal presence of God.

This unfathomable idea of an actual identity exchange is implicit in conversion. Jesus described the process in terms his hearers could understand. To Nicodemus he called it being "born again" or "born from above," indicating that spiritual life requires an identity change as drastic as a person's first entrance into the world.

As a result of this stuff-exchange, we carry within us not just the image of, or the philosophy of, or faith in, but the actual substance of God. One staggering consequence credits us with the spiritual genes of Christ: as we stand before God, we are judged on the basis of Christ's perfection, not our unworthiness. "If anyone is in Christ, he is a new creation; the old has gone, the new has come!... God made him who had no sin to be sin for us, so that in him we might become the righteousness of God" (2 Corinthians 5:17, 21). Elsewhere, Paul underscored, "Your life is now hidden with Christ in God" (Colossians 3:3). We are "in him" and he is "in us."

Just as the complete identity code of my body inheres in each individual cell, so also the reality of God permeates every cell in Christ's Body, linking us members with a true, organic bond. I sense that bond when I meet strangers in India or Africa or California who share my loyalty to the Head; instantly we become brothers and sisters, fellow cells in Christ's Body. I share the ecstasy of community in a universal Body that includes every man and woman in whom God resides.

Along with the incredible benefits of our identity transfer come some sobering responsibilities. When we act in the world, we quite literally subject God to that activity. Paul applied the body analogy to impress upon promiscuous Corinthians the full extent of their new identity. "You are members of Christ's Body," he warned. "Shall I then take the members of Christ and unite them with a prostitute? Never! Do you not know that he who unites himself with a prostitute is one with her in body?" And, he concluded, "You are not your own; you were bought at a price. Therefore honor God with your body" (1 Corinthians 6:15–16, 19–20).

I cannot imagine a more sobering argument against sin. Paul appeals not to a guilt-inducing "God is watching you" argument, but to a mature realization that we literally incarnate God in the world. It is indeed a heavy burden.

The process of joining Christ's Body may at first seem like a renunciation. I no longer have full independence. Ironically, however, renouncing my old value system — in which I had to compete with other people on the basis of power, wealth, and talent — and committing myself to Christ, the Head, abruptly frees me. My sense of competition fades. No longer do I have to bristle against life, seizing ways to prove myself. In my new identity my ideal has become to live my life in such a way that people around me recognize Jesus Christ and his love, not my own set of distinctive qualities. My worth and acceptance are enveloped in him. I have found this process of renunciation and commitment to be healthy, relaxing, and wholly good.

# Chapter 6

# SERVICE

*It is in giving that we receive, it is in pardoning that we are*
*pardoned, it is in dying that we are born again to eternal life.*

Saint Francis of Assisi

⟝⟞

I close my eyes and reflect on my life, flashing back through my
memories to recall rare moments of intense pleasure and fulfillment. To my surprise, my mind passes by hedonistic recollections
of great meals, thrilling vacations, or awards ceremonies. Instead,
it settles on instances when I have been able to work closely with
a team and our work has allowed us to serve another human being.
Sometimes our work has helped to improve sight, arrest crippling
effects of leprosy, or save a leg from amputation. At the time, some
of those acts involved apparent sacrifice. Surgeries were performed
in primitive situations on a portable table, in 110-degree heat, with
a young assistant beside me holding a flashlight. But those times of
working together, when I focused all my concentration on the goal
of helping another, glow with an unusual luster.

I remember one patient particularly, Sadagopan, or Sadan as his
friends called him. Born of an artistic, high-caste family in South
India, he was educated and refined, but leprosy had made him an
outcast. Passersby on the street, noticing his sores, would call him

names, shrinking from him in disgust. Cafés would not serve him; buses would not admit him.

Sadan came to our hospital at Vellore filled with despair. Though his face looked normal, his fingers were shortened and paralyzed, and his ulcerated feet left damp spots on the floor wherever he stepped. Constant infection in the bones had reduced his feet to half their normal length. Sadan was well advanced in the classic leprosy process of losing all use of hands and feet, a process our medical team had been desperately fighting to reverse.

We were convinced that most foot destruction of this type resulted from the stress of walking on feet without sensation. Simple observation had indicated that, for we were able to match up nails and rough spots in patients' shoes with the ulcers on their feet. If only we could spread the stress evenly over the whole surface of the foot, perhaps the skin could bear it and our patients could walk without further damage.

Sadan was an ideal person to test our theory. He eagerly agreed to live in a mud-and-thatch hut in our New Life Center and volunteered for anything that might improve his condition. We put him to bed until his ulcerous feet had healed and then fitted him with soft sandals. Excitedly, he began to walk. But in less than a week a runny red blister appeared on his foot, and Sadan returned to bed. We all remained cheerful, however, for the program was still experimental; we merely needed to keep seeking the right footwear.

There is no way to compress into a few paragraphs our accumulating emotions of hope and despair that seesawed through the next three years. We tried plaster casts, wooden clogs, and plastic shoes formed from wax molds. I traveled to Calcutta to learn how to mix polyvinyl chloride and to England to test spray-on plastics.

I felt as though I was trying, and failing, to sustain the life of two cherished friends. One was the theory, a conviction born and nurtured in my own mind, that leprosy deformity could be prevented. The disease attacked nerves primarily, I believed, so we only had to find a way to protect patients from self-destruction. We had collected much supporting evidence and had achieved successes with less severe cases. More than a cold, scientific theory, the idea was almost like our own child. In the face of opposition from older, more experienced doctors, our little group at Vellore was fighting for a cause that could conceivably overturn ancient prejudice against leprosy. Now, over months and ultimately years, as Sadan tried shoe after shoe and we saw the ulcers recur and heal and recur again, our idea was dying.

But there was another friend to sustain: Sadan himself. After all, it was his feet we were studying. We gambled with ideas; Sadan offered his body and hope. I got to the point where I could hardly bear to meet him and remove his socks, though I knew I would never hear a complaint from him. I had come to love Sadan, and I knew he loved me and clung to me as his last hope. I often thought that for his sake I should give up and amputate his feet. At least then, with wooden legs, he could return to his home and family.

After each failure we would start with a new design — a high, firm boot or a flexible, springy sole — and then each evening we would meet with rising hope.

Sometimes a month would go by. "Sadan, now we've really found it!" I would exclaim when I could find no sign of infection. But finally, inevitably, the signal of failure appeared.

I would relieve pressure on an area where there had been an old problem only to have the foot rub in a new area. Our team comforted Sadan; he comforted us. We all wept on our own and tried not to let our despair show.

Besides the shoe's design, I also had to contribute hard manual work. After a day of teaching and surgery I would make my way to the New Life Center and revive my old trade of carpentry. With a set of chisels and gouges and rasps I would shape a block of wood into a clog, then thin it down to a copy of Sadan's foot. As he sat on the bench, I would match every bump on his foot with a hollow in the clog. Finally I would sandpaper the finish to a smooth, polished texture that could not damage his feet. After fastening leather straps, I would launch Sadan on another period of experimental walking.

During the next weeks I would check pressures and feel his feet for signs of inflammation, adjusting the clogs accordingly. Finally Sadan would bring me one of the clogs and point to a blood stain near one end. "I'm sorry," he would say. I too would mumble "I'm sorry," and we would start over again.

Amid all the despondency, though, there were some good moments. We learned that all the most successful shoes had a "rocker" — a rigid bar under the sole of the shoe that made the foot rock, like a seesaw on a pivot, instead of bend. Most importantly, I discovered I could feel signs of damage in the foot. Although Sadan could not sense pain, my hands could detect an area of heat in the tissues. I quickly learned that this indicated early damage, and in a day or two that spot would break down. By finding these spots early, I could alter the shoe or give the foot a rest so the skin could recover.

Soon after this discovery the periods of successful walking grew longer and the breakdowns were less frequent. An almost breathless hope began to replace our despair. Sadan went for months without trouble and was walking better than he had for years.

Then came an almost blinding insight. One day I was feeling his feet, which I had come to know better than my own, rejoicing that they were cool and free from inflammation. Suddenly I realized that his skin felt different. Sadan's skin had always seemed solid and warm and tense, whereas now it was loose and cool, almost shrunken. Then it hit me. These were Sadan's normal feet coming through for the first time. In all the years I had known him, a residue of chronic infection and recurrent damage had kept his feet swollen and inflamed. Now, after several damage-free months, the protein fluids were being absorbed, leaving skin and bone free from inflammation and thus able to move and adjust to outside pressures.

At least part of our earlier problem had stemmed from the fact that Sadan's feet had never returned to normal between his troubles. The very tissue his body had developed to fight infection also made him vulnerable to mechanical stress. We had him walking too soon after each apparent healing, but with dulled nerves, Sadan did not notice. Over the months I had learned to feel the pain he could not feel.

Today when I visit India I make a small detour to visit my dear friend Sadan, his wife Kokela, and their fine family. He is proud and independent, earning his living as a hospital record librarian. He walks on a type of rocker boot, now used in many parts of the world for leprosy patients, diabetics, and others with insensitive feet.

When we meet, Sadan always takes off his boots and enthusiastically displays his feet that have remained free of ulcers for many years. His skin is loose and free, and his feet are cool. I run my fingers over every familiar contour. When our eyes meet, we remember our days of despair and tears. But we remember most vividly the ecstasy of that day when we knew his real feet had at last won through. I call them my feet now, as he says my hands are his, because only through them can he feel.

When Jesus described the Christian life, often his invitation to it sounded more like a warning than a sales pitch. He spoke of "counting the cost," of selling all and "taking up a cross" to follow him. While that attitude used to puzzle me greatly, I now believe he was simply underscoring the need for loyalty, which in biological terms means the need for individual cells to offer up service for the whole body. Sometimes following the Head may involve a sort of self-denial, including some pain. But I have learned, through rare instances like my experience with Sadan, that service also opens up levels of fulfillment far exceeding any others I have encountered. We are called to self-denial, not for its own sake, but for a compensation we can obtain in no other way.

Our culture exalts self-fulfillment, self-discovery, and autonomy. But according to Christ, it is only in losing my life that I will find it. Only by committing myself as a "living sacrifice" to the larger Body through loyalty to him will I find my true reason for being.

We cling to a self-serving feeling of martyrdom about such a life of service. In actual fact, we are called to deny ourselves in order to open up to a more abundant life. In the exchange, the advantage clearly rests on our side: crusty selfishness peels away to reveal the love of God expressed through our own hands which, in turn, reshapes us into God's own image. "To refuse to deny one's self" said Henry Drummond, "is just to be left with the self undenied."

The concept of service is best communicated through a personal example rather than through an abstract discussion, and a powerful memory edges into my mind of a strange-looking Frenchman named Abbé Pierre. He arrived at the leprosy hospital at Vellore wearing his simple monk's habit and carrying a blanket over his shoulders and one carpetbag containing everything he possessed. I invited him to stay at my home, and there he told me his story.

As a Catholic friar he had been assigned to work among the beggars in Paris after World War II. At that time beggars in that city had nowhere to go, and in winter many of them would freeze to death in the streets. Abbé Pierre began by trying to interest the community in the beggars' plight, but was unsuccessful. He decided the only recourse was to show the beggars how to mobilize themselves. First, he taught them to do their tasks better. Instead of sporadically collecting bottles and rags, they organized into teams to scour the city. Next, he led them to build a warehouse from discarded bricks and start a business in which they sorted vast amounts of used bottles from big hotels and businesses. Finally Pierre inspired each beggar by giving him responsibility to help another beggar poorer than himself. Then the project really began to succeed. An organization called Emmaus was founded to perpetuate Pierre's work, with branches in other countries.

Now, he told me, after years of this work in Paris, there were no beggars left in that French city. Pierre believed his organization was about to face a serious crisis.

"I must find somebody for my beggars to help!" he declared and had begun searching in other places around the world. It was during one of those trips that he had come to Vellore. He concluded by describing his dilemma. "If I don't find people worse off than my beggars, this movement could turn inward. They'll become a powerful, rich organization and the whole spiritual impact will be lost! They'll have no one to serve." As we walked out of the house toward the student hostel to have lunch, my head was ringing with Abbé Pierre's earnest plea for "somebody for my beggars to help!"

We had a tradition among the medical students at Vellore about which I warned all guests in advance. All lunchtime guests would stand and say a few words about who they were and why they had come. Like students everywhere, ours were lighthearted and ornery, and they had developed an unspoken three-minute tolerance rule. If any guest talked longer than three minutes (or became boring before that time was up), the students would stamp their feet and make the person sit down.

On the day of Pierre's visit, he stood up and I introduced him to the group. I could see the Indian students eyeing him quizzically — this small man with a big nose and nothing attractive about him, wearing a peculiar old habit. Pierre started speaking in French, and a fellow worker named Heinz and I strained to translate what he was saying. Neither of us was well-practiced in French, since no one in that part of India spoke it, so we could only break in here or there with a summary sentence.

Abbé Pierre began slowly but soon speeded up, like a tape recorder turning too fast, with sentences spilling over each other, gesticulating all the while. I was extremely tense because he was going into the whole history of the movement, and I knew the students would soon shout down this great, humble man. Worse, I was failing miserably to translate his rapid-fire sentences. He had just visited the UN headquarters where he had listened to dignitaries manipulate fine-sounding, flowery words to express insults to other countries. Pierre was saying that you don't need language to express love, only to express hate. The language of love is what you *do.* Then he spoke faster and faster, and Heinz and I looked at each other and shrugged helplessly.

Three minutes passed, and I stepped back and looked around the room. No one moved. The Indian students gazed at Pierre with piercing black eyes, their faces rapt. He went on and on, and no one interrupted. After twenty minutes Pierre sat down, and immediately the students burst into the most tremendous ovation I ever heard in that hall.

Completely mystified, I had to question some of the students. "How did you understand? No one here speaks French."

One student answered me, "We did not need a language. We felt the presence of God and the presence of love."

Abbé Pierre had learned the discipline of loyal service that determines the body's health. He had come to India and found leprosy patients to fulfill his desperate search to find someone worse off than his beggars, and when he found them, he was filled with love and joy. He returned to his beggars in France, and they and Emmaus worked to donate a ward at the hospital in Vellore. They had found people who needed their help so the spiritual motives of their lives continued on. The Emmaus movement thus flourished as a serving part of Christ's Body.

# Chapter 7

# MUTINY

*An enormous technology seems to have set itself the task of making it unnecessary for one human being ever to ask anything of another in the course of going about his daily business. We seek more and more privacy, and feel more and more alienated and lonely when we get it.*

Philip Slater

A t the central railway station in Madras (renamed Chennai), India, lay a beggar woman more pitiful than the others I saw there. She had positioned herself alongside the stream of passengers hurrying to catch their trains. Businessmen with briefcases passed by her, as did wealthy tourists and government officials.

Like many Indian beggars, the woman was emaciated, with sunken cheeks and eyes and bony limbs. But, paradoxically, a huge mass of plump skin, round and sleek like a sausage, was growing from her side. It lay beside her like a formless baby, connected to her by a broad bridge of skin. The woman had exposed her flank with its grotesque deformity to give her an advantage in the rivalry for pity. Though I saw her only briefly, I felt sure that the growth was a lipoma, a tumor of fat cells. It was a part of her and yet not, as if some surgeon had carved a hunk of fat out of a three-hundred-pound person, wrapped it in live skin, and deftly sewed it on this woman. She was starving; she feebly held up a spidery hand for alms. But her tumor was thriving, nearly equaling the weight of the rest of her body. It gleamed in the sun, exuding health, sucking life from her.

Fat cells: the Madras beggar's tumor was composed entirely of an orgiastic community of them. In our figure-conscious Western culture, the word "fat" connotes a lack of discipline, an unnecessary aggregation of cells that should be reduced.

From the surgeon's vantage point, however, as he draws a knife across the skin, exposing oleaginous layers of fat cells, the evil connotation is balanced by a sense of the value of fat. It insulates against cold, and for that reason billions of fat cells congregate just below the skin. (Because of this, fat people can survive cold air and water better than thin people.) Fat cells pitch their tents wherever they find space around internal organs and muscles and between layers in the body. Their presence helps cushion those vital parts against jarring shocks.

Nothing influences appearance as much as fat. Why are young women so pleasing to the eye? An abundance of fat cells fills in the irregularities of bone and muscle, giving their skin a sleek, smooth contour.

But there is more to fat's function than insulation and contouring. Each fat cell is a storehouse containing a yellow globule of oil which crowds out the cell nucleus. Most of the time the cell lies dormant, while the body eats enough food to fuel its needs. Come famine, people with plenteous fat cells will be able to sit by while others starve. And that is the most strategic function of fat.

When all is going well, the body takes in just enough food to maintain itself, grow, and replace worn cells. But when the supply diminishes, as when a person mowing the lawn delays supper in order to utilize the summer light, a signal sounds in the body's fat cells. To the liver short of glycogen and the blood short on glucose, the fat cells freely yield their oily treasure. By being the body's storehouse, the fat cells free other cells to do their job more efficiently. For example, if every muscle cell had to include a pouch-like reservoir of energy, our bodies would be deformed lumps and nodules.

Some fat is readily expendable: it goes first when a person starts a diet. Other fat, such as that around the kidney and in the palm of the hand, holds out because of its important secondary functions. When the body is starving, however, even these high priority fat cells must relinquish their important contents.

I like to think of fat cells as the banker cells of the body. In times of plenty they bulge with excess, as the body deposits more than it withdraws. In times of want they channel their chemical wealth back into the bloodstream.

Sometimes a dreaded thing occurs in the body — a mutiny — resulting in a tumor lipoma such as the one attached to the Madras beggar. A lipoma is a low-grade, benign tumor. It derives from a single fat cell, skilled in its lazy role of storing fat, that rebels against the leadership of the body and refuses to give up its reserves. It accepts deposits but ignores withdrawal slips. As that cell multiplies, daughter cells follow its lead and a tumor grows like a fungus, filling in crevices, pressing against muscles and organs. Occasionally a lipoma crowds a vital organ like the eye, pushing it out of alignment or pinching a sensitive nerve, and surgery is required.

I have removed such lipoma tumors. Under a microscope they seem composed of healthy fat cells, bulging with shiny oils. The cells function beautifully except for one flaw — they have become disloyal. In their activity they disregard the body's needs. And so the beggar woman in Madras gradually starved while a lipoma that was part of her engorged itself.

A tumor is called benign if its effect is fairly localized and it stays within membrane boundaries. But the most traumatizing condition in the body occurs when disloyal cells defy inhibition. They multiply without any checks on growth, spreading rapidly throughout the body, choking out normal cells. White cells, armed against foreign invaders, will not attack the body's own mutinous cells. Physicians fear no other malfunction more deeply: it is called cancer. For mysterious reasons, these cells — and they may be cells from the brain, liver, kidney, bone, blood, skin, or other tissues — grow wild, out of control. Each is a healthy, functioning cell, but disloyal, no longer acting in regard for the rest of the body.

Even the white cells, the dependable palace guard, can destroy the body through rebellion. Sometimes they recklessly reproduce, clogging the bloodstream, overloading the lymph system, strangling the body's normal functions — such is leukemia.

⌐

Because I am a surgeon and not a prophet, I tremble to make the analogy between cancer in the physical body and mutiny in the spiritual body of Christ. But I must. In his warnings to the church, Jesus Christ showed no concern about the shocks and bruises his Body would meet from external forces. "The gates of hell shall not prevail against my church," he said flatly (Matthew 16:18). He moved easily, unthreatened, among sinners and criminals. But he cried out against the kind of disloyalty that comes from within.

I must concentrate on how I, as an individual cell, should respond to the crying needs of the Body of Christ in other parts of the world. Beyond that, I cannot and should not make sweeping judgments about what the response of other Christians should be.

But I must say, from the perspective of a missionary who spent eighteen years in one of the poorest countries on earth, the contrasts in resources are astonishingly large. At Vellore we treated leprosy patients on three dollars per patient per year; yet we turned many away for lack of funds. Then we came to America where some churches were heatedly discussing their million-dollar gymnasiums and the cost of landscaping and fertilizer and a new steeple ... and sponsoring seminars on tax shelters for members to conserve their accumulated wealth. As I saw those churches' budgets for foreign missions and for inner city work, I could not force a telling image from my mind — the memory of the Madras woman slowly starving to death while her lipoma grew plump and round.

The problem is not just an American problem, or even a Western problem. I could easily point to examples of hoarding in every society I've seen: in the cruel Iks of Africa, in China, in the disparity within the Christian community in India. The warning applies to all of us. My only message is the caution of a doctor: remember, the body will have health only if each cell regards the needs of the whole body.

I wonder if perhaps we in the West get caught up in a competitive spiral with "cells" around us and become oblivious to the stark needs of the rest of the world. In the Body of Christ ownership of property and money is no sin; it is an important function of certain members. And when I liken wealthy people to fat cells, I use the image positively, as an admiring doctor who appreciates the role of fat. Hospitality and generosity are made easier by wealth. Reserves can help the Body care for itself and fuel its muscular activity in a hurting world. However, the control of fat is a difficult problem, both in biology and in religion.

I will cite two sets of statistics and then leave the application to you.

First, wealth is not only material in nature. A huge percentage of all the full-time Christian workers in the world work in North America among less than 8 percent of the world's population. On Sunday morning in rural Louisiana I can flip a radio dial to ten different church services, while elsewhere entire countries have no Christian witness.

Second, consider the world as if it were shrunk down to a village of 100 persons:

In our town of 100 —

There would be 60 Asians, 12 Europeans, 13 Africans, and 14 from the entire Western Hemisphere.

25 live in substandard housing, 20 suffer from malnutrition, 26 of the adults are unable to read.

20 people possess 90 percent of the town's wealth. Of the rest, almost half get by on less that two dollars a day.

2 have a college education, and 4 own a computer.

How does the fortunate group use its incredible wealth? Well, as a group they spend less than 1 percent of their income to aid the lower land. In the United States, for example, of every $100 earned, $2.66 is given for all religious and charitable uses, and only a small part of that goes outside the U.S.

I realize these issues have complex economic and cultural factors behind them. But I am impressed with how decisively the early church responded to pressing needs: the apostle Paul took months out of his schedule to collect money from Greek Christians to aid impoverished Jewish Christians in Jerusalem.

We need to pause and look carefully at ourselves. Christ's Body needs all types of cells: fat and thin, rich and poor, simple and complex. But that Body only needs loyal cells. And in the area of using resources, Jesus, our Head, had many unsettling things to say. God save us from being a cancer within his Body.

# BONES

# Chapter 8

# A FRAME

*Bone is power. It is bone to which the soft parts cling, from which they are, helpless, strung and held aloft to the sun, lest man be but another slithering earth-noser.*

Richard Selzer

The setting was worthy of a horror movie. Each morning I threaded through dark, narrow corridors until I came to a winding stairway which led to the ancient attic. There I found rows of boxes, layered with dust, containing six hundred skeletons. Each day I hunkered over the boxes in the dimly lighted, creaking room, sorting through bones. In all, I spent seven days crouched in the musty attic of the old house in Copenhagen.

The house served as a museum for Dr. Möller Christiansen, a medical historian, who had invited me there because the six hundred skeletons once belonged to people with leprosy. After discovering the bones on an island off the coast of Denmark and diligently studying them, Dr. Christiansen had written an extraordinary book on leprosy. Those of us who worked with the disease could hardly believe it when we learned he had never observed a living patient. All his insights into the disease were drawn from the five-hundred-year-old skeletons in his attic; yet he had taught us many facts about leprosy and had made good suggestions about its treatments.

Picking over his clattery bones, much as a child rummages through a box of precious toys, Dr. Christiansen would locate certain favorites and proudly show me their features. Many skeletons, for example, had loose or missing front teeth, caused by leprosy's tendency to attack first the body's cooler parts. Together we examined bones of feet and hands, speculating what injuries could have caused their deformities.

One morning, working alone in the attic, I came across some boxes of skeletons that had been dug up from a monastery. I was soon to be reminded of a lecture given by anthropologist Margaret Mead, who spent much of her life studying primitive cultures. She asked the question, "What is the earliest sign of civilization?" A clay pot? Iron? Tools? Agriculture? No, she claimed. To her, evidence of the earliest true civilization was a healed femur, a leg bone, which she held up before us in the lecture hall. She explained that such healings were never found in the remains of competitive, savage societies. There, clues of violence abounded: temples pierced by arrows, skulls crushed by clubs. But the healed femur showed that someone must have cared for the injured person — hunted on his behalf, brought him food, and served him at personal sacrifice. Savage societies could not afford such pity. I found similar evidence of healing in the bones from the churchyard. I later learned from Dr. Christiansen that an order of monks had worked among the victims: their concern came to light five hundred years later in the thin lines of healing where infected bone had cracked apart or eroded and then grown back together.

After a week I left that eerie attic feeling as though I had watched a slide show on an ancient civilization. My clues for visualizing it had been tiny projections and furrows on the surfaces of bones exhumed from the dust of history, but they had taught me much. Faces, hair, and clothes, which consume so much cultural energy, had all rotted away, leaving bones as the only mementos of that settlement.

The bulky pelvis, for instance, quickly betrayed the sex of the person who owned it. A broad and shallow one with a smooth inner ring obviously belonged to a woman. The oval opening precisely matched the size and shape that a baby's head would need to squeeze through. The pelvis beside it, a man's, was narrower, more heart-shaped, and formed with heavier bones. Hard, nub-like projections on its inner ring marked where muscles and ligaments had once been attached.*

A closer look at bones such as those in Copenhagen shows surfaces which are not even and shiny, but coarsely filled with grooves for blood vessels and slick areas for gliding tendons. The very thickness of a bone may divulge its former use. Discus throwers and weight lifters have the densest bones because an exercised bone collects more calcium for needed strength. By carefully studying the stress lines of individual bones under a microscope, even a person's occupation can be guessed at. A horseback rider leaves definite clues in leg bones and pelvis. A porter who lugs heavy suitcases in his right hand will bear the effects of this stress in hip and shoulder.

Shakespeare said, "The good [men do] is oft interred with their bones." More than good is interred there. A field of science, forensics, exists to unravel the clues hidden in bones. Experts can determine a

---

*The female runner still lags behind the male, and blame rests on the pelvis. The projections on the man's pelvis allow for more powerful muscles, but a woman equipped with them could not bear a child. Similarly, a man's hip sockets are closer together, nearer the center of gravity, which enables more efficient movement. If a woman's were similarly designed, there would be no room for the baby's head to extrude. So the odd pelvic bone represents a summation of many different requirements. When a woman wishes she could run faster or sway less or have a narrower base, let her know that the survival of the human race depends upon her being just the shape she is.

skeleton's age by how hard or "ossified" the cartilage has become. By age fifteen, for example, the foot is fully formed, at twenty-five the collarbone is fused to the breastbone, and by age forty, three-fourths of the seams in the skull have coalesced.

Simple laboratory experiments reveal the components of bones. Burning a bone in a fire will flare away all organic material, leaving an object the same shape and appearance as the bone but consisting of minerals only. If baked long enough, the bone will crumble between the fingers.

Hydrochloric acid does the opposite: it dissolves all minerals, leaving the organic substance collagen, again in the original shape. The treated object looks the same but is no longer bone. It has lost its hardness and cannot support weight. Such a bone can be tied into a knot and, when untied, will spring back into its shape. (Collagen makes even untreated bone surprisingly elastic: Arab children play with bows made from the ribs of camels.) Grit and glue — those are the ingredients of bone. We need both.

No Exxon researcher has yet discovered a material as well-suited for the body's needs as bone, which comprises only one-fifth of our body weight. In 1867 an engineer demonstrated that the arrangement of bone cells forms the lightest structure, made of least material, to support the body's weight. No one has successfully challenged his findings. As the only hard material in the body, bone possesses incredible strength, enough to protect and support every other cell. Sometimes we press our bones together like a steel spring, as when a pole vaulter lands. Other times we nearly pull a bone apart, as when my arm lifts a heavy suitcase.

In comparison, wood can withstand even less pulling tension, and could not possibly bear the compression forces that bone can. A wooden pole for the vaulter would quickly snap. Steel, which can absorb both forces well, is three times the weight of bone and would burden us down.

The economical body takes this stress-bearing bone and hollows it out, using a weight-saving architectural principle it took people millennia to discover; it then fills the vacant space in the center with an efficient red blood cell factory that turns out a trillion new cells per day. Bone sheaths life.

I find bone's design most impressive in the tiny, jewel-like chips of ivory in the foot. Twenty-six bones line up in each foot, about the same number as in each hand. Even when a soccer player subjects these small bones to a cumulative force of over one thousand tons per foot over the course of a match, his living bones endure the violent stress, maintaining their elasticity. Not all of us leap and kick, but we do walk some sixty-five thousand miles, or more than two and one-half times around the world, in a lifetime. Our body weight is evenly spread out through architecturally perfect arches which serve as springs, and the bending of knees and ankles absorbs stress. Unfortunately, we coax our feet to assume the shape of footwear fashion, sometimes tilting our heels high and canceling all the effects of that balanced design.

Bone's strength is quiet, dependable. It serves us well, without fanfare, and comes to our attention only when we encounter a rude, fracturing stress that exceeds its own high tolerance.

⟋.

In order to appreciate the invisible frame each of us wears inside, we must pause to consider the progression of skeletons in nature, which offers abundant variations. Much of the earth's hard surface, sedimentary rock, was left to us by microscopic creatures who died and cemented together, pooling their skeletons to form rock. Of these simple creatures, perhaps the most exquisite are the saltwater *Protozoa* called *Radiolaria*.

Recall the most perfect snowflake you have ever seen: a large, unblemished one that floats like a feather on a frosty day. It has only six sides, but an abundance of symmetrical cusps gives it beauty. Now imagine a three-dimensional snowflake with hundreds of crystalline shapes sprouting from its center. Such is a *Radiolaria* skeleton, billions of which float through our oceans.

The ocean is a hungry place, and skeletons there are as likely to be required for protection as for movement. So for the *Radiolaria*, mollusks, scallops, nautiluses, crabs, lobsters, and starfish a skeleton becomes a place of refuge.

On land, however, dominated by the incessant tug of gravity, movement is everything. The fastest rabbit evades the coyote and the fleetest African cat dines on gazelle. Several million species mimic their oceanic counterparts with external skeletons, notably the vast insect world. But these can only grow so large or the burden of armor becomes insupportable. The largest insects, with their excreted exoskeletons, barely approach the size of the smallest birds or mammals.

Thus, we're back to the old distinction: higher and lower. The highest animals, called vertebrates, rule even in the ocean. An internal, *living* skeleton allows revolutionary advances. No longer need an animal outgrow his home and risk a vulnerable molting period. Rather, the skeleton grows with the animal, and because of the hundreds of muscles attached to internal scaffolding, heretofore unheard-of feats can be performed.

Insects and spiders can run, jump, and fly, but only with an internal skeleton can an animal as large as a barn swallow flaunt gravity with his skydiving, or a creature like a condor support a ten-foot wingspan and soar on thermals for hours. Only with an internal skeleton can an elephant charge like thunder across the grasslands or an elk hoist his rack of antlers proudly towards the sky. Without bones, locomotion tends to revert to the most primitive: the segmented scrunching of an earthworm or the lubricated slide of a slug.

Bones do not burden us; they free us.

# Chapter 9

# HARDNESS

*There are an infinity of angles at which one falls, only one at which one stands.*

G. K. Chesterton

P eople are never born without bones, but some are born with defective bones in a condition called brittle bone disease. When this occurs, the victim's bone consists of deposits of calcium without the organic material welding them together — the grit without the glue. A fetus with this disorder may survive the pressures of birth, but with half its bones broken. Just diapering such a child may break his or her fragile legs; a fall could break dozens of bones.

At our Carville hospital a patient was given massive doses of steroids during treatment of her leprosy, and as a result her bones became soft. She could fracture her foot by walking too briskly. Whenever I examined the woman and checked her X-rays for fractures, I was reminded that the most important feature of bone is its hardness. That one property separates it from all other tissue in the body, and without hardness bone is virtually useless.

An analogous body as advanced and active as the Body of Christ's followers also needs a framework of hardness to give it shape, and I see the church's doctrine as being just such a skeleton.

Inside the Body lives a core of truth that never changes — the laws governing our relationships to God and to other people.

Do I hear a groan? Our age smiles kindly on musings about unity and diversity and the contributions of individual cells. But the drive which stirred church councils and framers of the Constitution has stalled. Bones are dusty, crumbling, dead, belonging in a musty museum display case. Other parts of the body are memorialized: the heart on Valentine's Day, the sexual parts and the muscles in magazines and fashion, the hands in sculptures. The skeleton is relegated to Halloween, a spooky remnant of the past, leeringly inhuman.

Today one can easily muster up sympathy and support for Jesus' ethics governing human behavior. But squeezed in between his statements on love and neighborliness are scores of harsh, uncompromising statements about our duties and responsibilities and about heaven and hell.

The modern world is still pictured as a courtroom scene, as described by the ancients, but not with God as Judge, setting the rules and arbitrating disputes. Rather, God stands indicted, and prosecutors are stalking across the stage jabbing their fingers, demanding to know why God allows such a miserable world to continue and what right Jesus has to make such grandiose claims. Don't all religions ultimately point to God? Isn't belief really an individual quest for ultimate meaning that each must find in his or her own way? What is this talk about "No man comes to the Father except by me" and "I am the way, the truth and the life"?

As I encounter the Body of Christ, I keep hitting against the hard tissue, the principles that do not change. Joining that Body involves a capitulation which defies my nature, an acknowledgment that someone else, not I, has already determined the way I should live. In some areas of my life I gladly accept restrictive laws. For instance, traffic laws inhibit my freedom (what if I don't want to stop?), yet I accept the inconvenience. I assume some skilled engineers calculated the number of one-way streets and red lights, and even if I doubt their ability, I prefer traffic laws to auto anarchy. But something within me rebels against being told how to live morally.

I came across this property of hardness when I was first taught about God. God is perfect, I was told, and cannot tolerate sin. God's character requires him to destroy sin whenever it is present, so I am branded an enemy of God. That fact, rooted in the first chapters of Genesis, is stressed throughout the Bible. God cannot ignore rebellion; his nature demands that justice be done, and nothing I can do will soften the inflexibility of that fact. I must meet God on his terms, not my own.

Later, I learned how justice was accomplished. God obtained it on our behalf by becoming a man and taking on himself all the sin and rebellion we had stored up against him. The debt of humankind was paid, but in a way that cost only God, not those of us who had piled it up. To the servant with a three-million-dollar debt Jesus announced, "It's forgiven; you owe nothing." And his message to the Prodigal Son: "The table is set; come join the party. The past may all be forgiven; all that counts is how you respond to what God has offered."

Even at its core, the hard, unchangeable part that does not flex, the gospel sounds almost like a fairy tale. "It's too good to be true," someone protested to George MacDonald. "No," he replied, "it's so good it has to be true."

⚊.

Others more skilled in theology than I must describe and interpret specific doctrines for us. Today some within the church attack law and doctrine. Situation ethics suggest that right and wrong often depend on the need and mood of the moment. I merely submit this single aspect of God's law: it must be consistent, like bone. Trust demands it.

I think back to an encounter with trust I had many years ago. Before I trained for surgery, I worked in the general practice of my father-in-law, near London. One day a woman came in with a list of complaints that exactly described gastritis. After a brief examination I told her my diagnosis, but she looked up at me with large, fear-filled eyes.

I repeated to her soothingly, "Really, it's not a serious condition. Millions of people have it, and with medication and care, you'll be fine." The fear did not fade from her face. Lines of tension were jerking in her forehead and jaw. To my "You'll be fine," she flinched as if I had said, "Your disease is terminal."

She quizzed me on every point, and I assured her I would be doing further tests to verify my diagnosis. She repeated to me all her symptoms and kept asking, "Are you sure? Are you sure?" So I ordered a barium meal and extensive X-rays.

When the test results came back, all pointed conclusively to gastritis. I saw the woman on one last visit. She trembled slightly as I spoke to her, and I used my most comforting and authoritative doctor's tone. "It is perfectly clear — no doubt — that you have gastritis. I thought so from the first visit, and now these tests have confirmed it. The condition is chronic and will require you to change diet and medication, but it should settle down. There is absolutely no reason for alarm."

The woman stared into my eyes with a piercing gaze for at least a minute, as if she was trying to see into my soul. I managed to hold her gaze, fearing that if I looked away she would doubt me. Finally, she sighed deeply, and for the first time her face relaxed. She sucked her breath in sharply and said, "Well, thank you. I was sure I had cancer. I had to hear the diagnosis from somebody I could trust, and I think I can trust you."

She then told me a story about her mother, who had suffered a long, painful disease. "One torturous night the family doctor made a house call while mother was groaning and pressing her hands to her stomach. She was feverish and obviously suffering. When the doctor arrived, Mother said, 'Doctor, am I really going to get better? I feel so ill and have lost so much weight . . . I think I must be dying.'

"The doctor put his hand on my mother's shoulder, looked at her with a tender expression, and replied, 'I know how you feel. It hurts badly, doesn't it? But we can lick this one — it is simply gastritis. If you take this medicine for a little while longer, with these tranquilizers, we will have you on your feet in no time. You'll feel better before you know it. Don't worry. Just trust me.' My mother smiled and thanked him. I was overwhelmed by the doctor's kindness.

"In the hallway, out of her hearing, the doctor turned to me and said gravely, 'I'm afraid your mother will not last more than a day or two. She has an advanced case of cancer of the stomach. If we keep her tranquilized, she will probably pass away peacefully. If there's anyone you should notify —'

"I interrupted him in mid-sentence. 'But, doctor! You told her she was doing fine!'

"'Oh, yes, it's much better that way,' he replied. 'She does not know, and so she won't worry. She'll probably die in her sleep.' He was right. My mother died that same night."

This woman, now a middle-aged patient herself, had first gone to that same family doctor with her stomach pains. He had put a hand on her shoulder and said gently, "Don't worry. It's only gastritis. Just take this medicine, and you'll be feeling fine very soon."

And he smiled the same paternal smile he had shown her mother. She had fled from his office in tears and would never see him again.

⟶

When people complain to me about the rigid, unbending laws of God, I think of that woman. The family doctor had obliterated all possibility of helping her because of his flexible attitude to truth. Only one thing could relieve her anxiety and despair: trust in someone who believed in truth that could not be twisted and bent.

Occasions will come when to be untruthful is more convenient or less offensive. But a respect for truth cannot be worn and then casually removed like a jacket; it cannot be contracted and then relaxed like a muscle. Either it is rigid and dependable, like healthy bone, or it is useless.

# Chapter 10

# FREEDOM

*Obedience is a particular means of joy and the only means of that particular joy.*

Charles Williams

He came to me as a patient in England: a brawny, burly Welsh-man who spoke lyrically and with a workman's vocabulary. "Mornin', doctor," he growled. As he removed his wool plaid jacket, I saw the reason for his coming. The upper part of his right arm was not pink skin, but grimy steel and leather — an awkward, brace-like contraption covered with black coal dust. I removed the brace. This was no artificial limb; his forearm was intact, but the flesh between his elbow and shoulder was flaccid. A long section of bone appeared to be missing. But if a mining accident had crushed his upper arm, how had his forearm survived?

After I studied the miner's records and X-rayed his arm, the puzzle fell into place. Years before, a bone tumor in his upper arm had led to a serious fracture which splintered large sections of bone there. Under the bright lights of the operating room his doctor had deftly stolen an eight-inch pipe of living bone and sewed back the muscles and skin around the space. As the miner lay recovering, his boneless arm seemed perfectly normal. Who would know the interior landscape had changed?

Everyone would know, the first moment this miner used the muscles, still strong and intact, in his upper arm. Bones and muscles work on a triangle principle: the joint provides the fulcrum, and two bones work with a muscle. To pull the hand up, the biceps muscle, attached to the upper arm, pulls on the forearm. The arm bends at the elbow, and the triangle is complete. But one muscle and one forearm bone do not make a triangle; this coal miner lacked the third element, the bone of the upper arm.

Ever since his surgery years before, whenever the miner contracted his biceps muscle his entire upper arm shortened, like an earthworm spastically pulling in towards its middle. The fixed, resistant bone between his elbow and shoulder had become a soft, collapsible space, canceling out the triangle that should have transferred force to his forearm. His ingenious Welsh doctor had fitted the miner with a crude exoskeleton, a bulky contraption of leather and steel which positioned stiff rods between his elbow and shoulder. When his biceps contracted, because these steel rods prevented his upper arm from merely shortening, the forearm could pull upward. The steel frame outside his arm worked much the same as the now-missing bone had inside his arm.

I have surgically removed such upper arm bones, though today we circumvent the awkwardness of an external skeleton by inserting a bone graft into the vacant space. A bone graft unites with the stumps above and below it, and gradually the arm will adjust to its new member. But this man's crude external brace had served him well for years, allowing him to work as a vigorous coal miner. He came to me asking for a new bone mainly because he was tired of having to buckle on his exoskeleton every day.

Because it is hard and sometimes subject to fracture, bone has acquired the reputation of a nuisance to human activity. Bone prohibits us from squeezing into small spaces and from sleeping comfortably on hard ground. And what prevents skiers from adding twenty meters onto the looping, graceful ski jump and what keeps the slalom course in the domain of a few experts? The old nemesis of broken bones. A person who breaks a leg skiing could wish for stronger bones. But stronger bones would be thicker and heavier, making skiing far more limited or impossible.

No, the 206 lengths of calcium our body is strapped to are not there to restrict us; they free us. In the same way that the Welsh miner's arm was able to move only when it contained a proper scaffolding, external or internal, almost all our movements are made possible because of bone — rigid, inflexible bone.

⟿

In the Body of Christ also the quality of hardness is not designed to burden us; rather, it should free us. Rules governing behavior work because, like bones, they are hard.

Moral law. The Ten Commandments. Obedience. Doing right. A "thou shalt not" negativism taints the words, and we tend to view them as opposites to freedom. As a young Christian, I cringed at such words. But later, especially after I became a father, I started thinking beyond my reflex reaction to the very nature of law. Are not laws essentially a description of reality by the One who created it? God's rules governing human behavior — are they not guidelines meant to enable us to live the very best, most fulfilling life on earth?

I do not slip easily into such reasoning. Laws are too encrusted with cultural barnacles that obscure their true essence. They can summon up in me deeply embedded memories of parental disapproval, and instead I crave another kind of freedom — freedom from law, not freedom by it.

I have discovered, however, that it is possible to see beyond the surface negativism of, for example, the Ten Commandments and to learn something of the true nature of laws. Rules soon seem as liberating in social activity as bones are in physical activity.

The first four of the Ten Commandments are rules governing a person's relationship to God: Have no other gods before me. Don't worship idols. Don't misuse my name. Remember the day set aside to worship me. As I contemplate these once-forbidding commandments, more and more they sound like positive affirmations.

What if God had stated the same principles this way:

I love you so much that I will give you myself. I am true reality, the only God you will ever need. In me alone will you find wholeness.

I desire a wonderful thing: a direct, personal relationship between myself and each of you. You don't need inferior representations of me, such as dead wooden idols. You can have me. Value that.

I love you so much that I have given you my name. You will be known as "God's people" on the earth. Value the privilege; don't misuse it by profaning your new name or by not living up to it.

I have given you a beautiful world to work in, play in, and enjoy. In your involvement, though, set aside a day to remember where the world came from. Your bodies need the rest; your spirits need the reminder.

The next six commandments govern personal relationships. The first is already stated positively: honor your father and mother, a command echoed by virtually every society on earth. The next five:

Human life is sacred. I gave it, and it has enormous worth. Cling to it. Respect it; it is the image of God. Whoever ignores this and commits the sacrilege of murder must be punished.

The deepest human relationship possible is marriage. I created it to solve the essential loneliness in the heart of every person. To spread what is meant for marriage alone among a variety of people will devalue and destroy that relationship. Save sex and intimacy for its rightful place within marriage.

I am entrusting you with property. You can own things, and you should use them responsibly. Ownership is a great privilege. For it to work, you must respect everyone else's right to ownership; stealing violates that right.

I am a God of truth. Relationships only succeed when they are governed by truth. A lie destroys contracts, promises, trust. You are worthy of trust: express it by not lying.

I have given you good things to enjoy: oxen, grains, gold, furniture, musical instruments. But people are always more important than things. Love people; use things. Do not use people for your love of things.

Stripped down, the commandments emerge as a basic skeleton of trust that links relationships between people and between people and God. As the Good Shepherd, God has given law as the way to the best life. Our own rebellion, from the garden of Eden onward, tempts us to believe God is the bad shepherd whose laws keep us from something good.

⚊

Yes, one might reply, the Ten Commandments can be twisted around to reveal a more positive side. But why didn't God state them that way? Why say, "You shall *not* murder. You shall *not* commit adultery. You shall *not* steal ..."?

I suggest two answers. First, a negative command is actually less limiting than a positive one. "You may eat from any tree of the garden except one" allows more freedom than "You must eat from every tree of the garden, starting with the one in the northwest corner and working along the outer edge of the orchard." "You shall not commit adultery" is more freeing than "You must have sex with your spouse twice a week between the hours of nine and eleven in the evening." "Do not covet" is more freeing than "I am hereby prescribing limits on ownership. Every man is entitled to one cow, one ox, three gold rings. . . ."

Second, people were not yet ready for an emphasis on the positive commands. The Ten Commandments represent a kindergarten phase of morality: the basic laws needed for a society to operate. When Jesus came to earth, he filled in the positive side. Quoting the Old Testament, Jesus summarized the entire law in two positive commands: "Love God with all your heart and with all your soul and with all your strength and with all your mind," and "Love your neighbor as you love yourself" (Luke 10:27). It is one thing not to covet my neighbor's property and not to steal from him. It is quite another to love him so that I care for his family as much as I care for mine. Morality took a quantum leap from prohibition to love. (Paul affirmed and developed this thought in Romans 13:8–10.)

Jesus' Sermon on the Mount puts the capstone on his attitude toward the law. There, he described the Ten Commandments as the bare minimum. They actually point to profound principles: modesty, respect, non-violence, sharing. Then Jesus submitted the ideal social ethic — a system governed by only one law, the law of love. He calls us toward that ideal. Why? So God can take a fatherly pride in how well the little experiment on earth is progressing? Of course not. These laws were not given for God's sake, but for ours. "The Sabbath was made for man, not man for the Sabbath," Jesus said, and "You will know the truth, and the truth *will set you free*" (Mark 2:27; John 8:32). Jesus came to cleanse the violence, greed, lust, and hurtful competition from within us *for our sakes*. His desire is to have us become like God.

The Ten Commandments were the fetal development of bone, the first ossification from cartilage. The law of love is the fully developed, firm, liberating skeleton. It allows smooth movement within the Body of Christ, for it is hinged and jointed in the right places.

If you examine one law, like a random bone plucked from a pile, it may seem strangely shaped and illogical because laws, like bones, are designed for the complex, connected needs of a whole body. For example, as we have observed, the pelvis is a crazily shaped structure. It represents a compromise of converging needs: to walk, to protect abdominal organs, to sit, to support the back, and, in the woman's case, to bear children. Its shape exists to serve the body, not to dominate it. Similarly, God's laws governing us are a combination of conflicting human desires and needs, chosen to allow us to live life most fully and healthily. God, knowing our weaknesses and human frailties, designed the dogma of faith and morality to give strength and stability where we need them.

The law requiring sexual faithfulness in marriage to many people appears oddly and needlessly restrictive. Why not allow interchangeability, with men and women enjoying each other freely? We have the biological equipment for such practices. But sex transcends biology; it intertwines with romantic love, need for stable families, and many other factors. If we break one law, gaining the freedom of sexual experimentation, we lose the long-term benefits of intimacy that marriage is intended to provide. As my Welsh miner proved, removing one bone can ruin complex motion.

I have known people who feel compelled to cast off every possible limitation. They are like spoiled children, dashing from one toy to another, searching bitterly for an even better thrill, unaware that their search is actually a flight. Where do they stop cheating on their income tax? At what point do they allow the truth to break open before a cuckolded spouse? At what lie will their children cease to believe anything they say? Their lives become an entangling web of deception and fear. Does such a person have freedom?

I conclude with G. K. Chesterton that "the more I considered Christianity, the more I found that while it had established a rule and order, the chief aim of that order was to give room for good things to run wild."[1] He used the example of sex: "I could never mix in the common murmur of that rising generation against monogamy, because no restriction on sex seemed so odd and unexpected as sex itself.... Keeping to one woman is a small price for so much as seeing one woman. To complain that I could only be married once was like complaining that I had only been born once. It was incommensurate with the terrible excitement of which one was talking. It showed, not an exaggerated sensibility to sex, but a curious insensibility to it. A man is a fool who complains that he cannot enter Eden by five gates at once. Polygamy is a lack of the realization of sex; it is like a man plucking five pears in mere absence of mind."[2]

⟵

A skeleton is never beautiful; its contributions are strength and function. I do not inspect my tibia and wish it to be longer or shorter or more jointed. I just gratefully use it for walking, thinking about where I want to go rather than worrying about whether my legs will bear my weight. I should respond that way to the basic fundamentals of the Christian faith and the laws governing human nature. They are merely the framework for relationships which work best when founded on set, predictable principles. Of course, we can break them: adultery, thievery, lying, idolatry, oppression of the poor have crept into every society in history. But the result is a fracture that can immobilize the entire Body. Bones, intended to liberate us, only enslave us when broken.

Chapter 11

# GROWTH

*Better a little faith, dearly won, better launched alone on the infinite bewilderment of truth, than perish on the splendid plenty of the richest creeds.*

Henry Drummond

---

I n rural India legs are important. Tourists visit India's cities and ride in automobiles, but missionaries who want to reach the village people go to places with no roads. Bullock carts, with large, steel-rimmed wheels like those on the covered wagons of American pioneers, carry people over rough ground, but they are slower than walking. So missionaries walk.

I viewed it as one of my most important jobs to get missionaries back on their feet after accidents, and when Mrs. S. arrived at the hospital in Vellore I examined her with great concern. Heat and anxiety had soaked her dress with perspiration, and the awkward angle of her right foot indicated a severe leg fracture. She told me of an accident some months before in which she had broken her thigh bone, the femur. A doctor in the mountains had set the bone, but so far his X-rays had shown incomplete healing. He had sent her to our medical college for examination.

This good woman, Mrs. S., politely insisted she had to get back to mission work in her rural area. Legs meant everything to her.

When I X-rayed Mrs. S.'s fracture site, I expected to see the wondrously familiar sight of healing bone. Although bone has come to symbolize death at Halloween and in museums, the surgeon knows the symbol lies, for the skeleton is a growing organ. When I cut bone, it bleeds. Most amazing of all, when it breaks, it heals itself. Perhaps an engineer will someday develop a substance as strong and light and efficient as bone, but what engineer could devise a substance that, like bone, can grow continuously, lubricate itself, require no shutdown time, and repair itself when damage occurs?

When bone breaks, an elaborate process begins. Excited repair cells invade in swarm. Within two weeks a cartilage-like sheath called callus surrounds the region and cement-laying cells enter the jellied mass. These cells are the osteoblasts, the pothole-fillers of the bone. Gradually they break down the callus and replace it with fresh bone. In two or three months the fracture site is marked by a mass of new bone that bulges over both sides of the broken ends like a spliced garden hose. Later, surplus material is scavenged so the final result nearly matches the original bone.

That is bone's normal healing cycle. But to my surprise I saw no evidence of this process in Mrs. S.'s X-rays. A clean line — a dreaded gap — appeared between the two broken ends of bones, with no mending material fusing them together.

I opened up her leg for a firsthand look and confirmed there was no vestige of healing. Resorting to the inferior, nonliving tools of science, I fixed the area of the spiral break with a steel bone plate screwed into both pieces of the bone, above and below. On the other side of the break I placed a grafted section of her tibia to promote new bone formation, then sutured the wound.

After months of casts and wheelchairs and crutches, Mrs. S. again underwent X-rays. They revealed the grafted bone was taking: a milky cloud of growing bone enveloped the new bone strip, joining it to her original femur. But between the ends of the two broken bones a clean division still yawned open. Then I knew we had something very strange. After researching Mrs. S.'s history, I learned that twenty years earlier a doctor had irradiated her mid-thigh to treat a small, soft-tissue tumor. Evidently the radiation had killed the tumor. It had also killed all her living bone cells at that site, and thus the two ends would never grow together.

The inactivity was driving Mrs. S. crazy. God had sent her to a place where she needed legs, she insisted, and she was determined healing must take place.

I saw one hopeful sign, however: the bone grafts had grown normally. So I performed another operation. I found the space between the two ends of her broken femur so distinct I could insert the edge of my knife and wiggle it. First I checked the steel plate. The two screws farthest from the fracture site were loose and easy to remove: her body had begun rejecting them. But the four screws nearest the fracture were as solid as if they had been drilled into mahogany because the bone there was dead. I had to strain to turn them.

Obtaining two more bone grafts, one from Mrs. S.'s other tibia and one from her pelvis, I surrounded her fractured bone with living bone, as if packing it in ice. Then I closed the wound and waited.

Mrs. S. recovered and rejoined her mission station in the mountains. She spent an active life trudging the dusty trails, and her improvised leg bone served her well. Seven years later when I had her in for a checkup, X-rays revealed that the original fracture site had never healed — in one little area between the grafted bones I could see light. But a living bone shell, like a huge knot on a tree, had joined the two pieces together and formed a misshapen bulge of bone. She walked entirely on grafts — her original bone above, grafted bone in the middle, and her original bone below.

—͢

Mrs. S. offered a rare example of dead and living bone tissue existing side by side. When I opened her leg, the two looked the same. Their crucial difference showed when living bone interacted organically with her body while the dead bone did not. Because Mrs. S. was a living person encountering stresses and forces that required bone renewal, the dead bone failed her. A living body cannot rely on dead bone.

The analogy from physical bone to a spiritual skeleton has already been drawn for us in a dramatic passage in Ezekiel 37. There we see the prophet touring a surrealistic valley piled high with "bones that were very dry" (v. 2). God addressed those bones: "I will attach tendons to you and make flesh come upon you and cover you with skin; I will put breath in you, and you will come to life. Then you will know that I am the LORD" (v. 6).

The bones Ezekiel saw symbolized a great nation, Israel, that had degenerated to the dead skeletal form of antiquity. Israel's obedience and faith in God existed only as a dry, lifeless memory. Yet even those ancient bones had value. Ezekiel watched breathlessly as bones rattled together and formed the framework for a new body. This new nation would come to life with a preexisting heritage and understanding of God.

The history of a long, personal relationship with God can be preserved in laws and scriptures and ceremonies, as it was with Israel, or in creeds and art and cathedrals, as it is in Western culture today. Some revere such skeletons for their antiquity, buying recordings of Mozart's Masses and purchasing religious art. But, clearly, the real value of a skeleton only comes to light when it supports a growing organism. Although our laws, scriptures, traditions, and creeds reveal truth in themselves, they exist to serve such an organism, the Body of Christ.

The grafted bone in Mrs. S.'s leg beautifully displayed the normal procedures of living bone. As surely as the skeleton ossifies and hardens, it simultaneously grows and renews itself. Bone is alive. It spends its days changing, flowing, correcting, shifting — like a river as well as a rock.

The same stages of growth that I watched in Mrs. S.'s bone graft work faithfully each day within the skeletons of children. The newborn baby has 350 bones which will gradually fuse together into the 206 carried by most adult humans. But many of the baby's bones are soft and pliable, hardly showing the qualities of bone. The birth event would be impossible if a baby were not so compressible and flexible.

As I watch bone ossifying, or becoming hard, in X-rays, I am reminded of my own skeleton of faith. As a newborn Christian my faith was soft and pliable, consisting of vaguely understood beliefs about God and my spiritual hunger. Over time God has used the Bible and other Christians to help ossify the framework of my faith. In the same way that osteoblasts lay down firm new minerals in a bone, the substance of my faith has become harder and more dependable. The Lord has become my Lord; doctrines that were cold and formal have become an integral part of me.

The evangelical wing of faith, especially, tends to convey that all answers can be codified in a comprehensive statement of faith. Those who doubt the basic doctrines are sometimes treated as aliens in the Body and made to grovel in guilt and rejection. For that reason, in the evangelical world doubt is often a private phenomenon. Those of us tempted toward that kind of rigidity must come back to the analogy of living bone. New believers need time for the bones of their faith to strengthen.

I have known many times of doubt. In India I was challenged by the attractions of other religions devoutly practiced by millions of people. In medical school I faced constant exposure to assumptions that the universe is based on randomness, without room for an intelligent Designer. As I have grappled with these and other issues — questions about the person of Christ, trust in the Bible, etc. — I have learned it is sometimes helpful to continue accepting as a rule of life something about which I have basic intellectual uncertainties. In other words, I have learned to trust the basic skeleton and use it even when I cannot figure out how various bones fit together and why some are shaped the way they are.

In medical school I was taught by such secular biologists as J. B. S. Haldane and H. H. Woolard, pioneers of evolutionary theory. I noticed that some churches nourished a kind of intellectual dishonesty on this subject. In the university their students took exams and recited the theories of evolution; when they joined the church, they declared their faith in a way that contradicted their exam answers. Ultimately this dichotomy led to a sense of intellectual schizophrenia.

Only after much research and long periods of reflection was I able to put together what I had learned at church and what I had learned at school. But in the meantime I determined that my faith was based on realities that could stand by themselves and that did not need to be subordinated to any explanation of science. Either I would discover that evolution was compatible with the God of my faith, or I would find that evolution was somehow wrong and I would stay with my faith. I operated on that assumption for years during which I was unable to fill in all the blanks about how creation and evolution fit together. (In recent years, new understanding of the nature of DNA has greatly strengthened the position of one who believes in a guiding supernatural intelligence.)

A certain bridge in South America consists of interlocking vines supporting a precariously swinging platform hundreds of feet above a river. I know the bridge has supported hundreds of people over many years, and as I stand at the edge of the chasm I can see people confidently crossing the bridge. The engineer in me wants to weigh all the factors — measure the stress tolerances of the vines, test the wood for termites, survey all the bridges in the area for one that might be stronger. I could spend a lifetime determining whether the bridge is fully trustworthy. But eventually, if I really want to cross, I must take a step. When I put my weight on that bridge and walk across, even though my heart is pounding and my knees are shaking, I am declaring my position.

In the Christian world I sometimes must live like this, making choices which contain inherent uncertainty. If I wait for all the evidence to be in, for everything to be settled, I'll never move. Often I have had to act on the basis of the bones of the Christian faith before those bones were fully formed in me and before I understood the reason for their existence. Bone is hard, but it is alive. If the bones of faith do not continue to grow, they will soon become dead skeletons.

# Chapter 12

# ADAPTING

*If I profess with the loudest voice and clearest exposition every portion of the truth of God except precisely that little point which the world and the devil are that moment attacking, I am not confessing Christ, however boldly I may be professing Christ.*

Martin Luther

—⁊

Bone, concealed as it is, does not display its flow of life to onlookers. I must turn to the microscope to see traces of the activity now occurring there. With enough magnification I can identify two types of active cells in bone.

We have already met one type, the osteoblasts, pothole-filling repair cells that attach themselves to fracture sites and lay down bone crystal. But the Blasts do not wait around for accidents. Billions of them labor diligently inside me, replacing overaged bone. When I was young, 100 percent of all the bone in my body was replaced each year. So the jawbone I had as a four-year-old did not contain a single remnant of my three-year-old jawbone. Thanks to the wisdom of bone's DNA the shape stayed the same, only larger.

Now only about 18 percent of my bone gets replaced every year. Old bone does not surrender territory easily, though. It must be dynamited and vacuumed out, and for this job the body has osteoclasts, the demolition team. Clasts are large, packed with an average of ten to thirty nuclei, as if they need all the instructions they can get for their sensitive task.

If I tried to renovate a brick wall by removing a line of bricks in a horizontal row, the entire wall would quickly collapse. If, on the other hand, I removed a brick over here by my left elbow and replaced it, then replaced a brick by my knee, then one up by my head, I could in time safely reconstruct the entire wall. Similarly, Clasts scavenge each bit of bone, one cell at a time. They tunnel through bone as easily as moles through a lawn, opening up holes for the Blasts to fill. Blasts rejuvenate, depositing a new supply of healthy fiber.

The reckless Clast cell leads a kamikaze life, boring through granite with such verve that it burns out after forty-eight hours and is itself escorted away as waste. To me, this cell is employed most beautifully in the bird family. In a brief, crucial span of time, Clasts gently invade the bird's bone to loosen up calcium so the mineral can be used to harden the shell of the egg about to be laid.

The Blasts and the Clasts race throughout a person's life. Blasts tend to dominate the first half, laying down new bone in the orderly design of growth. But demolition Clasts eventually outstrip the weary Blasts. And so in old age teeth sockets decrease in size, the chin protrudes, the jaw angles in, and the elderly are left with more severe, pointed faces. That is why a fracture causes trauma for the elderly: their Blasts, barely up to the rigors of routine repair, heal bones slowly.

As old bone is renewed, Blasts factor into their design necessary adjustments for stress. All bone elements are arranged in perfectly engineered, intersecting lines of stress, like the girders on a steel bridge. If I break a foot and the pain of healing makes me adjust my walk so I take shorter steps, gradually those lines of stress in the heel bone will change and will end up at a new angle to the leg. The Blasts will accommodate to meet the new challenges.

If I start weight-lifting, a supporting leg bone like the femur might reasonably be expected to buckle or bend. Instead, it becomes thicker and develops extra struts on the stress side. In fact, stress stimulates bone growth. Rest in a hospital bed for a prolonged time and you may lose up to 50 percent of the calcium in your bones. The astronauts in outer space, freed from gravity, lost up to 20 percent of their calcium. Walking, lifting, flexing — any activity sends electrical currents through bone to generate growth.

⟵

When I consider the spiritual Body of Christ, and especially its skeleton of rules governing human behavior, I am conscious of a parallel type of renewing, adapting activity. The principles God has laid out, sometimes capsulized as in the Ten Commandments and the Sermon on the Mount, do not change, but their specific application certainly changes as the Body of Christ encounters new stresses. Many of the laws and observances of the Bible were geared to a society and culture alien to our own. A continuing need exists for prophets and teachers to interpret unchanging principles in light of the peculiar conditions of their day.

Consider the following list of direct instructions, all given to Christians in New Testament times and recorded for us in the Bible. Some of them are still followed or at least subscribed to by most Christians. Others are practiced by only a few denominations who strive to conform literally to New Testament practices. Nevertheless, I know of no group that obeys all of these instructions.

1. Greet one another with a holy kiss (Romans 16:16).
2. Abstain from food sacrificed to idols (Acts 15:29).

3. Be baptized (Acts 2:38).
4. A woman ought to have a veil on her head (1 Corinthians 11:10).
5. Wash one another's feet (John 13:14).
6. It is disgraceful for a woman to speak in the church (1 Corinthians 14:35).
7. Sing psalms, hymns, and spiritual songs (Colossians 3:16).
8. Abstain from eating blood (Acts 15:29).
9. Observe the Lord's Supper (1 Corinthians 11:24).
10. Remember the poor (Galatians 2:10).
11. Anoint the sick with oil (James 5:14).
12. Permit no woman to teach men (1 Timothy 2:12).
13. Preach two by two (Mark 6:7).
14. Eat whatever is put before you without raising questions of conscience (1 Corinthians 10:27).
15. Prohibit women from wearing braided hair, gold, pearls, or expensive clothes (1 Timothy 2:9).
16. Abstain from sexual immorality (Acts 15:29).
17. Do not look for a wife (1 Corinthians 7:27).
18. Refrain from public prayer (Matthew 6:5–6).
19. Speak in tongues privately and prophesy publicly (1 Corinthians 14:4).
20. Lead a quiet life and work with your hands (1 Thessalonians 4:11).
21. Lift up holy hands in prayer (1 Timothy 2:8).
22. Give to those who beg from you (Matthew 5:42).
23. Only enroll (for aid) widows who are over sixty, have been faithful to their husbands, and are well-known for good deeds (1 Timothy 5:9–10).
24. Wives, submit to your husbands (Colossians 3:18).
25. Show no partiality toward the rich (James 2:1–7).

26. Owe no man anything (Romans 13:8).
27. Abstain from the meat of animals killed by strangulation (Acts 15:29).
28. If a man will not work, he shall not eat (2 Thessalonians 3:10).
29. Set aside money for the poor on the first day of every week (1 Corinthians 16:1–2).
30. If you owe taxes, pay taxes (Romans 13:7).[1]

A biblical scholar can research those commands viewed as temporary or occasional and explain why the Bible writer applied the principle in just that peculiar way to a stress. For example, the apostle Paul gave many instructions on eating meat that had passed through heathen ceremonies in the temples, a problem not common today in Western nations. Also, in those days in a church like the one at Corinth, women were judged by powerful social customs. If a woman spoke out in a public meeting, the group would naturally assume she was a prostitute or pagan priestess; the same inference was drawn about women who wore their hair in certain styles.

Paul realized the need to adapt lines of stress depending on what group he was with. He refused to let Jewish Christians force Gentiles to be circumcised unwillingly, yet he went through purification rites in the Jerusalem temple (Acts 21) to win the trust of Jewish Christians.

Today we are facing our own particular stress lines. When the human race was young on a planet of unbelievable expanse and few people, the law "Be fruitful and multiply" was obviously appropriate. But we have obeyed that one command so well that all life is now endangered. We need to place new emphasis on our responsibility for the soil and wildlife and perhaps slow down on our multiplying.

Now that we can separate the enjoyment of sex from the risk of increasing the number of children, we need new ways to emphasize the Christian view that sex is a means to an end and not an end in itself. If it is not always a step toward the making of a child, how can it be reaffirmed as a symbol of the continuing love that binds a marriage together, and not as a haphazard expression of lust?

Some in the church are trying to adapt to stresses created by the medical profession. When major diseases assailed health, rules to prolong life were developed. Today science has an ability to prolong life almost indefinitely, even when that life is meaningless, without consciousness or hope of recovery, yet not meeting any of the old criteria of death.

These issues do not call for sweeping revisions of creeds and beliefs, but they do evince a need for some members of the church to reflect, study the Bible, and pray, and then lead the way in reinterpreting the will of God for their own generation. These people, prophets and teachers, serve as living bone cells in Christ's Body, laying down the inorganic minerals that go into our frame. They should possess humility and a commitment to preserve the great principles of the Christian faith. Yet they should have equal concern that the principles be relevant and give strength just where it is needed.

⟝

In 1892 Julius Wolff first noticed lines of stress in the cellular arrangement of the human skeleton, leading to Wolff's Law, which every medical student learns. Caught up in his enthusiasm, Wolff declared that bones were in a state of great flux, adapting readily to changes in environment and function. Actually, when I visit a museum and compare skeletons throughout the centuries, I am chiefly impressed by their uniformity. Adaptations to stress are minor knobs and slight ridges along bones that have consistently maintained a definite length and shape.

Behind each of the adaptations of divine law applied to a specific culture in the Bible stands a basic principle. Respect for life must be cherished, although today we redefine life in light of new medical advances. Modesty must be protected, but today a woman's short hair is not immodest. The bone endures; the Body simply adapts to new stresses.

# Chapter 13

# INSIDE-OUT

*Thy bone is marrowless, thy blood is cold.*

Shakepeare's *Macbeth*

—✐

Twice a year a strange fever rolls like a fog from the bayous, spreading across the flatlands of Louisiana. Hand-painted signs are propped up outside dilapidated restaurants: FRESH CRAWFISH NOW! Schoolboys, barefoot and sweaty, scramble up the gullies dragging tin pails crawling with dozens of the prehistoric-looking creatures. Each pail contains a writhing mass of crushed antennae, flexing pinchers, and clicking skeletons.

You can find crayfish (or crawfish) in almost any river, pond, or ditch in Louisiana and in most other states. High-banked ditches running east and west are the most likely places, since crayfish shy away from the hot sun and that alignment provides them more shade. Early morning or evening, squat down beside the creek and wait. Soon your eyes will adjust to the shimmering surface and you can focus on the underwater world. Probably you won't see crayfish right away. They are subtle, and a green or brownish coloration camouflages them masterfully.

As you stare, you gradually see a monster. First are two armored claws, hinged, hooked at the elbow and menacing-looking. Crayfish claws, half its body length, give it an unbalanced, militaristic appearance, like a gunboat with two oversized howitzers protruding over its bow. Two gleaming black eyes jut out between the claws, eyes that protrude on the ends of stalks — *movable* stalks. If the crayfish wants to see you from a better angle, he does not tilt his head, but jerks his eyestalks as easily as you raise an eyebrow.

If catfish are the garbage collectors of ponds, crayfish are the trash compactors. Anything goes into their mouths: snails, other crayfish, plants, frogs, fish — living or dead, fresh or carrion. Their elder brothers, the lobsters, contentedly munch hardshell crabs, clams, and mussels. This devouring of things stony is made possible by some ingenious equipment, including two segmented, short limbs called *foot-jaws* which crush and tear whatever is placed between them. Inside, the crayfish stomach features three hard, bony teeth that continue the mastication process.

The rest of the crayfish duplicates in miniature the familiar lobster: plates of overlapping armor ending in a broad, fan-shaped tail.

In 1879 Thomas Henry Huxley wrote a classic book about crayfish. He told of the vile habits of a species that may attack its own babies or devour its spouse after a vigorous mating session. He reported the amazing process of regeneration whereby a crayfish with a missing claw will miraculously sprout a new one. He described the unique qualities of crayfish blood, colorless, which adjusts to the temperature of the surrounding water. The clear liquid draining from a wounded crayfish hardly brings to mind the river of life, but to a crayfish red blood probably seems extravagant.

I write of crayfish not because of their blood or bad tempers or capacity for regeneration, but because of their skeletons. Crack open a crayfish and you'll find soft, white meat, begging to be dipped in butter. No bones grow there to annoy a gourmand — the shell *is* its skeleton. When crayfish season arrives in Louisiana, local restaurants will bring you platters of thirty or so of the boiled creatures, their shells tinted a bright red by the cooking process. After an hour of popping and scraping and digging, you leave a plateful of skeletons — thin, crayfish-shaped exteriors which, if propped up in a lifelike pose, would look like a complete crayfish.

A crayfish has an exoskeleton. Its muscles work against a skeleton surrounding it, and the hardness of the crayfish becomes its chief offense and defense in a competitive world.

After devoting several chapters to the essential property of hardness in the bones (doctrines and principles) of Christ's Body, I must, for the sake of balance, insert a strong warning. I sense the need for that warning best when I compare the crayfish and lobster family to human beings. The difference is obvious, especially when you try to shake hands with both. A human feels soft, warm, responsive. If you shake hands with a crayfish, you'll feel inflexibility, coldness, and probably pain. A good-sized lobster can break your finger with a quick pinch of its claw.

As I look at the history of the church, failures loom large — failures which can be traced to a misunderstanding of the place of the skeleton in the Body of Christ. Some Christians who realize the importance of law and discipline unfortunately wear their skeletons on the outside. When you meet these people, their dogma stands out as obtrusively as does a crayfish's shell.

Examples leap to mind: the "athletes for God" monks who wished to display their dedication to God publicly and convincingly. Simon Stylites, who died in A.D. 459, led the way: he perched on a pillar east of Antioch for thirty-six years and is said to have touched his feet with his forehead more than 1,244 times in succession. Other monks subsisted by eating only grass. Theodore of Sykeon, a seventh-century saint, spent most of his life suspended from a rock in a narrow cage, exposed to the storms of winter, starving himself while soulfully singing psalms.

Some of these practitioners sought a personal way of demonstrating their commitment to God. Others, however, strained to make a public display of their zeal in order to impress onlookers — exactly the error which Jesus blasted in the Pharisees (see Matthew 23 and Luke 11).

Today the most rigorous expressions of faith are seen in the religions of the East, where zealots walk on hot coals and lie on beds of nails. But subtle means of displaying exoskeletons persist in Christianity.

Find a non-Christian walking the streets of your city or town. Pull him aside and ask him what impressions he has of truly committed Christians — not the church-on-Sunday kind but the earnest, born-again kind. Fleeting images will likely cross his mind. He may mention cartoons of the doomsday, sandwich-board prophets who have become a cliché in magazines like the *New Yorker*. He may refer to radio preachers who assail him with threats of hell. Or, he may identify Christians around him by a certain lifestyle, a list of things they do not do: smoking, drinking, swearing, attending movies, or dancing.

How is an evangelical identified in today's world? Often they are perceived as people who obey strict rules. Psychiatrists excoriate them as guilt-inducers, declaring that over half their patients got messed up in church. Somehow we keep producing variations on pole-sitting Christians. We tend to retreat into our exoskeletons and define our place in the world by how different we are from the rest.

I am often tempted to view legalism as a harmless diversion of the faith. So what if one denomination chooses to ban an innocent activity? Isn't it merely humorous that churches overseas, whose members readily drink and smoke, recoil in horror at the idea of Christians wearing blue jeans or chewing gum? Perhaps some of our cultural quirks are harmless diversions.

But legalism contains enough inherent dangers to elicit the strongest warnings in the Bible. No other issue — not pornography, adultery, violence, or the things which most rankle Christians today — inspired more fiery outbursts from Jesus.

Strangely, the people who made Jesus livid with anger were the ones the modern press might call Bible-belt fundamentalists. This group, the Pharisees, devoted their lives to following God. They gave away exact tithes, obeyed each minute law in the Old Testament, and sent out missionaries to gain new converts. Almost no sexual sin or violent crime was visible among the Pharisees. Yet Jesus denounced these model citizens. Why?

To answer that question, I go back to the humble crayfish creeping along the creek bottoms of Louisiana. In comparing its exoskeleton with my more advanced internal skeleton, several differences suggest themselves and throw light on Jesus' strong statements in Matthew 23 and Luke 11 about the dangers of legalism.

First, the crayfish relies almost exclusively on its skeleton for protection. Its dependable armor plating can ward off enemies. Humans, in contrast, have soft, vulnerable exteriors. But as the rules God gave to free Christ's Body begin to calcify, we tend to hunker down inside them for protection. We develop a defensive exoskeleton. In his *Letters to an American Lady*, C. S. Lewis said, "Nothing gives a more spuriously good conscience than keeping rules, even if there has been a total absence of real charity and faith."

Legalists fool you. Like the Pharisees and the "athletes for God," they impress you with their unquestioned dedication.

Surely, you think, they have a high view of God. But I learned as I grew up in a legalistic environment that legalism actually errs by lowering sights. It spells out exactly what a person has to do to meet God's approval. In so doing, legalists can miss the whole point that the gospel is a gift freely given by God to people who don't deserve it.

A meticulous researcher named Merton Strommen surveyed seven thousand Protestant youths from many denominations, asking whether they agreed with the following statements:

"The way to be accepted by God is to try sincerely to live a good life." More than 60 percent agreed.

"God is satisfied if a person lives the best life he can." Almost 70 percent agreed.

"The main emphasis of the gospel is on God's rules for right living." More than half agreed! One would think the apostle Paul and Martin Luther had never opened their mouths, or that Jesus had never come to die. Christians — a majority of young ones — still believe that following a code of rules gets you accepted by God.[1]

What else but our relentless, harping insistence on strict rules could cause this phenomenon? Shouldn't we devote equal time to explaining that rules are merely joints and bones to make our Body effective, and not a ladder to God?

➤

A second danger of legalism is that it limits our growth by forming a hard, crusty shell around the accepted group.

An adult crayfish only has the opportunity to grow about once a year. Growth entails an arduous, tortuous procedure called molting that exposes the creature to deadly dangers. The confining exoskeleton must be shed. Warming up for this traumatic experience, the crayfish rubs its limbs against one another, moves each separately, then flips onto its back, flexing its tail up and down. These movements give it a little play inside its shell.

After several spasms of agitation, the crayfish pushes mightily and its top plate of armor pops free, staying connected only at the mouth. Gingerly, it removes its head, with special care for the eyes and antennae, which are sometimes damaged in the process. Next, legs are yanked out, often with one breaking off. Finally, with a sudden spring forward, the crayfish unsheathes its abdomen and lies there naked and weak.

After resting, prostrate, from the demands of shedding its shell, the crayfish slinks toward some protection. Its body is no longer a stiff, lacquered sheet of chitin; now it has the consistency of wet paper. Often the molting crayfish will make the discarded skeleton its first meal, ingesting minerals it will need to grow a new shell.

During the next few weeks, the crayfish does all its growing for a year. It may add as much as an inch to its length before the new shell hardens and locks it into the shape and size of the new skeleton.

I have undergone a parallel process of Christian molting. I started in a close-knit group holding rigid ideas of what a Christian was and who was worthy of fellowship. As I traveled and gained breadth of experience, I realized that not all Christians were of my race with my style of worship and my footnoted doctrinal statement. So I grew a new shell, until the next experience came along. I tended to lapse into seeing the Christian family as an exclusive set of *people like me* encased in a shell. Inside, all was warm and comfortable; outside, the shell protected us from "the world."

But Jesus never described anything resembling an exoskeleton which would define all Christians. He kept pointing to higher, more lofty demands, using words like love and joy and fullness of life — internal words. When someone came to him for a specific interpretation of an Old Testament rule, usually he pointed instead to the principle behind it.

Jesus understood that rules and governing behavior are meant to free movement and promote growth as a vertebrate skeleton does, not to inhibit growth as an exoskeleton does.

⟿

Perhaps the most pernicious effect of legalism is its influence on groups outside the legalistic community. Lobsters and crayfish make unappealing pets because of their external shells. If doctrines and rules are worn externally, as a show of pride in spiritual superiority, the exoskeleton obscures God's grace and love, making the Christian gospel ugly and unattractive.

Earlier in this century in India and other Asian countries, the missionaries' tendency to Westernize the church created a hard exoskeleton that offended the local society and limited the church's influence.

In America too, examples persist. Find a person once deeply involved in church who has chosen to leave it, and you will likely hear that something harsh obtruded into that person's faith. Perhaps it was some Christians' judgmental attitude about a marriage situation. How many divorced persons have left the church when made to feel like second-class citizens? Or perhaps it was disapproval of a habit, like smoking. Having treated emphysema and removed cancerous lungs, I hate smoking. And I hate what divorce does to its victims, especially the children. But I must not allow my views on smoking or divorce to drive people away. For a model, I must look to Jesus, who opposed the sin but loved the sinner.

Though he openly declared God's laws, somehow he conveyed them with such love that he became known as the friend of sinners.

Do we drive people away from the riches of God's love because of our ideas of what behavior should be? Rules about behavior certainly have a function; the Bible swells with them. But they are meant to be worn on the inside, not on the outside as a display of superiority.

A troubling phenomenon recurs among young Christians reared in solid homes and sound churches. After living their early years as outstanding examples of Christian faith, many become spiritual dropouts. Did they fail because they concentrated on the exterior, visible Christian life? Did they learn to mimic certain behaviors, nuances of words, and emotional responses? Crayfish-like, did they develop a hard exterior that resembled everyone else's and conclude such was the kingdom of God, while inside they were weak and vulnerable?

When Christianity is an external exercise, it can be cast aside in the manner of a crayfish flinging off its shell. In fact, many crayfish perish from the molting ordeal, either because of exhaustion or because of their vulnerability to outside enemies.

An outside shell may seem attractive, trustworthy, and protective. It certainly has advantages over a dead, useless skeleton or over no skeleton at all. But God desires for us a more advanced skeleton that serves as it stays hidden.

# SKIN

# Chapter 14

# VISIBILITY

*What is it, then, this seamless body stocking, some two yards square, this our casing, our facade, that flushes, pales, perspires, glistens, glows, furrows, tingles, crawls, itches, pleasures and pains us all our days, at once keeper of the organs within, and sensitive probe, adventurer into the world outside?*

Richard Selzer

In India, while leprosy research consumed my time, my wife Margaret trained as an ophthalmologist and became an expert eye surgeon. Because many of the neediest people could not travel to the hospital, she and a team of helpers took a well-stocked mobile unit on monthly circuits into rural areas. On a certain date a designated building, perhaps a school or an old rice mill, would receive a stream of Indians afflicted with runny eyes or blindness. The staff worked under crude conditions, sometimes in stifling heat, devising an assembly line of treatment. If no building was available, they would even set up portable operating tables under a banyan tree. Sometimes two doctors performed over one hundred cataract operations a day.

In 1956, Margaret's team staffed a camp for several weeks in an area of India that had been devastated by drought. Crops had failed for five years, and the wells were dry of drinking water. People straggled in from every direction, begging for food. Assuming they would have to stay at the camp to receive food, many volunteered for needless surgery — to the extent of asking that one of their eyes be removed — in order to get something to eat.

Young boys volunteered to assist at that hectic camp, and Margaret was assigned a shy, dark boy about twelve years old. He stood on a box, with an impressive but baggy hospital gown wrapped around him, charged with strict instructions to hold a three-battery flashlight so that the light beamed directly on the cornea of the patient's eye. Margaret was dubious: could a young village boy who had never watched any surgery endure the trauma of seeing people's eyes sliced open and stitched together again?

The child, however, performed his task with remarkable aplomb. During the first five operations he scrupulously followed Margaret's instructions on when to shift the angle of light, aiming the beam with a steady, confident hand. But during the sixth case he faltered. Margaret kept saying softly, "Little brother, show the light properly," which he would momentarily do, but soon it again would dangerously bob away from where she was cutting. Margaret could see that he simply could not bear to look at the eye being worked on. She stopped and asked if he was feeling well.

Tears ran down his cheeks and he stuttered, "Oh, doctor — I– I cannot look. This one, she is my mother."

Ten days later the boy's suffering was over. His mother's stitches were removed, and the team gave her eyeglasses. She first tried to blink away the dazzling light, but finally adjusted, focused, and for the first time in her life saw her son. A smile creased her face as she reached out to touch him. "My son," she said, "I thought I knew you, but today I see you." And she pulled him close to her.

⬋

In her poignant way, the Indian woman expressed that her son at last had become a recognizable image to her. Before, she had known the sensation of touching him and the sound of his voice. Now she had a literal image of his shape and appearance. If he entered her dreams at night, she would know him. Yet she had seen only one organ of his body, the skin. Our impressions and memories of each other come packaged in that one visible organ by which we judge others and convey our own responses.

Sometimes I envy my wife's field of medicine which is confined to two transparent ovals not shielded by the opaque fabric of skin. She can peer inside without cutting, and if she must cut, can later observe healing with an unobstructed view. Only the eyes expose to the doctor moist, living cells inside the body: corpuscles shooting through capillaries, and sometimes traces of bacteria and cancer as well.

Yet in more subtle ways the skin is, like the eye, a window. On it we read the health of the activities within. Anemia shows in the nails and skin, drawing a ghostly pallor across its victims. Jaundice yellows the skin, while a form of diabetes shades it bronze. Some drugs transform the skin into an iridescent tattoo-blue; we have such patients at Carville. Lack of oxygen in the blood casts a purple tint. Scurvy, beriberi, glandular malfunctions — the skin reveals their presence and many other deficiencies.

When its rainbow is depleted, the skin turns to other signals. Leprosy shows itself when nerve endings fall silent. Cancers leak out in a rash or an aggravating mole. An allergist can crack the secret code of your body's likes and dislikes merely by mapping out a grid on your back and pricking the skin with pin-sized potions. Is it dog hair? Pollen? Shellfish? Your skin will unriddle the mysterious vomiting or sneezing.

⊸

Skin also provides a window to the emotional world within. We have relatively few voluntary muscles on our skin — we cannot twitch it at will, as can a horse. But we do have control over our faces, and there volumes are written. Pains from childhood are sometimes stamped onto the contours of skin like carved initials scarring a tree trunk. A slight downward curve of the lips can warn a spouse to walk on eggshells.

Sometimes the body revolts and shows its true sentiments in spite of us. Mark Twain said, "Man is the only animal who blushes — or needs to." Blush. It connotes a sudden heat, a steamy swelling of vessels which involuntarily, rebelliously even, rush fifty times more blood to the skin. (Imagine a city water supply responding to an instantaneous 5000-percent increase in demand.) The young blush more than the old, women more than men. No one is exempt: blind people blush; all races blush, including the darkest ones (their albinos prove it). Blushing acts upon the skin to alert an observer to underlying sentiments.

⊸

There is no organ like the skin. Averaging a mere nine pounds, it flexes and folds and crinkles around joints, facial crags, gnarled toes, and fleshy buttocks. It is smooth as a baby's stomach here, rough like a crocodile there. A bricklayer's hands may be horny, taut, and layered with sandpaper, but flaccid, pliable folds shroud his abdomen. Intricate spot-welds fasten a leg's wrap, holding it tautly to the muscle layer; an elbow droops loosely, like the skin of a cat that can be tossed by the scruff of its neck.

Choose sections of the scalp, the lip, the nipple, the heel, the abdomen, and the fingertip to view through a laboratory microscope. They are as different as the skins of a host of species — a patchwork somehow growing in a continuous sheet over the body. Tiny ridges crisscross skin's surface to provide traction, much as a snow tire does. Amazingly, for no apparent reason, each of us is given a different pattern for the ridges, a flourish which the FBI capitalizes on in its fingerprint files. The ridges themselves give texture and the power to grasp a slippery object.

We have a love affair with skin, and our chief response, curiously, is to adorn it. Males perform a daily morning ritual to chop off a night's growth from hair follicles. They rearrange other hairs atop their heads, perhaps worry over a few pimples, and inspect a mole or two. Females expand the ritual, countering the hard work of dense oil glands on the nose by powdering them dry, curling hairs around the eye, plucking others, and outlining that organ with traces of bright colors. Some daub the skin like canvas, hiding it under a paste of color; most shade the lips to match the day's attire. And then, alone of all the animals on God's earth, we sense the need to swathe large patches of that skin, supporting a multi-billion-dollar fashion industry in the process.

I can best understand the urge to adorn by studying the competition, the several million other species with whom we share this planet. Choose any class of animal — snakes, insects, birds, mammals — and flip through a color photograph book of its members. Brightness and design leap from the pages. It is as if the Creator began with exhilaration, splurging on a macaw and a killer whale and a coral snake, took a breather with greyish lizards and dull sparrows and game fish, then lavished tropical fish with just-invented pigments, splashed a cardinal and a jay and a magpie before settling down to the more intricate designs of reptile scales, zebra stripes, and cheetah spots. Then, creativity exhausted and pigment running dry, the designer settled on blandly uniform flesh colors for the human species — with interesting variegations of yellows, browns, and reds, to be sure — nevertheless solid and one-colored except for a wash of coral across lips and nipples.

How skilled is the Creator? Consider the line drawings, paintings, sculptures, and photographs that have, since cave dwellers, eloquently expressed our unending fascination with plain human skin.

By studying skin's biochemistry, I can fathom how a few molecules here and there, interacting with sunlight, can change a color (the Negroid race derives its rich shade from a mere one-thirtieth of an ounce of melanin). I can comprehend the process by which moist, gelatinous cells march to the surface to flatten out and dry into keratin, a protective, flaky coating, before being shed. I can understand the complex process of keratin producing rigid fingernails and horses' hooves. But no amount of training will lessen my astonishment as I watch a single stalk of keratin push its way out of a follicle, grow erect and proud and shockingly unfurl as a peacock feather. What was chemistry becomes beauty. It is as if a brilliant Appalachian quilt springs from a rock, as if a desert suddenly births a gang of cavorting porpoises.

⌐

Compared with other finely decorated animals, the human seems naked, vulnerable, incomplete. More than that of any other species, our skin is designed not so much for appearance as for relating, for being touched. And this aspect of skin summons up the basic function of skin within the Body of Christ. In that Body, skin becomes the presence of Christ himself, the membrane lining that defines our community and enshrouds God's Body in the world. We have seen that Christians sometimes err by displaying their skeletons before a watching world. Christ condemned that trend. Instead, he held before us the principle of love, saying, "All men will know that you are my disciples, if you love one another" (John 13:35).

The analogy of skin — soft, warm, and touchable — conveys the message of a God who is eager to relate in love to his creations. Christ was saying to us: Let the world first see the beauty and feel the softness and warmth of the Christian community, and then let it realize the underlying internal framework.

As the world encounters Christ's Body, what is its texture, its appearance and "feel" — its skin? Do people see "love, joy, peace, patience, kindness, goodness, faithfulness, gentleness and self-control" (Galatians 5:22–23)? We judge people by appearance, studying facial expressions for some hint of mood or glimpse into them. In the same way, we as a Body are being scrutinized and evaluated. Others are drawing a picture of Christ from our appearance. The atmosphere in a church will, skinlike, reveal the substance underneath.

# Chapter 15

# PERCEIVING

*The greatest sense in our body is the touch sense. We feel, we love and hate, are touchy and are touched, through the touch corpuscles of our skin.*

J. Lionel Taylor

In 1953 I toured the United States on a Rockefeller Foundation grant, studying under renowned hand surgeons and pathologists to explore why leprosy causes paralysis. My trip ended in New York where I was to speak on assignment for the American Leprosy Mission and visit several surgeons. During the meeting with ALM, I began to feel nauseated and dizzy. I managed to deliver the address, but the fever continued to rise as I made my way to the subway station. At one point I swayed and fell to the floor of the subway car, too dizzy to sit or stand. Other passengers, probably assuming I was drunk, simply ignored me.

Somehow I staggered to my hotel. I dully realized I should call a doctor, but the hotel room had no telephone and the illness overwhelmed me so that all I could do was curl up on the bed and moan. For several days I stayed that way, with a bellboy daily fetching me orange juice and milk and aspirin.

I recovered, though weak and unsteady, in time for my ship's voyage back to Southampton, England. After landing at Southampton, I rode a train to London, sitting in a cramped corner, hunched over and wishing the interminable trip would end.

At last I arrived at my aunt's house, emotionally and physically drained. I collapsed like a sack of potatoes into a chair and pulled off my shoes. Then came probably the bleakest moment of my entire life. As I leaned forward and pulled off my sock, I became aware of the horrible fact that my left heel had no feeling.

A dread fear worse than nausea gripped my stomach. After seven years of working with leprosy patients, had it finally happened? Was I now to be a patient myself?

I stood stiffly, found a straight pin, and sat down again. I lightly pricked a small patch of skin below my ankle. I felt no pain. I jabbed the pin deeper, longing for a reflex, but there was none — just a speck of blood oozing out the pinhole. I put my face between my hands and shuddered, longing for pain that would not come.

For seven years my team and I had joined in the battle against centuries of tradition to gain new freedom for leprosy patients. We had tried to combat fear, had helped tear down the ugly barbed-wire fence around the leprosy village at Vellore.

I had assured new staff members that the disease was the least contagious of all communicable diseases and that proper hygiene would practically guarantee they would not contract the disease. Now I, their leader ... a *leper*. That vicious word I had banned from my vocabulary rose up like a monster with new meanings. How glibly I had encouraged patients to overcome the stigma of the past and forge a new life for themselves by surmounting society's prejudices.

My mind roiled. I would have to separate myself from my family, of course — children of patients were the most susceptible group. Perhaps I should stay in England. But what if word somehow leaked out? I could envision the headlines. And what would happen to my leprosy work? How many would now risk becoming social outcasts to help unfortunate victims?

I lay on my bed all night, fully clothed except for shoes and socks, sweating and breathing heavily from tension. Scenes flickered through my mind — poignant reminders of what I would lose as a leprosy patient. Although I knew that sulfone drugs would probably arrest the disease quite quickly, I could not avoid imagining the disease spreading across my face, over my feet, and to my fingers. My hands were my stock in trade. How could I use a scalpel on living organs without exquisite finger control and response to pressure? My career as a surgeon would soon end.

So much of beauty would also slip away. I had always found my greatest relaxation working in a garden. I loved to pulverize the soil with a hoe, then bend down and squeeze it. Crushing the dirt through my fingers brought a wealth of sensations: hardness in the clods, dew on the grass, and a sense of the soil's dampness or clay-like qualities. I might lose that sensitivity.

I would no longer feel the pleasing softness of petting a dog, or the flutter of a June beetle cupped in my hands, or the prenatal stirrings of a caterpillar throbbing ominously against a rough cocoon. Feathers, frogs, flowers, wool — touch sensations filled my world. Because I worked with leprosy patients who had lost most of these sensations, I cherished them more consciously than most people.

Dawn finally came, and I arose, unrested and full of despair. I stared in a mirror for a moment, summoning up courage, then picked up the pin again to map out the affected area. I took a deep breath, jabbed in the point — and yelled aloud. Never has a feeling been so delicious as that live, electric jolt of pain synapsing through my body. I fell on my knees in gratitude to God.

I laughed aloud and shook my head at my foolishness of the night before. Of course, it all made perfect sense now. As I had sat on the train, weakened enough to forego the usual restless motion of muscles in a cramped place, I had numbed a nerve in my leg. Exhausted, I had exaggerated my fears and jumped to false conclusions. There was no leprosy, only a tired, nervous traveler.

━

That dismal experience, which I was too ashamed to mention to anyone for years, imprinted in me profound lessons about pain and sensitivity. Since then I have purposefully tried to feel, *really* feel the extravagant number of objects surrounding me. Forests, animals, cloth, sculpture, paintings — these beg for eager explorations by sense-hungry fingertips.

The skin does not exist merely to give the body an appearance. It is also a vital, humming source of ceaseless information about our environment. Most of our sense organs — the ears, the eyes, the nose — are confined to one spot. The skin is rolled thin like pie dough and studded with half a million tiny transmitters, like telephones jammed together waiting to inform the brain of important news.

Think of the variety of stimuli your skin monitors each day: wind, particles, parasites, changes in pressure, temperature, humidity, light, radiation. Skin is tough enough to withstand the rigorous pounding of jogging on asphalt, yet sensitive enough to have bare toes tickled by a light breeze. The word *touch* swells with such a plethora of meanings and images that in many dictionaries, including the *Oxford English*, its definition runs the longest of any entry. I can hardly think of a human activity — sports, music, art, cooking, mechanics, sex — that does not vitally rely on touch. (Perhaps pure mathematics?)

Touch is the most alert of our senses when we sleep, and it is the one that seems to invigorate us emotionally: consider the lovers' embrace, the contented sigh after a massage, the cuddling of a baby, the sting of a hot shower. Read the thoughts of Helen Keller — a *cum laude* graduate of Radcliffe and author of twelve books — and you will see what the brain can accomplish with no input but a sense of touch.

Although scientists disagree on exactly how touch works, they can calibrate how well it works. One tap of the fingernail can tell me if I am touching paper, fabric, wood, plastic, or steel. A normal hand can distinguish between a smooth plane of glass and one etched with lines only 1/2500 of an inch deep. A textile feeler can readily recognize burlap by the friction — that's easy; but he can also pick satin over silk, blindfolded. By rubbing his hands over a synthetic fabric, he can detect if the nylon blend has been increased by 5 percent.

Those seemingly useless hairs blanketing our bodies act as levers to magnify the sensation of touch. We can discern a thousandth of an ounce of pressure on the tip of a half-inch hair.*

⭲.

The skin's advanced ability to inform helps me understand one of the chief duties of the front line of the Body of Christ: to

---

*A good friend of mine, Dr. Khonalker of Bombay, learned firsthand about the sensitivity of hairs when he tested a group of women to seek the normal threshold of sensitivity. He discovered that the women who did not usually shave their legs were very insensitive in the area shaven for testing for awhile, as insensitive as leprosy patients. But gradually their skin adapted. The skin had a potential for greater sensitivity, but suppressed it as long as hairs were present. When shaving removed the hairs, the body noticed silent areas on the legs and "turned up the volume" on touch-sensitive cells there.

sensitively perceive the people it contacts. Beginning counselors, eager to help people, are warned, "First, you must listen. Your wise advice will do no good unless you begin by carefully listening to the person in need." Skin provides a more basic kind of listening, a tactile perception from thousands of sensors. Love for others starts with this primal contact.

If there is a change in the air pressure, or in the texture of cloth, or in the temperature, skin sensors fire off messages to the brain. In the same way the Christian church being, as Jesus said, "in the world but not of the world," encounters a constant stream of signals about the qualities and needs of its environment. The Body is large, universal, and its sensors report in simultaneously from lakeshore apartments in Chicago, the slums of Harlem, the jungles of Peru and Sri Lanka, and the deserts of Russia and Arabia.

In Christ's Body, some members are specifically designated to monitor the changing needs of the world. Today, for example, Christian missions have become more sensitive to the physical and social needs of people as well as their spiritual needs.

The early days of missions were sometimes marked by people who were unresponsive to new environments. They did not sense the worth and beauty already present in strange cultures. They responded to bare-breasted, drum-beating Africans as if they were inchoate Europeans, swaddling them in inappropriate clothes and teaching them Martin Luther's favorite hymns.

Condescending love intrudes on the scene with a slick solution devised in a place far away from the human need. The best, most effective kind of love begins with a quiet listening, a tactile awareness.

Of all the senses, touch is most trustworthy. A baby first relates to the world through the sense of touch. Give him an object to play with and he will finger it, then bring it to his mouth and tongue it. To him, auditory and visual senses are secondary; not until later will he primarily value visual sense. But even we adults somehow believe our tactile senses more readily. "Tangible" proof is easier to accept. Thomas doubted visual reports of Christ's resurrection, declaring, "Unless I see the nail marks in his hands and put my finger where the nails were, and put my hand into his side, I will not believe it" (John 20:25).

A child touches a magician's props to see if they are real — she cannot trust her eyes. A mirage can fool the eye and the brain, but not the skin's touch.

I recall one incident when my daughter Mary, three years old, was trying to overcome a fear of violent thunderstorms. She understood we were safe inside our house, and yet as the lightning streaked closer and closer, she ran to me and put her tiny hand in mine. "We aren't afraid, are we, Daddy?" she said in an uncertain voice.

Just then a tremendous clap of thunder crashed nearby and all our lights went out. Mary, breathing in short gasps, fearfully cried out, "Daddy! We aren't afraid, are we?" Her words were brave, but I could feel her true thoughts in her stiffened hand, trembling with fear. Skin communicates to skin.

We shall observe qualities of skin that allow for quick adaptation to changes. But these qualities are useless if the receptors of skin are numbed. God chose to establish a tangible presence in the world where he, like men and women, felt — through skin — fatigue, pain, and ultimately death. No better model of tactile love exists than Jesus, God's Son. And now we are called to be his sensitive "skin" in the world.

# Chapter 16

# COMPLIANCY

*No one but kings and princes should have the itch, for the*
*sensation of scratching is so delightful.*

King James I

---

As an intern in London I had the great privilege of training under Dr. Gwynne Williams, a surgeon who unfailingly emphasized the human side of medicine. He strolled through the halls of poorly heated hospital wards with his right arm Napoleonically tucked inside his coat which, unknown to his patients, concealed a hot water bottle.

"You can't rely on what patients tell you about their intestines," Dr. Williams would admonish us interns. "Let their intestines talk to you." The hot water bottle made his hand a better listener. He taught us to kneel by a patient's bedside and gently slip a warm hand under the sheets onto the person's belly. "If you stand," he explained, "you'll tend to feel only with the downward-pointing fingertips. If you kneel, your full hand rests flat against the abdomen. Don't start moving it immediately. Just let it rest there."

We learned to feel an instant tightening of the patient's abdominal muscles — a protective reflex. A cold hand assured those muscles would remain tight, but a warm, comforting hand could coax them to relax. We gently caressed the abdomen, earning tactile trust. Once muscles had softened, we could sense the organs' movement, responding to the simple act of breathing.

Dr. Williams was right: there is no need to ask questions. A trained hand gently exploring the abdomen can detect tautness, inflammation, and the shape of tumors that more complicated procedures merely confirm. Touch is my most precious diagnostic tool.

⌐.

We have called touch a "basic" sense, but that word can mislead. Actually touch is one of our most complex senses.

Every square inch of the body has a different response to touch. Scientists such as Maximilian von Frey have mapped the nerves as meticulously as Rand McNally has mapped the world. Von Frey measured the threshold of touch, the amount of gram weight it takes for a person to sense that an object has come in contact with the skin. The soles of the feet, thickened for a daily regimen of abuse, do not report in until a weight of 250 milligrams per square mm is applied. The back of the forearm is triggered by 33 milligrams of pressure, the back of the hand by 12 milligrams. The really sensitive areas are the fingertips (3 milligrams) and the tip of the tongue (2 milligrams).[1]

All touch sensors seem sluggish compared to those in the cornea of the eye, transparent, deprived of blood and thus incredibly vulnerable. The cornea fires off a response if just two-tenths of a milligram of pressure is applied. A stray eyelash can make a baseball pitcher stop the game — he can concentrate on nothing else. In contrast an eyelash on his forearm would go unnoticed. Similarly, a wise mosquito will land on the forearm, not the sensitive hand, to go undetected. And only a foolhardy insect would attempt a secret landing on soft lips.

Touch distribution was not handed down at a blackjack table ("God does not play at dice," said Einstein): the sensitivity of each square inch is programmed to fit the function of that body part. Our fingertips, tongues, and lips are the portions of the body used in activities that need the most sensitivity.

Scientists compose their charts based on "normal" reactions to stimuli. Actually, touch changes constantly with its environment. The skin, for example, responds by adapting. A 100-milligram weight is lowered onto my forearm. Blindfolded, I realize that something is touching me. The sensation stays for four seconds, then fades. My nervous system has adapted; I no longer notice the weight. My body has filtered out the messages coming from nerve endings on my forearm, deciding there is no evident danger and no need to clog up the circuits with useless information about weights on my arm. Involuntarily, I lose awareness of the weight — that is, until the weight is removed, at which time my brain will clearly report a change on my forearm. Were it not for this extraordinary volume switch through which my sensations pass, I could not wear wool or other coarse clothing — my body would constantly remind me of its scratchy presence, and I could hardly concentrate on anything else.

I experience skin's adaptation whenever I lower myself into a hot bathtub. I run the water so hot I can barely stand it and gradually lower my body, first reacting as if I am easing myself into a patch of stinging nettles. Within ten seconds my body has adjusted, and the same water actually feels soothing and comfortable. I can continue raising the temperature of the water, and my body will adapt — up to a maximum point of 115° F, beyond which I will feel constant, nonadapting pain.

▬.

What prompts such a complex system of perception? Is the brain starved of sensation, desiring a circuit-jamming report from the world outside? Do the body's senses accumulate information out of curiosity? No, the purpose of all this is to prepare the body parts to respond wisely.

The elaborate mechanisms producing touch, for instance, prepare the skin to adapt to changing surfaces. Bioengineers use the word compliancy to denote this response. Compliancy describes the capacity of skin to flow around whatever surface it contacts, a quality skin exhibits better than any comparable material. Compliancy gives the body freedom to move around in any environment, to expose itself to changing conditions and yet keep an unbroken, protective surface. Leather clothes and shoes are highly valued (and priced) because they, as animal skins, have flexibility and elasticity as well as an ability to "breathe."

As I have tried to design shoes and tools for the feet and hands of leprosy patients who lack the basic sensitivities of touch, I have spent hundreds of hours researching the anatomy of living skin. Underneath the skin in the palm of the hand lie globules of fat with the look and consistency of tapioca pudding. Fat globules, so soft as to be almost fluid, cannot hold their own shape, and so they are surrounded by interwoven fibrils of collagen, like balloons caught in a supporting rope net. Collagen occurs in greater quantity where it is most needed — in those parts that need structure and support. The cheeks and the buttocks have more fat and less collagen, as anyone who has struggled with a double chin or sagging figure unfortunately knows. But where stress occurs, such as on the palm of the hand, fat is tightly gathered and enveloped by fibrous tissue in a design resembling fine Belgian lace.

I grasp a hammer in the palm of my hand. Each cluster of fat cells changes its shape in response to the pressure. It yields but cannot be pushed aside because of the firm collagen fibers around it. The resulting tissue, constantly shifting and quivering, becomes compliant, fitting its shape and its stress points to the precise shape of the handle of the hammer. Engineers nearly shout when they analyze this amazing property, for they cannot design a material that so perfectly balances elasticity with viscosity.

If my skin tissue had been made harder, I might insensitively crush a goblet of fine crystal as I hold it in my hand; if softer, it would not allow a firm grip. When my hand surrounds an object — a ripe tomato,* a ski pole, a kitten, another hand — the fat and collagen redistribute themselves and assume a shape to comply with the shape of the object being grasped. This response spreads the area of contact, preventing localized spots of high pressure, limiting stress while giving firm support.

Take a clattery hand of bone — such as the hand of a human skeleton on display in a biology classroom — and wrap it around a hammer. Against such a hard surface, the hammer handle will contact only about four pressure points. Without my compliant skin and its supporting tissues, those four pressure points would inflame and ulcerate if I pounded the hammer just a few times. But because of compliancy, my entire skin-covered hand absorbs the impact.

Compliancy, a word with special meaning to my engineering colleagues, is a good word biologically and a pregnant word spiritually. I need the inflexibility of my skeleton to keep me upright and to impose my will on the environment, but when I grasp

---

*Tomatoes demonstrate the superior qualities of human skin. Commercial tomatoes are bred with thick skins so that insensitive mechanical pickers, which do not have compliant surfaces, won't destroy them. I exult in my own vine-ripened tomatoes, with thinner skins and better taste, which I can pick when they are most succulent because my skin is so compliant.

something it is good that my bones do not contact the object. The compliant tissues covering my bones assume the shape — awkward or smooth — of the object. I do not demand that the object fit the shape of my hand; my hand adapts, distributing the pressure.

The art of Christian living, I believe, can be glimpsed in this concept of compliancy. In daily activity as my shape moves into contact with other, foreign shapes, how does my skin respond? Whose personality adapts? Do I, as does my grasping hand, become square to those things that are square, round to those things that are round? The apostle Paul finished the analogy for us in 1 Corinthians 9:19–22: "Though I am free and belong to no man, I make myself a slave to everyone, to win as many as possible. To the Jews I became like a Jew, to win the Jews. To those under the law I became like one under the law (though I myself am not under the law), so as to win those under the law. To those not having the law I became like one not having the law (though I am not free from God's law but am under Christ's law), so as to win those not having the law. To the weak I became weak, to win the weak. I have become all things to all men so that by all possible means I might save some."

# Chapter 17

# TRANSMITTING

*In the midst of bloody persecution under Idi Amin's rule in Uganda, a missionary society in England wrote a bishop there, "What can we send your people?" The answer came back: Not food, not medicine; 250 clerical collars. This was the explanation: "It is your Western prejudice which thinks this an odd request. You must understand, when our people are being rounded up to be shot, they must be able to spot their priests."*

Paul Seabury

D r. Harry F. Harlow loved to stand by the animal cages in his University of Wisconsin laboratory and watch the baby monkeys. Intrigued, he noticed that the monkeys seemed emotionally attached to cloth pads lying in their cages. They caressed the cloths, cuddled next to them, and treated them much as children treat a teddy bear. In fact, monkeys raised in cages with cloths on the floors grew huskier and healthier than monkeys in cages with wire mesh floors. Was the softness and touchability of the cloth an important factor?

Harlow constructed an ingenious surrogate mother out of terry cloth, with a light bulb behind her to radiate heat. The cloth mother featured a rubber nipple attached to a milk supply from which the babies could feed. They adopted her with great enthusiasm. Why not? She was always comfortingly available, and, unlike real mothers, never roughed them up or bit them or pushed them aside.

After proving that babies could be "raised" by inanimate, surrogate mothers, Harlow next sought to measure the importance of the mother's touchable, tactile characteristics. He put eight baby monkeys in a large cage that contained the terry cloth mother plus a new mother, this one made entirely out of wire mesh. Harlow's assistants, controlling the milk flow to each mother, taught four of the babies to nurse from the terry cloth mother and four from the wire mesh mother. Each baby could get milk only from the mother assigned to it.

A startling trend developed almost immediately. All eight babies spent almost all their waking time (sixteen to eighteen hours per day) huddled next to the terry cloth mother. They hugged her, patted her, and perched on her. Monkeys assigned to the wire mesh mother went to her only for feeding, then scooted back to the comfort and protection of the terry cloth mother. When frightened, all eight would seek solace by climbing onto the terry cloth mother.

Harlow concluded, "We were not surprised to discover that contact comfort was an important basic affectional or love variable, but we did not expect it to overshadow so completely the variable of nursing; indeed the disparity is so great as to suggest that the primary function of nursing is that of insuring frequent and intimate body contact of the infant with the mother. Certainly, man cannot live by milk alone."[1]

In other experiments, some baby monkeys were raised in cages with only a wire mesh mother. They too approached her only for feeding, and many of these babies did not survive. Those who did reacted to stress by cowering in a corner, screaming, or by hiding their faces under their arms.

⟶

Anthropologist Ashley Montagu reports on these and many other similar experiments in his elegant and seminal book *Touching.* He found close physical contact with a mother animal to be essential to the normal development of young animals. Except for man, all mammals spend great amounts of time licking their young. Animals will often die if they are not licked after birth; they never learn to eliminate waste, as one consequence. Montagu concludes that the licking is not for cleanliness, but for essential tactile stimulation.

As pet owners know, animals do not outgrow the urge to be touched. A cat arches its back and brushes it gently across its owner's leg. A dog wriggles on the carpet, begging for a belly scratching. A monkey meticulously grooms and combs the hair on its fellow tribe members.

Montagu even suggests that human fetuses need the massive tactile stimulations of labor. Only the human species goes through such a long, arduous birth process. Montagu believes the fourteen hours or so of uterine contractions, which have been described from the mother's viewpoint but never from the fetus's, may be important stimuli to finish off maturation of certain body functions. Could this explain, he wonders, why babies delivered by Caesarean section have a higher death rate and a greater incidence of hyaline membrane disease?[2]

Although the role of tactile stimulation during birth remains speculative, the need for touching after birth has been dramatically, and tragically, demonstrated. As late as 1920, the death rate among infants in some foundling hospitals in America approached 100 percent. Then Dr. Fritz Talbot of Boston brought from Germany an unscientific-sounding concept of "tender loving care." While visiting the Children's Clinic in Düsseldorf, he had noticed an old woman wandering through the hospital, always balancing a sickly baby on her hip. "That," said his guide, "is Old Anna. When we have done everything we can medically for a baby and it still is not doing well, we turn it over to Old Anna, and she cures it."

When Talbot proposed this quaint idea to American institutions, administrators derided the notion that something as archaic as simple touching could improve their care. Statistics soon convinced them. In Bellevue Hospital in New York, after a rule was established that all babies must be picked up, carried around, and "mothered" several times a day, the infant mortality rate dropped from 35 percent to less than 10 percent.

Despite these findings, even today touching is often viewed as an unavoidable part of the more important tasks of feeding and cleaning the baby. Seldom is it considered an essential need in itself without which a baby may never mature. Jewish people are highly tactile, as are Latins, but Anglo-Saxons and Germanic people are low on the scale. In general, though, the higher the social strata, the less parents touch their infants. Perhaps we have reached the extreme in America, where mothers carry their babies at arms' length in plastic carriers and fathers spend an average of thirty seconds per day in tactile contact with their children.

Among some severely disturbed children, forceful and persistent touching may represent the only hope for a cure. An autistic child needs almost constant touching and rubbing to trigger a release from his self-hugging isolation.

Montagu decisively concludes that the skin ranks highest among the sense organs, higher even than eyes or ears. Skin not only conveys information about the world, but also perceives basic emotions. Am I loved and accepted? Is the world secure or hostile? The skin osmotically absorbs these concepts and the worldview they provide.

Words of touch have edged into our vocabulary as expressions of the way we relate to others. We rub people the wrong way, or conversely, we stroke them. A gullible person is a soft touch; a volatile one we handle with kid gloves. We are thin-skinned, thick-skinned; we get under each other's skins. We relate tactfully or tactlessly.

The sex act is our most massive cutaneous experience. We touch so intimately that two organisms become, for an instant, one. And in the West, a visual-oriented culture, some express a need for sex (often mistakenly equated with love) by exposing larger areas of skin, as if the daring wearer is begging to be touched.

As we grow older, skin offers us the most natural medium for communicating basic emotions, such as love. It is our chief organ of contact with others. Skin cells offer a direct path into the deep reservoir of emotion we metaphorically call "the human heart."

Touching includes risk. It can evoke the cold, armorlike resistance of a hurt spouse refusing to be comforted or the lonely shrug of a child who insists, "Leave me alone!" But it can also conduct the electric tingling of lovemaking, the symbiosis of touching and being touched simultaneously. A kiss, a slap on the cheek — both are forms of touching, and both communicate.

━

The skin of the Body of Christ, too, is an organ of communication: our vehicle for expressing love.

I think back on how Jesus acted while inhabiting a human body on earth. He reached out a hand and touched the eyes of the blind, the skin of the person with leprosy, and the legs of the cripple. When a woman pressed against him in a crowd to tap into the healing energy she hoped was there, he felt the drain of that energy, stopping the noisy crowd and asking, "Who touched me?" His touch transmitted power.

I have sometimes wondered why Jesus so frequently touched the people he healed, many of whom must have been unattractive, obviously diseased, unsanitary, smelly. With his power, he easily could have waved a magic wand. In fact, a wand would have reached more people than a touch. He could have divided the crowd into affinity groups and organized his miracles — paralyzed people over there, feverish people here, people with leprosy there — raising his hands to heal each group efficiently, en masse. But he chose not to. Jesus' mission was not chiefly a crusade against disease (if so, why did he leave so many unhealed in the world and tell followers to hush up details of healings?), but rather a ministry to individual people, some of whom happened to have a disease. He wanted those people, one by one, to feel his love and warmth and his full identification with them. Jesus knew he could not readily demonstrate love to a crowd, for love usually involves touching.

In chapter 7 I mentioned the need for us as Christ's Body to devote resources to aid the whole Body by distributing food and medicine throughout the world. Having been at the front lines of such activity overseas, I firmly believe such love is best expressed person to person, through touch. The further we remove ourselves from personal connections with people in need, the further we stray from the ministry Jesus modeled for us.

In India, when I would treat a serious case and prescribe some drug, sometimes the relatives of the patient would go and purchase the medicine, then bring it back and ask me to give it to the patient "with my good hands." They believed the medicine was more able to help the patient if it was given by the hand of the physician.

⟶

I live on the grounds of the only leprosarium in the continental United States. Carville has a vivid history. The hospital began after the Civil War when an order of Catholic nuns, the Daughters of Charity, expressed a specific calling to serve leprosy patients. Because no one wanted to live near a leprosarium, a remote plot of swampland was purchased on the Mississippi River under the guise of establishing an ostrich farm. Early patients were smuggled in at night on coal barges, blackened and hiding under tarpaulins.

Word about the leprosarium soon leaked, however, and immediately construction workers quit their jobs. Misconceptions of the disease struck such fear that no one would risk exposure to it. But a calling is a calling, the nuns decided. Under the direction of a stout and courageous Mother Superior, they took up the hoes and shovels themselves, digging canals to drain the swamp. With no prior construction experience, teams of sisters in starched, sweltering habits, dug foundations and erected buildings. Only they cared enough to touch and treat the disfigured patients who came to them in the darkness of night.

Now, nearly a century later, I treat leprosy patients at that same hospital. For many of them, whatever they touch — furniture, fabric, grass, asphalt — feels the same. When they put their hands on a hot stove because it feels the same as a cool one, I must treat their damaged hands.

I hate leprosy. Victims who are not treated feel the disease slowly creep over the hands and feet and they then experience the worst effect of all: they lose the ability to sense human contact. Many cannot even feel when another person holds their hands or caresses them. Because of ignorance and superstition, this disease destroys social contact between victims and their friends, employers, and neighbors. Leprosy is a devastatingly lonely disease.

As at Carville, many of the great advances in leprosy research have come about because of Christian action, especially by the Leprosy Mission and its counterpart, the American Leprosy Mission. I have sometimes wondered why leprosy merits its own mission; I know of no "Malaria Mission" or "Cholera Mission." I think the reason is the starving need of leprosy patients for human touch. It is a unique and terrible need, and Christian love and sensitivity meet it best.

Medical teams at places like Vellore, India, can do great things for leprosy patients. They treat the raw ulcers and painstakingly reconstruct feet and hands through tendon transfers and plastic surgery. They transplant new eyebrows to replace missing ones, repair useless eyelids, and sometimes even restore sight. They train patients in constructive jobs and give them new life.

But of all the gifts we can give to leprosy patients, the one they value most is the gift of being touched. We don't shrink away. We love them with our skin, by touch.

# Chapter 18

# LOVING

*Christianity is not a statistical view of life.*

Malcolm Muggeridge

---

A simple woman named Mother Teresa was awarded a Nobel Peace Prize for her work in Calcutta among members of India's lowest caste. The order of nuns who carry on her work cannot save all India, so they seek the least redeemable, the dying. When they find them, in the gutters and garbage dumps of Calcutta's alleys, they bring them to the hospital and surround them with love. Smiling women daub at their sores, clean off layers of grime, and swaddle them in soft sheets. The beggars, often too weak to talk, stare wide-eyed at this seemingly misdirected love offered so late in their lives. Have they died and gone to heaven? Why this sudden outpouring of care — why the warm, strengthening broth being gently spooned to their mouths?

A newsman in New York — properly outfitted in a three-piece suit, taking cues from an off-camera Teleprompter — once confronted Mother Teresa with a similar line of questioning. He seemed pleased with his acerbic probing. Why indeed should she expend her limited resources on people for whom there was no hope? Why not attend to people worthy of rehabilitation? What kind of success rate could her hospital boast of when most of its patients died in a matter of days or weeks? Mother Teresa stared at him in silence, absorbing the questions, trying to pierce through the facade to discern what kind of a person would ask them. She had no answers that would make sense to him, so she said softly, "These people have been treated all their lives like dogs. Their greatest disease is a sense that they are unwanted. Don't they have the right to die like angels?"

━━

Malcolm Muggeridge, who wrote a book on Mother Teresa, struggled with these questions also. He observed the filth and poverty of Calcutta and returned to England to write about it with fire and indignation. But, he comments, the difference between his approach and Mother Teresa's is that he returned to England … while she stayed in Calcutta. Statistically, he admitted, she did not accomplish much by rescuing a few stragglers from a cesspool of human need. Then he concludes with the statement, "But then Christianity is not a statistical view of life."

Indeed it is not. Not when a shepherd barely shuts the gate on his ninety-nine before rushing out, heartbroken and short of breath, to find the one that's missing. Not when a laborer hired for only one hour receives the same wage as an all-day worker (Matthew 20:1–16). Not when one rascally sinner decides to repent and ninety-nine upstanding citizens are ignored as all heaven erupts in a great party (Luke 14:4–7).

Christian love, *agape*, giving love, is not statistical either. Perception by the skin is more basic than perception through an eye or an ear. It senses a need and responds instinctively, personally.

I do not believe mission work necessarily becomes more effective as it grows more specialized and impersonal. Sometimes the increase in technology may be inevitable, as in a Christian medical college, but I have watched good Christian medical agencies in India gradually lose their original mission as they become institutionalized, with buildings and staff to support. The "quality" of their treatment rises, but so does the expense. To make the work more self-supporting, they branch out into techniques that attract patients who can pay. Meanwhile, the poor and unloved, who can no longer afford the mission hospital, must turn to the government clinic for help.

In contrast, I look at the impact my parents had. Although they went to India to preach the gospel, by living in tactile awareness of people's needs they began to respond on several levels. Within a year they were involved in the fields of medicine, agriculture, education, evangelism, and language translation. Their perception of needs determined the form (compliancy) their love assumed.

My mother and father worked for seven years before anyone converted to Christianity, and, in fact, that first conversion came as a direct result of their healing love. Villagers would often abandon their sick outside our home, and my parents would care for them. Once when a Hindu priest was dying of influenza, he sent his own frail, sickly, nine-month-old daughter to be raised by my parents. None of his swamis would care for the sick child; they would have let her die. But my parents took her in, nursed her to health, and adopted her as their own. I gained a stepsister, Ruth, and my parents gained an unexpected response of trust. The villagers were so moved by this example of Christian love that a few soon accepted Christ's love for themselves.

Years later, when my mother, universally called "Granny Brand," was eighty-five, long after my father had died, she helped forge a medical breakthrough. She had often treated gross abscesses on the legs of mountain people by draining the pus and excising a long, thin guinea worm. Distressed by the frequency of those abscesses, she studied the problem and learned that the worm's life cycle included a larval stage spent in water. If she could help break that cycle, she would eradicate the worm. Knowing the people's habits well, she quickly deduced that wading in water was probably the means of transmission. Cashing in on the trust and love she had built up through decades of personal ministry, she rode her horse from village to village, urging the people to build stone walls around their shallow wells and to prevent foot contact with the water. In a few years this old lady had single-handedly caused the eradication of all such worms, and their resulting abscesses, in two mountain ranges.

◥

My wife Margaret had a similar experience with a terrible condition afflicting the eyes of children. Whenever she encountered this condition, I could read it in the despair on her face that night. I would look at her and sympathetically murmur one word, "Keratomalacia?" and she would nod yes.

The condition resulted from a deficiency of vitamin A and protein among young children between one and two years old. A baby would be well-nourished as long as it was breast-fed, but soon a new brother or sister would push it from its mother's breast. A steady diet of rice failed to provide needed vitamins, making small bodies especially susceptible to infection. Finally, an attack of conjunctivitis — usually one of the easiest infections to treat in a well-nourished person — would begin to eat away at the malnourished child's eyes. Looking into those eyes, we would see a jellied mass of softness and sogginess, as if a strange heat ray had melted all the parts. Contact with one of those children, fearfully squinting to keep out light, never failed to overwhelm Margaret, regardless of how many successful procedures she had performed that day.

Then, spurred by Margaret's sense of need, some medical college researchers discovered that a common green herb, which grew wild all over our area, contained a remarkably high concentration of vitamin A. They also realized that peanuts, a local crop grown for peanut oil, possessed the missing protein. After mashing the nuts to produce oil, the villagers had been feeding the peanut residue to their pigs.

Now the task became one of education. Margaret and public health nurses spread the word, and soon mothers were excitedly telling their neighbors that the green herb and peanuts could prevent their children's blindness. The news traveled like gossip through the villages, soon protecting children from the dreaded keratomalacia.

These two examples are unusual, of course. Much of mission work consists of exhausting labor with less dramatic results. But they both demonstrate possible results of tactile Christian love. Government data banks, advanced hospitals, and agricultural experts had sufficient knowledge to attack keratomalacia and the guinea worm, but they had not gained the trust of villagers. Impetus for a medical advance came, instead, from workers who were "in touch with" the suffering people and who had built up enough trust and respect to effect the remedy.

An old Chinese proverb says: "Nothing can atone for the insult of a gift except the love of the person who gives it." If I go up to a man who looks poor, press a ten-dollar bill in his hand, and walk away, I really am insulting that person. My action says, "You can't take care of yourself—here's a gift for you." But if I involve myself in his life, recognize his need, and stand alongside him, sharing what resources I have with him, he is not offended.

I wonder how effective Granny Brand would have been had she dropped leaflets from an airplane explaining the need for stone walls around wells.

⬥

Every week my mailbox bulges with appeals for help from Christian organizations involved in feeding the hungry, clothing the naked, visiting the prisoners, healing the sick. They describe to me the horrible condition of a hurting world and request my money to help relieve the pain. Often I give, because I have lived and worked among the world's suffering and because I know most of these organizations conscientiously shed love and compassion abroad. But it saddens me that the only thread connecting millions of giving Christians to that world is the distant, frail medium of direct mail. Ink stamped on paper, stories formula-edited to achieve the best results — there is no skin involved, no sense of touch.

If I only express love vicariously through a check, I will miss the incredible richness of response that a tactile loving summons up. Not all of us can serve in the Third World where human needs abound. But all of us can visit prisoners, take meals to shut-ins, and minister to unwed mothers or foster children. If we choose to love only in a long-distance way, *we* will be deprived, for skin requires regular contact if it is to remain sensitive and responsive.

Again, the best illustration of this truth is Jesus Christ, the embodiment of God living on this planet. The Book of Hebrews sums up his experience on earth by declaring that we now have a leader who can be *touched* with the feelings of our weaknesses (Hebrews 4:15). God saw the need to come alongside us, not just love us at a distance. How could a God who was spirit fully manifest love except through human flesh? Jesus is said to have "learned obedience from what he suffered" (Hebrews 5:8). A stupefying concept: God's Son learning through his experiences on earth. Before taking on a body, God had no personal experience of physical pain or of the effect of rubbing against needy persons. But God dwelt among us and touched us, and Jesus' time spent here allows him to more fully identify with our pain.

The ideal, then, is to give love to someone you can touch — a neighbor, a relative, a needy person in your community. I was able to do that in India. Now, I look for people in Carville to love through touch. Of course, I still have great concern for the needs of the people of India, and I seek out others who can love the Indians through touch. I support these people and their organizations with my gifts and prayers.

Touch can be secondhand, both in the human body and in the church. Touch corpuscles are located deep inside my skin, and the activities on the surface can indeed reverberate through other cells, conveying the sense of touch. I give to India through medical workers at the leprosy hospital there. They apply my love in person, and I expect from them a sensitive report on the results of that love. It is my responsibility to enter into their work by learning about them, reading their reports, and praying for them. As I pray for those cells on the front lines, I sense their pain and struggle. We can all keep contact with members of the Body overseas and use them as our own personal touch corpuscles.

━

The world's needs are increasing like molten lava in an overdue volcano. Each day we watch a litany of news reports of famines, wars, and epidemics, often even as we are deftly shoveling in the abundance of our own food. We casually flip past the advertisement appeals picturing babies with stomachs bloated by malnutrition. The needs are so overwhelming that, instead of shocking us to action, they make us callous, insensitive.

In some ways we are acquiring an intolerable burden of guilt that could immobilize us. Again, I think back to the ministry of Jesus. He healed people, but in a localized area. In his lifetime he did not affect the Celts or the Chinese or the Aztecs. Rather, he set in motion a Christian mission which was to spread throughout the world, responding to human needs everywhere. We must begin with our resources, our neighborhood, our theater of service. Although we cannot change the whole world individually, together we can fulfill God's command to fill the earth with Christ's presence and love. When we stretch out a hand to help, we stretch out the hand of Christ's Body.

# Chapter 19

# CONFRONTING

*No one has greater love than the one who lays down his life for his friends.*

Jesus

———

I would be remiss if I left the impression that skin's only functions are to inform us of our environment and relate to it by touch and appearance. Nature is never so lavish. Skin exists chiefly as a barrier, a Maginot Line that keeps the inside in and the outside out. Without it some of our body parts would slosh around like Jell-O and we would lose our definition as an organism.

If I had to choose skin's most crucial contribution, I might opt for waterproofing. Sixty percent of the body consists of fluids, and these would soon evaporate without the moist, sheltered world provided by skin. Or without skin, a warm bath would kill: fluids would rush in like water over a flooded spillway, swelling the body with liquid, diluting the blood, and waterlogging the lungs. Skin's tight barrier of shingled cells fends off such disasters.

Modern civilization taxes skin's capacities. We scrub with harsh detergents and soaps (which, ironically, may alter skin's acidic base and promote bacterial growth). On any Saturday we can subject our skin to the abuse of swimming in a chlorinated pool, spilling kerosene on hands as a barbecue fire is lighted, cleaning paint brushes with turpentine and scouring it all off with abrasive powder and a roughened pad. But somehow skin survives.

Skin also offers a frontline defense against the hordes of bacteria and yeast that pepper its surface. Lennart Nilsson's superb microscopic photos of the body's surface reveal the tiny perforations of sweat pores and oil ducts as mammoth, jagged caverns providing entry into the deeper parts of the dermis. On the lips of these caves lurk glowing green bacteria and wildly spreading yeast. A single bacterium, which only lives for twenty minutes or so, can reproduce to a million in eight hours. Each one of us carries as many of these creatures on the surface of our bodies as there are people inhabiting this planet. Skin draws from an array of chemicals, electro-negative charges, and bands of defending cells to keep the marauders at bay.

Larger animals crawl in the fissures too. Until this century in developed countries, mites, fleas, bedbugs, and lice were an accepted part of the skin's landscape. Thomas à Becket's hair shirt was studded with wriggling lice; Samuel Pepys had to return a wig that came from the hairdresser full of nits. The gentry of France, always concerned about proper behavior, frowned on cracking fleas between the nails in public unless the gathering was a group of intimate friends.

Even today an eight-legged creature just a third of a millimeter long, the *Demodex folliculorum*, squirrels its way inside hair follicles and contentedly lives out its days in its burrow of choice, the eyelash. This mite, cigar-shaped and seemingly harmless, is found on almost every human examined. Male and female Demodexes merrily mate in the tunnel beside the hair, and as many as twenty-five of the creatures can congregate in one warm, oily fat gland.

Skin must also counter attacks by larger creatures, such as Portuguese men-of-war, scorpions, ticks, fleas, blister beetles, and biting flies. Some insects, thirsty for human juices, rush to constricted parts of the body where pressure squeezes the skin close to underlying blood vessels. Thus a chigger scampers across the body at a speed of three inches a minute until it reaches the constriction of underwear elastic. Ah, the epidermis is so thin and inviting there; it gorges on blood.

Large blows such as poundings and bruisings spread their impact across thousands of skin cells which spring back like a trampoline to absorb forces that could irreparably damage hidden organs.

It is a rough world out there, and the epidermis provides a continuous rain of sacrificed cells. This outer, horny layer is poised like curling cornflakes, ready to scale off and make room for moist, fresh cells from underneath. People who count such things estimate we lose ten billion skin cells a day. Just shaking hands or turning a doorknob can produce a shower of several thousand skin cells; one trembles to calculate the effect of a game of racquetball.

Dead cells linger on the surface of an arm which has been covered by a plaster cast for several weeks. But where do all the rest go? Pools of skin collect underneath sheets and some is lost to the breeze, but much stays around home. Up to 90 percent of all household dust consists of dead skin — friendly scrapings of you, your family, your guests, waiting to be smoothed together with a soft cloth and shaken outdoors without a moment of gratefulness for the sacrifice represented. Replacement cells will grow back mainly between 12:00 P.M. and 4:00 A.M. while much of the body rests.

Once I was consulted by an enthusiastic young student just learning to play the guitar. With lines of worry in his face, he asked me to examine his fingertips; they were red and swollen and sometimes would bleed when he played. "Are they too weak to play — will I never be a guitarist?" he asked plaintively.

I had to laugh at the way he had been inspecting his own skin cells. Though they were part of him, working loyally on his behalf, he viewed them as a manager would his employees, wondering whether they were really contributing. I advised him to slow down. His skin was working furiously to keep pace with intense new pressures that scraped off the paper-thin epidermal layer before new cells could be marshaled. Soon the multiplication rate of his cells would catch up and layer his fingertips with hard calluses.

Of all the organs, skin seems to me the most sacrificial; it is no wonder one-fourth of a general practitioner's patients come because of skin ailments. Skin absorbs incredible abuse to maintain the equipoise of vital organs inside, which cannot tolerate a changing environment. A temperature increase of just seven or eight degrees would kill the whole body; thus, the skin is called on to act as a radiator, rushing fluids to the surface to evaporate and cool the body. Increased blood supply to the skin's surface dissipates the heat. On a summer day, as much as two gallons of perspiration may be shed to cool the active body.

In one sense, because the whole community of followers represents Christ's Body to the world, all Christians participate in the appearance function of skin. At times each of us also encounters the friction of being the advance guard of Christ's Body to the world. Yet I believe that just as our bodies must protect the delicate cells in the eye or the liver from harsh realities of the external environment, so the church includes individuals who need to be sequestered and allowed times of quiet contemplation. Others need protection during particularly vulnerable periods of their lives. On behalf of all these, some members of the Body of Christ take up the front line, the exposed positions, and endure the trauma for the rest of us.

The skin is not a place for beginners. It is an advanced organ, programmed with the body's immunity and disease-fighting system. Allergies, smallpox, and tuberculosis are tested on its surface because it can represent the internal parts of the body and protect them. Christians, anxious to "put on a good front" for a watching world, eagerly push new converts to become the visible organ. Many are not wise or mature enough to handle the shock. I could rattle off a list of sports heroes who started out as featured speakers on the Christian athlete circuit and who fell away and today have no interest in Christian matters. They remind me of the tender, swollen cells of the young guitar player, still not adjusting to the increased stress of being pulled across steel wire.

New converts, especially susceptible to the dangers of their alien environment, need protection to learn the ways of the Body. If the apostle Paul needed a lengthy time of reflection, should not we ask the same for new Christians today?

Not all of us will be called to the front lines. And those involved in more humble service inside the Body face their own unique danger: they feel inferior to the parts of the Body that are more visible. Can typing or cleaning hospital rooms contribute to the kingdom in the same way as the activities of the visible representatives of the faith? The Bible often focuses on those rare people who were called on to lead the way and forge new territory for religious faith and practice. They are important models for us, to be sure. But we will not all be apostles, and there is no hint in the Bible that we should be. On the whole, the church is populated by ordinary citizens who are different mainly because of the allegiance of their lives.

Some are called to the front, such as members of the persecuted church, relief workers in places of famine and war, medical workers fighting AIDS in Africa. From us they deserve support and prayer, not envy, for life on the surface of the Body is never easy.

The history of the church is dotted with cells who were willing to live at the touch-point of friction; these men and women did not shrink from bruisings or scorching heat or unbearable stresses. I read the list of heroes in Hebrews 11 as a roll call of martyrs who fought on the front lines, "Who shut the mouths of lions, quenched the fury of the flames, and escaped the edge of the sword; whose weakness was turned to strength; and who became powerful in battle and routed foreign armies. Women received back their dead, raised to life again. Others were tortured and refused to be released, so that they might gain a better resurrection. Some faced jeers and flogging, while still others were chained and put in prison. They were stoned; they were sawed in two; they were put to death by the sword. They went about in sheepskins and goatskins, destitute, persecuted and mistreated — the world was not worthy of them. They wandered in deserts and mountains, and in caves and holes in the ground" (Hebrews 11:33–38).

I think of my own mother, from a society home in suburban London, who went to India as a missionary. When Granny Brand reached sixty-nine she was told by her mission to retire, and she did ... until she found a new range of mountains where no missionary had ever visited. Without her mission's support she climbed those mountains, built a little wooden shack, and worked another twenty-six years. Because of a broken hip and creeping paralysis she could only walk with the aid of two bamboo sticks, but on the back of an old horse she rode all over the mountains, a medicine box strapped behind her. She sought out the unwanted and the unlovely, the sick, the maimed, and the blind, and brought treatment to them. When she came to settlements who knew her, a great crowd of people would burst out to greet her.

My mother died in 1974 at the age of ninety-five. Poor nutrition and failing health had swollen her joints and made her gaunt and fragile. She had stopped caring about her personal appearance long ago, even refusing to look in a mirror lest she see the effects of her grueling life. She was part of the advance guard, the front line presenting God's love to deprived people.

━

Another woman, also serving on the front lines, captures for me in a single image all the elements of the skin of Christ's Body. I visited a nun, Dr. Pfau, in the 1950s outside Karachi, Pakistan, in the worst human squalor I have ever encountered. Long before I reached her place, a putrid smell burned my nostrils. It was a smell you could almost lean on.

Soon I could see an immense garbage dump by the sea, the accumulated refuse of a large city that had been stagnating and rotting for many months. The air was humming with flies. At last I could make out human figures — people covered with sores — crawling over the mounds of garbage. They had leprosy, and more than a hundred of them, banished from Karachi, had set up home in this dump. Sheets of corrugated iron marked off shelters, and a single dripping tap in the center of the dump provided their only source of water.

But there, beside this awful place, I saw a neat wooden clinic in which I found Dr. Pfau. She proudly showed me her orderly shelves and files of beautifully kept records on each patient in the dump. The stark contrast between the horrible scene outside and the oasis of love and concern inside her tidy clinic burned deep into my mind. Dr. Pfau was daily exhibiting all the properties of skin: beauty, sensitivity to needs, compliancy, and the steady, fearless application of divine love through human touch. All over the world people like her are fulfilling Christ's command to fill the earth with his presence.

# MOTION

# Chapter 20

# MOVEMENT

*In the absence of any other proof, the thumb alone would convince me of God's existence.*

Isaac Newton

A kindly looking old gentleman with a more-than-prominent nose and a face seamed with wrinkles crossed the stage. His shoulders slumped and his eyes seemed sunken and cloudy — he was over ninety years old. He sat on a stark black bench, adjusting it slightly. After a deep breath, he raised his hands. Trembling slightly, they poised for a moment above a black and white keyboard. And then the music began. All images of age and frailty slipped quietly from the minds of the four thousand people gathered to hear Arthur Rubinstein.

His program that night was simple: Schubert's *Impromptus*, several Rachmaninoff Preludes, and Beethoven's familiar *Moonlight Sonata*, any of which could be heard at a music school recital. But they could not be heard as played by Rubinstein. Defying mortality, he wedded a flawless technique to a poetic style, rendering interpretations that evoked prolonged shouts of "Bravo!" from the wildly cheering audience. Rubinstein bowed slightly, folded those marvelous nonagenarian hands, and padded offstage.

I must confess that a bravura performance such as that by Rubinstein engrosses my eyes as much as my ears. Hands are my profession; I have studied them all my life. A piano performance is a ballet of fingers, a glorious flourish of ligaments and joints, tendons, nerves, and muscles. I must sit near the stage to watch their movements.

From my own careful calculations I know that some of the movements required, such as the powerful arpeggios in *Moonlight's* third movement, are simply too fast for the body to accomplish consciously. Nerve impulses do not travel with enough speed for the brain to sort out that the third finger has just lifted in time to order the fourth finger to strike the next key. Months of practice must pattern the brain to treat the movements as subconscious reflex actions — "finger memory" musicians call it.

I marvel too at the slow, lilting passages. A good pianist controls his or her fingers independently, so that when striking a two-handed chord of eight notes, each of the fingers exerts a slightly different pressure for emphasis, with the melody note ringing loudest. The effect of a few grams more or less pressure in a crucial pianissimo passage is so minuscule only a sophisticated laboratory could measure it. But the human ear contains just such a laboratory, and musicians like Rubinstein gain acclaim because discriminating listeners can savor their subtlest nuances of control.

～

Often I have stood before a group of medical students or surgeons to analyze the motion of one finger. I hold before them a dissected cadaver hand, almost obscene-looking when severed from the body and trailing strands of sinew. I announce that I will move the tip of the little finger. To do so, I must place the cadaver hand on a table and spend perhaps four minutes sorting through the intricate network of tendons and muscles. (To allow dexterity and slimness for actions such as piano playing, the finger has no muscles in itself; tendons transfer force from muscles in the forearm and palm.) Finally, when I have arranged at least a dozen muscles in the correct configuration and tension, with a delicate movement I can maneuver them so the little finger firmly moves without the proximal joints buckling.

Seventy separate muscles contribute to hand movements. I could fill a room with surgery manuals suggesting various ways to repair hands that have been injured. But in forty years of study I have never read a technique that has succeeded in improving a normal, healthy hand.

I remember my lectures as I sit in concert halls watching slender fingers pump up and down or glissade across the keyboard. I revere the hand; Rubinstein took its function for granted. Hands were his obedient servants; often he closed his eyes or gazed straight ahead and did not even watch them. He was not thinking about his little finger; he was contemplating Beethoven and Rachmaninoff.

Scores of other muscles lined up as willing reinforcements for Rubinstein's hands. His upper arms stayed tense, and his elbows bent at nearly a ninety-degree angle to match the keyboard height. Shoulder muscles rippling across his back contracted to hold his upper arms in place, and muscles in his neck and chest stabilized his shoulders. When he came to a particularly strenuous portion of music, his entire torso and leg muscles went rigid, forming a firm base to allow the arms leverage. Without these anchoring muscles, Rubinstein would topple over every time he shifted forward to touch the keyboard.

⌐

In order to observe the types of artificial hands that scientists and engineers have developed through years of research and millions of dollars of technology, I have visited facilities that produce radioactive materials. With great pride scientists demonstrate their skilled machines that allow them to avoid exposure to radiation. By adjusting knobs and levers they can control an artificial hand whose wrist supinates and revolves. Recent models even possess an opposable thumb, an advanced feature reserved for primates in nature. (Only we humans, though, can join the tips of our index fingers with our thumbs, allowing us to grasp, retain, and handle objects easily and precisely.) Smiling like a proud father, the scientist wiggles the mechanical thumb for me.

I nod approvingly and compliment him on the wide range of activity the mechanical hand can perform. But he knows, as I do, that compared to a human thumb his atomic-age hand is clumsy and limited, even pathetic — a child's Play-Doh sculpture compared to a Michelangelo masterpiece. A Rubinstein concert proves that.

⌐

Six hundred muscles, which comprise 40 percent of our weight (twice as much as bones), burn up much of the energy we ingest as food in order to produce all our movements. Tiny muscles govern the light permitted into the eye. Muscles barely an inch long allow for a spectrum of subtle expression in the face — a bridge partner or a diplomat learns to read them as important signals. Another, much larger muscle, the diaphragm, controls coughing, breathing, sneezing, laughing, and sighing. Massive muscles in the buttocks and thighs equip the body for a lifetime of walking. Without muscles, bones would collapse in a heap, joints would slip apart, and movement would cease.

Human muscles are divided into three types: smooth muscles control the automatic processes which rumble along without our conscious attention; striated muscles allow voluntary movements, such as piano-playing; and cardiac muscles are specialized enough to merit their own category. (A hummingbird heart weighs a fraction of an ounce but beats eight hundred times a minute; a whale heart weighs one thousand pounds — in contrast to either, the human heart seems dully functional, but does its job well enough to get most of us through seventy years with no time off for rest.)

Surrounded as we are by man-made motion — airplanes, dune buggies, color dots dancing across a TV screen — we can grow numb to the sheer exaltation of movement made possible by muscles. But even lower forms of animal life display impressive feats. A common housefly's muscles respond in one-thousandth of a second, which is why not many are caught with the bare hand. The despised flea performs acrobatic leaps and somersaults, which, if factored up to human size, would make our best Olympians quit in dismay. Visit a zoo with an underwater window and watch the seals and sea lions, awkward and ponderous on land, infuse the word "graceful" with new meaning. Stand in a farmyard and watch a swooping swallow redefine flight.

As is often the case, the human being has a more conservative, scaled-down range of movement. We cannot see like an eagle, hear like an owl, or glow like a firefly, nor can we run like a dog, leap like a gnat, or fly like a goose. But we do have enough potential packed in our muscles to allow the Bolshoi Ballet and the sports of ice skating and gymnastics. On TV the performers are models of weightless beauty, gliding through the air, pirouetting on a single toe, dismounting from a high bar with a light spring. But in person, close to the event, the grace is seen as a by-product of hard work. It is *noisy* there, all shocks and thuds and creaking boards and panting, sweating bodies. That humans can transform such strenuous muscular activity into fluidity and grace is a tribute to the dual nature of motion: robust strength and masterful control.

# Chapter 21

# BALANCE

*Christianity got over the difficulty of combining furious*
*opposites, by keeping them both, and keeping them both furious.*
G. K. Chesterton

The movements of a Rubinstein or a Michael Jordan do not come cheaply. The motor cortex of the brain, on which will be written all the coding for intentional movement, starts out blank as a washed chalkboard. Although the seeds of instinctive behavior are there, an infant, dominated by gravity, cannot hold her head or trunk upright. Her hand and leg movements are abrupt and jerky, as in an old silent movie. She learns fast, however, lifting her head in one month and her chest in two. In seven months, if all goes well, she sits upright without support. At age eight months the infant can stand unassisted, but on the average it takes seven more months for her to walk smoothly at the speed of one footstep per second, without consciously thinking of the action.

If we traced all the bodily signals involved in walking, we would find in that grinning, perilously balanced toddler a machine of unfathomable complexity. Over one hundred million sense cells in each eye compose a picture of the table she is walking toward. Stretch receptors in the neck relate the attitude of her head to the trunk and maintain appropriate muscle tension. Joint receptors fire off messages that report the angles of limb bones. The sense organs inside the ear inform the brain of the direction of gravity and the body's balance. Pressure from the ground on each toe triggers messages about the type of surface on which she is walking.

Just for the toddler to stand, the muscles which oppose each other in the hip, knee, and ankle must exert an equal and opposite tension, stabilizing the joints and preventing them from folding up. "Muscle tone" describes the complex set of interactions that keeps all the infant's muscles in a mild state of contraction, making her erect posture as active and strenuous as the movements that follow it.

A casual glance down to avoid a toy on the carpet will cause all these sense organs to shift dramatically: the image of the ground moves rapidly across the retina, but the inner ear and stretch receptors assure the brain the body is not falling. Any movement of the head alters the body's center of gravity, affecting the tension in each of the limb muscles. The toddler's body crackles with millions of messages informing her brain and giving directions to perform the extraordinary feat of walking.

⟼

Muscles rely on an advanced hierarchy to organize the individual cells. Muscle cells — long, sleek bodies with dark nuclei — perform just one action: they contract. They can only pull, not push, as two protein molecules interact and the molecules slide together like the teeth of two facing combs. Cells unite in strands called fibers, resembling coils of rope, and fibers report to a further hierarchy called a motor unit group.

One motor nerve controls a motor unit group, wrapping its end plates around the muscle group as an octopus would encircle a pole. When that nerve gives a signal, all of its muscle fibers immediately become shorter and fatter. Some fibers are fast-twitch for short bursts of energy while others, long-twitch, are less quickly fatigued. Muscle fibers adhere to what is called the "all or none" principle. They do not have a variable throttle of energy, but a simple on-off switch. Variations of strength, as when a pianist lightly taps a key or pounds it mightily, occur because of the quantity of motor units firing off at any moment.

Conductors of large choirs warn their singers not to take breaths at the end of a pianissimo measure, since the sound of many singers inhaling would be audibly distracting. Rather, they should gasp for air in the middle of a measure, staggering their breathing so that the full choir continues singing while just a few members inhale at any one instant. Similarly, to vary the intensity, the biceps simply alters the number of participants. Each motor unit takes a rest when needed, but the muscle's contraction stays steady.

Rarely will all the motor units in a large muscle fire simultaneously. Occasionally, adrenaline induces feats of great strength, called hysterical strength, such as a mother lifting a car off her child — perhaps then all the motor units are galvanized into action.

The muscle "choir" can be literally heard if a needle is inserted into a muscle and attached to a machine that transforms electrical energy into sound. Click-click-click: a constant stream of messages reports the activity of muscle tone. Slowly flex the biceps, and the volley of clicks accelerates. Move the arm abruptly, and the clicks crescendo to machine-gun frequency. The cells never stop clicking, and they adjust instantly, within fractions of a second, when the brain calls for sudden activity.

As the meter records the stream of static flowing from just one muscle area the size of a needle point, hundreds of other muscles go wholly undetected. A crucial group of them fire off whether or not we think about them: the automatic muscles controlling our eyelids, breathing, heartbeat, and digestion. It is as if the wisdom of the body does not trust the forgetful, erratic free will with these life-or-death functions. So protected are they that we can not voluntarily stop our heartbeat or breathing. No one can commit suicide by holding his or her breath; accumulating carbon dioxide in the lungs will trigger a mechanism to override conscious desire and force the muscles of ribs, diaphragm, and lungs to move.

Consider the electrical network linking every home and building in metropolitan New York City. At any given second lights are turned on and off, toasters pop up, microwave ovens begin their digital countdowns, water pumps lunge into motion. Yet that enormous interlinking of decisions and activities is marked by the randomness of individual users. A far more complex switching system is operating in your body at this second as you read this book, and it is perfectly controlled and orderly. When you reach the end of this page, you will turn it with your fingers, still only vaguely aware of the complex systems that allow such an act.

⚊

In the physical body as well as the spiritual, a muscle must be exercised to continue growing. If, through paralysis, we lose movement, atrophy will set in and muscles will shrink away until they are absorbed by the rest of the body. Similarly, Christ's Body shows its health best by acting in love toward other human beings. When it cuts back on active response to pain and injustice, it begins to waste away and weaken.

One aspect of motion in Christ's Body continues to puzzle me, though. Even when it is being exercised in history, it seems marked by a confused, convulsive nature. Pick any century, and the history of the church then will include splits and divisions, heated debates about the role of social concern, and sadly excessive reactions to non-Christian influences. Because church history includes these tentative, spastic flailings of activity, we easily discount the effectiveness of the Body's motion.*

As I look closer at the biology of motion, though, I can better grasp how seemingly disconnected spurts of energy can actually contribute to fluidity. In the human body a motion does not result from all parts unanimously contributing the same activity; in fact, every action has an equal and opposite reaction. We have seen that muscles are paired antagonistically so that when the triceps contracts the biceps relaxes, and vice versa. But one of the pioneers of neurophysiology, Sir Charles Sherrington, demonstrated that *all* muscular activity involves inhibition as well as excitation. In every muscular sentence there is a balancing "but."

The knee jerk, which involves only two muscles, illustrates Sherrington's principle. When a doctor taps a patient's knee, the muscle on the front of the thigh springs into action, excited. But the action is not possible unless the back of the thigh, which bends the knee, is actively inhibited and chooses not to contract. Two stimuli are equally powerful; one leads to action, one to inaction. In complex movements, like walking or hitting a baseball, hundreds of opposing reactions occur simultaneously. All muscular action, therefore, involves this policy of give-and-take. Sherrington expounded on this concept: "It has been remarked that Life's aim is an act, not a thought. Today the dictum must be modified to admit that, often, to refrain from an act is no less an act than to

---

*At least a part of the confusion stems from the fact that the visible, organized church may be very different at any given time from the true church — the Body of Christ. A pastor or even a bishop may at some moment of history have been outside of the Body and working against it.

commit one, because inhibition is coequally with excitation a nervous activity."[1] Not to decide to act is to decide.

A harmony of inhibitions synchronizes the whole body, coordinating heartbeats with breathing and breathing with swallowing, setting muscle tone, adjusting to all changes in movement. In short, inhibition keeps one part of the machine out of the way of the other.

This biological principle may help explain what at first glance appears as a troubling recurrence in the history of the church. The Body of Christ has moved by extreme, exaggerated reflexes. On the very issue of activity versus inactivity, debate broke out in the early years of the church. In behavior, as Charles Williams has pointed out, there are two opposite tendencies. "The first is to say: 'Everything matters infinitely.' The second is to say: 'No doubt that is true. But mere sanity demands that we should not treat everything as mattering all that much.'"[2] The rigorous view leads to a sharpened, intense view of the world that sees all actions as having eternal consequences. In its worst forms it can evolve into Pharisaical legalism and the intolerance of "holy" crusades. The relaxed view, contributing sanity, can at its worst drift toward inactivity, a "who cares?" attitude toward injustice and sin.

The apostle Paul, notably in Galatians and Romans, fought a pitched battle against both extremes, on the one hand excoriating legalists for perverting God's grace and on the other hand upholding Christian works as a normal outgrowth of new life.

In relating to the larger world too, Christians have oscillated between opposing forces. In the first two Christian centuries, the Way of Affirmation and the Way of Negation sprang up, each attracting ardent followers. The Way of Affirmation established strict church policy: "If any bishop or priest or deacon, or any cleric whatsoever, shall refrain from marriage and from meat and from wine ... let him be either corrected or deposed and turned out of the Church."[3]

Abstainers from marriage and feasting were labeled "blasphemers against creation," and the affirmers had many targets, what with all the athletes of God running around thin and naked in the desert. The paradox was hardly new: Jesus pointed out that John the Baptist had been blasted for his asceticism while he, the Son of God, was gossiped about as a winebibber and glutton (Matthew 11:19). Each tendency extracted something good from the conflict: The Way of Affirmation bequeathed us great art and romantic love and philosophy and social justice while the Way of Negation contributed the profound documents of mysticism that could only come from undisturbed contemplation of the holy.

Christians today are trying to balance the church's aesthetic appreciation against critical needs in an increasingly overpopulated world. Is it possible to maintain beautiful art and lavish architecture in view of the resources such activities consume? Some are rediscovering the need for community, which, in a society as stubbornly democratic as the West, may need a highly structured form. Mission leaders constantly struggle with the tensions created between their twin goals of ministering spiritually and materially through evangelism and social concern. Even a tiny congregation may reflect the counterbalancing tendencies.

If I visit a Christian community of young political radicals who strongly oppose the American government and advocate total pacifism and intentional poverty, I may come away with a distorted view of what Christian activity in the world should look like. Yet such a Christian counterculture can, by the process of inhibition, temper the activity of the institutionalized church, smoothing out its insensitive movements, calling it back to a radical awareness of justice. Perhaps their contribution can keep theBody from toppling over to one side.

The unifying factor in such debates must be a common commitment to the Head, Jesus Christ. We will disagree on interpretations of what he said and meant and what is the best means of accomplishing those goals in a hostile society. But if we fail to find fellowship in our mutual obedience to Christ, our actions will be seen not as reciprocal, counterbalancing forces necessary for movement, but as futile, spastic contractions.

# Chapter 22

# Dysfunctions

*Our faculties are like those smelting works that can only take ore of a high degree of impurity; when the light is too bright we cannot see.*

Malcolm Muggeridge

A man entered my office in India, a blubbering hulk of a man. He was a successful Australian engineer who had worked in India for many years. But his neck twitched so violently that every few seconds his chin smashed into his right shoulder. He had spasmodic torticollis, or twisted neck syndrome, a peculiarly debilitating condition usually caused by a deeply rooted psychological disorder.

Between the spastic flingings of his chin, my patient described his despair. To compound his reasons for self-pity, he was short and fat and had a history of alcoholism. The torticollis, he said, had begun soon after a visit to Australia. A confirmed bachelor throughout his time in India, he had returned from Australia with a wife—a gorgeous woman, taller and younger than he, who immediately became the object of much village gossip. What had she seen in him? What had prompted such a mismatch?

I referred the engineer to a psychiatrist, for I could do nothing except sedate him temporarily. The psychiatrist confided to me his suspicion that the engineer's condition had developed out of his anxiety over not being able to measure up to his new wife. He offered a diagnosis, but no hint of a cure. The engineer returned to me in a few weeks, even more weighted down with despair. Slovenly kept, with his neck wrenching spasmodically, he was an object of great pity.

When he sat alone, unnoticed by anyone, his neck rarely contorted. But as soon as someone began a conversation with him, his chin would shoot over to his shoulder, aggravating a chronic, spongy bruise. I researched the condition and worked with him, but nothing helped other than sedation and the temporary relief that followed an injection of his nerve roots with novocaine. Finally he reached the point of utter despondency and attempted suicide. He insisted, with a firm and resolute edge to his voice, that he would try again and again until he succeeded. He could no longer continue living with his anarchic neck.

I tried to send him abroad, since there was no neurosurgeon in India, but he refused. Reluctantly I agreed to attempt a dangerous and complicated operation that involved exposing his spinal cord and the base of his brain. I had never tried a procedure quite so complex, but the man insisted his only alternative was suicide.

I cannot recall an operation plagued with as many mishaps as that one. We had improvised an extension to a regular operating table so that the patient could lie face down, as on a neurological table. Unfortunately, this made it difficult for the anesthetist to replace the tube in his trachea when it became dislodged. The resulting poor oxygenation made bleeding profuse, and the cautery short-circuited at the critical time when we most needed it to control bleeding. Then all the hospital lights failed, and I was left with only a hand-held flashlight and no cautery just when the spinal cord was coming into view. To add to the stress, I had neglected to empty my bladder before surgery and was most uncomfortable throughout.

Between these distractions, I tried to concentrate on some very delicate cutting. After exposing the spinal cord and lower brain, I traced the hair-like nerves that supplied the spastic muscles in his neck. Any slight quiver of the scalpel could have cut a bundle of nerves, destroying movement or sensation.

Somehow, in spite of these difficulties, the surgery proved successful. When the engineer awoke, his back humped with a bandage, he discovered that the feared neck movement no longer plagued him. It couldn't, of course, for I had cut the motor nerves which led from the spinal cord to the muscles that turned his neck; he could not make the movement that had previously dominated him. That group of muscles had been totally rejected because of their rebellion against orders from the brain. Gradually, through lack of use, they were absorbed into the body.

⟋

When people see someone with a spastic muscle, they often assume the muscle itself is malfunctioning. Actually, the muscle is perfectly healthy, not diseased. In fact, it is well-developed because of frequent use. The malfunction stems from the muscle's relationship to the rest of the body; it demonstrates its strength at the wrong times, when the body neither needs nor wants it to function. A spastic muscle may, as in the case of the Australian engineer, cause embarrassment, pain, and deep despair.

Just as aberrant fat cells can lead to a harmful tumor by hoarding the body's resources, so spastic muscles can interfere with the body's normal movement. Quite simply, a spastic muscle disregards the needs of the rest of the body; its dysfunction is closer to rebellion than disease.

Acts of love — healing, feeding, educating, proclaiming Christ — are the spiritual Body's proper functions of movement. Even these motions, though, which appear wholly good, can fall prey to a dangerous dysfunction. Like the spastic muscle, we can tend to perform acts of kindness for our own benefit, for our sakes and reputations. In ministering to physical and emotional needs, we are especially susceptible to the temptations of "playing God" and self-contented pride. Love, having become a god, seeks to become a demon. Those of us in Christian work, I have found, consistently come against this subtle tendency toward pride. Someone comes to me for spiritual counsel, and I give it. But before they have walked out of my room I'm congratulating myself on what a fine counselor I am.

Jesus' disciples, the first trainees to represent him, consistently stumbled at this point. They argued about such petty issues as who was the greatest disciple and who would have the greatest honor in heaven (Matthew 20:20–23). Jesus lectured them on the need for self-sacrifice, pulled children from the crowd to picture the meek attitude they should have, even washed their dirty feet to illustrate service. It did not seem to sink in — not until after that dark day on Calvary.

⟍⟋

I have no desire to make judgments or name Christians today who seem to be exercising their muscles in a self-serving rather than a Body-serving way. But I do wonder about the dangers of the electronic church. This powerful "muscle" can reach millions of people and also collect millions of dollars in revenue. But does the medium give some leaders too much leverage and power? As a former missionary in a helping role, I know too well the human weaknesses that lead to spiritual pride. Media evangelists and Christian speakers and performers have described to me their unique pressures. They can easily bask in the glow of warm acceptance and ego-satisfying comments from adulating fans. Executives in Christian corporations and pastors are subject to the same temptations of pride and status.

None of us is exempt. Radical Christians who urge action in the inner city, politically conservative Christians who give large sums of their investments to missions, seminary students who glory in their new-found knowledge, church members who fill out committees within the church — all of us need to come back to the image of the Son of God kneeling on a hard floor and unbuckling sandals covered with choking dust. We cannot find real fulfillment by demonstrating individual strength as a muscle unit in Christ's Body. Rather, our activity must be for the sake of the Body. If we loyally serve Christ, and applause or even fame results, we will need special grace to handle it. But if we consciously seek applause or fame or wealth, for whatever end result, the effect will be like the spastic contraction of a once-healthy muscle. Like Ananias and Sapphira, we will have turned a good act into an impure act because of our impure motive.

Movement in the Body, then, requires the smooth and willing cooperation of many parts who gladly submit their own strength to the will of the Head. If they act apart from the Head's orders, their action, though powerful and impressive, will not benefit the body.

Motion also involves another severe problem which can cripple the body. When parts work together closely, they generate friction. I was reminded of this danger when a famous pianist in England consulted me. She said a specific pain was interrupting all of her performing. No longer could she concentrate on the flow of music or the rhythm. Instead her mind focused on the pain that would shoot through her hand whenever the thumb moved at a certain angle to her wrist. She had recently canceled a series of concerts because of that grating pain, even though all her other skills — music interpretation, muscle action, sense of touch, and timing — were intact.

I told her that the trouble emanated from a small, rough arthritic area between the two wrist bones at the base of her thumb. I suggested she continue to play but try to move that joint minimally. "But how can I think about Chopin when I have to worry about the angle of my thumb?" she protested. Each time she started to play, her attention riveted on the painful friction of that one roughened little joint.

Treating patients such as this pianist prompted me to study the type of lubrication our joints use and I learned that one of the most astonishing things about our bodies is how our joints ordinarily work so smoothly and free of pain. At the Cavendish laboratory in Cambridge, England, a team of chemists and engineers compared the frictional properties of the cartilage lining our joints with that of materials the engineers use for bearings. They were seeking a material suitable for use in artificial hips. Initially, they calculated that the friction present in the knee of an ox was one-fifth that of highly polished metal — about the same friction as ice on ice. It did not seem possible that biology could offer a joint five times more efficient than anything engineering science had ever achieved.

They researched further and found that joint cartilage is filled with tiny channels full of a synovial fluid. The cartilage is compressible, and as a joint moves, the part of the cartilage bearing the strain compresses, causing jets of fluid to squirt out from these canaliculi. The fluid forms a sort of forced pressure-lubrication which lifts the two surfaces apart. When the joint moves further, a different part of the surface bears the stress; fluid in the new area squirts out while the area just relieved of pressure expands and sucks its fluid in. Thus in active movement the joint surfaces do not really touch, but float on jets of fluid. The engineers were astonished, for boundary lubrication and pressure lubrication were recent developments in engineering — they had thought.

In the Body of Christ, joints are those special areas of potential friction where people work together in some stressful movement. In a body at rest there is little need for resistance against friction, but as soon as muscles and bones start producing activity, joints become critical attention points. Considering how soon joints and bearings need attention in a new machine, my joints amaze me with their ability to last for decades without squeaking or grinding. But despite their remarkable powers of lubrication, joints can break down as their gliding surfaces are injured or start to wear thin.

Quite commonly in old age friction will begin to cause joints to ache and throb — a natural response to years of wear. In Christ's Body, this natural wear is sometimes seen in the intolerant way older, wiser Christians may judge those who have a new enthusiasm for the faith but much to learn about behavior or doctrine. In recent years the church has absorbed a large influx of new people, especially waves of charismatic Christians and younger people who prefer a different worship style. Some older Christians have found themselves getting irritable and intolerant in their relationships with these new members. Sometimes the grace of God must come in the form of little squirts of synovial fluid that help the old to understand and get along with the young and that help the young to understand what it must be like to have thin cartilage.

⟵ ⟶

Far more serious than this natural ailment of the joints is the condition of rheumatoid arthritis, which may cripple even the young. We really do not know the cause of this disease which somehow produces a hypersensitivity in the cells of the joints. Suddenly a joint becomes flooded with enzymes that normally occur only when bacteria and foreign protein call for defense mechanisms. A usually healthy reaction turns cannibalistic, and the cells of the synovial membrane respond as if they were inflamed by infection. When we open up the joints and examine them, we can find no enemies, just the angry presence of defensive cells vainly attacking the body's cartilage and ligaments. A dreadful civil war has broken out: the defense mechanism itself has become the disease.

Various theories attempt to explain rheumatoid arthritis. One proposes that there really is an enemy, but we have not isolated and identified it yet. Whatever theory is true, this overreaction causes painful, irreversible harm. Even if a real enemy is present, that enemy would most likely inflict less damage than these cells do by reacting against it.

Spiritual rheumatoid arthritis sometimes attacks the work of the Christian church. Members become hypersensitive, taking offense at imagined criticism. Their own dignity and position become more important than the harmony of the group. Or, they may choose a minor doctrinal issue and make agreement on it the determinant of spiritual unity.

The lesson here is so obvious that it hardly needs to be clarified; yet it does, certainly, need to be applied. Do friction and tension flare up in my environment? Could they result from my own righteous indignation against wrong within my family or colleagues or church? Could my anger be causing more harm than the wrong I am angry about?

Arthritis strikes at joints because there the friction caused by movement takes its toll. Some may think Christians are less susceptible to friction because of the ideals and goals they hold in common. But in fact Christian work can increase friction as the pressures to "be spiritual" compound normal working tensions. At the Christian Medical College in India we had a psychiatrist whose clients frequently were missionaries. Being highly motivated, working in lonely places, often with just one partner, missionaries seem to fall prey to acute personal tensions. Often they refuse to admit their problems until friction has undone all the good they have accomplished.

Two women will serve in one station together, with only each other for fellowship. While they face a tremendous task together, what wrecks them is not the size of the task but the grating, everyday frictions of working together. And they won't express the tension because they believe that to be unchristian and they don't like to admit a real problem exists. So they bury it, channeling it into emotional and physical damage. When the frictions finally come out, they may root back to such trivial things as an ill-timed joke, a tendency to snore, or the way a roommate picks her teeth.

People sometimes assume the Christian life brings with it a natural immunity against friction, but it clearly does not. The human body goes to incredible lengths to prevent friction, and the Body of Christ should be as careful to lubricate possible conflicts as we move in common activity.

# Chapter 23

# HIERARCHY

*The neuron is like a miniature person — having a personality, having an array of unlike parts, having actions both spontaneous and upon stimulation. . . . It speaks finally with one voice, which integrates all that went before.*

Theodore H. Bullock

I have casually referred to the linking force that races through the body as electricity. Electricity? Today's assumption was yesterday's wild adventure. The very word, charged with lightning bolts and immolated bodies, was as terrifyingly mysterious to former generations as atomic energy is to ours. Today we manufacture electricity, with local utility boards determining how many dollars should be exchanged for the prompt conveyance of it to our homes. But still a thousand jagged streaks of fire assault the earth every minute in the form of lightning. Only a brave man flaunts Zeus.

What relevance could that dreaded juice of the heavens have to the billions of tiny nerve cells unifying me? Luigi Galvani, an Italian who lived thirty years after courageous Ben Franklin, launched his kite in the labyrinth of human nerves. Before Galvani, every scientist and doctor since A.D. 130 had faithfully followed the theory of the Greek physician Galen, who elegantly described communications in the body as an uninterrupted flow of ethereal "animal spirits" through a network of hollow tubes. His theory served the age well. What era but our own would attempt to reduce the tingle of a lover's desire, the surge of response to Vivaldi's music, and the holy mysticism of a saint to the quantifiable formulas of chemical actions and electrical impulses?

Galvani, poor soul, could not anticipate the reductionist lengths his discovery would lead to; he merely brought a few frogs home for dinner one cloudy day and hung them on his porch. Following one of those crazy, implausible hunches that have formed the history of science, he beheaded the frogs, skinned them, and ran a wire from a lightning rod to the frogs' exposed spinal cords. He recorded what happened next as a summer thunderstorm growled across the Bologna sky: "As the lightning broke out, at the same moment all the muscles fell into violent and multiple contractions, so that, just as does the splendor and flash of the lightning, so too did the muscular motions and contractions ... precede the thunders and, as it were, warn of them."[1]

Galvani was a scientist; had he been a writer he would have described the anxious astonishment on the faces of his guests who watched beheaded frogs jerk and twitch as if they were kicking across a pond. Electricity in the atmosphere had flowed through the nerves of the frogs and stimulated movement in otherwise dead animals.

Galvani performed many other experiments on frogs, some of which have been so embellished over the years that it is hard to know what really did occur. A shy man, he published his findings relatively late in life, letting his nephew defend most of his theories in public. But his most consequential discovery came one bright day when he hung several beheaded frogs on copper hooks above the iron railing on his porch. Whenever one of the frog legs drifted toward the railing and made contact, it jerked violently.

Dead frogs jumping during a lightning storm are one thing, but high-kicking on the porch on a sunny day — that's the kind of discovery to set the scientific community on its ears. And so it did.

Galvani's rival, Alessandro Volta, concluded that the electric current had nothing to do with the frogs and everything to do with two dissimilar metals joined by a conductor. He went on to invent the battery, and we have him to thank for exploding scoreboards, the electric news ticker on Times Square, the floodlit Wrigley building in Chicago, and a battery that starts a car on a below-zero morning.

Galvani stubbornly insisted the reaction came from "animal electricity," and we have him to thank for EKG monitors, biofeedback machines, electric shock treatment, and untold millions of dead frogs' legs hopping madly in medical school laboratories.

Another century and a half would pass before body explorers finally came up with a reasonable explanation of how electricity travels through the body. Obviously, it couldn't flow like the current sputtering behind each wall receptacle, not over nerves so fine that a hair-width bundle of them contains 100,000 separate "wires." Rather, electric current inside us passes through the chemical interactions of sodium and potassium ions, and now medical textbooks portray colorful drawings of nerve cells with plus signs outside the membrane and minus signs inside, illustrating how molecules carry the nervous messages like runners passing a torch.

~

A cell called the neuron is the most important unit in communication inside the body. Twelve billion neurons are poised for action at birth. Every other cell in the body dies away and is replaced every few years, but not the neuron. How could we function if the reservoirs of memory and our information about the world were periodically sloughed away? By unanimous decree of medical specialists, the neuron is declared the most significant and interesting cell in the entire organism.

Biology textbooks picture single neurons, plucked out of the body and stained in idealized form as they never appear in nature. But even from such caricatures one can sense the neuron's grandeur. It begins with a maze of incredibly thin, lacy extensions called dendrites which, like the root-hairs of a tree, funnel to a single shaft. On afferent neurons, which carry messages to the brain, these dendrites extend to whatever part of the body they are reporting stimulation from. On efferent neurons, which control muscles, branches wrap around muscle fibers, terminating in the end plates that directly control muscular activity.

The medical student who has studied acetate renderings of organs, neatly labeled and layered, is in for a rude shock the first time he or she opens a cadaver and finds a mess of bloody organs all looking approximately alike and nudging each other for room. Likewise, a surgeon never encounters a neuron standing in stark relief apart from the body. He sees hundreds, perhaps thousands, joined together in rope-like strands leading to thicker cables and finally to the spinal cord itself. The dendrites interweave so intricately that even with a microscope it is nearly impossible to discern where one ends and another begins. I liken the sight to standing on the edge of a forest on a winter day. Before me marches a line of several hundred trees, each thrusting black lengths of snow-laced branches up and out. If all those trees could be compressed together into a few square yards, with their branches intact and somehow filling up the spaces without actually touching each other, the resulting image would resemble a nerve bunch in the body.

A great debate raged in neurophysiology for decades: Do the branches, or dendrites, actually touch? In the electrical wiring of a home, of course, every live wire is joined by a wire nut to every other wire, so the system is, like plumbing, a completely closed loop. But in the body each of the twelve billion neurons stops just short of its neighboring neurons, forming a precise gap called a synapse.

The synapse allows staggering complexity. Take just one motor neuron controlling one muscle fiber in one hand. Along the length of that one nerve cell, at thousands of separate points, knobs from other neurons form synapses. (On a large motor nerve ten thousand separate contacts are made, and a brain neuron may have as many as eighty thousand.) If a signal stimulates that motor nerve into action, immediately thousands of other nerve cells in the vicinity are put on alert. The single cells pictured in the biology texts extend to every square millimeter of skin, every muscle, every blood vessel, every bone.

I want to move my hand. Is the stimulus from the brain strong enough to contract the muscle? How many muscle fibers are necessary for the appropriate strength? Are opposing muscles properly inhibited? The single nerve carries all these electrical messages, up to one thousand separate impulses a second, with an appropriate pause between each. Every impulse is monitored and affected by all the ten thousand synaptic connections along the path. The click-click-click auditory image of muscular action, then, is a kindergarten concept. Actually a stupendous crackling wildness surges in all of us at every moment.

Should we do something to alleviate the incessant hysteria of communication? Should I rest from my typing to allow my finger neurons to recover from their frenetic activity? To the contrary, our bodies seem to require an incredible volume of stimuli. Experimental subjects have deprived their bodies of normal daily stimuli with disastrous results. Some have locked themselves in dark, padded boxes; some have floated blindfolded and motionless in a tank of warm water. If nature abhors a vacuum, the brain abhors silence. It begins to break down, quickly filling the void with hallucinations. The volunteer begs for relief after a few hours, unable to stay sane without the stimuli.

—.

The brain cannot directly order each decision in the body — that would defy the management principle of delegation. Instead, a dependable reflex system handles many situations.

When I tap the tendon below a patient's knee, his leg flies up toward my face until muscle tension stops it. I tap it again, this time after telling the patient to stifle the reflex. He fails; the leg recoils anyway. What sinister force in his tendon dares to oppose his brain? It is simply a built-in protection system. Small, spindle-shaped structures, embedded near that tendon, stretch with the muscles, alerting nerve fibers to hurry the message to the spinal cord. Normally (in fact, almost always except in the case of the doctor's reflex test), sudden tension in that tendon means his leg has just been burdened by a heavy weight. Usually this happens when he is about to fall, and the process of stumbling triggers a reflex that automatically straightens his leg. The brain delegates such protections to the reflex arc. A reflex is built-in, unwavering.

It shows good management principles, this delegation to sneeze, cough, swallow, salivate, and blink. Blink. I have already mentioned the tragic blindness that afflicts leprosy patients who have lost eyelid reflexes. Nothing alerts them when the cornea has dried out and needs a lubricating blink. We can sometimes prevent the blindness by teaching the patients to blink. One would think patients with eyesight at stake would be eager learners, but conscious reflexes are not so simple. Patients must be trained with placards and stopwatches, drilled, scolded, praised, cajoled. The advanced brain informs them it cannot be bothered with something so elementary as a reflex (who would force a supercomputer to count to ten every thirty seconds?). Some patients do not learn, and their eyes eventually dry out.

⚊

Some functions, though, do not fit the rigid, robotlike response of reflex. In the brain stem lies the next level of guidance, the subconscious regulators of breathing, digestion, and heart action. These need more attention than reflexes: simply breathing entails the cooperation of ninety chest muscles. And, the body's requirements change quickly; for example, heartbeat and breathing spurt wildly when I race up the stairs.

Highest of all in the hierarchy of the nervous system are the cerebral hemispheres of the brain, the holy of holies of the body — most protected by bone, most vulnerable to injury if the protection is ever breached. There ten billion nerve cells and one hundred billion glia cells (which provide the biological batteries for brain activity) float in a jellied mass, sifting through information, storing memories, creating consciousness. In the brain lies our proclivity to evil and rage as well as our impetus toward purity and love.

Already researchers can control rage, can, with a transmitter implanted in the brain of a charging bull, electrically switch him into a harmless, cuddly pet. Some love to take complex notions, like romantic love, altruism, or an idea of God, and smilingly explain them away in terms of potassium ions and chemical balances and memory-association cells in the brain. But the logic is circular. How do I know that the idea of God isn't merely a series of electrical impulses in my brain? Answer: How do I know that electrical impulses are not God's chosen device for communicating to me a spiritual reality that could not otherwise be known?[2]

⟶

The hierarchy seems neatly ordered. But one messy problem keeps popping up, throwing a pencil into the well-lubricated gears of motion. The final decision, the localized "will" that controls muscles and movement, resides not in the magnificent crevasses of the brain, but in the humble, singular nerve cell or neuron that controls the muscle fibers. Sir Charles Sherrington discovered this discomfiting feature and grandiosely labeled it "the final common path."

The cell body of this neuron receives a spray of impulses from surrounding nerve centers. It stays alert to muscle tension, the presence of pain, the action of opposing muscles, the degree of strength required for any given activity, the frequency of stimuli, the oxygen available, the body temperature, the fatigue factor. Orders from the brain flood in: lift your arm — the box is heavy, so be ready to enlist a squadron of motor units. But after all the signals have accumulated in a giant contradictory pool of advice and recommendations, the motor neuron itself, down in the spinal cord, decides whether to contract or relax. It, after all, is best equipped for such a decision, being in intimate contact with thousands of local synapses as well as the brain.

Professor Bullock of the University of California in San Diego sums up the process: "The degrees of freedom available even at this low level can provide for an almost unlimited degree of complexity." Now that we have figured out the sequenced hierarchy of the body, it reduces to the simple fact that the neuron does whatever it thinks is best. Who said nature is not a democracy? Particle physicists have been telling us that for decades, and now our brain and its agents confirm the fact.

Only the "final common path" can decide between incompatible commands and reflexes, and we should be glad. I stand on a cliff on one of the sheer granite hulks in the Rocky Mountains. Ahead of me, just beyond my reach, is a delightful wildflower I have never seen before. I reach forward, peering through my camera under instructions from my brain, after carefully planting my feet. My close-up lens is within inches of the wildflower when suddenly a string is jerked and, like a marionette, I tip backward away from the flower. My heart is pounding, and I look around to see who interrupted my photography. No one is there, save a raucous, scolding jay.

Ever since I peered over the edge of the cliff to the ravine two thousand feet below, my cells have been chemically flooded with a heightened awareness of the potential danger. My conscious brain wanted a picture of the flower; my subconscious reflexes picked up a slight, precarious tilt in the balancing organs of my ear and short-circuited the orders, by sending *urgent* messages directly to the nerve cells that controlled the muscles, abruptly yanking me backward.

The same saving rebellion takes over when I walk barefoot around the grounds of the Carville Hospital. (I am a great advocate of barefootedness, believing it makes for healthy, strong feet and opens up a whole world of sensation and awareness of the ground I walk on.) If I step on a thorn, my foot will stop in mid-step, pulling itself back even before the pain registers in my brain. But if I were escaping a burning plane, my cells would know that the brain was calling on them to bear some unusual stresses to prevent much more traumatic stress. I could then step on a flaming shard of metal because the normal reflex would be short-circuited for the sake of the more pressing goal of escape.*

The nervous system's hierarchy serves my sense of survival. Sometimes my brain overrules; sometimes it delegates. Always the results of its orders depend on the local, autonomous cell — the final common path.

---

*Jim Corbet, who wrote about India, described one remarkable case of willpower overcoming pain in a time of stress. Upon examining the scene of a tiger attack, he found that a lady had gripped a tree branch so resolutely that the skin of her hands stayed on the branch while the tiger tore her body from it.

# Chapter 24

# GUIDANCE

*To will one thing, then, can only mean to will the Good,*
*because every other object is not a unity, and the will that only*
*wills that object, therefore, must become double-minded.*

Søren Kierkegaard

W̶e have charted the hierarchy within the body: cell to neuron
to reflex to conditioned reflex to brain stem to higher brain,
then back down the final common path to the controlling neuron.
Despite the complex interactions of thousands of synapses, the system shows a basic simplicity of design. It combines freedom with
cooperation. Actions as ordinary as squashing a mosquito or photographing a flower tax the full capacity of this amazing system.

I cannot imagine a more striking parallel to the network of
communication that unites the members of Christ's Body. All of
us have declared allegiance to the Head, who is Christ. But God,
with a deep, implicit regard for freedom, has left the final choice of
action to individuals who are as fully independent as the final common path.

The body offers one obvious lesson: all levels of communication are important. Life would be hopelessly complex if my brain
had to give conscious orders for every muscle contraction. As I walk

to work in the morning, I am free to think about my patients or about the birds chirping in the branches. My legs need no conscious direction; their muscles follow the sequence of reflex activity that has been programmed into them. Motor units rest in turn rather than all at once, so my action can be continuous rather than sporadic. My neurons, alert to all other parts of my body, will slow my pace if my heart complains or take immediate action if I stumble.

A healthy body is a beautiful, singing harmony between the central nervous system and the tissues it controls. Yet in all this harmony every neuron must determine its own action based on the many impulses that come in. The microscopic computer in each nerve cell gauges my intentions, consults other muscles, analyzes hormones, energy availability and the inhibition of fatigue or pain, and fires a yes or no order to its muscle group.

Think of yourself as a motor unit in Christ's Body, one of millions. How do you decide how and when to act? What is true guidance? Should a "higher" impulse always supersede a "lower" impulse?

⟶

Each cell's most numerous and immediate connections link it to local neurons. Some feed in from other motor cells, some from pain cells, pressure cells, temperature cells, muscle tone cells. All of these transmit waves of data which inform the individual neuron how to act in community. I believe that God has similarly delegated certain controls to the local church. How should the church respond to a decaying inner city? To the increasing pressures tearing families apart? To a disastrous flood? God has laid out principles governing the response of the whole Body, but has also designated that local groups of Christ-followers determine the role of each individual cell.

The Bible lists the various spiritual gifts that should be used in organizing a hierarchy among the local members. Interestingly, when it outlines church offices, it does not recommend seeking out technically skilled people. There are no suggestions that a leader be a good manager or a sharp accountant or even show leadership potential. The essential qualities are spiritual qualities: How committed are they to God? Can they control their own temperaments? What are their families like? The key ingredient for all church offices listed in the Bible is not ability but loyalty. God seems to say, I will work with any people you give me as long as they are loyal. Having entrusted us with freedom, God needs leaders among us who are prone to exercise that freedom by aligning it with his will. A skilled but disloyal cell may initiate a wonderfully impressive action, but, like the spastic muscle, it will be useless unless it matches the body's needs.

Those of us raised in Western democracies, which highly value autonomy and freedom, readily respond to the image of the body as a composite democracy with the ultimate decision resting in individual cells. But that is only part of the story. As Bishop Lesslie Newbigin has stated it, "The goal of his [God's] purpose is not a collection of individual spirits abstracted one by one.... Such a thought is irreconcilable with the biblical view of God, of man, and of the world. The redemption with which he is concerned is both social and cosmic, and therefore the way of its working involves at every point the re-creation of true human relationships and of true relationship between man and the rest of the created order. Its center is necessarily a deed wrought out at an actual point in history and at a particular place. Its manner of communication is through a human community wherein men are reborn into a new relation one with another, and become in turn the means of bringing others into that new relationship."[1] Often God speaks to us not just through a direct approach to our own souls, but through fellow members of Christ's Body. That very process binds us together with them.

Some Christian leaders have developed this mutual relationship to other cells in challenging ways. John Wesley's "Methodists" got their name from organized methods of making individuals responsible to others. In regular bands that met weekly, each member would answer to the group, "Have you faced temptations this week? Did you give in? How did you spiritually grow this week? What in your life needs prayer?" Early Methodists took seriously the chain of command which, in Christ's Body as in physical bodies, extends horizontally as well as vertically.

Daily each of us as individual cells face a myriad of choices: what to have for breakfast, what radio station to listen to, what toothpaste to use, which neighbors to see, which phone calls to make. Beyond these trivia are numerous ethical choices: How can I love my neighbor as myself? Is it wrong for me to use this excess income on a new shirt? How scrupulous should I be on my income tax return? How do I get God's guidance on these decisions? Psychiatrists can give many examples of well-meaning religious people who have been paralyzed by just such perplexing questions. Our brains can be so occupied sorting through the blizzard of information that our response is helpless inactivity.

For this reason, I think, the Bible encourages us to ground ourselves in contact with God and the Word so thoroughly that our Christian actions become like reflexes to us. If I must decide whether to tell the truth in the face of every situation, my life is hopelessly complex. But if I have a reflex of truthfulness that responds without orders from higher up, I can learn to "walk" as a Christian without having to think about each individual step.

Paul summarized the process of our being imprinted with proper spiritual reflexes in this passage: "Do not conform any longer to the pattern of this world, but be transformed by the renewing of your mind. Then you will be able to test and approve what God's will is — his good, pleasing and perfect will" (Romans 12:2). From there he goes on to the first full mention in the New Testament of the Body analogy, followed by a list of abrupt commands telling what God's will includes: Hate what is evil; cling to what is good. Honor one another above yourselves. Share with God's people who are in need. Don't be proud. Live at peace with everyone.

Paul never dwells on subtle psychological distinctions or explores all the family and sociological factors that would make such obedient behavior difficult. He doesn't coax us toward right living. He simply states what it is and admonishes us to "renew our minds." I would paraphrase that as "reminding individual cells of their new identity in Christ." We have a tendency to forget, to substitute our educated selves for Christ as the Head. Paul recommends a process of mental purging, a conscious identification with the hierarchy God has set up.

Quite often I meet Christians who tend to wear their spirituality as an aura of otherworldliness. According to some, the most spiritual Christian is one who confidently asserts, "God told me it's time to buy a new dress," or "I'm positive God wants our church to use our money this way." "God told me" can become a casual manner of speech. Actually, I believe most of what God has to say to me is already written in the Bible and the onus is on me to diligently study his will revealed there. For most of us, mysterious direct messages from a hotline to God are not the ordinary ways of discerning his will. Guidance mediated through circumstances or modified on the advice of wise Christian friends, though it may seem less spectacular, is not at all inferior.

College graduates agonize over what decisions to make for the future, waiting for God to alert them with a jolting, custom-made plan dropped into their laps. In the Bible God indeed employed the supernatural means of angels and visions and the like to convey his will. But, if you look closely at those incidents, you will note that few of them came in response to a prayer for guidance. They were usually unrequested and unexpected.

Consider the oft-cited Macedonian call of Paul as an example. Spectacular, yes, since a vision of a man beckoned Paul to change his travel plans and head toward Macedonia. Note carefully, however, that the vision prompted Paul to *change* his plans. You would expect Paul to plan his future in a godly way, but this incident indicates that Paul had gone off on his missionary journey without any visions or inner voices from the Spirit. Most likely, he looked over the situation and chose the route that seemed the most sensible. But the Holy Spirit wanted him to go into a whole new region — and so intervened spectacularly. It was exceptional guidance, obviously not the kind Paul normally relied on.

When grasping for analogies to describe the growing faith of the individual believer, Paul often turned to athletics: running, boxing, wrestling. Athletes demonstrate well the discipline that can train the body toward predictable, dependable actions. Chipper Jones can count on his muscles springing into action to snare a screaming line drive because he has built that response into the neurons through hours of practice. An athlete's body knows what his mind wants and is equipped and experienced to effect that desire. Similarly, the individual Christian would better spend his time working on practical, daily obedience to what God has already revealed rather than fervent searches for some magic secret, elusive as the Holy Grail.

⟶

After stressing guidance from community and from trained reflexes, I must quickly add that each individual neuron does have a direct access to the brain. Although the pathway may not often be used in spectacular ways, it is present, and its synaptic connection can provide stirring, life-changing moments.

Such an experience happened to me my first year in India. I had had a general feeling I was supposed to be a missionary, so after my medical training I agreed to journey to India, the country of my birth. When the medical college first proposed my going, I stipulated a one-year contract because I was still tentative about my whole future. I went and taught, performed surgery, and filled whatever daily functions came up on the hospital staff.

Then, after being there a few months, I visited Dr. Robert Cochrane, a renowned skin specialist, at the leprosy sanitarium in Chingleput a few miles south of Madras. My own hospital did not admit leprosy patients, and I had seen none professionally. Dr. Cochrane showed me around the grounds of his hospital, nodding to the patients who were squatting, stumping along on bandaged feet, or following us with their unseeing, deformed faces. Gradually my nervousness (a result of my childhood memories) melted into a sort of professional curiosity, and my eyes were drawn to the hands of the patients.

Hands waved at me and stretched out in greeting. I study hands as some people study faces — often I remember them better than faces. But these were not the exquisite paradigms of engineering I had studied in medical school. They were twisted, gnarled, ulcerated stumps. Some were stiff like metal claws. Some were missing fingers. Some hands were missing altogether.

Finally I could restrain myself no longer. "Look here, Bob," I interrupted his long discourse on skin diseases, "I don't know much about skin. Tell me about these hands. How did they get this way? What do you do about them?"

Bob shrugged and said, "Sorry, Paul, I can't tell you. I don't know."

"Don't know!" I responded with obvious shock and amazement. "You've been a leprosy specialist all these years and you don't know? Surely something can be done for these hands!"

Bob Cochrane turned on me almost fiercely, "And whose fault is that, if I may ask — mine or yours? I'm a skin man — I can treat that part of leprosy. But you are a bone man, the orthopedic surgeon!" More calmly, with sadness in his voice, he went on to tell me that not one orthopedic surgeon had yet studied the deformities of the fifteen million leprosy victims in the world.

As we continued our walk, his words sank into my mind. Far more people were afflicted by leprosy than those deformed by polio, or those mangled by auto accidents world-wide. But not one orthopedist to serve them? Cochrane told me why he thought that was true: simple prejudice. Leprosy was surrounded by an aura of black magic. Most doctors would not get close to the leprosy patients. The few who did were idealistic or were priests and missionaries.

A few moments later I noticed a young patient sitting on the ground trying to take off his sandal. His disabled hands would not cooperate as he attempted to wedge the sandal strap between his thumb and the palm of his hand. He complained that he could never grasp things — they always slipped from his hand. On sudden impulse, I moved toward him. "Please," I asked in Tamil, "may I look at your hands?"

The young man arose and, smiling, thrust his hands forward. I held them in mine, almost reluctantly. I traced the deformed fingers with my own and studied them intently. Finally, I pried his fingers open and placed my hand in his in a handshake grip. "Squeeze my hand," I directed, "as hard as you can."

To my amazement, instead of the weak twitch I had expected to feel, a sharp intense pain raced through my palm. His grip was like a vise, with fingers digging into my flesh like steel talons. He showed no paralysis — in fact I cried out for him to let go. I looked up angrily but was disarmed by the gentle smile on his face. He did not know he was hurting me. And that was the clue. Somewhere in that severely deformed hand were powerfully good muscles. They were obviously not properly balanced, and he could not feel what force he was using. Could they be freed?

I felt a tingling as if the whole universe was revolving around me. I knew I had arrived in my place.

That single incident in 1947 changed my life. From that instant I knew my calling as surely as a cell in my body knows its function. Every detail of that scene — the people standing around the grounds, the shade of the tree, the questioning face of the patient whose hand I was holding — is still etched into my mind. It was my moment, and I had felt a call of the Spirit of God. I was made for that one moment in Chingleput, and I knew when I returned to my base I would have to point my life in a new direction. I have never doubted it since.

# Chapter 25

# A PRESENCE

*The Holy Spirit is the force in the straining muscles of an arm,*
*the film of sweat between pressed cheeks, the mingled wetness on*
*the backs of clasped hands. He is as close and unobtrusive as that,*
*and as irresistibly strong.*

John V. Taylor

As a junior doctor on night duty in a London hospital I called on eighty-one-year-old Mrs. Twigg. This spry, courageous woman had been battling cancer of the throat, but even with a raspy, hoarse voice she remained witty and cheerful. She had asked that we do all we could medically to prolong her life, and one of my professors removed her larynx and the malignant tissue around it.

Mrs. Twigg seemed to be making a good recovery until about two o'clock one morning when I was urgently summoned to her ward. She was sitting on the bed, leaning forward, with blood spilling from her mouth. Wild terror filled her eyes. Immediately I guessed that an artery back in her throat had eroded. I knew no way to stop the bleeding but to thrust my finger into her mouth and press on the pulsing spot. Grasping her jaw with one hand, I explored with my index finger deep inside her slippery throat until I found the artery and pressed it shut.

Nurses cleaned up around her face while Mrs. Twigg recovered her breath and fought back a gagging sensation. Fear slowly drained from her as she began to trust me. After ten minutes had passed and she was breathing normally again, with her head tilted back, I tried to remove my finger to replace it with an instrument. But I could not see far enough back in her throat to guide the instrument, and each time I removed my finger the blood spurted afresh and Mrs. Twigg panicked. Her jaw trembled, her eyes bulged, and she forcefully gripped my arm. Finally, I calmed her by saying I would simply wait, with my finger blocking the blood flow, until a surgeon and anesthetist could be summoned from their homes.

We settled into position. My right arm crooked behind her head, supporting her. My left hand nearly disappeared inside her contorted mouth, allowing my index finger to apply pressure at the critical point. I knew from visits to the dentist how fatiguing and painful it must be for tiny Mrs. Twigg to stretch her mouth open wide enough to surround my entire hand. But I could see in her intense blue eyes a resolution to maintain that position for days if necessary. With her face a few inches from mine, I could sense her mortal fear. Even her breath smelled of blood. Her eyes pleaded mutely, "Don't move — don't let go!" She knew, as I did, if we relaxed our awkward posture, she would bleed to death.

We sat like that for nearly two hours. Her imploring eyes never left mine. Twice during the first hour, when muscle cramps painfully seized my hand, I tried to move to see if the bleeding had stopped. It had not, and as Mrs. Twigg felt the rush of warm liquid surge up in her throat she gripped my shoulder anxiously.

I will never know how I lasted that second hour. My muscles cried out in agony. My fingertip grew totally numb. I thought of rock climbers who have held their fallen partners for hours by a single rope. In this case the cramping four-inch length of my finger, so numb I could not even feel it, was the strand restraining life from falling away.

I, a junior doctor in my twenties, and this eighty-one-year-old woman clung to each other superhumanly because we had no choice — her survival demanded it.

The surgeon came. Assistants prepared the operating room, and the anesthetist readied his chemicals. Mrs. Twigg and I, still entwined together in our strange embrace, were wheeled into the surgery room. There, with everyone poised with gleaming tools, I slowly eased my finger away from her throat. I felt no gush of blood. Was it because my finger could no longer feel? Or had the blood finally clotted firmly after two hours of pressure?

I removed my hand from her mouth and still Mrs. Twigg breathed easily. Her hand continued to clutch my shoulder and her eyes stayed on my face. But gradually, almost imperceptibly at first, the corners of her bruised, stretched lips turned slightly up, forming a smile. The clot had held. She could not speak — she had no larynx — but she did not need words to express her gratitude. She knew how my muscles had suffered; I knew the depths of her fear. In those two hours in the slumberous hospital wing, we had become almost one person.

⟜

As I recall that night with Mrs. Twigg, it stands almost as a parable of the conflicting strains of human helplessness and divine power within us. In this case, my medical training counted very little. What mattered was my presence and my willingness to respond by reaching out and contacting another human being.

Along with most doctors I know, I often feel inadequate in the face of real suffering. Pain strikes like an earthquake, with crushing suddenness and devastation. A woman feels a small lump in her breast, and her sexual identity begins to crumble. A child is stillborn, and the mother wails in anguish: "Nine months I waited for this! Why do so many mothers abort their babies while I would give my life to have a healthy one?" A young boy is thrown through the windshield of a car, permanently scarring his face. His memory flickers on and off like a faulty switch — doctors, ever cautious, can't offer much hope.

When suffering strikes, those of us standing close by are flattened by the shock. We fight back the lumps in our throats, march resolutely to the hospital for visits, mumble a few cheerful words, perhaps look up articles on what to say to the grieving.

But when I ask patients and their families, "Who helped you in your suffering?" I hear a strange, imprecise answer. The person described rarely has smooth answers and a winsome, effervescent personality. It is someone quiet, understanding, who listens more than talks, who does not judge or even offer much advice. "A sense of presence." "Someone there when I needed him." A hand to hold, an understanding, bewildered hug. A shared lump in the throat.

We want psychological formulas as precise as those techniques I study in my surgery manuals. But the human psyche is too complex for a manual. The best we can offer is to be there, to see and to touch.

Several themes have recurred throughout this book: the need to serve the Head loyally, the unobtrusive nature of the Body's firm skeleton, the softness and compliancy of the skin, and the healing activity of Christ's Body. Taken together, these provide a sense of presence to the world — God's presence.

Sometimes I, as a member of Christ's Body, feel as if I am back in the room with Mrs. Twigg. All my parts — bone, muscle, blood, brain — collaborate beautifully to allow me to stave off certain death in my patient. Yet I must also fend off a sense of helpless futility. The most I can do is dam the flow of blood for a short while, delaying the further invasion of her terminal cancer. I wish, instead, for a miracle.

⟶

Is God's plan to possess the earth through a Body composed of frail humans adequate in light of the sheer enormity of the world's problems? Such a question deserves the full treatment of a book much longer and wiser than this one. I can, however, capture a glimpse of God's style of relating to our planet by reviewing the progression of metaphors in the Bible.

All language about God is, of course, symbolic. "Can one hold the ocean in a teacup?" Joy Davidman asked. Words, even thoughts, cannot carry Godness. In the Old Testament, symbols for God most often expressed "otherness." God appeared as a Spirit, so full of light and glory that anyone who approached was struck dead or returned with an unhuman glow. Moses saw only God's back; Job heard a voice from a whirlwind; the Israelites followed the shekinah glory cloud.

Is it any wonder that the Jews, accustomed to such mystery and afraid to say aloud or write the name of God, recoiled at the claims of Jesus Christ? "Anyone who has seen me has seen the Father," Jesus said (John 14:9), words that grated harshly on Jewish ears. He had, after all, spent nine fetal months inside a young girl and had grown up in a humble neighborhood. In Chesterton's words, "God who had been only a circumference was seen as a center; and a center is infinitely small."[1] Visibly at least, Jesus seemed too much like any other human. Their suspicions were confirmed when he succumbed to death. How could God be contained inside the flesh and blood of humanity? How could God die? Many still wonder, long after a resurrection that convinced and ignited his followers.

But Jesus departed, leaving no body on earth to exhibit the Spirit of God to an unbelieving world — except the faltering, bumbling community of followers who had largely forsaken him at his death. *We* are what Jesus left on earth. He did not leave a book or a doctrinal statement or a system of thought; he left a visible community to embody him and represent him to the world. The seminal metaphor, Body of Christ, hinted at by Christ and fully expanded by Paul could only arise *after* Jesus Christ had left the earth.

The apostle Paul's great, decisive words about the Body of Christ were addressed to congregations in Corinth and Asia Minor that, in the next breath, he assailed for human frailty. Note that Paul, a master of simile and metaphor, did not say the people of God are "like the Body of Christ." In every place he said we *are* the Body of Christ. The Spirit has come and dwelt among us, and the world knows an invisible God mainly by our representation, our "enfleshment."

"The Church is nothing but a section of humanity in which Christ has really taken form," said Bonhoeffer.[2] Too often we shrink from both clauses of that summary. Dismayed, we blast ourselves for continuing to manifest our flawed humanity. Disheartened, we in practice, if not in faith, deny that Christ really has taken form in us.

Three dominant symbols — God as a glory cloud, as a Man subject to death, and as a Spirit melding together his new Body — show a progression of intimacy, from fear to shared humanity to shared essence. God is present in us, uniting us genetically to himself and to each other.

Where is God in the world? What is God like? We can no longer point to the Holy of Holies or to a carpenter in Nazareth. *We* form God's presence in the world through the indwelling of God's Spirit. It is a heavy burden.

⮕

After World War II German students volunteered to help rebuild a cathedral in England, one of many casualties of the Luftwaffe bombings. As the work progressed, debate broke out on how to best restore a large statue of Jesus with his arms outstretched and bearing the familiar inscription, "Come unto me." Careful patching could repair all damage to the statue except for Christ's hands, which had been destroyed by bomb fragments. Should they attempt the delicate task of reshaping those hands?

Finally the workers reached a decision that still stands today. The statue of Jesus has no hands, and the inscription now reads, "Christ has no hands but ours."

I show you a mystery: "In him you too are being built together to become a dwelling in which God lives by his Spirit" (Ephesians 2:22).

# NOTES TO FEARFULLY AND WONDERFULLY MADE

CHAPTER 2
[1] Annie Dillard, *Pilgrim at Tinker Creek* (New York: Harper's Magazine Press, 1974), 94.
[2] Lewis Thomas, *The Medusa and the Snail* (New York: Viking Press, 1979), 155–57.

CHAPTER 3
[1] Frederick Buechner, *Telling the Truth* (New York: Harper & Row, 1977), 57–58.
[2] C. S. Lewis, *God in the Dock* (Grand Rapids, Mich.: Eerdmans, 1970), 62.

CHAPTER 10
[1] G. K. Chesterton, *Orthodoxy* (Garden City, N.Y.: Doubleday, 1959), 95.
[2] Ibid., 58.

CHAPTER 12
[1] Adapted from Mont Smith, "The Temporary Gospel," *The Other Side* (November–December 1975).

CHAPTER 13
[1] Merton P. Strommen, *Five Cries of Youth* (New York: Harper & Row, 1974), 76.

CHAPTER 16
[1] R. J. Christman, *Sensory Experience* (Scranton, Pa.: Intext Educational Publishers, 1971), 359.

CHAPTER 17
[1] Ashley Montagu, *Touching* (New York: Columbia University Press, 1971), 30.
[2] Ibid., 82.

CHAPTER 21

[1] Jonathan Miller, *The Body in Question* (New York: Random House, 1978), 310.

[2] Charles Williams, *The Descent of the Dove* (London: Longmans, Green and Company, 1939), 31.

[3] Ibid., 57.

CHAPTER 23

[1] Robert Galambos, *Nerves and Muscles* (Garden City, N.Y.: Doubleday, 1962), 23.

[2] Robert Farrar Capon, *The Third Peacock* (Garden City, N.Y.: Doubleday, 1971), 48.

CHAPTER 24

[1] Lesslie Newbigin, *The Household of God* (New York: Friendship Press, 1954), 109–10.

CHAPTER 25

[1] G. K. Chesterton, *The Everlasting Man* (Garden City, N.Y.: Image Books, 1955), 174.

[2] Dietrich Bonhoeffer, *Ethics* (London: SCM Press, 1971), 64.

# In His Image

# IMAGE

# Chapter 1

# LIKENESS

*What a piece of work is a man! how noble in reason! how infinite in faculties! in form and moving how express and admirable! in action how like an angel, in apprehension how like a god!*

William Shakespeare

Curtains screened my group of ten interns and medical students from the rest of the forty-bed ward. Externally, the Christian Medical College Hospital in Vellore resembled a modern Western facility, but inside it was all Indian. Activity throbbed just beyond our curtain: patients' families bringing in home-cooked food and nurses chasing away the scavengers that followed — crows and an occasional monkey.

Those of us inside the curtains, however, were giving full attention to our young colleague as he made his diagnosis. He was half-kneeling, in the posture I had taught him, with his warm hand slipped under the sheet and resting on the patient's bare abdomen. While his fingers probed gently for telltale signs of distress, he continued a line of questioning that showed he was weighing the possibility of appendicitis against an ovarian infection.

Suddenly something caught my eye — a slight twitch of movement on the intern's face. Was it the eyebrow arching upward? A vague memory stirred in my mind, but one I could not fully recall. His questions were leading into a delicate area, especially for demure Hindu society. Had the woman ever been exposed to a venereal infection? The intern's facial muscles contracted into an expression combining sympathy, inquisitiveness, and disarming warmth as he looked straight in the patient's face and asked the questions. His very countenance coaxed the woman to relax, put aside the awkwardness, and tell us the truth.

At that moment my memory snapped into place. Of course! The left eyebrow cocked up with the right one trailing down, the wry, enticing smile, the head tilted to one side, the twinkling eyes — these were unmistakably the features of my old chief surgeon in London, Professor Robin Pilcher. I sucked in my breath sharply and exclaimed. The students looked up, startled by my reaction. I could not help it; it seemed as if the intern had studied Professor Pilcher's face for an acting audition and was now drawing from his repertoire to impress me.

Answering their questioning looks, I explained myself. "That is the face of my old chief! What a coincidence — you have *exactly* the same expression, yet you've never been to England and Pilcher certainly has never visited India."

At first the students stared at me in confused silence. Finally two or three of them grinned. "We don't know any Professor Pilcher," one said. "But Dr. Brand, that was *your* expression he was wearing."

Later that evening, alone in my office, I thought back to my days under Pilcher. I had thought I was learning from him techniques of surgery and diagnostic procedures. But he had also imprinted his instincts, his expression, his very smile so that they too would be passed down from generation to generation in an unbroken human chain. It was a kindly smile, perfect for cutting through the fog of embarrassment to encourage a patient's honesty. What textbook or computer program could have charted out the facial expression needed at that exact moment within the curtain?

Now I, Pilcher's student, had become a link in the chain, a carrier of his wisdom to students some nine thousand miles away. The Indian doctor, young and brown-skinned, speaking in Tamil, shared few obvious resemblances with either Pilcher or me. Yet somehow he had conveyed the likeness of my old chief so accurately that it had transported me back to university days with a start. The thought gave me a crystalline insight into the concept of image.

—.

The word *image* is familiar to us today, but the meaning of the word has leaked away so that now it connotes virtually the opposite of its former meaning of "likeness." Today, a politician hires an image-maker, a job applicant dresses for image, a corporation seeks the right image. In all these usages, image has come to mean the illusion of what something is presented to be, rather than the essence of what it really is.

In this book entitled *In His Image* I want to reinforce the original meaning of image as an exact likeness, not a deceptive illusion. We must return to the concept of likeness to understand the "image of God" we are intended to carry. Glimpses into that former meaning still endure. For instance, when I gaze at a nerve cell through a scanning electron microscope, I study the neuron's image. I am looking not at the neuron itself — its small size precludes that — but at a reassembled image that faithfully reproduces it for my eye. In this case the image enhances, rather than distorts, the essence of the cell.

Similarly, photographers use the word *image* to describe their finished product. The image of a sequoia redwood grove flattened onto a small black-and-white rectangle surely does not express the totality of the original, but when developed by a master like Ansel Adams it may convey the original essence with great force.

Or, think of a ten-pound bundle of protoplasm squirming fitfully in a blanket. The baby's father weighs fifteen times as much and has a vastly larger range of ability and personality. Yet the mother announces proudly that the baby is the "spitting image" of his father. A visitor peers closely. Yes, a resemblance does exist, evident now in a dimple, slightly flared nostrils, a peculiar earlobe. Before long, mannerisms of speech and posture and a thousand other mimetic traits will bring the father unmistakably to mind.

These usages of image, applied to the microscope and photograph and offspring, carry a meaning similar to the "image" of Professor Pilcher that I unwittingly passed along to scores of Indian students. All are true images, a likeness of one subject expressed visibly through another. And all shed light on the grand and mysterious phrase from the Bible: the image of God. That phrase appears in the very first chapter of Genesis, and its author seems to stutter with excitement, twice affirming a concept just mentioned in the preceding verse: "So God created man in his own image, in the image of God he created him" (1:27). The image of God — the first man on earth received it, and in some refracted way each one of us possesses this quality wondrous strange.

How can visible human beings express the image of God? We certainly cannot look like God, sharing characteristic features of eyebrow or earlobe, for God is invisible spirit. Philosophers and theologians have long speculated on all that could be contained within the mystery of that single phrase. Predictably, they tend to project onto their definitions the principal concerns of their own era. The Enlightenment age assures us the image of God is the ability to reason, Pietists identify it as the spiritual faculty, Victorians claim it as the capacity to make moral judgments, and Renaissance thinkers locate the image of God in artistic creativity. As for our own psychology-dominated age? What else could that image be, we are now advised, than our capacity for relationships with other people and with God.

Because even professional theologians have failed to reach a consensus over the centuries, I will not attempt a comprehensive definition saying the image of God is *this* and not *that*. But since it stands for all that is unique about humanity among God's creations, the phrase deserves a few moments' reflection.

In the Genesis narrative, the concept "image of God" appears at the consummation of all creation. At each stage of progress, Genesis notes punctiliously, God looks back on creation and pronounces it good. But creation still lacks a creature to contain God's own image. Only after all that preparation does God announce the culmination of life on earth: "Let us make man in our image, in our likeness, and let them rule over the fish of the sea and the birds of the air, over the livestock, over all the earth, and over all the creatures that move along the ground" (1:26).

Among all God's creatures, only humanity receives the image of God, and that quality separates us from all else. We possess what no other animal does; we are linked in our essence to God. (Later, as God discusses with Noah the extent of human dominion over the animals, this quality of the image of God looms up again, as a decisive and awesome demarcation between man and other creatures. Killing an animal means one thing; killing a fellow human is an entirely different matter, "for in the image of God has God made man" [9:6].)

﹅

One of the supreme artists of history rendered the Creation sequence on the vaulted stone ceiling of the Sistine Chapel in Rome. Michelangelo chose as the centerpiece of his great work the precise moment when God awakened man into his image.

I have visited the Sistine Chapel, in its contemporary ambiance far different from what Michelangelo probably had in mind as a setting for his art. Tourists are admitted in groups running to several hundred, many of them clasping white plastic headphones to their ears like painful growths. They are listening to a recording that guides them through the chapel. Instead of looking up when they walk into that splendid room, they look down, following the trail of red tape that marks off an area where the recording is being transmitted.

Nothing can quite prepare the visitors for what they see when, on cue, they raise their heads. Magnificent works of art cover every inch of the large room: the division of light and darkness, the creation of the sun and planets, the days of Noah, the last judgment. And in the focal center, the calm eye in the swirl of frescoes, Michelangelo has painted the creation of man.

Adam's muscular body reclines on the ground in the classical pose of the ancients' river gods. Slumberous, he is lifting up his hand, stretching it out toward heaven from where God reaches down. The hands of God and Adam do not actually touch. A gap separates their fingers, like a synapse across which the energy of God is flowing.

In some respects, Michelangelo captured man's creation as no artist ever has. The very word Adam in Hebrew refers to ground or dust, and Adam is set on the physical earth. Yet Michelangelo also expressed Adam's dual nature by portraying the instant when God reached across the void to convey spiritual life. The second account of man's creation, in Genesis 2, adds more detail: "And the LORD God formed man from the dust of the ground and breathed into his nostrils the breath of life, and man became a living being" (v. 7).

When I heard that verse as a child, I imagined Adam lying on the ground, perfectly formed but not yet alive, with God leaning over him and performing a sort of mouth-to-mouth resuscitation. Now I picture that scene differently. I assume that Adam was already biologically alive — the other animals needed no special puff of oxygen, nitrogen, and carbon dioxide to start them breathing, so why should man? The breath of God now symbolizes for me a spiritual reality. I see Adam as alive, but possessing only an animal vitality. Then God breathes into him a new spirit, and infills him with God's own image. Adam becomes a living soul, not just a living body. God's image is not an arrangement of skin cells or a physical shape, but rather an in-breathed spirit.

This single act of special creation, God breathing into man "the breath of life," distinguished humanity from all other creatures. We share with the animals a biological shell composed, in our case, of bone, organs, muscle, fat, and skin. In truth, we fall short in direct comparison to the strictly biological features of some animals. Who would compete in beauty with a splashy macaw or even a lowly luna moth? A horse easily outruns us, a hawk sees far better, a dog detects odors and sounds imperceptible to us. The total sum of our sheer physical qualities is no more godlike than a cat's.

And yet, *we* are made in the image of God. For us, the shell of skin and muscle and bones serves as a vessel, a repository for God's image. We can comprehend and even convey something of the Creator. Our cellular constructions of proteins arranged by DNA can become temples of the Holy Spirit. We are not "mere mortals." We are, all of us, immortals.

—,

I began with the image of Professor Robin Pilcher, my old surgical chief from London. As a young student I absorbed something from his image that I carried nine thousand miles to India and in turn transferred to scores of Indians. Today, those former students work in hospitals all over the world. An exact copy of Pilcher's expression may appear at critical moments in Borneo, in the Philippines, in Africa. Pilcher died years ago, but that one aspect of him — a small pattern of facial muscles appropriate for a particular medical situation — remains alive and visible on my face and the faces of my students.

What God has in mind for us is similar, but far greater. God is asking us to be the chief bearers of his likeness in the world. As spirit, God remains invisible on this planet, relying instead on us to give flesh to that spirit, to bear the image of God.

# Chapter 2

# MIRRORS

*Materialists mistake that which limits life for life itself.*
Leo Tolstoy

⌐

In forty years of surgery I have encountered my share of human drama, but nothing has surpassed my early experiences as a surgical student during the German bombings of London in World War II. Daily, squadrons of ugly, fat Luftwaffe bombers filled the sky, their engines growling like unbroken thunder, their bomb bays belching out cargoes of destruction.

Several scenes scarred my memory so that forty years later they still come to me vividly. I remember one direct hit on a Turkish bathhouse in the Imperial Hotel. The raid had come without much warning, and the baths were still full when the bomb exploded. When I arrived at the site I found a scene straight out of Dante. Partitions in the baths had all been glass, and now shattered glass literally paved the streets. Enormously fat men, stark naked, were climbing out of the glowing rubble and stumbling onto the glass-strewn street. Blood from dozens of small cuts flecked their bodies; on some, blood spurted from huge gashes. In the background, air-raid sirens howled a belated, plangent wail. Everything was glistening: the blood, the naked, pinguid flesh, the eerily shining streets. Ambulance workers did their best to calm the injured, carefully picking shards of glass from skin and binding up the worst wounds, while we interns rushed to our hospital to prepare for treatment.

Another night, I was watching from my hospital roof when a bomb fell into the infant ward at the nearby Royal Free Hospital, causing the upper floors to collapse into smoldering ruins. I ran to the scene. There, volunteers dug for the newborns, most of them less than a week old, and found both survivors and casualties covered with blood, grime, and glass. Rescuers set up a human chain, like a fire brigade, to pass the bundled infants out from the hospital rubble to waiting ambulances. The babies' thin cries seemed a pathetically inadequate response to the horror of that scene. To the side, mothers in bathrobes watched with fear and despair flickering across their faces. Had their babies survived? All the infants looked alike in the smoke and darkness.

To this day, when I hear the undulating pitch of a siren that approximates the air-raid warning in London, adrenaline floods my body, resurrecting the fear and tension.

During one period, the *Luftwaffe* attacked our city on fifty-seven consecutive nights, with the raids lasting as long as eight hours without pause. Fifteen hundred planes came each night, in waves of 250. In those dark days, we could not help believing that everything we cherished—our freedom, our nation, our families, our civilization—would be buried in the wasteland created by those hated bombers. Only one thing gave us hope: the courage of Royal Air Force pilots who rose in the skies each day to battle the Germans.

We could watch the aerial confrontations from the ground. RAF Hurricanes and Spitfires, tiny and maneuverable, looked like mosquitoes pestering the huge German bombers. Although their cause seemed futile, and more than half of their own fighters were soon shot down, the RAF pilots never gave up. Each day they sent a few more of the dreaded bombers cartwheeling in flames toward the earth, and all of us spectators cheered loudly. Eventually, Germany could not sustain further losses from the increasingly accurate fighter pilots and Hitler called off the raids. London slept again.

I cannot possibly exaggerate the adoration that Londoners gave to those brave RAF pilots. Winston Churchill, if anything, understated our gratitude when he said, "Never in the history of human conflict has so much been owed by so many to so few." I doubt whether a more adulated group of young men has ever lived. They were the cream of England, the brightest, healthiest, most confident and dedicated, and often the handsomest men in the entire country. When they walked the streets in their decorated uniforms, the population treated them as gods. All eyes turned their way. Young boys ran up to touch them and to stare at close range. All girls envied the few who were fortunate enough to walk beside a man in Air Force blue.

I came to know some of these young men, though in far less idyllic circumstances. The Hurricane, agile and effective as it was, had one fatal design flaw. The single propeller engine was mounted in front, a scant foot or so from the cockpit, and fuel lines snaked alongside the cockpit toward the engine. In a direct hit, the cockpit would erupt in an inferno of flames. The pilot could eject, but in the one or two seconds it took him to find the lever, heat would melt off every feature of his face: his nose, his eyelids, his lips, often his cheeks. I met the RAF heroes swathed in bandages as they began the torturous series of surgeries required to refashion their faces. I helped treat the damaged hands and feet of the downed airmen, even as a team of plastic surgeons went to work on their burned faces.

Sir Archibald McIndoe and his plastic surgeons performed miracles of reconstruction, inventing many new procedures along the way. For facial work they usually used skin grafts from the abdomen and chest. In the days before microvascular surgery, full thicknesses of skin and fat could not simply be sliced away from one part of the body and stitched onto another. Swatches of skin had to be coaxed away, with one end remaining attached to the old blood supply while the other was connected to the graft site until new vessels grew to nourish it. Often surgeons used a two-stage process, temporarily attaching one end of the patient's abdominal skin flap to an arm until a blood supply developed on the arm. They then cut the flap of skin from the abdomen so that it dangled only from the arm, and sewed the loose end to the forehead or cheek or nose. Eventually a blood supply would develop on the facial graft site and the skin could be cut free from its temporary host, the arm.

As a result of these complex techniques, bizarre sights flourished in the wards: arms growing out of heads, a long tube of skin extending from a nasal cavity like an elephant trunk, eyelids made of skin flaps so thick they could not open. An airman commonly endured twenty to forty such surgical procedures before being ready for dismissal.

Throughout the tedious progression of surgeries, morale remained surprisingly high among the pilots, who were fully aware of their patriotic contribution. Wonderful nurses did their best to create an atmosphere of cheerfulness and warmth. The pilots discounted the pain and teased each other about their elephant-man features. They were ideal patients.

But gradually, as the last few weeks of recuperation drew to a close, a change would set in. We noticed that many of the pilots kept asking for minor alterations: a nose flap tucked in just a bit, a mouth turned up some at the corner, a slight thinning down of the right eyelid. Soon the realization dawned on all of us, including the patients, that they were simply stalling. They could not face the world outside.

Despite the miracles wrought by McIndoe with his marvelous techniques, each face had changed irreparably. No surgeon could possibly restore the protean range of expression of a handsome young face. Although technically a good piece of work, the new face was essentially a scar. You cannot appreciate the flexible, nearly diaphanous delicacy of the eyelid until you try to fashion one out of coarser skin from the abdomen. That bulgy, stiff tissue will protect the eye adequately, but without beauty.

I especially remember an RAF pilot named Peter Foster, who described to me his mounting anxiety as the release day approached. Your fears and concerns, he said, come to a focus in the mirror. For some months you use the mirror daily, as an objective measuring device, to scrutinize the progress your surgeons have made. You study scar tissue, the odd wrinkling of the skin, the thickness of lips and shape of the nose. From this survey, you ask for certain adjustments to improve appearance, and the doctors tell you whether your request is reasonable.

But nearer the day of release, your view of the mirror changes. Now, as you gaze at the reflection of a new face, not the one you were born with but an inferior imitation, you try to see yourself as strangers will see you. In the hospital you have been an object of pride, supported by the camaraderie of your friends and the ministrations of the staff. On the outside, you will be a freak. Fear creeps in. Will any girl dare to marry that face? Will anyone give it a job?

At that critical moment, concluded Foster, as each airman contemplated the new image of himself as viewed by the rest of the world, one factor alone mattered: the response of family and intimate friends. The surgeons' relative success in remaking the face counted for little. The future hinged on the reactions of family members to the news that the surgeons had done all they could and the face before them would never improve. Did the airman sense loving acceptance or recoiling hesitance?

These distinctly different reactions cleaved the airmen into two groups in as dramatic a demarcation as I have ever seen. Psychologists followed their progress. In one group were some whose girlfriends and wives could not accept the new faces. These women, who once had idolized their heroic lovers, quietly stole away or filed for divorce. Airmen who encountered this reaction changed in personality. They stayed indoors, refusing to venture outside except at night, and looked for some kind of work to do at home. In contrast, those whose wives and girlfriends stuck by them went on to tremendous success — they were, after all, the elite of England. Many became executives and professionals, leaders of their communities.

Peter Foster gratefully admitted belonging to the fortunate group. His own girlfriend assured him that nothing had changed but a few millimeters' thickness of skin. She loved *him*, not his facial membrane, she said. The two got married just before Peter left the hospital.

Naturally, Peter encountered painful rejection from some. Many adults quickly looked away when he approached. Children, cruel in their honesty, made faces, laughed, and mocked him.

Peter wanted to cry out, "Inside I am the same person you knew before! Don't you recognize me?" Instead, he learned to turn toward his wife. "*She* became my mirror. She gave me a new image of myself," he said with appreciation. "Even now, regardless of how I feel, when I look at her she gives me a warm, loving smile. That tells me I am OK."

⟶

Years after I worked with the airmen, I read a profoundly disturbing article entitled "The Quasimodo Complex" in the *British Journal of Plastic Surgery*. In it, two physicians reported on their study of 11,000 prison inmates who had committed murder, prostitution, rape, or other serious crimes. They carefully documented a trend that I will summarize with one overall comparison. In the normal adult population, 20.2 percent of all people may be said to have surgically correctable facial deformities (protruding ears, misshapen noses, receding chins, acne scars, birthmarks, eye deformities). But research revealed that among the 11,000 offenders fully *60 percent* showed such characteristics.

The authors, who named the phenomenon after Quasimodo, Victor Hugo's "hunchback of Notre Dame," ended the article with some disquieting questions. Had these criminals encountered hostility and rejection from classmates in grammar school and high school because of their deformities? Could the cruel japery of other children have pushed them toward the state of emotional imbalance that ultimately led to criminal acts?

The authors went on to propose a program of corrective plastic surgery for prison inmate volunteers.* If the surface appearance had made society reject these people and possibly push them toward crime, they reasoned, perhaps changing that surface appearance would help rehabilitate them by changing their self-image.

---

*Due partly to the authors' (F. W. Masters and D. C. Greaves) findings, many U.S. states have instituted comprehensive programs of free plastic surgery for prisoners with deformities.

Whether a murderer on death row or a crack pilot in the RAF, a person forms a self-image based largely on what kind of image other people mirror back.

The report on the Quasimodo complex reduces to statistics a truth that haunts every burn victim, handicapped person, and leprosy patient. We humans give inordinate regard to the physical body, or shell, that we live in. It takes a rare person indeed, someone like Peter Foster's wife, to look through that shell and acknowledge the inherent human worth, the image of God inside.

As I have pondered the Quasimodo complex I realize that in subtle and not-so-subtle ways I too have judged and labeled people by their external appearances. I think back to an old family tradition I used to practice with my children. Each year during summer holidays I devised a serial adventure story that featured every member of the family by name and character. Continuing the story each night at bedtime, I tried to weave in some helpful aspects: the children heard of themselves showing unexpected displays of courage and unselfishness that perhaps they would later try to exercise in real life.

Yet the stories contained villains also. I heightened tension and excitement from day to day by having these villains lure the children into impossible situations from which they would somehow have to extricate themselves. Now, as I recall these stories, I remember with a wince that my chief villains, who reappeared in the stories annually, bore the names Scarface and Hunchback. One had an ugly scar across his face; the other was short with a hump on his back. In the running plots, the two would attempt to disguise these features, but sooner or later one of the children would see through the disguises and unmask the villains.

Why, I now wonder, did I give the bad men of my stories those names and characteristics? Undoubtedly I followed the universal stereotype of equating ugly with bad and beautiful with good. Did I inadvertently encourage my own children to equate ugliness with evil, possibly as a result making it harder for them to love those bearing deformities or scars?

Medieval princes used to collect midgets, monsters, and hunchbacks for their own entertainment. Our sophistication does not allow that sort of practice, but do we slip into subtle kinds of rejection just as powerful? After reading about the Quasimodo complex and recognizing overtones of labeling and judgment in my own storytelling, I started noticing more carefully the cultural influences that determine our standards for human worth and acceptance. In America the national ideal is a tall, handsome, and confident male or a slender-yet-shapely, smiling female. Advertisements for body-building programs, diet plans, facial makeovers, and clothes for "the right image" underscore our cultural commitment to physical beauty. If we judged the American population by the images that appear in magazines and on television, we would conclude we live in a society of gods and goddesses.

I have seen the long-term impact of our devotion to physical perfection on my leprosy patients, who will never achieve the image of an Olympic athlete or a Miss America. And I have watched more subtle forces at work in my own children as they have attended public schools. Somehow our cultural ideals have placed us in such bondage that we find no room for a child who is clumsy, shy, or unattractive. Those children meet constant, unrelieved rejection. The "mirrors" around them determine their self-images, and they do not measure up. How many Salks or Pasteurs have been lost because of this deadly process of rejection by peers? We too have much to learn about mirroring.

⌐

I have spent my life in medicine trying to improve the "shells" of my patients. I strive to restore their damaged hands, feet, and faces to the body's original design specifications. I have felt deep satisfaction in seeing those patients relearn how to walk and use their fingers and then return to their communities and families with an opportunity to live a normal life.

Yet increasingly I have come to realize that the physical shell I devote so much energy to is not the whole person. My patients are not mere collections of tendons, muscles, hair follicles, nerve cells, and skin cells. Each of them, regardless of deformed appearance and physical damage, contains an immortal spirit and is a vessel of the image of God. Their physical cells will one day rejoin the basic elements of earth, the *humus* that constitutes the material part of humanity. But their souls will live on, and my effect on those souls may have far more significance than my attempts to improve their physical bodies.

Although I live in a society that honors strength, wealth, and beauty, God has placed me among leprosy patients who are often weak, poor, and unattractive. In that environment, I have learned all of us are, like Peter Foster's wife, mirrors. Each of us has the potential to help summon up in the people we meet the image of God, the spark of Godlikeness in the human spirit. Or, instead, we can ignore or squelch that image and judge only on the basis of external appearance. I pray that when I see a person I will see the image of God inside, and ultimate worth, not just the cultural "image" that we all strive to attain.*

---

*The author of Proverbs points to the inherent worth in every person in this intriguing statement: "He who oppresses the poor shows contempt for their Maker, but whoever is kind to the needy honors God" (14:31).

Mother Teresa used to say that when she looked into the face of a dying beggar in Calcutta, she prayed to see the face of Jesus so that she might serve the beggar as she would serve Christ. In an often quoted passage, C. S. Lewis expressed a related thought: "It is a serious thing to live in a society of possible gods and goddesses, to remember that the dullest and most uninteresting person you talk to may one day be a creature which, if you saw it now, you would be strongly tempted to worship, or else a horror and a corruption such as you now meet, if at all, only in a nightmare. All day long we are, in some degree, helping each other to one of these destinations."

# Chapter 3

# RESTORATION

*The Christian ideal changed and reversed everything so that, as the gospel puts it, "That which was exalted among men has become an abomination in the sight of God." The ideal is no longer the greatness of Pharaoh or of a Roman emperor, not the beauty of a Greek nor the wealth of Phoenicia, but humility, purity, compassion, love. The hero is no longer Dives, but Lazarus the beggar; not Mary Magdalene in the day of her beauty, but the day of her repentance.*

Leo Tolstoy

I am standing in the sublime Sistine Chapel. Most tourists have left, twilight approaches, and the light has ripened to a golden hue. My neck aches slightly from supporting my head at odd angles, and I wonder fleetingly how Michelangelo felt after a day of working on these ceiling murals.

My eyes keep drifting back to the pivotal scene which shows God imparting life to man. The image of God stands for all that gives worth and dignity to individual men and women, and nothing could better display that indwelling power than the paintings that surround me. And yet even as I stare at the creation scene something troubles me. Michelangelo succeeded wonderfully at depicting human duality and the drama of creation. But he clearly failed, as all artists must, at portraying God. Michelangelo's God is no spirit, but a God made in the image of man.

Six centuries before Christ, the Greek philosopher Xenophanes observed that "If oxen and horses and lions had hands or could draw with hands and create works of art like those made by men, horses would draw pictures of gods like horses, and oxen of gods like oxen. . . . Aethiopians have gods with snub noses and black hair; Thracians have gods with grey eyes and red hair." Michelangelo's God has the shape and texture of humanity — even a sloping Roman nose just like Adam's. The artist portrayed the likeness between God and man literally and physically, not spiritually. In fact, if you took Adam's face in the painting, aged it around the eyes, and crowned it with flowing white locks and a beard, you would have Michelangelo's depiction of God the Father.

How can an artist possibly represent a God who is spirit? And if we cannot see God, how can we contemplate God's image? Our vocabulary, superb and precise when describing the material world, falls silent before the inner processes of spirit. The very word "spirit" in many languages means nothing more than breath or wind. But the entire Old Testament insists upon the central truth that God is spirit and that no physical image can capture God's essence.

The second of the Ten Commandments forbids drawing a picture or making a sculptured image intended to represent God. Whenever the Jews tried, God viewed it as profanation. After living in a country where graven images and idols abound, I can well understand the prohibition.

Hinduism has over a thousand different images, and I could hardly walk a block in an Indian town without seeing an idol or representation. As I watched the effects of those images on the average Indian, I observed two common results. For most, the images trivialize the gods. The gods lose any aura of sacredness and mystery and become rather like mascots or good luck charms. A taxi driver mounts a goddess statue on his taxicab and offers flowers and incense as a prayer for safety. For other Indians, the gods may become grotesque symbols that evoke an attitude of fear and bondage. Calcutta's violent goddess Kali, for example, has a fiery tongue and wears a garland of bloody heads around her waist. Hindus may worship a snake, a rat, a phallic symbol, even a goddess of smallpox; such images crowd the ornate temples.

Wisely, the Bible warns us against reducing the image of God to the level of physical matter; such an image too easily limits our concept of God's real nature. We may begin to think of God as a bearded old man in the sky, like the figure in Michelangelo's painting. Being a spirit, present everywhere, God can have no confining shape. "To whom, then, will you compare God?" asks Isaiah. "What image will you compare him to?" (40:18)*

⟶

We have, therefore, a God who cannot be captured in a visible image. But what does God look like? How can I find him? Where is God's image? Somehow the essence of God entered the bodies of the first created humans, and *they* bore his image on this planet. For a time the two natures, the physical nature of organs and blood and bone and a spiritual nature allowing direct communion with God, fit together in harmony. Sadly, that condition failed to last.

An event recorded in Genesis 3 disrupted the harmony between the two natures. Adam's and Eve's rebellion forever marred the

---

*See Isaiah 44 for a speech from God that gives a forceful and yet witty summary of the foolishness of making idols.

image of God they carried, and at that moment a huge gulf fissured open, destroying the unity between God and mankind. Now when we gaze on human beings we find lurking among them the likes of Genghis Khan, Josef Stalin, and Adolf Hitler. And, yes, dramatic evidence of the broken image spills out of every one of us. Individual human beings can no longer express adequately a likeness to God; history proves darkly our unlikeness to God.

It is not enough for us to mirror forth the residue of spirit and worth inside each person. We need something greater, far greater, to know what God is like. We need a new image, a new demonstration of God's likeness on our planet.

Christians believe we got such an image in the person of Jesus Christ, the Second Adam, whose coming proved so revolutionary that it became the exact center of a new religion. God the spirit agreed to become a human being. Inside a body of skin and bone and blood, the divine lived in matter as a microcosm, like the sun in a drop of water.

In three places the New Testament applies the word image to Jesus Christ (2 Corinthians 4:4; Colossians 1:15; Hebrews 1:3). Jesus is, says the Hebrews passage, "the radiance of God's glory and the exact representation of his being." Christ came to earth to offer us an image in the purest sense of the word: a precise reflection of what the Father is like, in bodily form. "In the Father," says Michael Ramsey, "there is no unChristlikeness at all."

Doctors warn against glancing into the sky to look at the brilliance of the sun, even for an instant. Doing so would overwhelm light-receptor cells so that even with our eyes closed the image of that star would still appear, seared into our retinas like a brand of fire. It is the same with Jesus Christ: in a form we can visualize he sears our perception with the image of God.

Here is a strange truth, though: the image Jesus revealed surprised nearly everyone. Most of us have heard and seen the Jesus story portrayed so often that we have firm, preconceived notions of what Jesus was like. We will never be able to recapture the shock, the cataclysmic shock of the incognito form God took on. For his grand entrance he bypassed Rome, of course, and even Jerusalem, selecting instead a tiny, jerkwater town. He missed the people's expectations of divinity so widely that some asked, incredulous, "Isn't this the carpenter's son?" The inevitable ethnic slur followed, "Nazareth! Can anything good come from there?" Even Jesus' brothers did not believe him; at least once they judged him insane. John the Baptist, who had foretold Christ and baptized him, wavered in faith toward the end. Jesus' closest follower cursed him.

Jesus claimed to be a king greater than David, but little about him suited the image of royalty. He carried no weapons, waved no banners, and the one time he permitted a processional he rode on a donkey, his feet dragging the ground. Clearly, Jesus did not measure up to the image expected of a king or a God.

We instinctively think of Jesus as a perfect physical specimen, and in art he is portrayed as tall, with flowing hair and fine features modeled after the accepted ideals of the artist's culture. But on what basis? From the evidence of Scripture, nothing about Jesus made him very special as a physical specimen either.

Once in my childhood my gentle Aunt Eunice came home from a Bible study in an absolute rage. Someone had read a description of Jesus, written by Josephus or another historian, that characterized him as a hunchback. Aunt Eunice trembled with shame and anger, and her face flushed scarlet. It was blasphemy, she declared. "Utter blasphemy! That is a horrid caricature, not a description of my Lord!" As an impressionable child, I could not help nodding in sympathetic indignation.

Although the notion shocked me greatly at that time, now it would not shock me at all to discover that Jesus was not a handsome, shining ideal in his personal looks and physique. Although the Bible does not include a description of Jesus' face and body, there is a description of sorts, in a prophecy of the suffering servant in Isaiah:

> "... there were many who were appalled at him —
>> his appearance was so disfigured beyond that of any man
>> and his form marred beyond human likeness....
> He had no beauty or majesty to attract us to him,
>> nothing in his appearance that we should desire him.
> He was despised and rejected by men,
>> a man of sorrows, and familiar with suffering.
> Like one from whom men hide their faces
>> he was despised, and we esteemed him not"
>
> (52:14; 53:2–3).

Socially, in his own teaching about himself, Jesus identified with the hungry, the sick, the estranged, the naked, and the imprisoned so totally that, he said, whatever we do for one of the least of those people, we do for him (Matthew 25:40). We meet the Son of God not in the corridors of power and wealth, but in the byways of human suffering and need. Christ chose to identify most intimately with those who appeared ugly and useless in the world's eyes.

It is this fact of Jesus' personal identification with the lowly, more than any other, that has taught me the stark distinctions in uses of the word *image*. In the image of the world — the image we exploit today in status games, beauty contests, advertising campaigns — God on earth made no special mark. Yet even one from insignificant Nazareth, a carpenter's son, a bruised body twitching on a cross — even he could express the image, the exact likeness of God.

I cannot tell you what impact that single truth can have when it fully dawns on a person who will never measure up — a leprosy victim in India, for example, unspeakably poor and physically deformed. For such a person Jesus becomes the only hope for restoration.

⟶

Jesus, the exact likeness of God in flesh, expressed the image of God in human form. But from the very beginning he warned that his physical presence was temporary. He had in mind a further goal: to restore the broken image of God in humanity.

God's activity on earth did not end with Jesus, and his image on earth did not vanish when Jesus departed. New Testament authors extend the term to a new Body that God is creating composed of "members" — men and women joining together to do the work of God. In referring to this Body, these writers pointedly use the same word that first described the spark of the divine in man and later described Christ. We are called, said Paul, to be "the likeness [image] of his Son, that he might be the firstborn among many brothers" (Romans 8:29).

This book is not primarily a treatise on the nature of individual men and women. We will not explore the psychological and mental attributes in each one of us that might reflect the image of God. Instead, following the analogy already begun, we will center on a community, that group of God's people who are called, more than two dozen times in the New Testament, Christ's Body. All of us joined to him are an extension of the Incarnation. God reproduces and lives out his image in millions of ordinary people like us. It is a supreme mystery.

We are called to bear that image as a Body because any one of us taken individually would present an incomplete image, one partly false and always distorted, like a single glass chip hacked from a mirror. But collectively, in all our diversity, we can come together as a community of believers to restore the image of God in the world.

For a pattern to follow, we need only look back at Jesus, that divine image seared into our consciousness. The surprising qualities he showed — humility, servanthood, love — become the model for his Body also. No longer must we struggle to build up our own images, to prove ourselves. Rather, we can focus our lives on showing forth his image. And what counts for great success in popular culture — strength, intelligence, wealth, beauty, power — means little to that image.*

I had never grasped the revolutionary pattern Jesus laid down until I began working among leprosy patients in India. Again and again I saw these people, so cruelly ostracized from society, somehow radiate the love and goodness of God far better than wealthy, handsome, and comfortable Christians I had known. Just as God had taken on a lowly image, so it seemed Jesus most faithful followers commonly revealed that same homeliness. They had a more natural right to anger and bitterness, yet the level of dedication and spiritual maturity among patients who came to know Christ shamed us doctors and

---

*Let not the wise man boast of his wisdom
    or the strong man boast of his strength
    or the rich man boast of his riches,
but let him who boasts boast about this:
    that he understands and knows me,
that I am the LORD, who exercises kindness,
    justice and righteousness on earth,
    for in these I delight (Jeremiah 9:23–24).

missionaries. I wrestled with the paradox that those who seemingly had least reason to be grateful to God showed his love best.

The trend appeared with such force and consistency that it drove me to examine biblical passages that I had never taken seriously and that, I confess, had caused me embarrassment. Describing the church in Corinth, Paul said, "Not many of you were wise by human standards; not many were influential; not many were of noble birth. But God chose the foolish things of the world to shame the wise; God chose the weak things of the world to shame the strong. He chose the lowly things of this world and the despised things — and the things that are not — to nullify the things that are, so that no one may boast before him" (1 Corinthians 1:26–29). Statements from Jesus also came to mind: the Sermon on the Mount, in which he enigmatically blesses the poor, the mourning, the persecuted; his comments on how difficult it is for the rich to enter the kingdom of heaven; his condemnation of pride and self-sufficiency.

Inevitably, as I read these passages now, my thoughts keep circling back to that single word we have been discussing: image. I strive with all my energy to improve the damaged self-images of the patients I treat. But when I approach Scripture, I encounter a new kind of image, one for which the same rules do not apply. If anything, the opposite principles hold true, a sort of reverse Quasimodo complex.

Human self-image thrives on physical attractiveness, athletic ability, a worthwhile occupation; I worked to give those gifts to injured fliers in Britain and leprosy patients in India and now America. But, paradoxically, any of those desirable qualities may raise a barrier against the image of God, for virtually any quality that a person can rely on makes it more difficult for that person to rely on the spirit of God. The beautiful, the strong, the politically powerful, and the rich do not easily represent God's image. Rather, God's spirit shines most brightly through the frailty of the weak, the impotence of the poor, the deformity of the hunchback. Even as bodies are broken, God's image can grow brighter.

Initially, I found this insight into the nature of Christ's Body jarring, perhaps because it brought a gnawing awareness that I had often sought to surround myself with the successful, the intelligent, and the beautiful. Too often I had judged by the image of people rather than the image of God. But as I have reflected on my life and the people who have most powerfully presented God's image to me, my mind keeps fixing on three people especially. And none of them met human standards of success.

As a child, I often attended large churches and retreat centers where I listened to some of the most famous Christian speakers in England, many of whom demonstrated great eloquence and erudition. But another kind of speaker holds a special place in my memory: Willie Long, a man I encountered in a Primitive Methodist church at a seaside resort. Willie would mount the pulpit in his blue fisherman's jersey, with the fish scales still clinging to its sides contributing a salty aroma to the church hall. Yet this uneducated man with a thick Norfolk accent, unconventional grammar, and simple faith probably did more to nudge my own faith in those formative years than the entire company of famous men. When he stood to speak of Christ, he spoke of a personal friend, and the love of God radiated from him, through his tears. Willie Long, of little consequence in the image of men, showed me the image of God.

Later, in India, I observed with awe the spiritual rapport that bonded patients to the surgeon Mary Verghese. Mary was unique: a paraplegic surgeon.

One of my most promising students, Mary had suffered a terrible automobile accident that left her paralyzed from the waist down. For months she lay in her hospital bed, resisting rehabilitation. She was staking her hopes on divine healing, she said, and rehabilitation exercises for paraplegia would merely waste her time. One day soon God would restore the full use of her legs.

Ultimately, however, Mary gained the courage to relinquish that demand for miraculous healing in exchange for the sense of the power of the Spirit revealed best in her weakness. Against all odds, she completed her surgery requirements and became a powerful spiritual force in the Christian Medical College Hospital.

In addition to the paraplegia, Mary had also suffered severe facial injuries. After a series of operations to rebuild the bony infrastructure of Mary's cheeks, the plastic surgeon had no choice but to leave a large, ungainly scar right across her face. As a result, she had an odd, asymmetrical smile. By standards of physical perfection, she did not rate high. Yet she had a profound impact on the patients at Vellore.

Dejected leprosy patients would loiter aimlessly in the hallways of their wards (at that time their movements in the main hospital were restricted). Suddenly they would hear a small squeak that signified the approach of Mary's wheelchair. At once the row of faces lit up in bright smiles as though someone had just pronounced them all cured. Mary had a power to renew their faith and hope. Thus, when I think of Mary Verghese, I see not her face, but its reflection in the smiling faces of so many others; not her image, but the image of God poured through her broken human body.

One last figure towers above all others who have influenced my life: my mother, known as Granny Brand. I say it kindly and in love, but in old age my mother had little of physical beauty left in her. She had been a classic beauty as a young woman — I have photographs to prove it — but not in old age. The rugged conditions in India, combined with crippling falls and her battles with typhoid, dysentery, and malaria had made her a thin, hunched-over old woman. Years of exposure to wind and sun had toughened her facial skin into leather and furrowed it with wrinkles as deep and extensive as any I have seen on a human face. She knew better than anyone that her physical appearance had long since failed her — for this reason she adamantly refused to keep a mirror in her house.

At the age of seventy-five, while working in the mountains of South India, my mother fell and broke her hip. She lay all night on the floor in pain until a workman found her the next morning. Four men carried her on a string-and-wood cot down the mountain path to the plains and put her in a jeep for an agonizing 150-mile ride over rutted roads. (She had made this trip before, after a head-first fall off a horse on a rocky mountain path, and already had experienced some paralysis below her knees.)

I soon scheduled a visit to my mother's mud-walled home in the mountains in order to persuade her to retire. By then she could walk only with the aid of two bamboo canes taller than she was, planting the canes and lifting her legs high with each painful step to keep her paralyzed feet from dragging on the ground. Yet she continued to travel on horseback and camp in the outlying villages in order to preach the gospel and treat sicknesses and pull the decayed teeth of the villagers.

I came with compelling arguments for her retirement. It was not safe for her to go on living alone in such a remote place with good help a day's journey away. With her faulty sense of balance and paralyzed legs, she presented a constant medical hazard. Already she had endured fractures of vertebrae and ribs, pressure on her spinal nerve roots, a brain concussion, a fractured femur, and severe infection of her hand. "Even the best of people do sometimes retire when they reach their seventies," I said with a smile. "Why not come to Vellore and live near us?"

Granny threw off my arguments like so much nonsense and shot back a reprimand. Who would continue the work? There was no one else in the entire mountain range to preach, to bind up wounds, and to pull teeth. "In any case," she concluded, "what is the use of preserving my old body if it is not going to be used where God needs me?"

And so she stayed. Eighteen years later, at the age of ninety-three, she reluctantly gave up sitting on her pony because she was falling all too frequently. Devoted Indian villagers began bearing her on a hammock from town to town. After two more years of mission work, she finally died at age ninety-five. She was buried, at her request, in a simple, well-used sheet laid in the ground — no coffin. She abhorred the notion of wasting precious wood on coffins. Also, she liked the symbolism of returning her physical body to its original humus even as her spirit was set free.

One of my last and strongest visual memories of my mother is set in a village in the mountains she loved, perhaps the last time I saw her in her own environment. She is sitting on a low stone wall that circles the village, with people pressing in from all sides. They are listening to all she has to say about Jesus. Heads are nodding in encouragement, and deep, searching questions come from the crowd. Granny's own rheumy eyes are shining, and standing beside her I can see what she must be seeing through failing eyes: intent faces gazing with absolute trust and affection on one they have grown to love.

I know that even with my relative youth and strength and all my specialized knowledge about health and agricultural techniques, I could never command that kind of devotion and love from these people. They are looking at a wrinkled old face, but somehow her shrunken tissues have become transparent and she is all lambent spirit. To them, she is beautiful.

Granny Brand had no need for a mirror made of glass and polished chromium; she had the incandescent faces of thousands of Indian villagers. Her worn-out physical image did nothing but enhance the image of God beaming through her like a beacon.

—.

Willie Long, Mary Verghese, Granny Brand — these are three in whom I have seen the image of God most clearly. I do not say that a Miss Universe or a handsome Olympian can never show forth the love and power of God, but I do believe that such a person is, in some ways, at a disadvantage. Talent, a pleasing physical appearance, and the adulation of crowds tend to shove aside the qualities of humility and selflessness and love that Christ demands of those who would bear his image.

The message is clear: "God has combined the members of the body and *has given greater honor to the parts that lacked it*, so that there should be no division in the body, but that its parts should have equal concern for each other" (1 Corinthians 12:24–25). In our own physical bodies, Paul points out, those parts that seem to be weakest prove indispensable and the unpresentable parts call for special modesty. In Christ's Body too, the analogy holds. When we join his Body, it is the image of God himself we must find, not our own. We find it not by proving ourselves, but by releasing that desperate dependence on our own self-images in favor of taking on God's glorious image.

I, Paul Brand, approaching my seventieth year with more wrinkles and less hair than I would prefer, can let go the anxiety about my health and appearance and abilities that are slipping away. The painful and competitive dependence on my own self-image yields to a freeing, joyful dependence on God's own image.

Admittedly, I lose some autonomy and a chance to nurture my ego. But belonging to Christ's Body offers its reward too. From God's viewpoint we members are in fact swallowed up, surrounded by Christ's Body — "in Christ," as Paul keeps repeating. New Testament authors stretch for metaphors to express the reality. We live or "abide" in him, they say (1 John 2:6). We are "the aroma of Christ" to God (2 Corinthians 2:15). We "shine like stars in the universe" (Philippians 2:15) and are "holy and blameless in his sight" (Ephesians 1:4). Those are just a sampling; the message resounds throughout the Epistles. We are God's delight and pride, his experiment on earth meant to display wisdom even to the "rulers and authorities in the heavenly realms" (Ephesians 3:10). A restoration of God's image on earth is underway, through us.

For membership in Christ's Body, God has drawn from all races and groups, since in him there is neither Greek nor Jew, slave nor free. A simple fisherman, a scar-faced pilot, a paraplegic, a crone can take their rightful places there with joy. It is Christ's glory we take on, not our own. The cost may increase for those with wealth, physical attraction, and security. But for all of us, the reward is the same: a chance to be judged not for what we are but for what Christ is. God looks upon us and sees his beloved Son.

"But we all, with unveiled face, beholding as in a mirror the glory of the Lord, are being transformed into the same image from glory to glory, just as from the Lord, the Spirit" (2 Corinthians 3:18 NASB).

# BLOOD

# Chapter 4

# POWER

*A fly is a nobler creature than the sun, because a fly hath life,*
*and the sun hath not.*

St. Augustine

My entire career in medicine traces back to one dreary night at Connaught Hospital in East London. Before that night I had stubbornly resisted all pressures to enter medical school. For some time my family had tried to influence me toward medicine, even to the extent of an uncle offering to pay all school expenses. And just before I left high school my mother's return from India gave us an opportunity for a serious talk about my future.

We sat together before a hissing gas fire in her bedroom. After a separation of six years, I was struck by her changed appearance. Twenty years in rural India had worn away the soft facade of British gentility and etched an unmistakable resolve in the lines of her face. Grief covered her face like a mask—my father had died of black-water fever that same year. She had come home a desperately broken person, seeking a place of refuge.

It seemed strange for me to be abruptly planning my future with someone I had not seen in six years. "You know how much your father loved the medical work in the mountains," she began gently. "He always wished he had become a doctor with a proper degree instead of having to rely on a short training course at Livingston College. If he had ... who knows, he might still be with us. He would have known how to treat the fever."

Her eyes filled up and she paused a few minutes, swallowing repeatedly. She went on to tell me of new laws in India that would prohibit all but qualified doctors from practicing medicine. Then she looked directly into my eyes and said gravely, "Paul, your father always dreamed that you could take up where he left off and return as a real doctor — "

"No, Mother!" I stopped her in mid-sentence. "I don't want to be a doctor. I don't like medical work. I'd rather be a builder. I could build houses and schools and even hospitals. Anyhow, I don't want to be a doctor."

Although she did not argue, I could sense a barrier had arisen between us. I mumbled some excuse and left, with a gnawing awareness that I was disappointing her as well as my father and my generous uncle by not studying medicine. I could not tell my mother, and probably did not even admit to myself at the time, the real reason: a visceral reaction against blood and pus. Memories had sickened me ever since childhood.

As small children in India my sister and I had shared in everything my parents did. Sometimes a patient came for treatment of a tumid abscess, and when Dad dressed the wound we held the bandages. If we were on camp, my father would cart his sterilizer out to a shady tree, boil the instruments, and prepare to lance the abscess. He had no anesthetics, so the patient would cling fiercely to a relative during the incision and drainage. My sister turned her head the instant she saw the flash of the knife. I laughed at her and boasted that boys were not afraid.

But I was afraid, and also repulsed by the sight of the blood and the pus. I hated those scenes and the sticky cleanup that followed. Vivid memories, years later, were still keeping me from becoming a doctor. I could not brave a whole lifetime of dealing with blood and pus and sickness.

⟶

Five years after my awkward conversation with Mother, I found myself unavoidably working at Connaught, a small hospital on London's East Side. I had kept my promise of learning the building trade, having apprenticed as a carpenter, a mason, a painter, and a bricklayer. I loved it. Evening classes in civil engineering had also exposed me to the theories behind construction. I chafed to return to India to practice my trade. The mission advised enrolling in the same Livingston College course in hygiene and tropical medicine that my father had taken. I was assigned to a local hospital to do dressings in the wards and to learn basic principles of diagnosis and treatment.

It was during one evening of my stint at Connaught that my whole view of medicine — and of blood — permanently shifted. That night hospital orderlies wheeled a beautiful young accident victim into my ward. Loss of blood had given her skin an unearthly paleness, and her brownish hair seemed jet-black in contrast. Oxygen starvation had shut down her brain into a state of unconsciousness.

The hospital staff lurched into their controlled-panic response to a trauma patient. A nurse dashed down a corridor for a bottle of blood while a doctor fumbled with the transfusion apparatus. Another doctor, glancing at my white coat, thrust a blood pressure cuff at me. Fortunately, I had already learned to read pulse and blood pressure. I could not detect the faintest flicker of a pulse on the woman's cold, damp wrist.

In the glare of hospital lights she looked like a waxwork Madonna or an alabaster saint from a cathedral. Even her lips were pallid, and as the doctor searched her chest with his stethoscope I noticed whitened nipples on her small breasts. Only a few freckles stood out against the pallor. She did not seem to be breathing. I felt sure she was dead.

The nurse arrived with a bottle of blood and buckled it into a metal stand as the doctor punctured the woman's vein with a large needle. They fastened the bottle high and used an extra-long tube so that the increase in pressure would push the blood into her body faster. The staff told me to keep watch over the emptying bottle while they scurried off for more blood.

Nothing in my memory can compare to the excitement of what happened next. Certainly the details of that scene come to me even now with a start. As the others all left, I nervously held the woman's wrist. Suddenly I could feel the faintest press of a pulse. Or was it my own finger's pulse? I searched again — it was there, a tremor barely perceptible, but regular. The next bottle of blood arrived and was quickly connected. A spot of pink appeared like a drop of watercolor on her cheek. It began to spread into a beautiful flush. Her lips darkened pink, then red, and her body quivered with a kind of sighing breath.

Then her eyelids fluttered lightly and parted. She squinted at first, and her pupils constricted, reacting to the bright lights of the room. At last she looked directly at me. To my enormous surprise, she spoke, asking for water.

That young woman entered my life for only an hour or so, but the experience left me utterly changed. I had seen a miracle: a corpse resurrected, the creation of Eve when breath entered into and animated her body. If medicine, if blood could do this....

I picked up the empty glass bottle, streaks of blood still smearing its side, and read the label. Who had given these pints of life? I wanted some mental picture of the donor who had made the miracle possible. In our registry I discovered the donor lived in Seven Kings, Essex, a town where I had worked for a building construction firm. With eyes closed I envisioned one of the burly workmen from that blue-collar neighborhood. At that moment he could have been out climbing ladders or laying bricks, exuding strength and vigor, oblivious to the frail young woman revived by his own blood cells miles away.

By the time I finished my year at Livingston College I was incurably in love with medicine. A short time later, feeling some shame at my vacillation, but compelled by an inner sense, I turned back and accepted my uncle's offer of support for medical school. The memory of shed blood had kept me out of medicine; the power of shared blood ultimately brought me to it.

For most of us, the organ of blood, if one can think of this fluid mass as an organ, comes to consciousness mainly when we begin to lose it. Then, the sight of it in tinted urine, a nosebleed, or a weeping wound provokes alarm. We miss the dramatic sense of blood's power that I saw demonstrated in the Connaught patient — the power that sustains our lives at every moment.

"What does my blood *do* all day?" a five-year-old child asked, peering dubiously at his scraped knee. Whereas the ancients would have responded with elegant references to ethers and humours borne in that "pure clear lovely and amiable juice," perhaps a technological metaphor would serve best today. Imagine an enormous tube snaking southward from Canada through the Amazon delta, plunging into oceans only to surface at every inhabited island, shooting out eastward through every jungle, plain, and desert in Africa, forking near Egypt to join all of Europe and Russia as well as the entire Middle East and Asia—a pipeline so global and pervasive that it links every person worldwide. Inside that tube an endless plenitude of treasures floats along on rafts: mangoes, coconuts, asparagus, and produce from every continent; watches, calculators, and cameras; gems and minerals; forty-nine brands of cereals; all styles and sizes of clothing; the contents of entire shopping centers. Six billion people have access: at a moment of need or want, they simply reach into the tube and seize whatever product suits them. Somewhere far down the pipeline a replacement is manufactured and inserted.

Such a pipeline exists inside each one of us, servicing not six billion but one hundred trillion cells in the human body. An endless supply of oxygen, amino acids, nitrogen, sodium, potassium, calcium, magnesium, sugars, lipids, cholesterols, and hormones surges past our cells, carried on blood cell rafts or suspended in the fluid. Each cell has special withdrawal privileges to gather the resources needed to fuel a tiny engine for its complex chemical reactions.

In addition, that same pipeline ferries away refuse, exhaust gases, and worn-out chemicals. In the interest of economical transport, the body dissolves its vital substances into a liquid (much as coal is shipped more efficiently through a slurry pipeline than by truck or train). Five or six quarts of this all-purpose fluid suffice for the body's hundred trillion cells.

When blood spills, it appears as a uniform, syrupy substance ranging in color from bright red to dark purple. The late Loren Eiseley, a naturalist and anthropologist, more accurately recognized it as a teeming population. Near the end of his life, he tripped while walking to his office one afternoon. He fell face downward, and blood spilled from a gash on his forehead. Somewhat dazed, Eiseley sat up and stared at the blot on the sidewalk. Later, he wrote:

> Confusedly, painfully, I murmured, "Oh, don't go. I'm sorry." The words were spoken to no one, but to a part of myself. I was quite sane, only it was an oddly detached sanity, for I was addressing blood cells, phagocytes, platelets — all the crawling, living independent wonders that had been part of me and now, through my folly and lack of care, were dying like beached fish on the hot pavement. I was made up of millions of these tiny creatures, their toil, their sacrifices, as they hurried to seal and repair the rent fabric of this vast being whom they had unknowingly, but in love, compounded. I was their galaxy, their creation. For the first time, I loved them consciously. It seemed to me then, and does now in retrospect, that I had caused to the universe I inhabited as many deaths as the explosion of a supernova in the cosmos.

A simple experiment confirms the composite nature of blood. Pour a quantity of red blood into any clear glass and simply wait. Horizontal bands of color will appear as various cells settle by weight, until the final multilayered result resembles an exotic cocktail. The deepest reds, comprising clumps of red cells, sink to the bottom; plasma, a thin yellow fluid, fills the top part of the flask; platelets and white cells congregate in a pale gray band in between.

What the telescope does to nearby galaxies, the microscope does to a drop of blood: it unveils the staggering reality. A speck of blood the size of this letter "o" contains 5,000,000 red cells, 300,000 platelets and 7,000 white cells. The fluid is actually an ocean stocked with living matter. Red cells alone, if removed from a single person and laid side by side, would carpet an area of 3,500 square yards.

Red cells and white cells make appearances in other portions of this book and are examined in detail elsewhere. But the body's survival depends just as surely on the cells with a delicate flower-like shape, the platelets. Their function remained hidden until recently. Now scientists recognize that platelets, which circulate only six to twelve days in the blood, play a crucial role in the life-saving process of clotting; they serve as mobile first-aid boxes by detecting leaks, plugging them, and tidying up the debris.

When a blood vessel is cut, the fluid that sustains life begins to leak away. In response, tiny platelets melt, like snowflakes, spinning out a gossamer web of fibrinogen. Red blood cells collect in this web, like autos crashing into each other when the road is blocked. Soon the tenuous wall of red cells thickens enough to stanch the flow of blood.

Platelets have a very small margin of error. Any clot that extends beyond the vessel wall and threatens to obstruct the vessel itself will stop the flow of blood through the vessel and perhaps lead to a stroke or coronary thrombosis and possibly death. On the other hand, people whose blood has no ability to clot live short lives: even a tooth extraction may prove fatal. The body cannily gauges when a clot is large enough to stop the loss of blood but not so large as to impede the flow within the vessel itself.*

---

*India has a very feared species of snake, the "eleven-step adder," so named because its toxic bite is said to allow the victim time for just eleven more steps. Like all vipers, it kills with a clotting toxin. If its fang penetrates a major vein, say, in the leg, all the blood in the channel between the heart and leg clots at once. If the toxin merely reaches a minor vessel, an amazing thing happens. The poison draws platelets to the tissue like a magnet. Elsewhere in the body platelets simply vanish so that the blood cannot clot anywhere. Then, the smallest scratch will kill the victim or he may bleed internally in the brain or intestine. Bleeding cannot be stopped. Thus a viper's toxin can kill in two opposite ways: a devastating clot or an equally devastating inability to clot. The Haffkeine Institute in Bombay (Mumbai) milks these adders and uses minute amounts of the dried toxin to treat excess bleeding in patients.

A view through a microscope clarifies the various components of blood but gives no picture of the daily frenzy encountered by each cell. Red cells, for example, never sit motionless. From their first entrance into the bloodstream they are pushed and shoved through rush hour traffic. Beginning the cycle at the heart, they take a short jaunt to the lungs to pick up a heavy load of oxygen. Immediately they return to the heart, which propels them violently over the Niagara Falls of the aortic arch. From there, highways crowded with billions of red cells branch out to the brain, the limbs, and vital internal organs.

Sixty thousand miles of blood vessels link every living cell; even the blood vessels themselves are fed by blood vessels. Highways narrow down to one-lane roads, then bike paths, then footpaths, until finally the red cell must bow sideways and edge through a capillary one-tenth the diameter of a human hair. In such narrow confines the cells are stripped of food and oxygen and loaded down with carbon dioxide and urea. If shrunken down to their size, we would see red cells as bloated bags of jelly and iron drifting along in a river until they reach the smallest capillary, where gases fizz and wheeze in and out of surface membranes. From there red cells rush to the kidneys for a thorough scrubbing, then back to the lungs for a refill. And the journey begins anew.

A person can live a day or two without water and several weeks without food, but only a few minutes without oxygen, the main fuel for our hundred trillion cells. Heavy exercise may increase the demand for oxygen from the normal four gallons up to seventy-five gallons an hour, prompting the heart to double or even triple its rate to speed red cells to the heaving lungs. If the lungs alone

cannot overcome the oxygen shortage, the red cells call up reinforcements. Instead of five million red cells in a speck of blood,
seven or eight million will gradually appear. After a person spends
a few months in the rarefied atmosphere of Colorado's mountains,
for example, up to ten million red cells will fill each drop of blood,
compensating for the thinner air.

The pell-mell journey, even to the extremity of the big toe, lasts
a mere twenty seconds. An average red cell endures the cycle of
loading, unloading, and jostling through the body for a half million
round trips over four months. In one final journey, to the spleen,
the battered cell is stripped bare by scavenger cells and recycled into
new cells. Three hundred billion such red cells die and are replaced
every day, leaving behind various parts to reincarnate in a hair follicle or a taste bud.*

The components of this circulatory system cooperate to
accomplish a simple goal: nourishing and cleansing each living cell.
If any part of the network breaks down—the heart takes an
unscheduled rest, a clot overgrows and blocks an artery, a defect
diminishes the red cells' oxygen capacity—life ebbs away. The
brain, master of the body, can survive intact only five minutes
without replenishment.

Blood once repulsed me. I saw it as the most distasteful part of
medical treatment. Now, however, I share the grateful sentiments

*The body provides the energy for the red cells' travels by employing the heart, an organ
that deserves a book exclusively devoted to it. Primitive artificial hearts are now available,
but I would like to see a government design specification sheet for a truly adequate
replacement.

BIDS ACCEPTED FOR:
— Fluid pump with 75-year life expectancy (2,500,000,000 cycles).
— No maintenance or lubrication required.
— Output: must vary between .025 horsepower at rest and short bursts of 1 horsepower
determined by such factors as stress and exercise.
— Weight: not to exceed 10.5 ounces (300 grams).
— Capacity: 2,000 gallons per day.
— Valves: each to operate 4,000–5,000 times per hour.

of Loren Eiseley. I feel like assembling all my blood cells and singing them a hymn of praise. The drama of resurrection enacted before me in Connaught Hospital takes place without fanfare in each heartbeat of a healthy human being. Every cell in every body lives at the mercy of blood.

Chapter 5

# LIFE

*The line between the living and the dead is a sharp line. When the dead atoms of Carbon, Hydrogen, Oxygen, Nitrogen, are seized upon by Life, the organism at first is very lowly. It possesses few functions. It has little beauty. Growth is the work of time. But Life is not. That comes in a moment. At one moment it was dead; the next it lived. This is conversion, the "passing," as the Bible calls it, "from Death unto Life." Those who have stood by another's side at the solemn hour of this dread possession have been conscious sometimes of an experience which words are not allowed to utter — a something like the sudden snapping of a chain, the waking from a dream.*

Henry Drummond

B lood spatters the pages of mythology and history. Drinking it gave strength and new life to the ghosts of the dead in *The Odyssey*, to the Roman epileptics who dashed onto the floor of the Colosseum to lap up the blood of dying gladiators, to Kenya's Masai tribesmen who still celebrate feast days by quaffing blood freshly drawn from a cow or goat.

In human relations, blood had a mysterious, almost sacred aura. An oath held more power than a person's word, but blood made a contract nearly inviolable. The ancients, unashamed to act out their symbols, sometimes sealed contracts by slashing themselves and commingling their blood.

We moderns have inherited quaint tokens of the intrinsic mystery of blood: a wedding ring placed on the "leech finger" that was once believed to contain a vein leading directly to the heart; a child's game of "blood brothers" by which two participants solemnly and unhygienically pledge their undying loyalty. We echo misconceptions too, when we use such terms as *pure blood*, *mixed blood*, *blood relations*, or *hot-blooded* and *cold-blooded*, harking back to the days when the liquid was presumed to carry heredity and temperament.

Even now, after it has been centrifuged in laboratories and demythologized, blood still retains mystic power, if only in the queasy sensation it evokes when we see it shed. There is something horribly unnatural, even nauseating, about watching the fluid of life pour uncontrollably from a living body. Little wonder religions throughout history have honored blood as a sacral substance. A ravaging plague, a minor drought, or, perhaps, a desire to triumph over enemies or decoy the gods' anger — anything of major import can prompt a bloody sacrifice in a primitive religion.

Although worshipers may feel uncomfortable with the fact, Christianity too is inescapably blood-based. Old Testament writers graphically describe blood sacrifices, and their New Testament counterparts overlay those symbolic rituals with theological interpretations. In their writings, they choose the word "blood" three times as often as the "cross" of Christ, five times as frequently as "death." And daily, weekly, monthly (or whenever, depending on denomination) we are called upon to commemorate Christ's death with a ceremony centered in his blood.

As a surgeon, I come into contact with blood almost daily. I read it as a measure of my patients' health. I suction it away from areas where I am cutting. I order neatly labeled pints of it from a refrigerator when a patient needs an extra supply. I know well the warm, slightly acrid substance pumping around inside each of my patients—blotches of it soil every lab coat I own.

But as a Christian, I confess I used to recoil instinctively from the blood symbol that suffuses our religion. Unlike our forefathers, we have not grown up in a cultural environment stocked with mystagogic religions and animal sacrifices. For most of us, blood is not an everyday metaphor, and over time blood-linked concepts may lose their meanings or, worse, unnecessarily repel people from the faith. A challenge arises. Can we discover insights into the biblical symbolism of blood that fit more naturally within our culture while preserving the essence of the metaphor?

Blood works as a religious symbol because of what it is, and the more we know about the properties of actual blood, the better we will grasp its metaphoric connotations. I have already described how the innate power of blood so impressed me that I changed careers. Because I am a surgeon and not a theologian, I will restrict the next few chapters to the specific functions of blood I have encountered in medicine. I will keep before me the actual warm and sticky fluid I wash off my gloves each day.

To people who practice medicine, blood represents life; that quality overarches all other aspects. Every time I pick up a scalpel I have an almost reverent sense of the vital nature of blood.

When performing surgery, I must continually control bleeding, for each quiver of the scalpel leaves a thin wake of blood. Most often it comes from a few of the millions of tiny capillaries, and I disregard them, knowing they will seal up of their own accord. Every minute or two a spurt of bright blood tells me an artery has been cut, and I must either clamp it or sear it with a cautery. The slow ooze of darker blood indicates a punctured vein, and I pay even closer attention. A cut vein is dangerous: with far less muscle in its wall than an artery, it cannot easily close itself off. To avoid these problems, I strive to locate each significant vessel before I make a cut. Then I can clamp it twice and slice between the clamps without the loss of a drop of blood. After years of surgical practice, all this routine proceeds without producing stress or emotion.

Despite all precautions, a different level of bleeding may occur — one that no surgeon ever gets used to. Sometimes, through an error of judgment or loss of manual dexterity, a really large vessel is cut or tears open and the wound gushes with blood. It wells up in a cavity like the abdomen or the chest and totally obscures the rip in the vessel from which it comes. The surgeon, fumbling in the sump of blood up to his wrists, shouts for suction and gauze sponges — inevitably, this is when the suction nozzle gets blocked or the lights go out. No surgeon goes through a career without such incidents.

I shall never forget the horror-struck face of one of my London students during one such experience. He was performing a routine procedure on a woman in our outpatient clinic, excising a tiny lymphatic node from her neck for biopsy. It was a minor procedure, performed with local anesthetic. I was working in an adjacent room. Suddenly, a nurse appeared in my doorway, her hands and uniform splashed with fresh blood. "Come quick!" she cried, and I dashed next door to find the intern, white as a corpse, working frantically on a woman from whose neck blood was gushing. It was hard to tell who was more terrified: my intern or the patient.

Fortunately, a wonderful teacher in England had drilled into me the appropriate reflexes. I ran to the woman's side and, quickly removing all instruments from the wound, grasped her neck and simply applied firm pressure on the wound with my thumb. As my thumb filled in the broken part of the blood vessel wall, bleeding stopped, and I stayed in that position until the woman calmed down enough for me to extend the anesthesia and repair the vessel. I learned that the intern had dissected the nodal area and had conscientiously tried to clip it free from all its roots. But in doing so he had inadvertently snipped off a small section of the jugular vein!

A crisis with blood — and it *will* occur sometime — tells a student whether or not to continue in the profession. If a young surgeon panics, he or she should move over to a branch of medicine less likely to produce fearsome situations.

My London teacher, who had the grand name Sir Launcelot Barrington-Ward, had diligently tried to prepare his students for just such an emergency. Sir Launcelot, surgeon to England's royal family, taught me pediatric surgery. As his assistant, I would hear him ask each fresh student, "In case of massive bleeding, what is your most useful instrument?" At first the newcomer would propose exotic surgical tools, and the old teacher would frown and shake his head. There was only one acceptable answer: "Your thumb, sir." Why? The thumb is readily available — every doctor has one — and offers a perfect blend of strong pressure and gentle compliancy.

Then Sir Launcelot would ask, "What is your greatest enemy when there is bleeding?" and we would say, "Time, sir." And he would ask, "What is your greatest friend?" and we would say again, "Time."

Sir Launcelot impressed on us the fact that as long as blood is being lost, time is the enemy. Second by second, life will leak away as the patient grows weaker and approaches the point of no return. The temptation is to panic, to grab at vessels and clamp them off with forceps here and there, often causing more damage.

But once I have my thumb on the bleeding point, time becomes my friend. There is no hurry; I can stop and plan what to do next. The body busies itself helping: clots form to repair the breach. I can take time to clean up and arrange a transfusion, or to send for a special instrument, or to call for an extra assistant, or to enlarge the incision to get a better view. (Once, I held a clump of blood vessels in my fist for twenty-five minutes while removing a diseased spleen, operating with one hand while I held off the flow of blood with the other.) All this can happen if my thumb is pressing firmly on the area of bleeding. Finally, when all is ready, I slowly remove my thumb while my other hand and my assistants are poised to take action — and I find that no action is needed. The bleeding has stopped.

At those moments, in the rush of adrenaline brought on by the crisis, I often have a sense of spiritual exaltation. I feel at one with the millions of living cells in that wound fighting for survival. I realize that, incredibly, the common thumb is the only thing between my patient and death.

After many such experiences in the electric atmosphere of the operating room, every surgeon learns to identify blood with life. The two are inseparable: you lose one, you lose both.

Why, then, does blood as a Christian symbol seem to contradict what I learn at such moments?

⟶

I admit at the outset that I sometimes find the associations of the blood symbol in Christendom distasteful. I switch on my radio on a Sunday morning while driving from my hospital in Carville to New Orleans. A heavy-breathing pastor is conducting a communion service in a church in the bayous. He gives a maudlin commentary on the final agony of Jesus on the cross. He vividly describes the scene of a cross being strapped to a back bloodied by whips. The congregation murmurs as he evidently holds up a four-inch thorn and illustrates how barbarously the soldiers jammed a crown of them onto Jesus' head. Every occasion for the word blood (which his drawl stretches into two syllables) — the nailing, the thud of the cross in the ground, the spear in the side — seems to give this preacher a fresh burst of energy.

The theme of death and unrelieved gloom hangs darkly over the entire hour. I drive along in bright Louisiana sunshine, glancing at the stately egrets, white as clouds, bobbing for food in the canals lining the highway. The preacher asks his parishioners to think of all their recent sins, one by one, and to contemplate the horrible guilt that led to such a bloody death on their behalf.

A ceremony follows, the sacrament itself. My mind, jarred from the solemn service on the radio, returns to the literal substance of blood — not the watery purple substance in the communion glasses but, the rich scarlet soup of proteins and cells that keeps my patients alive. Again I wonder; has something been lost over the centuries, something foundational? Has the intent and meaning of the symbol evaporated? The Louisiana pastor concentrates exclusively on blood that was *shed* — but does not the sacrament center also on blood that is *shared*?

William Harvey, the seventeenth-century British scientist who revolutionized our understanding of circulation and blood, stated the medical fact: "Blood is the cause not only of life in general but also of longer or shorter life, of sleep and watching, of genius, aptitude and strength. It is the first to live and the last to die." Medically,

Right: Paul, age nine, as he first arrives in London in 1923.

Below: Paul taught leprosy patients to rely on cats for protection against rats biting their insensitive limbs during the night.

Right: Paul in 1990, age seventy-six.

Above: The Brand family's first furlough to England, in 1952. Clockwise from upper left: Christopher, Paul, Jean, Estelle, Margaret, Mary.

Left: Paul and Margaret's wedding at Emmanuel Church, Northwood, Middlesex, England, on May 29, 1943.

Left: The Brand family just prior to leaving India for furlough in 1952. Clockwise from top: Paul, Christopher, Jean, Mary, Estelle.

Below: Entire family in India, 1961. Back row: Margaret, Evelyn "Granny" Brand, Paul, Christopher, Jean, Mary; Middle row: Estelle; Front row: Patricia, Pauline.

Above: Paul and his parents in the Kolli Hills of South India, 1921. Paul, age seven, is in the foreground; his father, Jesse Brand, is riding a horse and wearing a white hat; his mother, Evelyn Brand, is barely visible on the right, being carried in a dholi.

Below: At the Women's Hostel, Christian Medical College, Vellore, India, Paul assists with the baptism of Ted Centerwall, the son of staff members. (The "baptistry" is actually a cement mixing container used during construction.)

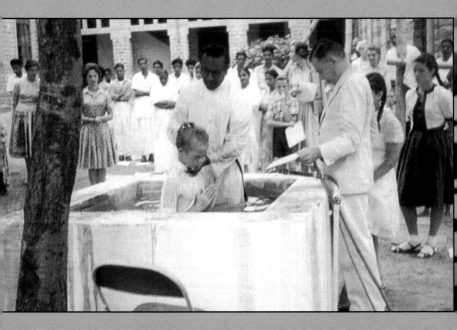

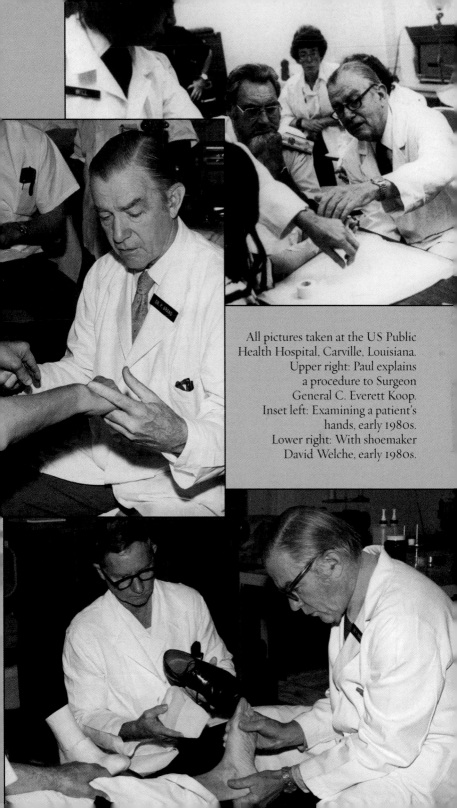

All pictures taken at the US Public Health Hospital, Carville, Louisiana. Upper right: Paul explains a procedure to Surgeon General C. Everett Koop. Inset left: Examining a patient's hands, early 1980s. Lower right: With shoemaker David Welche, early 1980s.

Above: Damien-Dutton Society Chairman of the Board, Rhoda Van der Clute awarding Drs. Brand with a plaque that reads:

THE 1977 DAMIEN-DUTTON AWARD PRESENTED TO DR. MARGARET E. BRAND AND DR. PAUL W. BRAND, UNITED STATES PUBLIC HEALTH HOSPITAL, CARVILLE, LOUISIANA, WHO HAVE DEVOTED THEIR LIVES TO PREVENTING AND CORRECTING DISABILITIES IN LEPROSY PATIENTS. MAY 12, 1977, BELLMORE, NEW YORK

Above: Paul at an informal gathering in 1998.

Right: Paul Brand preaching at the Union Protestant Chapel on the hospital grounds in Carville, Louisiana, in 1983.

Left: An avid hiker and birdwatcher, Paul enjoys the wilderness of Crane Island in the Puget Sound, at age eighty-one.

Below: Paul being interviewed for the book *The Gift of Pain* in the early 1990s.

Lower Right: Paul and Margaret visiting the India coast south of Madras in 1990.

Above: Paul with granddaughter Evelyn Brand exploring tidepools in West Seattle, 1990.

Above: Margaret and Paul, Puget Sound, 1996.

Right: Paul near Mount Rainier, 1992.

blood signifies life and not death. It feeds and sustains every cell in the body with its precious nutrients. When it seeps away, life falters. Has our modern interpretation of the symbol, as exemplified by the radio preacher's fixation on death, strayed so far from the original meaning?

We must find the decisive clue of meaning not from medicine but from Jesus and from the authors of the Bible who introduced that symbol. To them, shed blood could stand for death ("[Abel's] blood cries out to me from the ground" Genesis 4:10). And yet, deep in every Jewish person's consciousness lay a fundamental association of blood with life. God had given it that meaning. As a new era of world history began, in a covenant with Noah, God commanded, "But you must not eat meat that has its lifeblood still in it" (Genesis 9:4). Later, in the formal legal code given to Moses and the Israelites, God reiterated his command as "a lasting ordinance for the generations to come." The reason? "For the life of a creature is in the blood" (Leviticus 3:17; 7:26–27; 17:11, 14; Deuteronomy 12:23).

Old Testament Jews, inured to violent death and capital punishment, were not squeamish about blood. Israel had no aseptic slaughter-houses for sheep and cattle, so each Jew must have viewed the bloody deaths of many animals. But still, every good Jewish housewife checked her meat to see that no blood remained. The rule was absolute: do not eat the blood, for it contains life. Kosher cuisine developed, using elaborate techniques to assure that no blood contaminated the meat.

So ingrained was this prohibition against ingesting blood that thousands of years later, when the apostles distilled what indispensable customs must be honored by the new gentile Christians, two rules about blood made the list of only four taboos (Acts 15:29). Though flexible on such long-held practices as circumcision, the apostles forbade drinking blood and eating meat improperly butchered (in strangled animals the blood would not have drained out).*

In view of this background of rigid Jewish assumptions about blood, consider the shocking, almost revolting message Jesus brought to that culture:

> I tell you the truth, unless you eat the flesh of the Son of Man and drink his blood, you have no life in you. Whoever eats my flesh and drinks my blood has eternal life, and I will raise him up at the last day. For my flesh is real food and my blood is real drink. Whoever eats my flesh and drinks my blood remains in me, and I in him. Just as the living Father sent me and I live because of the Father, so the one who feeds on me will live because of me. (John 6:53–57)

A call for gross immorality would hardly have jolted Jesus' followers more severely. His words, coming at the peak of his popularity just after the feeding of the five thousand, signaled a drastic turning point in his public acceptance. The Jews became so confused and outraged that a crowd of thousands, who had pursued Jesus around a lake in order to crown him king forcibly, silently melted away. Many of his closest disciples deserted him; his own brothers judged him insane; plots to kill him suddenly sprang up. This time, Jesus had simply gone too far.

At least those first hearers caught the dramatic sweep of what Jesus had done. He had siphoned from the word *blood* four thousand years of deeply felt associations. No Jew ingested blood—only savages and the uncircumcised did that. Blood was always poured out before God as an offering, for life belonged to God; it

---

*Curiously, even the most literalistic Christians today ignore this direct command to the New Testament church.

was sacred. Yet to those very people Jesus said, "Drink my blood." Is it any wonder the Jews bristled and the disciples slunk away?

A question looms. Knowing — as he must have known — the offense his words would cause, why did Jesus say them? Why not draw a more reasonable parallel to Jewish sacrifice? If he had said, "Eat my flesh and pour out my blood," or "Eat my flesh and sprinkle my blood," his hearers would not have been offended. But they would not have grasped Jesus' intent. Instead, he told them, "Drink it."

Jesus spoke as he did not to offend, but to effect a radical transformation in the symbol. God had said to Noah, if you drink the blood of a lamb, the life of the lamb enters you — don't do it. Jesus said, in effect, if you drink my blood, my life will enter you — do it! Thus, I believe Jesus intended our ceremony to include not only remembrance of his past death but also realization of his present life. We cannot live without the nourishment his life provides.

The ceremony we call Eucharist (or Lord's Supper or Holy Communion) formally traces back to Jesus' last night with the disciples before his crucifixion. There, amid a stuffy roomful of his frightened disciples, Jesus first said the words that have been repeated millions of times: "This is my blood of the new covenant, which is poured out for many for the forgiveness of sins" (Matthew 26:28). Jesus commanded his disciples to drink the wine, representing his blood. The offering was not merely poured out, but rather taken in, ingested. He repeated those shocking words, "Drink from it, all of you" (v. 27).

That same evening Jesus used another metaphor, perhaps to shed light on the meaning of shared blood. "I am the vine; you are the branches," he declared. "If a man remains in me and I in him, he will bear much fruit; apart from me you can do nothing" (John 15:5 — note parallel wording to John 6:56). Surrounded by the vineyard-covered hillsides that ringed Jerusalem, the disciples could more easily comprehend this metaphor. A grape branch disconnected from the nutrients of the vine becomes withered, dry, and dead, useless for anything except kindling. Only when connected to the vine can it grow, prosper, and bear fruit.

Even in the doom-shrouded atmosphere of that last night, at the meal from which the sacrament derives, the image of life welled up. For the disciples, the wine was to symbolize Jesus' blood that could vitalize them much as the sap does the grapevine.*

If I read these accounts correctly, they correspond to my medical experience exactly. It is not true that blood represents life to the surgeon but death to the Christian. Rather, we come to the table also to partake of his life. "For my flesh is real food and my blood is real drink. Whoever eats my flesh and drinks my blood remains in me, and I in him" (6:55–56) — at last those words make sense. Christ came not just to give us an example of a way of life but to give us life itself. Spiritual life is not ethereal and outside us, something that we must work hard to obtain; it is in us, pervading us, as blood is in every living being.

⟵

Theologian Oscar Cullmann, in *Early Christian Worship*, presents a fresh interpretation of an event that has often puzzled Bible scholars: Jesus' first miracle, when he turned water into wine at a wedding banquet in Cana. Cullmann says this miracle or "sign," like all others in John's gospel, points to a deeper spiritual teaching.

---

*The earliest Christians seemed to get the meaning: their Eucharist feasts invariably celebrated the risen Christ, memorializing not so much the Last Supper as the Easter meals when Jesus shared fish and broke bread with the disciples. Works of art lining the one hundred miles of dark corridors in the Roman Catacombs vividly illustrate that point. Among twenty thousand frescoes amateurishly painted on those stone walls, not a single death theme or cross appears. Whenever the Eucharist is portrayed, fish, a symbol of life, is always present on the table.

Relying on key phrases such as "My time has not yet come" (John 2:4), he concludes that the Cana story points to the new covenant to come with Christ. As the bread in John 6 connects to the bread of the Last Supper, the wine here may point to the wine of the Last Supper.

I will leave to Bible scholars the judgment on Cullmann's interpretation. If true, the setting could hardly be more appropriate to introduce this great symbol: a wedding feast, filled with joyous music, the laughter of guests, the clink of pottery, the sounds of excitement as two families are joined together. Sharing the wine that stands for Christ's blood fits in much better with that tone than with the dreary sounds I heard on my radio in Louisiana. Eucharist, celebrated in memory of the death of Jesus, is also a toast, if you will, to the Life that conquered even death and that is now offered freely to each of us.

Chapter 6

# CLEANSING

*Do you want to punish him fearfully, terribly, with the most awful punishment that could be imagined, and at the same time to save him and regenerate his soul? If so, overwhelm him with your mercy! You will see, you will hear how he will tremble and be horror-struck. "How can I endure this mercy? How can I endure so much love? Am I worthy of it?" That is what he will exclaim.*

Fyodor Dostoyevsky

---

I turn up the collar of my wool topcoat and lower my head against the moisture-laden wind. Snow is gradually transforming the tired modern city of London into a Dickensian Christmas card. On a deserted street I stop under an ancient streetlamp and look up. Snowflakes arc from the light like an endless shower of electrical sparks, then float down to cover potholes, gutter, cars, and sidewalk with a coat of softly glowing white.

From somewhere I hear music, the muffled tones of brass and what seems like human voices. On a night like this? I walk toward the sound, the music growing louder with each step, until I round a corner and see its source: a Salvation Army band. A man and a woman are playing a trombone and trumpet, and I wince as I imagine metal pressed against lips in the numbing wind. Three others, evidently new recruits, are lustily singing a hymn based on a poem by William Cowper.

Only two other people are listening: a drunkard who is propping himself against the stone porch of a Georgian-style townhouse and a businessman on the corner who keeps glancing at his pocket watch.

The words of Cowper's hymn are familiar to me:

There is a fountain filled with blood
  Drawn from Emmanuel's veins;
And sinners, plunged beneath that flood,
  Lose all their guilty stains....

An unavoidable smile crosses my face as I hear those words. I have just come from hospital rounds where real blood was being drawn from some veins, transfused into others, and diligently scrubbed off surgical smocks and nurses' uniforms. With my church background, I understand the origin and meaning of the Christian symbol. But these two bystanders, listening halfheartedly — what images fill their minds as they hear that hymn? Would not such a phrase as "washed in the blood of the Lamb" seem to the modern Englishman as bizarre as a report of animal sacrifice in Papua, New Guinea?

In addition to our culture's resistance to the intrusion of blood in religion, an even greater barrier blocks Cowper's blood symbol from modern hearers. Consider the phrase "washed in the blood": nothing in modern culture corresponds to the idea of blood as a cleansing agent. We use water, with soap or detergent, to clean. Blood, in contrast, soils or stains. It is something we try to scrub *off*, not scrub with. What possible meaning could the hymn writer, and Bible writers before him, have intended?

Blood's quality of cleansing appears throughout the Bible, from the earliest books to the latest. In Leviticus 14, for example, a priest sprinkles cleansing blood on a person with an infectious skin disease and on the mildewed walls of a house. New Testament authors often refer to Jesus' blood "cleansing" us (e.g., 1 John 1:7), and Revelation describes a multitude who "have washed their robes and made them white in the blood of the Lamb" (7:14).

Does this frequent reference to blood indicate primitive Christianity's remoteness from modern culture? To the contrary, modern medical science has shown that the symbol of cleansing conforms closely to the function of the actual substance. Presumably biblical writers did not know the physiology behind their metaphor, but the Creator chose a theological symbol with an exact analogue in the medical world. All that we have learned about physiology in recent years confirms the accuracy of the still-jarring linkage of blood and cleansing. The theological image immortalized by William Cowper's hymn makes for good biology as well.

If you truly wish to grasp the function of blood as a cleansing agent, I suggest a simple experiment. Find a blood pressure test kit and wrap the cuff around your upper arm. Have a friend pump it up to about 200 mm. of mercury, a sufficient pressure to stop the flow of blood in your arm. Initially your arm will feel an uncomfortable tightness beneath the cuff. Now comes the revealing part of the experiment: Perform any easy task with your cuffed arm. Merely flex your fingers and make a fist about ten times in succession, or cut paper with scissors, or drive a nail into wood with a hammer.

The first few movements seem quite normal at first as the muscles obediently contract and relax. Then you feel a slight weakness. Almost without warning, after perhaps ten movements, a hot flash of pain strikes. Your muscles cramp violently. If you force yourself to continue the simple task, you will likely cry out in absolute agony. Finally, you cannot force yourself to continue; the pain overwhelms you.

When you release the tourniquet and air escapes from the cuff with a hiss, blood rushes into your aching arm and a wonderfully soothing sense of relief floods your muscles. The pain is worth enduring just to experience that acute relief. Your muscles move freely, soreness vanishes. Physiologically, you have just experienced the cleansing power of blood.

The pain came because you forced your muscles to keep working while the blood supply to your arm was shut off. As muscles converted oxygen into energy, they produced certain waste products (metabolites) that normally would have been flushed away instantly in the bloodstream. Because of the constricted blood flow, however, these metabolites accumulated in your cells. They were not *cleansed* by the swirling stream of blood, and therefore in a few minutes you felt the agony of retained toxins.

The body performs its janitorial duties with such impressive speed and efficiency that I cannot resist at least a summary of them. Hold the theological metaphor of cleansing in abeyance while I indulge in a quick scan of the body's cleansing processes.

No cell lies more than a hair's breadth from a blood capillary, lest poisonous by-products pile up and cause the same ill effects demonstrated in the tourniquet experiment. Through a basic chemical process of gas diffusion and transfer, individual red blood cells drifting along inside narrow capillaries simultaneously release their cargoes of fresh oxygen and absorb waste products (carbon dioxide, urea, uric acid, etc.) from these cells. The red cells then deliver the hazardous waste chemicals to organs that can dump them outside the body.

In the lungs, carbon dioxide collects in small pockets to be exhaled with every breath. The body monitors the expiration cycle and makes instantaneous adjustments. If too much carbon dioxide accumulates, as when I burn more energy by climbing a flight of stairs, an involuntary switch increases my breathing to speed up the process.

Complex chemical wastes are left to a more discriminating organ, the kidney. I must restrain myself from writing long, rhapsodic chapters about the kidneys. Some observers judge them second in complexity only to the brain. The body obviously values them greatly, for one-fourth of the blood from each heartbeat courses down the renal artery to the twin kidneys. That artery divides and subdivides into a tracery of tubules so intricate as to bedazzle the finest Venetian glassblower.

Filtering is what the kidney is all about, but in very little space and time. The kidney manages speed by coiling the tubules into a million crystal loops, where chemicals can be picked over one by one. Since red cells are too bulky for those tiny passageways, the kidney extracts the sugars, salts, and water from the blood and deals with them separately. This segregation process roughly compares to a master mechanic who has a garage too small to fit a whole car inside. To repair a car engine, he hoists it out of the car, carries it to the garage, disassembles and scours each individual valve, piston, and ring, then reassembles the hundreds of parts minus the grime and corrosion.

After the kidney has removed the red cell's entire payload to extract some thirty chemicals, its enzymes promptly reinsert 99 percent of the volume into the bloodstream. The 1 percent remaining, mostly urea, is hustled away to the bladder to await expulsion, along with whatever excess water the kidney deems expendable. One second later, the thunder of the heart resounds throughout the body and fresh blood surges in to fill the tubules.

An elite coterie of people view the kidney with an attitude approaching reverence. These are the few without kidneys or with useless kidneys. Thirty years ago all of those people would have died. Now they have time to contemplate the wonders of the kidney — too much time. Three times a week for five hours they lie or sit motionless while a tube drains all their blood through a noisy, clanging machine the size of a large suitcase. The function of this technological monster, a kidney dialysis machine, crudely approximates the intricate work of the soft, bean-shaped human kidney. Our natural one, however, weighs only one pound, works around the clock, and normally repairs itself. Just to be safe, our body provides a spare — one kidney would do the job just fine.

Other organs enter into the scavenging process also. A durable red cell can only sustain the rough sequence of freight-loading and unloading for a half million circuits or so until, battered and leaky as a worn-out river barge, it nudges its way to the liver and spleen for one last unloading. This time, the red cell itself is picked clean, broken down into amino acids and bile pigments for recycling. The tiny heart of iron, "magnet" for the crucial hemoglobin molecule, is escorted back to the bone marrow for reincarnation in another red cell. A new cycle of fueling and cleansing begins.

This seeming digression into the process of cleansing actually leads back to the meaning of the metaphor. Medically, blood sustains life by carrying away the chemical by-products that would interfere with it — in short, by cleansing. As I reflect on the Body of Christ, the blood metaphor offers a fresh and enlightening perspective on a perpetual problem in that Body: sin.

To some, the word *sin* has become dusty, timeworn, and freighted with unfortunate connotations. And the metaphors commonly used to describe God's relationship with sinful creatures have faded too. God is the judge, we the accused — although biblically accurate, that metaphor loses force as the modern legal system grows less trustworthy and more capricious. Metaphors age over time; as culture and language change, sometimes they crack and the concept inside them leaks away.

In blood, however, we have the perfect analogue to reveal the nature of sin and forgiveness with startling clarity. Medical knowledge has only enhanced our understanding. Just as blood cleanses the body of harmful metabolites, forgiveness through Christ's blood cleanses away the waste products, sins, that impede true health.

Too often we tend to view sin as a private list of grievances that happen to irk God the Father, and in the Old Testament God seems easily irritated. But even a casual reading of the Old Testament shows that sin is a blockage, a paralyzing toxin that restricts our realization of our full humanity. God gave laws for our sakes, not his own. In the midst of a withering attack on Israel recorded in Jeremiah, God makes this poignant observation: "They pour out drink offerings to other gods to provoke me to anger. But am I the one they are provoking? . . . Are they not rather harming themselves, to their own shame?" (7:18–19).

Pride, egotism, lust, and covetousness are simply poisons that interfere with our relationship to God and to other people. Sin results in separation: separation from God, other people, and our true selves. The more we cling to our private desires, our thirsts for success, our own satisfactions at the expense of others, the further we will drift from God and others.

The Old Testament Israelites had a stark pictorial representation of this state of separation between God and humanity. God's presence rested in a Most Holy Place, approachable only once a year (the Day of Atonement) by one man, the high priest, who had purified himself through an elaborate ritual. Jesus Christ made that ceremony obsolete by a historical once-for-all sacrifice. "This is my blood of the covenant, which is poured out for many *for the forgiveness of sins*" (Matthew 26:28), he said as he instituted the Last Supper.*

The Lord's Supper, or Mass, as celebrated today contrasts sharply with that Old Testament ceremony on the Day of Atonement. No longer must we approach God through a ritually purified high priest, no longer await the Day of Atonement to enter the most Holy Place. On the day Christ died, the thick temple veil of separation split from top to bottom. Now all of us can enter into direct communion with God: "We have confidence to enter the Most Holy Place by the blood of Jesus, by a new and living way opened for us through the curtain, that is, his body" (Hebrews 10:19–20).

The Lord's Supper dramatizes that the effect of Christ's sacrifice is continuous and ongoing. Wine is taken personally, symbolizing that the same living blood that bathes every cell with the

---

*The author of Hebrews explains the theological shift that has taken place: "When Christ came as high priest of the good things that are already here, he went through the greater and more perfect tabernacle that is not man-made, that is to say, not a part of this creation. He did not enter by means of the blood of goats and calves; but he entered the Most Holy Place once for all by his own blood, having obtained eternal redemption. The blood of goats and bulls and the ashes of a heifer sprinkled on those who are ceremonially unclean sanctify them so that they are outwardly clean. How much more, then, will the blood of Christ, who through the eternal Spirit offered himself unblemished to God, cleanse our consciences from acts that lead to death, so that we may serve the living God!" (Hebrews 9:11–14).

nutrients of life also carries away all the accumulated waste and refuse. By his blood we are forgiven, made clean.

⟶.

The word *repentance* describes the process each cell undergoes in that cleansing action. C. S. Lewis reminds us that repentance "is not something God demands of you before He will take you back and which He could let you off if He chose; it is simply a description of what going back is like." The past hanging thickly over us needs to be remembered in order to be forgotten. In the terms of our analogy, in repentance each cell willingly avails itself of the cleansing action of blood. Repentance is for our sakes, not to punish us, but to free us from the harmful effects of accumulated sins. "This is Christ's body, broken *for you*" ... *for your* gossiping, *your* lust, *your* pride, *your* insensitivity ... broken to remove all those and replace them with his perfect obedience.

Why do any of us go to church and sit on rather uncomfortable furniture, in stiff clothes, lined up in rows as in a high school classroom, singing songs unlike any we have heard all week? Is it not because in each of us a spark of hope has been lit — a hope to be known, to be forgiven, to be healed, to be loved? Something like this yearning lies at the heart of the ceremony of the Lord's Supper.

Symbols are weaker than the reality behind them. But Christ has given us the wine and the bread as proof that we are forgiven, healed, and loved. The symbol works its way inside us, becoming material as well as spiritual nourishment, carrying its message to individual cells throughout each body.

In the Eucharist, we are reminded of the overarching forgiveness accomplished in Christ's sacrifice that made obsolete the whole Jewish sacrificial system. And we also experience the particular, cell-by-cell cleansing of toxins that have accumulated and will not easily release their grip. "For if, when we were God's enemies, we were reconciled to him through the death of his Son, how much more, having been reconciled, shall we be saved through his life!" (Romans 5:10). If sin is the great separator, Christ is the great reconciler. He dissolves the membrane of separation that grows up every day between ourselves and others, ourselves and God. "Now in Christ Jesus," said Paul elsewhere, "you who once were far away have been brought near through the blood of Christ. For he himself is our peace" (Ephesians 2:13–14).

Near the end of his life, François Mauriac, the French Catholic novelist who received the Nobel Prize for Literature, reflected on his own love-hate history with the church. He detailed the ways in which the church had not kept its promise: the petty rifts and compromises that have always characterized it. The church, he concluded, has strayed far from the precepts and example of its Founder. And yet, added Mauriac, despite all its failings the church has at least remembered two words of Christ: "Your sins are forgiven you," and "This is my body broken for you." The Lord's Supper brings together those two words in a quiet ceremony of healing by cleansing individual cells in his Body of all impurities.

Chapter 7

# OVERCOMING

*If our God were a pagan god or the god of intellectuals — and for me it comes to much the same — He might fly to His remotest heaven and our grief would force Him down to earth again. But you know that our God came to be among us. Shake your fist at Him, spit in His face, scourge Him, and finally crucify Him: what does it matter? ... It's already been done to Him.*

George Bernanos

Each day we live at the mercy of organisms one-trillionth our size. Medical author Ronald J. Glasser concludes rather humbly, "No matter how we may wish to view ourselves, despite all our fantasies of grandeur and dominion, all our fragile human successes, the real struggle ... has always been against bacteria and viruses, against adversaries never more than seven microns wide."

Wars, fires, and earthquakes get far more press coverage today than this war of microbes, but it was not always so. The great plague of the fourteenth century, for example, killed one-third of all people in Europe. Over a million pilgrims visited Rome the Easter of 1348; 90 percent went home infected, spreading its horror and death around the world. Ships drifted crewless at sea. Vast estates went untended. Traffic disappeared from highways.

Early in the twentieth century the "war to end all wars" cost the greatest toll in the history of human conflict: eight-and-a-half million lives. But during the year of armistice an influenza epidemic broke out that would eventually triple the carnage — twenty-five million deaths worldwide. And now AIDS threatens to decimate an entire generation in sub-Saharan Africa.

Battle imagery is particularly appropriate to describe what happens inside our bodies, for with an array of menacing weapons and defenders, our bodies, quite simply, declare war on invaders. At the first sign of invasion, a chemical Paul Revere alarm sounds, and numerous body systems hasten into action. Capillaries dilate, like inflatable tunnels, to allow a swarm of armed defenders into the combat zone. White blood cells of five distinct types form the initial assault forces. Transparent, bristling with weapons and possessing a Houdini-like ability to slip between other cells, the white cells are the body's chief fighters.

Flattened on a microscope slide, white cells resemble fried eggs sprinkled with pepper, each dot marking a deadly chemical weapon. As the white cells circulate in the body they assume roughly spherical shapes and resemble pale glass eyes aimlessly adrift in the blood vessels. When an invasion hits, they abruptly come alive.

Some white cells, armed with crude chemicals, serve as shock troops and attempt to overwhelm the invaders through sheer numbers. Others with massively shielded cell walls roll in with heavier ammunition, like battle tanks. Attack strategy differs also. Some white cells free-float in the bloodstream, sniping at strays. Some stalk the vital organs, alert for any invader that may slip through initial defenses. Others try to corral invaders into a fortresslike lymph gland for execution. And still others, the sanitary corps, linger until the battlefield is strewn with bits of cells and leaking protoplasm, then move in to clean up after the melee.

During healthy periods, twenty-five billion white cells circulate freely throughout the blood and twenty-five billion more loiter on blood vessel walls. When an infection occurs, billions of reserves leap from the marshes of bone marrow, some in inchoate form like beardless young recruits pressed into service. The body can quickly mobilize ten times the normal number of white cells; in fact, doctors use a census of them as a diagnostic blood test to judge the severity of infection.

We need vast numbers of white cells for one reason: some lymphocytes are "specific" defenders, programmed against only one type of disease. In truth the battle within resembles not so much a one-on-one infantry assault as a furious mating dance in which white cells crowd against the bacteria or viruses seeking the right "fit" before calling up reserves. The average white cell lives merely ten hours. But a select few live for sixty or seventy years and preserve the chemical memory of dangerous invaders, all the while checking in at their assigned lymph gland every few minutes. These master cells safeguard the chemical secrets that remind the body how to respond to any invader previously encountered.

A white cell must somehow home in on the actual invaders who are camouflaged by the chemical smoke-screen of battle and the rubble of leaking cells, clotting agents, and broken membranes. Antibodies (a misleading name, since no substance in the body is so pro-body) guide the white cell through the fray to its intended target. Only 1/1000 the size of bacteria, antibodies cling to the enemy like moss to a tree, softening them up for the approaching white cells and neutralizing their destructive spike shapes. A single antibody protects against only one disease; for example, measles antibody has no effect against infantile paralysis.

Because of the staggering range of invaders confronting a person in a lifetime, the body must stockpile an enormous arsenal of weapons. Immunologists share a little joke which they cite when asked how the body can possibly prepare every type of antibody required in our parlous world: "GOD," they reply. In this case GOD is an acronym for Generator of Diversity, expressing the body's astounding ability to manufacture whatever defense is needed. Dr. Ronald Glasser calls the process "a mixture of mystery and chemistry ... a combination of physics and grace down at the molecular level."

If I cut my hand, roaming antibodies tag the known invaders, or antigens, almost immediately. In the event a new one is spotted, a circulating lymphocyte cell touches it, memorizes its shape, and rushes to the nearest lymph node. There, that lymphocyte transmogrifies into a veritable chemical factory and conveys the newly acquired information to thousands of other lymphocytes that in turn produce billions of antibodies. Once the lymph produces an antibody, it permanently stores the formula so that a subsequent invasion will incite a fast-motion repeat of the process.*

Occasionally, a new antigen comes along with a shape utterly different from any previously known. The lymph cells fumble around for the precise combination, trying and abandoning formula after formula. Meanwhile the mystery invader, oblivious to the stunned and feckless white cells, wreaks havoc. The great plague of the fourteenth century was caused by such a newcomer.

---

*The body faces its most hazardous moments when a baby emerges from a sterile uterus into a deadly world, having had no exposure to germs. For that event too, the body provides a life-preserving system. Just before the birth, the mother's placenta floods the fetus's bloodstream with gamma globulin containing agents to fight scarlet fever, whooping cough, typhus, typhoid, pneumonia, diphtheria, tetanus, chicken pox, mumps, measles, polio — any disease, in fact, that the mother has already encountered. Even more immunities flow from the mother's milk until the infant begins to manufacture its own antibodies.

European blood had no previous experience with such a disease, which had migrated from Asia.

Still today, diseases like measles and influenza, minor annoyances in developed countries, can sweep through remote cultures with devastating impact. Gradually, however, bodies accumulate a culturally shared knowledge of such diseases, lessening the impact of successive outbreaks.

╼

Timing presents by far the biggest challenge to the body's protective system. Because bodily defenses are strictly that, defenses, and always counterattack, never attack, we must live in the perilous time gap between infection and adequate response. Antibiotic drugs merely buy precious hours for the body's own mobilization. (Antibiotics indiscriminately slaughter millions of invaders, but some survivors will always slip through the chemical barrier. And if just one bacterium survives, a million offspring can generate in just eight hours. To win, the body must kill 100 percent of invading microbes, a task as difficult as killing all mosquitoes in a given city. No antibiotic can accomplish that task, as shown by the fact that antibiotics prove ineffective for people with immuno-deficiency diseases like AIDS.)

For centuries humanity lived at the mercy of this deadly time gap, which sometimes resulted in the annihilation of entire populations. But one technique ingeniously solved the time problem and has done more to conquer disease than any other medical procedure. Called "immunization," it derives from brilliant pioneering work by Jenner, Pasteur, and others. Diseases that once held nations hostage and struck terror into every village and hamlet are now virtually unknown in developed countries. Yellow fever, diphtheria, smallpox, rabies, cholera, typhus, typhoid, polio, measles — each of these has killed and maimed more people than a world war; now immunization gives us the tools to defeat them all.

Normally, the body loses crucial hours while breaking the code of a new invader and manufacturing appropriate antibodies to combat it. With immunization, a prior injection exposes the body to polio or smallpox virus in a safe form: either a weakened or "tired" virus or a "killed" virus with its outer shell intact to stimulate antibody production. Immunization gives the body an advantage: with antibodies targeted against polio or smallpox now strategically deployed, the time gap shrinks. When invaded, the body can flood the scene with a prepared assortment of antibodies and quickly overwhelm the intruders.

The story of smallpox vaccination, one of the proudest chapters in medical history, wonderfully typifies the success of the vaccination procedure. Smallpox ravaged the world and was often more feared than the Black Death, bubonic plague. Wrote Thomas Babington Macaulay in his *History of England*, "The havoc of the plague had been far more rapid; but plague had visited our shores only once or twice within living memory; and the smallpox was always present, filling the churchyard with corpses, tormenting with constant fears all whom it had not yet stricken, leaving on those whose lives it spared the hideous traces of its power, turning the babe into a changeling at which the mother shuddered, and making the eyes and cheeks of a betrothed maiden objects of horror to the lover."

The disease ravaged Europe for centuries. When introduced to an unexposed population, smallpox showed even more ferocity. One of Cortés's warriors, wounded and left behind after a skirmish, infected the Aztec Indians with smallpox. In two years, four million died, far more than were destroyed by all Cortés's soldiers.

In Missouri, the Mandan Indian tribe, with no natural immunities, was reduced from thirty thousand to thirty people. Incredulous traders and scouts of the time filed reports of whole villages huddled in their tents, all dead. Vast prairies displayed no rising smoke, no signs of life, only corpses. This one disease killed 500 million people in the nineteenth century alone.

One man, Edward Jenner, a pastor's son, changed all that. Just as Pasteur was forever haunted by the memory of a rabid wolf, Jenner carried with him dreadful memories of the summer of 1757. That year, at the age of eight, he was chosen for a procedure called "buying the pox," a crude attempt to ward off an epidemic. For six weeks the town doctor bled the boy repeatedly and virtually starved him. Then, at the village apothecary the physician scratched his arm with a knife and placed over the fresh cut the dried scab of a smallpox victim. For the sake of observation Jenner was kept in a stable, surrounded by other boys in various stages of "cure." After a month he recovered, forever immune to smallpox, but the terror of that summer never left him.

Jenner's doctor was utilizing what had been known about smallpox for centuries: once infected with a mild case, a person became immune to the disease. Unfortunately, the unsterile procedures and the virulence of the microbe made the practice only marginally safer than an epidemic.

A stray bit of peasant wisdom started Jenner down the path to scientific immortality. After years of studying the disease in the British Isles, Jenner came across a milkmaid who calmly told him she had no fear of smallpox because she had once had cowpox. The idea ignited Jenner. Could the mild disease of cowpox somehow make a person immune to smallpox? He collected data, performed experiments (some flawed), coined the term "vaccination," perfected his procedures, and presented his findings to the Royal Society in

London. Rather predictably, the stuffy medical establishment scoffed at the young researcher's conclusions and refused to publish his paper.

Debate over Jenner's procedure raged for over a century. Some countries banned it, while others made it compulsory.*

⎯

In the year 1802, smallpox broke out among the Indians and Spanish settlers of Bogota, Colombia. Aware that the disease could easily decimate an unprotected population, the ruling council of Bogota petitioned Spain's King Carlos IV for help. Their letter described a city paralyzed by the fear of a disease which was spreading epidemically through its neighborhoods.

King Carlos (though remembered by historians as an incompetent ruler) had an active interest in the new technique of vaccination. His three children had received the treatment, and the king had endorsed Jenner's controversial theories. But how could cowpox vaccine be transported to the New World? Within Europe, vaccinators ran threads or quills through cowpox sores and stored them in glass vials for delivery to other countries, but the virus would dry up long before a ship could cross the Atlantic.

---

* The following poem appeared in the British magazine *Punch* in 1881:

To vaccinate or not, that is the Question!
Whether 'tis better for a man to suffer
The painful pangs and lasting scars of smallpox,
Or to bare arms before the surgeon's lancet,
And by being vaccinated, end them. Yes!
To see the tiny point, and say we end
The chance of many a thousand awful scars
That flesh is heir to — 'tis a consummation
Devoutly to be wished. Ah! soft, you, now,
The vaccinator! Sir, upon your rounds
Be my poor arm remembered.

At last one of the king's advisers suggested a daring and innovative plan. Why not mount an expedition and recruit enough volunteers to assure that the vaccine could be incubated throughout the trans-Atlantic voyage? The king balked at the expense of such a plan until his adviser reminded him of the potentially devastating economic impact of an epidemic in the colonies.

An expedition was born, with the grandiloquent name Real Expedición Maritima de La Vacuna (Royal Maritime Expedition of the Vaccine), headed by the physician Francisco de Balmis. Soon the Spanish ship *Maria Pita* left port with a human cargo of twenty-two boys, aged three to nine, from a nearby poorhouse, as well as a few cows to serve as backup hosts. De Balmis vaccinated five boys before departure; the others would form a human chain to keep the virus alive.

Five days into the voyage, vesicles — small craters with raised edges and sunken centers — appeared on the infected boys' arms. On the eighth day the vesicles reached maximum size: they were rounded and bulging, volcanoes of lymph ready to erupt. The tenth day lymph flowed freely from the mattering sores — it was ready to harvest. De Balmis carefully scraped that valuable lymph into the scratched arms of two uninfected boys. Every ten days two new boys were selected, vaccinated with the live virus, and quarantined until their harvesting time.

(Politics sometimes edges out pure medical rectitude. The royal ship with its cargo of festering sores sailed into San Juan, Puerto Rico, in February, where its proud physician proceeded to boast to local authorities of his life-saving mission. A near brawl broke out when a local physician insisted to de Balmis that his island had already received smallpox immunity from a vaccination source on the Danish island of St. Thomas. Incensed that his expedition was being devalued, de Balmis kept his ship at anchor for a month while challenging the physician to prove his population's immunity. The local doctor succeeded and de Balmis, chastened and running out of time, set sail.)

By the time the *Maria Pita* reached Puerto Cabello, Venezuela, the very last boy was keeping the vaccine alive. He represented the only hope for staving off further epidemics. De Balmis selected twenty-eight more boys from the local population and stayed long enough to vaccinate twelve thousand people. From there, the expedition divided. De Balmis's assistant headed for the original destination, Bogotá, now in desperate straits due to the long delays. A moment of panic struck when his ship wrecked on the way, but the carriers of live vaccine survived. Everyone in Bogotá was vaccinated, smallpox soon faded away, and the assistant went on to immunize Peru and Argentina.

Meanwhile, de Balmis himself journeyed to Mexico, where he launched a frenzied vaccination campaign. After crisscrossing the country, he organized a new boatload of volunteers for the dangerous voyage to the Philippines. Those islands, too, eventually received protection from the unbroken human chain that stretched all the way back to the orphanage in La Coruña, Spain. Hundreds of thousands of people lived because of those original twenty-two orphans.

I have stood at the foot of the great bronze memorial to those young boys, in modern Bogotá, and reflected on their stirring sacrifice. History books, which devote pages to petty wars of the time that destroyed human life, rarely mention those twenty-two or the thousands of lives they helped save. Yet the Vacuna Expedición strikingly symbolizes the greatest advance in medicine: the capability to recruit defensive properties of one person's blood to help protect another person.

Edward Jenner received the ultimate accolade in the twentieth century when the World Health Organization decided to use a variation of his procedure in a campaign to obliterate smallpox from the world. Unlike some diseases, smallpox uses no animal hosts; contact must be human to human. Therefore, WHO workers reasoned, if every person proximate to an infected person was vaccinated, smallpox would disappear.

A twenty-year effort saw WHO workers scouring the villages of India and visiting isolated hamlets in South American and Asian jungles, in short, mounting the most extensive public health campaign ever. The African nation of Somalia harbored the last naturally occurring case in 1977 — workers had to interrupt a border war to track the person down.

Officially, smallpox has vanished, though some countries still vaccinate against it because of the terrorist threat. Once the most feared killer, it has become the only disease in recorded history to disappear. What an individual body must do to conquer any disease — destroy every invading microbe — has been accomplished on a global scale. The history of struggle against smallpox has ended in triumph, not because of drugs or advanced technology, but because of the proper application of the skills of human cells. People from every race have learned to share their defenses against it.

—

As a child in India I experienced the full force of person-to-person transmission because of the relatively unsophisticated manner in which my parents vaccinated for smallpox. My parents had very limited quantities of vaccine, and no facilities for cold storage, so they relied on the same source as did de Balmis: previously vaccinated human beings. Runners would bring the vaccine up mountain paths and hand the precious lymph to my father. Even before the runner caught his breath, Father would break the little tubes of lymph and begin vaccinating the waiting crowd. Later, from one infected arm he would draw enough lymph to vaccinate ten other Indians. Those ten yielded enough to vaccinate a hundred more. The blood of each vaccinated person locked away the memory of the pox virus so that any contact with smallpox alerted an army of defenders capable of overcoming the threat.

This property of blood, which can be shared from person to person, gives meaning to a word used in the Bible that has otherwise seemed puzzling to me: the word *overcome*. In one of the visions in Revelation the apostle John describes a violent confrontation between the forces of good and of evil. Satan is hurled down, and the victors, people who have come into eternal life, are described this way: "They overcame him by the blood of the Lamb" (12:11).

How can such a word be applied in that sense to blood? I have learned to accept blood as a symbol for life, not death, and even learned to appreciate blood's cleansing properties. But this juxtaposition of words, "overcome by blood," seems at first hopelessly incongruous. "Overcome" connotes strength and commanding power: a terrorist with a knife or gun *overcomes* an airplane crew; a huge Japanese sumo wrestler *overcomes* his opponent. On the other hand, "blood" connotes weakness and failure — a bleeding person has *been* overcome.

Why does the apostle use this jarring combination of words? The answer, I believe, lies in the biological pattern of how blood overcomes. It reveals something of cosmic significance about how God operates in the world and also enriches my understanding of the symbol of blood. To grasp the meaning, we must look at a few biblical uses of the word *overcome*.

At a very tender moment, during his last evening with the disciples before his crucifixion, Jesus said this: "In this world you will have trouble. But take heart! I have overcome the world" (John 16:33). At that time the declaration with its heady ring of victory did seem heartening. To those of us who read those words in retrospect, however, the words have a strangely hollow tone. For even as Jesus spoke them, Judas was sealing the fateful contract and Pilate's soldiers were buckling on their swords. Upon reflection, Jesus' timing, mere hours before his arrest and execution, seems almost bizarre. Those triumphant words must have soured for the disciples as they cowered in the darkness watching his pale body glimmer on the cross. "We had hoped that he was the one who was going to redeem Israel," two of them would later report with great sadness (Luke 24:21).

When the power of God confronted the power of men, Jesus, who could have called on angelic reinforcements, chose to yield to a handful of soldiers with their whips and nails. The distinction between overcoming and being overcome has blurred.

Later, in the book of Revelation the image of a lamb appears again and again to represent Christ. We too easily miss the irony of the weakest, most helpless animal symbolizing the Lord of the universe—and not only that, but a lamb "looking as if it had been slain" (5:6). This, then, provides the background for the strange phrase "overcome by the blood of the Lamb."

God's visit to our planet is primarily remembered not for its display of raw power but for its example of representative suffering. A pattern emerges through the refining fire of suffering: God responds to evil not by obliterating it, but by making evil itself serve a higher good. He overcame evil by absorbing it, taking it on himself, and, finally, by forgiving it. Jesus overcame as the One who goes before, by going right through the center of temptation, evil, and death.

Think of a scientist, staring through his microscope's eyepiece at a microbe population gone berserk and threatening the world. He longs for a way to remove his lab coat, shrink down to micron size, and enter that microbe world with the genetic material needed to correct it.

In the context of our own analogy, imagine God, after looking with great sadness on the virus of evil that has infected creation, casting aside divine prerogatives to take on the shell of a victim cell of that abhorrent virus in order to vaccinate humanity against the death and destruction that are sure to follow. An analogy points to truth weakly; nothing could have more force than the simple assertion, "He became sin for us."

━

The profound symbolic meaning of blood as an agent of overcoming must filter down from this kind of abstract theological discussion to a personal application I can reflect on while receiving the Eucharist. That ceremony is, more than anything, a personal reenactment of the theological reality of Christ's life and death.

I come to the Lord's Table directly and without the elaborate form specified in the Old Testament. Jesus Christ made that change possible, and the author of Hebrews summarizes what he accomplished:

> Since the children have flesh and blood, he too shared in their humanity so that by his death he might destroy him who holds the power of death — that is, the devil — and free those who all their lives were held in slavery by their fear of death.

For surely it is not angels he helps, but Abraham's descendants. For this reason he had to be made like his brothers in every way, in order that he might become a merciful and faithful high priest in service to God, and that he might make atonement for the sins of the people. Because he himself suffered when he was tempted, he is able to help those who are being tempted. (2:14–18)

Somehow, by drawing on the resources of Christ, I become better equipped to meet temptation. Let me explain what happens, using the analogy of blood.

Some years ago an epidemic of measles struck Vellore and one of my daughters had a severe attack. We knew she would recover, but our other infant daughter, Estelle, was dangerously vulnerable because of her age. When the pediatrician explained our need for convalescent serum, word went around Vellore that the Brands needed the "blood of an overcomer." We did not actually use those words, but we called for someone who had contracted measles and had overcome it. Serum from such a person would protect our little girl.

It was no use finding somebody who had conquered chicken pox or had recovered from a broken leg. Such people, albeit healthy, could not give the specific help we needed to overcome measles. We needed someone who had experienced measles and had defeated that disease. We located such a person, withdrew some of his blood, let the cells settle out, and injected the convalescent serum. Equipped with "borrowed" antibodies, our daughter fought off the disease successfully. The serum gave her body enough time to manufacture her own antibodies. She overcame measles not by her own resistance or vitality, but as a result of a battle that had taken place previously within someone else.

There is a sense in which a person's blood becomes more valuable and potent as that person prevails in numerous battles with outside invaders. After antibodies have locked away the secret of defeating each disease, a second infection of the same type will normally do no harm. A protected person has "wise blood," to use a term Flannery O'Connor originated. Could this process cast light on the description of Christ being "made perfect through suffering" (Hebrews 2:10)? Recall the just-quoted passage from Hebrews: "Because he himself suffered when he was tempted, he is able to help those who are being tempted" (2:18). And again, "We do not have a high priest who is unable to sympathize with our weaknesses, but we have one who has been tempted in every way, just as we are — yet was without sin" (4:15).

The blood of Jesus Christ has overcome. It is as if he went out of his way to expose himself to temptation, to encounter the stress and strain you and I will meet — to gain wise blood for our benefit. Beginning with his personal struggle with Satan in the wilderness, Jesus declined to use naked power to overcome temptations toward success, power, and an escape from the limitations of humanity. In the garden of Gethsemane those temptations put him to the ultimate test, but "for the joy set before him [he] endured the cross, scorning its shame" (Hebrews 12:2).

Today, when we partake of Communion wine, it is as though our Lord is saying to us, *This is my blood, which has been strengthened and prepared for you. This is my life which was lived for you and can now be shared by you. I was tired, frustrated, tempted, abandoned; tomorrow you may feel tired, frustrated, tempted, or abandoned. When you do, you may use my strength and share my spirit. I have overcome the world for you.*

An overwhelming, sudden temptation can catch even the strongest Christian off guard. We need to be prepared, and the symbol of the blood reveals how: by relying on the wise and powerful blood of the One who goes before.

# Chapter 8

# TRANSFUSION

*Wilt Thou forgive that sin where I begun,*
*Which is my sin, though it were done before?*
*Wilt Thou forgive those sins through which I run,*
*And do run still, though still I do deplore?*
*When Thou hast done, Thou hast not done,*
*    For I have more.*

John Donne, "A Hymn to God the Father"

---

The history of blood transfusion, like that of so many other medical techniques, began perilously and quickly sped toward disaster. In 1492, the same year Columbus set sail, a Jewish doctor in Italy tried transfusing blood from three young boys into ailing Pope Innocent VIII. All three donors died of hemorrhaging, while the thrice-punctured pontiff barely outlived them.

Two centuries later, interest in transfusion resurged, especially in France under the leadership of Jean Baptiste Denis, personal physician to Louis XIV. After successfully transfusing blood from one dog to another, Denis went on to restore a dying boy with an eight-ounce injection of lamb's blood. A second blood recipient, spirits revived, headed to a tavern to celebrate and promptly dropped dead. Denis's mixed results merely confirmed what every reputable physician already believed: withdrawing blood, not inject-ing it, offered the best hope for recovery. After all, M. Cousinot, the royal physician who immediately preceded Denis, had been cured of rheumatism after sixty-four blood-lettings in eight months. And one eminent physician had gained renown all over France by over-seeing the letting of a total of twenty million pints of blood. Thus, the nation quickly adopted a law forbidding the heresy of transfu-sion; this law would stand for a century.

Italian and English physicians did not give up so easily. One Italian physician puzzled over a set of Siamese twins who shared circulatory systems: food swallowed by one of them somehow nourished the other. Could he not similarly borrow the blood of one person for use by the body of another? In those days, blood was viewed not only as an agent for nutrition but also as a vital essence, brimming with "humours" or soluble personality traits. Some suggested using transfusions to inject sanity into an insane person or to modify personality types. Indeed, would marital strife end forever if the blood of quarreling spouses could be blended through transfusion?

Not until the nineteenth century did medicine achieve some success with the mysterious procedure of transfusion. In England, Dr. James Blundell saved the lives of eleven of fifteen women who were hemorrhaging after childbirth. Extant etchings record the dra-matic scene: a solemn Blundell looks on as one woman, standing, delivers her blood through a tube directly into the vein of a dying woman. Those etchings poignantly capture the human-to-human essence of shared life which today gets lost in the formality of com-puter-matched blood banks and sterile containers.

Despite their evident value, for many years blood transfusions involved horrible risks. Sometimes, perhaps a third of the time, the recipient's body inexplicably decided not to accept a donor's blood;

a violent reaction often killed such patients. Decades of bewilderment passed before researchers sorted out the crucial vagaries of blood typing and Rh factors, along with proper techniques for storage and the prevention of clotting.

Finally, during World War I, the benefits of blood transfusion began to outweigh its risks. Medics carried a wooden box containing two large jars of the precious juice onto the battlefields. Word spread rapidly among the troops: "There's a bloke who pumps blood into you and brings you back to life even after you're dead!"

An African-American named Charles Drew solved many problems of blood storage and shipping, making possible a nationwide Blood for Britain campaign during the second great war. Since then a labyrinthine network of blood supply depots, refrigerated blood banks, trucks, and planes has grown up — an ironic technological mimicry of the body's own circulatory system.

⚊

The dramatic experience of watching a blood transfusion at London's Connaught Hospital had drawn me into medicine. Twelve years later, with medical and surgical training behind me, I found myself back in India amid people who still reacted with fear and revulsion to the prospect of giving blood.

I arrived as an orthopedic surgeon at the Christian Medical College in Vellore just as the college was recruiting specialists from all over the world. Among these was Dr. Reeve Betts, from the Lahey Clinic in Boston, who was to become the father of thoracic surgery for all of India. When Betts first arrived, he ran up against an immediate roadblock: the lack of a blood bank. In some surgeries we had been relying on a Rube Goldberg device I designed to suction out and recirculate a patient's own blood. But chest surgery required a prepared supply of five or more pints of blood which in turn entailed an efficient collection and storage procedure. Betts had the experience and skill to save the lives of patients who began streaming to Vellore from all over India, but he could do nothing without blood.

Thus, in 1949, a blood bank became my number one priority. I had to learn the skills needed for typing, cross-matching, and screening of donors for health problems. We had to develop ways to provide pyrogen-free water and to sterilize all our reusable equipment. In the hot, dusty atmosphere of Vellore, where so many people were afflicted with parasites or a hidden virus of hepatitis, we had to struggle constantly to make our system foolproof. Time after time we suffered heartbreak when a transfusion intended to bring health damaged the patient. Those accustomed to the smooth efficiency of blood banks today should pause and be thankful for the pioneers who tackled the many hazards of the transfusion process.

However, the attitudes of Indian people themselves offered the biggest challenge. To them, blood is life, and who can tolerate the thought of giving up lifeblood, even to save someone else?* I have vivid memories of scenes that transpired again and again as Reeve Betts collided with ancient prejudices. "How could anyone refuse to give blood that would save his own child?" he would mutter darkly after emerging from a lengthy family council.

Usually a whole tribe of relatives would accompany a patient facing major surgery, so there was never a lack of family to consult with, but the prolonged dialogue through a translator into a local

---

*Only one category of Indians responded eagerly to our call for donors. Rickshaw drivers, often of the Untouchable caste, saw blood donations as an easy way to earn the equivalent of a day's wages. As our regular donors showed up weaker and weaker, we investigated and discovered some had been donating blood at other hospitals also—sometimes up to a pint each week! Ultimately, to prevent them from harming themselves, we had to institute a skin tattoo system to keep track of how often they gave.

dialect took endless patience. It went like this in the case of a twelve-year-old girl with a very bad lung. Reeve first informed the family that the lung must be removed to save the patient's life. The family members nodded with appropriate gravity. Reeve continued: The surgery required at least three pints of blood, and we had only one, so the family must donate two more. At that news, the family elders huddled together, then announced a willingness to pay for the additional pints.

I watched Reeve flush red. The veins in his neck began to bulge, and his shining bald head was an excellent barometer of his remaining tolerance. Working to control his voice, he explained that he had no other source of blood — it could not be purchased. They might as well take the girl home and let her die. Back to the conference. After more lively discussion the elders emerged with a great concession. They pushed forward a frail old woman weighing perhaps ninety-five pounds, the smallest and weakest member of the tribe. The family has decided to offer her as a transfusion donor, they reported. We could bleed her.

Reeve fixed a stare on the sleek, well-fed men who had made the decision, and then his anger boiled over. His bald pate blazed. In halting Tamil he blasted the dozen cowering family members. Few could understand his American accent, but everyone caught the force of his torrent of words as he jabbed his finger back and forth from the husky men to the frail woman.

Abruptly, with a flourish Reeve rolled up his own sleeve and called over to me, "Come on, Paul — I can't stand this! I won't risk that poor girl's life just because these cowardly fellows can't make up their minds. Bring the needle and bottle and take my blood." The family fell silent, and watched in awe as I dutifully fastened a cuff around Reeve's upper arm, swabbed the skin, and plunged the needle into his vein. A rich red geyser spurted into the bottle and a great "Ahhh!" rustled through the spectators.

At once there was a babble of voices. "Look, the sahib doctor is giving his own life!" Onlookers called out shame on the family. I reinforced the drama by warning Reeve not to give too much this time because he had given blood last week and the week before. "You will be too weak to do the operation!" I cried.

In this case, as in most others, the family got the message at last. Before the bottle was half full, two or three came forward and I stopped Reeve's donation and took their trembling, outstretched arms. Ultimately I had to end the routine Reeve had developed in full sincerity because, although he never lost much blood at one time, he gave with such regularity that his blood-forming cells strained to keep up. Nevertheless, his reputation spread: if a family refused blood, the great doctor himself would contribute.

⟿

As I ponder the ancient symbolism behind the word "blood" in the Christian religion, especially as suggested in Jesus' statements, I keep returning to the modern procedure of blood transfusion. Obviously, Jesus and the biblical authors did not envision a Red Cross blood supply depot when they used the word. And yet out of my experience blood transfusion has emerged as a kind of summary image of the Christian symbol, incorporating all of the meanings we have explored.

In a time when blood transfusion was unknown, Jesus chose the perplexing figure of drinking his blood. Ever since, Christians have wrestled with the theology of the Eucharist. Who can describe the process by which Christ's body and blood become a part of my own? We are brought near to him; we participate in him; he feeds us — any of these phrases only hints at the mystery. Jesus used the analogy of branches attached to a vine. The more contemporary metaphor of blood transfusion opens the way for me to grasp the underlying meaning.

I will never forget the night I saw a woman resurrect before my eyes when connected to a bottle of donated blood at Connaught Hospital. My experiences with blood transfusion, the purest example of shared life, call up for me the life-giving power of blood. The Communion service reminds me that Christ is not dead and removed from me, but alive and present in me. Every cell in his Body is linked, unified, and bathed by the nutrients of a common source. Blood feeds life.

The infusion of fresh blood also helps explain the process of cleansing. I focus on the toxins accumulating in scattered cells of my body and the happy relief that comes when blood washes away those poisons.

And finally, I imagine the furious intercellular warfare within my body and the climactic effect of a serum injection on that struggle. Jesus, the One who went before, earned "wise blood" which he freely shares.

Thus, the Lord's Supper has become for me, not an embarrassing relic from primitive religion, but an image of startling freshness. I can celebrate the sensation of coming to life through the symbol of Christ's blood transfused into me. The Connaught woman escaped death because of the shared resources of a nameless donor; Reeve Betts's patients gained new hope through the contributions of individual family members; similarly, I receive in the Eucharist an infusion of strength and energy by availing myself of Christ's own reserves.

Some have asked, "The meaning, yes, but why the ceremony? Why must we repeat this ritual?" Robert Farrar Capon answers such an objection against formality with his own questions. "Why go to a party, when you can drink by yourself? Why kiss your wife, when you both know you love her? Why tell great jokes to old friends who've heard them before? Why take your daughter to lunch on her birthday, when you're going to have supper together anyway?" The real question, Capon concludes, is "Why be human?" Or, as one British theologian put it, sex is to marriage what the sacraments are to Christianity: the physical expression of spiritual reality.*

Under the old covenant, worshipers brought the sacrifice — they gave. In the new, believers *receive* tokens of the finished work of the risen Christ. "My body, which was broken *for you* ... my blood which was shed *for you*...." In those phrases, Jesus spans the distance from Jerusalem to me, cuts across the years separating his time from mine.

When we come to the table we come with light breath, a weakened pulse. We live in a world far from God, and during the week

---

\* Lady Helen Oppenheimer's *Incarnation and Immanence* is helpful here. In it, she says: "The physical rite, the partaking of bread and wine, is not a magical spell nor a kind of psychological pressure, but a material vehicle for the presence of God, His 'real presence' indeed. How after all can any personal relationship be effectively carried on without some such material expression? One needs to utter words, aloud or on paper, to smile or frown, move or keep still; but more than that, one practically needs the handshake or the kiss, the formal standing up, comfortable sitting or perhaps reverent kneeling, to express oneself or understand what other people are trying to convey. It might be possible to define a sacrament as 'a point of intersection of the personal and the material,' and if so human life is sacramental through and through; and frequently material things are used as 'elements.' Wedding rings and badges of rank, prizes, medals and birthday presents are not just attractive objects wanted for their own sake, nor 'merely' symbolic like a souvenir 'of sentimental value only'; but when given in the approved context are truly a sort of human 'means of grace,' properly conferring the reality they symbolise, whether a change of status, goodwill, affection, honour or whatever it may be....

"But what authenticates the continuing gift of Christ's presence in the bread and wine is his death and resurrection. He could give his body and blood because he did give his body and blood, and he could give them by his chosen material means of a sacramental meal because by rising from the dead he had shown himself Lord of the created universe."

we catch ourselves doubting. We muddle along with our weak-nesses, our repeated failings, our unconquerable sins, our aches and pains. In that condition, bruised and pale, we are beckoned by Christ to his table to celebrate life. We experience the gracious flow of his forgiveness and love and healing — a murmur to us that we are accepted and made alive, transfused.

"I am the Living One," Christ said to the awestruck apostle John in a vision. "I was dead, and behold I am alive for ever and ever!" (Revelation 1:18). The Lord's Supper sums up all three tenses: the life that was and died for us, the life that is and lives in us, and the life that will be and will come for us. Christ is no mere example of living; he is life itself.

Jesus Christ did not convey himself genetically. If he had, his offspring would have been one-half Christ, one-fourth Christ, one-sixteenth Christ, on through his distant descendants of modern times when faint evidence of his bloodline would remain. Rather, he chose to convey himself personally and nutritiously, offering to each one of us the power of his own resurrected life. No other New Testament image, such as shepherd, building, or bride, expresses the concept of "Christ in you" so well as does blood.

Recall the words that scandalized his followers, "Whoever eats my flesh and drinks my blood has eternal life, and I will raise him up at the last day. For my flesh is real food and my blood is real drink. Whoever eats my flesh and drinks my blood remains in me, and I in him. Just as the living Father sent me and I live because of the Father, so the one who feeds on me will live because of me."

He is real food and real drink.

Who knows not Love, let him assay
And taste that juice, which on the cross a pike
Did set again abroach; then let him say
    If ever he did taste the like.
Love is that liquor sweet and most divine,
Which my God feels as blood; but I, as wine.
                  *George Herbert, "The Agonie"*

# HEAD

# Chapter 9

# PATHWAYS

*Earth's crammed with heaven,*
*And every common bush afire with God;*
*But only he who sees takes off his shoes,*
*The rest sit round it and pluck blackberries.*

Elizabeth Barrett Browning

I am sitting in my cluttered office, leaning back in my chair, gazing vacantly out the window. Supposedly, five trillion chemical operations are occurring in my brain at this second. It certainly does not seem so on this lazy day.

I decide to concentrate on my senses, starting with my eyes. Around me, stacks of journals, notes for future books, and unanswered correspondence collect in ragged, top-heavy piles. They oppress me, so I pad over to a window. I glance at my vegetable garden and pangs of guilt remind me I have not watered and fertilized it recently. But over to the right, the plant I take greatest delight in, a fig tree, is bearing fruit in full glory.

Pendulous figs in velvety shades ranging from green to purple dangle so thickly off every branch that the entire tree bows down. Each year when the figs ripen an enormous population of admiring butterflies suddenly appears, all of one species, wearing bars of

331

black, orange, and white in a design not unlike the monarch's. Thousands of them encircle my fig tree in a shifting corona of color. Outdoors, you can actually hear the papery sound of their beating wings.

I watch as the butterflies test each tempting fruit with a "tongue" smaller in diameter than a thread. They light on the unripe figs momentarily, linger a few seconds at those just turning red, and settle in to gorge themselves on the figs two days past perfect ripeness. I have learned a foolproof method of selecting perfect figs: pick the ones butterflies loiter on but do not penetrate.

Various trivial sounds reach my ears: my dog snuffling around in a corner, the soft throb of a ship on the Mississippi River, the distant chatter of a lawnmower, classical music wafting in from the living room.

The lawnmower sound accompanies a pungent, vernal aroma of cut grass. If I tilt my head a bit and sniff, I can also smell the sweet fermentation of figs on the ground. Both these scents are partly spoiled by a more pervasive, sulfurous odor from the petrochemical factory just down the river.

On one level, nothing much is happening today. Yet, as I attend to it, I realize very much is happening. My nose, eyes, and ears had been recording all those sensations even before I consciously tuned in to them. These senses are so significant in forming my view of the world that each deserves a brief summary.

⚊⚊

"God gave man two ears," observed Epictetus the Stoic, "but only one mouth, that he might hear twice as much as he speaks." Compared to some animal protuberances, human ears seem small, and underdeveloped. They capture a smaller share of the auditory

range than a dog's or horse's ear, and offer no competition to those
animals' talents for ear expressiveness — we move ours only as a
party trick.

Even so, the human faculty of hearing is impressive. Ordinary
conversation causes air molecules to vibrate and move the eardrum
a mere ten-thousandth of a centimeter, but with enough precision
for us to differentiate all the sounds of human speech. The eardrum
membrane has the flexibility to register the drop of a straight pin
as well as the noise of a New York subway one hundred trillion
times louder. It could hardly be more sensitive; if ear sensitivity
increased by a tiny amount, we would hear the movement of air
molecules as a constant whishing sound (this affliction actually
plagues some people, with disastrous hallucinatory effects).

Survivors of high-school biology should know what happens
after the eardrum vibrates: three tiny bones, informally known as
the hammer, anvil, and stirrup, transfer that vibration into the
middle ear. I have worked with most of the bones in the human
body, and none are more remarkable than these three, the body's
smallest. Unlike every other bone, these do not grow with age — a
one-day-old infant has them fully developed. They are in constant,
unrelieved motion, since every sound that reaches us causes these
bones to swing into action. Working together, they magnify the
force that vibrated the eardrum until it is twenty times greater than
when it entered.

Inside an inch-long chamber known as the organ of Corti, the
force that began with molecules of air and was converted to a
mechanical pounding finally ends up as a turbulent fluid force. The
action of the three bones sets up pulsating waves in the viscous liquid inside the sealed organ of Corti. Everything we know as sound
depends on this seismic chamber.

How do I distinguish two different sounds, such as the buzz of a fly droning about in my room and the rumble of the lawnmower a block away? Every distinct sound has a "signature" of vibrations per second. (A tuning fork shows the process clearly; when struck, its tines visibly move back and forth.) If you hear a wave of molecules oscillating 256 times per second, for example, you are hearing the musical "middle C." The average person can detect vibrations from 20 to 20,000 cycles per second.

Inside the organ of Corti, 25,000 sound receptor cells line up to receive these vibrations, like strings of a huge piano waiting to be struck. Seen through a scanning electron microscope, the cells resemble rows of baseball bats standing upright together. Each cell is designed to respond to a certain pattern of sound. A few of these cells will fire off signals to the brain when a 256-cycle vibration reaches them, and I thus "hear" a middle C. The others will await their own programmed frequency. Imagine the moiling chaos of cell activity when I sit in front of a full orchestra and hear twelve different notes at once, as well as the variety of musical "textures" from the different instruments. In all, the human ear distinguishes some 300,000 tones.*

In considering the brain, the most important fact about hearing is that the vibration itself never reaches the brain. The process resembles a compact disk or cassette tape which records sound not as mechanical vibration but as a series of electrical and magnetic codes. Once the vibration excites its appropriate sound receptor cell, the force inside the head changes from mechanical to electrical. Thousands of wires, or neurons, lead from the patch of 25,000

---

*In nature, survival needs take precedence over aesthetics, and animals that rely on sound for acquiring food exhibit an even greater range of specialization. A bat emits and receives radar at 50,000 to 100,000 cycles per second. Even the family dog can hear better, and with wider range, than its master. An owl has the unique feature of omnidirectional sound: one ear points forward, the other backward, giving it a 360-degree locator sense so accurate that a blindfolded owl can easily pinpoint a mouse rustling in the straw of a large barn.

cells into the auditory part of the brain. There the frequencies are received in a sequence of on-or-off blips. Our experience of sound depends on which of these cells transmits its signal, how often, and in cooperation with what other cells. The brain pieces together these messages and we "hear."

After receiving the electrical code from the sound receptors, the brain makes its own contributions of meaning and emotion. I experienced this in a most poignant way in 1983 when my wife and I celebrated our fortieth wedding anniversary. The phone rang, and Margaret and I picked up extensions simultaneously. "Hello, Mom. Hello, Dad. Congratulations!" we heard. It was our son Christopher in Singapore. Then, to our surprise, we heard the same words again, this time from our daughter Jean in England. And then again from Mary in Minnesota, and Estelle in Hawaii, and Patricia in Seattle, and Pauline in London. Our six children had conspired to place a globe-girdling conference call.

I had not experienced such intense emotion in years. It transported me back to scenes around the dinner table when we had laughed and teased together. The sounds of their voices instantaneously brought tears to my eyes and filled me with joy. Though separated by thousands of miles, we felt like a family again. All the warmth of my love for them and the history of our shared experiences somehow surged up at once in my brain. The sounds, which began as mechanical forces faraway, had touched the "I," the person inside the computer, the "ghost in the machine."

I look with even greater amazement on a further phenomenon of the brain. If I let my mind drift I can hear in my mind the four crashing chords of Beethoven's *Fifth Symphony*, the melodious voice of my daughter Pauline, the piercing tones of a London air-raid siren complete with its unbidden sense of anxiety. There is no force, no vibration of molecules, no firing of sound receptor cells, but still I can hear them. My mind creates sounds out of what exists only in the complex of nerve cells jammed into every cubic inch of white matter.

⌐⌐

I write of hearing with a sense of wonder but of smell with near incredulity. Smell leaves the world of quantifiable physics and approaches mystery.

Consider a moth who comes across just one molecule of a pheromone emitted by a mate three miles away. He will not eat or rest until he finds the female who tantalizes him, and one molecule a mile gives sufficient clues to track her down. Or consider a salmon who leaves a river near Portland, Oregon, as a mere fingerling and voyages far into the ocean, thousands of miles from home. Without a map, without visual signposts, without any clues other than its sense of smell — its receptors bizarrely scattered in random sites all over the fish's squamous body — the adult salmon will find its way back to the stream of its birth. A pig will excavate earth like a bulldozer in pursuit of a truffle; a bear will rip down a tree and brave a hundred stings for a drop of honey. A boll weevil will attempt to mate soft fields of cotton all day long, passionately, when those fields are sprayed with his female's scent. Like no other sense, smell impels.

We moderns have devalued smell, and, alas, a large portion of our brain atrophies. We forget that smell (and its companion sense, taste) played a leading role in human history. Were it not for a European craving for spices and Columbus's brave quest for more, America might have lain undiscovered for another century. Most of us have far more capacity for smell than we ever exercise (except those few professionals whose livelihoods depend on their tasting of wine or coffee or tea or smelling of incense or perfume). Were we forced to live in the wild and depend on smell for survival, that dormant portion of our brains would awaken, directing the relentless search for food and warning of the nocuous odors of putrefaction, bitter poisons, and vile, smoky vapors.

Smell operates by direct chemical action: tiny olfactory receptors perform elaborate chemical tests on any stray molecules that float by. In flies and cockroaches, these receptors harbor disgustingly on the creatures' feet; in moths, fuzzy smell antennae work similarly to TV antennae, by increasing the reception capability; in humans a penny-sized patch of receptive tissue lies at the top of our nasal cavities. For a good analysis we must sniff in, forcing the molecules up to the sensitive spot and then trapping them in the sticky moisture of the nasal lining. Even with our more primitive systems, we can detect one garlic molecule in the waftage of 50,000 other molecules.

The amount of substance needed to trigger smell defies belief. No DuPont laboratory can perform an analysis with one-hundredth the speed and accuracy of a bloodhound's nose. A detective holds a sock before the baleful dog. He sniffs deeply a few times, sorting out stale cigarette smoke, the artificial odor of Dr. Scholl's footpads, the complex history of a piece of leather, traces of bacterial action and, somewhere, pieces of the man himself, the criminal. He finds a trail through the woods and shuffles along, snorting and evaluating. Suddenly a yelp. He has sniffed in another piece. The pine needles, the dust, the men around him, the thousand smells of the forest floor — none of these interfere with his singular determination to follow the one molecular structure imprinted on his brain. He will follow that spoor through creeks and swamps, across logs, down city sidewalks, up apartment stairs — wherever it leads — one day, two days, even a week after the criminal has left the telltale bits.

I know of no laboratory in the world that would agree to distinguish one human from another by analyzing bits of two socks, let alone track that smell through such conditions.

The nose also is an organ of nostalgia. The smell of coffee, a whiff of briny seashore, the faintest lingering trace of a certain perfume, or the etheric odor of a hospital corridor can stop you like a bullet. You relive that former moment in a flash, jerked backward in time by the fragrance locked away in your brain. I experience this whenever I visit India, a country that appreciates the sense of smell (Columbus's original destination, after all). In 1946, as a young doctor I sailed into the Bombay (Mumbai) harbor after a twenty-three-year absence. A tremendous surge of long-neglected childhood memories swept over me as the fantastic scents of that country drifted across the sea. The steam-powered trains, bazaars, exotic people, spicy food, sandalwood, Hindu incense — all these rushed through me as the air of India reached my nose. Something similar happens today whenever I step off a plane and inhale India.

Yet just a few days later these overpowering sensations fade into a barely noticeable background atmosphere. The brain faithfully squelches odors after an initial heightened period — "nasal ennui" Richard Selzer calls it. Smell is primarily a sentinel warning and, once warned, why should the brain be troubled with redundancy? Fish merchants, tanners, garbage collectors, and paper mill employees gratefully accept this mercy of habituation. "You get used to it," they say with total accuracy.

Certain phrases keep recurring in textbook descriptions of smell: "difficult to explain," "not yet determined," "it is still not understood precisely how." We humans possess baffling powers capable of discriminating some 10,000 different odors, yet is there any sense we attend to less or take for granted more?* We have foundations and self-help groups for those who have lost hearing or sight, but I know of no National Foundation for Olfactory Deficiency.

Taste deserves mention, of course, as one of the five great senses. "Gastronomy rules all life," wrote nineteenth century French epicure Jean Anthelme Brillat-Savarin. "The newborn baby's tears demand the nurse's breast, and the dying man receives, with some pleasure, the last cooling drink." But taste suffers in comparison to smell and, in fact, relies mostly on smell, as any chef or any eater with a stopped-up nose can confirm.

An electron microscope scan of the tongue's dense mat of taste buds reveals splendid structures: dramatic cliffs and caverns, cactus flowers, clusters of tall, waving stalks, exotic leaves. They work well enough to afflict most of us with lavish appetites and insatiable cravings. But it takes twenty-five thousand times as much of a substance to register on a stubby taste bud as it does to register on a smell receptor. And for some mysterious reason, taste buds live a mere three to five days, then die off, so the only "experienced" taste exists in the fortress of the brain.

Lest taste and smell appear mere flourishes without a strict utilitarian function, consider this hospital fact: when a patient is receiving

---

*One person did not take the sense lightly. Helen Keller wrote: "Smell is a potent wizard that transports us across thousands of miles and all the years we have lived. The odors of fruit waft me to my southern home, to my childhood frolics in the peach orchard. Other odors, instantaneous and fleeting, cause my heart to dilate joyously or contract with remembered grief. Even as I think of smells, my nose is full of scents that start awake sweet memories of summers gone and ripening fields far away."

food directly into the stomach or intravenously, the body will absorb more nourishment if the patient "primes" it by tasting food first. The experience of taste stimulates the gastric juices in the same way the smell of sizzling steak or frying bacon can awaken in us a sudden, unexpected hunger.

My brief survey of the senses and their connections to the brain would be incomplete if I omitted sight, the sense which more than any other shapes our understanding of the world (the sense of touch was covered in *Fearfully and Wonderfully Made*). As the husband of an eye surgeon, I hear daily of the virtues of the eyes, which take up a mere one percent of the weight of the head, and of the tragedies resulting from their malfunction.

"Who would believe," asked Leonardo da Vinci, "that so small a space could contain the images of all the universe? O mighty process ... what talent can avail to penetrate a nature such as this? What tongue will it be that can unfold so great a wonder? Truly none!"*

The human eye's characteristic coloring comes, of course, from the iris, comprising radial and circular muscles that assist in opening

---

*Even the skeptic David Hume, one not given to expounding the argument from design, said, "Anatomize the eye, survey its structure and contrivance; and tell me, from your own feeling, if the idea of a contriver does not immediately flow in upon you with a force like that of a sensation!" No doubt Hume was referring specifically to the human eye. I equally enjoy studying other prototypes in nature: the sea urchin with vision-sensitive spots scattered about its body, or the scallop with bright blue ones rimming its shell like a row of landing lights; the crayfish which scrapes along the mud-flats with eye-spots studding the surface of its abdomen, or the Copilia, with its single-celled roving TV camera; the common fly with thirty-thousand autonomous eye units. A nautilus eye functions like a primitive pinhole camera, whereas a high-flying kestrel has four times as many eye cells as humans do — with that much greater acuity, useful for spotting prey. Every animal possesses some component of vision, if only the amoeba's and earthworm's instinctive tropism away from light.

and closing the pupil, thus increasing or decreasing the amount of light permitted by a factor of sixteen. A camera f-stop shutter duplicates this mechanical function, but nothing duplicates the lovely texture of those exquisite muscles that ripple and flute like the gills of a tropical fish. Inside, a precision lens, made of living tissue, is slung with transparent protectors and kept in position by a clear liquid that renews itself constantly to nourish the cells and kill stray germs. In children, the lens has a startling crystalline transparency. Later, protein deposits accumulate, harden, and scumble the clear lens, causing a condition called *cataracts* because the effect reminds one of looking out through a waterfall.

The complexity of perceptual cells beggars the imagination. In humans, 127,000,000 cells called rods and cones line up in rows as the "seeing" elements that receive light and transmit messages to the brain. Rods, slender and graceful tentacles that reach out toward light, outnumber the bulbous cones 120,000,000 to 7,000,000. These rod cells are so sensitive that the smallest measurable unit of light, one photon, can excite them. Under optimum conditions the human eye can detect a candle at a distance of fifteen miles. Yet with rods alone, we would see chiaroscuro, only shades of black and gray, and would not get the focal resolution allowed by the more complex cones.

Squeezed into the dense forest of rods, the larger cones tend to concentrate in the precise spot in the eye where focusing is most acute.* Although cones are one thousand times less sensitive to light, they make possible all perception of colors and fine details. (The diversity of animal vision depends largely on the distribution

---

*The center of our eye focuses on only about 1/1000 of the visual field. We see clearly an angle of only four degrees — less than the angle at the point of a pin. Stare at a single word on this page. Other words around it trail off into a blur, and the rest of the page and surrounding room are mere background shapes.

of these two cells. Owls have far more rods to allow for superb night vision. In contrast, a chicken has only cones, for detecting tiny insects; beyond a certain range, a chicken is nearly blind.) Our assortment of rods and cones lets us see objects at the ends of our noses and also stars light-years away.

Plato mistakenly believed that vision consisted of particles squirting out of the eye and falling on external objects. We now accept the reverse: light of a given wavelength — whether particles or waves of energy the physicists are still debating — streams through the sky and bounces off external objects, then enters the eye. To that extent, the eye does operate like a camera, with precise shutter and focusing mechanisms to admit and record the light. A variable pinhole lets in mountains, fig trees, a skyscraper, a giraffe, a flea. But at the back of the eye, in a coin-sized patch called the retina, the camera analogy becomes obsolete, for the actual physical image stops with the retina. From there on, everything is electricity. In effect, we do not actually see with the eye, but rather with the help of it.

For a more accurate analogy, we could look to the spacecraft that rockets off our planet and hurtles across our solar system to circle Venus or Jupiter or Mars. We have all seen the remarkable pictures with their details of satellites and rings and planetary landscapes. Yet as we read the accompanying article we learn that we are not seeing an image recorded on film, but rather a translation of an image. The spacecraft takes a picture and converts it by computer program into thousands of bits of information about shading, shape, and color. That data comes back to earth in the form of radio messages: blips and bleeps broadcast across the solar system. On earth, scientists receive and translate those codes, electronically enhancing the messages, and produce a photograph that looks as if the spacecraft had pointed a camera at the planet and snapped a picture on high-contrast film. We have "seen" not Jupiter, but a recon-struction of bits of information about Jupiter.

Similarly, our brains do not receive photographic images of anything. Rather, some of the 127,000,000 rods and cones get "excited" by light waves and fire off messages into the 1,000,000 fibers of the optic nerve, which coils like a thick television cable back into the recesses of the brain. Impulses from the retina race along the fibers of the optic nerve, fan out in the brain, and finally slam into the visual cortex, stimulating the miracle of sight.

The cortex has no easy task, since one billion messages a sec-ond stream in from the retina. Only in the last few years have sci-entists gained a glimpse into how the visual cortex sorts out these electrical signals, by observing the process in anesthetized animals, usually cats or monkeys.

A researcher opens up a cat's head, locates the visual cortex in the brain, and attaches an unimaginably slender microelectrode to a single brain cell. Then the researcher places a variety of shapes and patterns of light and movement before the animal's eye and meticulously records which objects or patterns cause that particu-lar cell to fire. The "receptive field" of a given cell is so specific that it may only fire when the cat is presented with a horizontal bar at a thirty-degree angle. Some cells are excited by a large spot, some by a small spot. Some fire only in the presence of a bar of light in the center region of the field; if the bar is tilted ten or twenty degrees, they will no longer fire. Some record a bright line moving on a dark background, and others only record the boundary regions between light and dark. Some cells respond only to motion.

The Nobel laureate who first charted these patterns in the brain cortex states with resigned humility, "The number of neurons responding successively as the eye watches a slowly rotating pro-peller is scarcely imaginable." As I read reports from such scientists, who spend their lives mapping out the visual cortex cell by cell, I am most impressed by this fact: when I see, I am totally unconscious of the process of cells encoding data and firing, then decoding and reassembling it within the brain. The fig tree outside my window with its swirl of butterflies comes to my consciousness not as a series of dots and light flashes, but as a fig tree, whole and intelligible and complete with meaning.

This ability to transpose units of messages — whether from the ear, the nose, the tongue, or the eye — into ever-higher strata of meaning is only possible because of the inner functions of the secluded brain. Cells inside that ivory fortress have no immediate experience of light, sound, taste, or odor. Yet every bit of data transmitted by sense organs terminates there. Indeed, no sensation truly registers until the brain has taken hold of it, translated it, and made sense out of it. The pathways of the senses now lead us inside that brain.

Chapter 10

# THE SOURCE

*All bodies, the firmaments, the stars, the earth and its king-
doms, are not equal in value to the lowest mind; for mind knows
all these and itself too; and these bodies know nothing.*

Blaise Pascal

I n all of medicine, there is no more shocking procedure than
brain surgery. It seems a violation, as terrifyingly sacrilegious as
bursting into the Holy of Holies. No one who opens a human skull
escapes this grim sense of defilement. For centuries the human
brain remained undrawn, or sketched only in rough caricature —
the mysterious organ daunted even the brave pioneer da Vinci, as
shown by his hesitant and inexact studies. (His successor Vesalius
had to plead with executioners for heads severed in decapitation,
still warm, to produce the first good anatomical drawings of the
brain.)

I was first given a human head containing a brain during my
medical training, when I chose as my senior project the task of
exposing the major nerves in a human head. I wanted to trace the
pathways of sense organs to their source.

Two years of medical school had not steeled me sufficiently
for the experience of getting my own cadaver head, whole and

perfectly preserved though shrunken slightly by the chemicals. It had belonged to a middle-aged man with plentiful hair and bushy eyebrows. When I slid back his eyelids with my thumbs, he stared out with gimlet eyes. What is the appropriate way to transport a cadaver head? Hold it by the ears? Grasp the scalp as you would pick up a kitten? Textbooks did not mention such things.

During the next month I spent most of my waking hours with the head of my nameless friend. I planned to do a complete dissection of the major nerves in his face, tracing them from the ear, the eye, the tongue, and the nose through the skull into the brain. "That skull had a tongue in it, and could sing once," Shakespeare wrote, and I had to push from my mind images of this hunk of wrinkled tissue on the table singing, talking, winking, smiling. I felt almost grateful for the pungent odor of the formaldehyde that had seeped through my skin and was affecting the taste of food, toothpaste, and everything else in my life during that month. It reminded me I was carving away not on a man but on a specimen of preserved tissue, a face that had fully served its time.

I knew how authentic brain surgeons proceeded. I had seen them slice through layers of scalp, muscle, and membrane and peel these back to reveal the gleaming bone inside. I had watched in amazement as those surgeons huffed and puffed, leaning heavily some twenty degrees off the vertical to force a whirring drill bit through the quarter-inch sheath of bone. A cloud of fine bone dust would sometimes form and float through the room. By the time they drilled and sawed through enough skull to lift a trap door into the brain, perspiration beaded their faces.

Nothing so well-fortified can be entered without a twinge of foreboding. My cadaver's skull was a nearly impregnable orb of granite that had sealed off its owner's brain from every nuance of sensation, temperature, moisture, or other disturbance in the outside world. Yet, paradoxically, that same brain had contained within it all his knowledge of the outside world, thanks to the frail white nerves leading to it, the nerves I now sought to uncover.

I began my exploration with the parts I knew best, the familiar shapes of eye, ear, nose, and tongue. I sliced away, peeling back skin, fat, and muscle until I found the inner structure with its nerves leading to the brain. Then I worked inward, like an explorer searching for the source of the Nile, following a small sliver of white through increasingly dense territory into the penetralia of the brain itself. Nerves resisted exposure: the fifth nerve, for example, began conveniently enough in the chin, but meandered wickedly through the jawbone before disappearing into the base of the skull.

Unlike the brain surgeon, I could not simply draw a cutting plan with a marking pen and start sawing. I had to chisel the facial skeleton in thin layers, coaxing out slivers of bone while taking care not to cut too deep and sever the nerve. Fortunately, I had worked as a stone mason for a full year, and after a little practice with a mallet and chisel the process of shaving away layers of bone the thickness of tissue paper seemed natural and even artistic. I strove to expose the nerves intact in their settings, leaving behind no obvious signs of forced entry.

The orbit of the eye consists of seven bones fused together in a protective socket. I had to slice through each of these, unsheathing the full depth of the glossy eyeball, then gently trace the optic nerve along its tunnel back into the brain. I remember being most impressed by the vast range of textures. I would pick up a scalpel to make a satiny slice through muscle and fat, holding my breath and keeping the blunt edge toward the nerve — one quiver of my finger and that nerve would snap. Then I would lay down the scalpel, pick up a mallet and chisel and attack the bone, hard as masonry, with all my force.

After I had spent several arduous weeks dissecting, one-half of my cadaver's face was unrecognizable. Fine streams of white led from the ear, eye, tongue, nose, larynx, and facial muscles and disappeared into the cavity that contained the brain. Finally, I was ready to enter the brain itself. After slashing through hairy scalp and sawing through bone, I reached the three membranes, or meninges, that sheathed the brain. I slit each one, remembering with a smile the arcane Latin names I had learned in anatomy class: *dura mater* (hard mother), *arachnoid* (cobweb), and *pia mater* (tender mother). The innermost membrane fit like Saran wrap over the convolutions of the brain, and when I punctured it a small piece of the brain bulged through the opening like a tiny fist. I stared at it a full five minutes before continuing.

At first sight the brain, coiled extravagantly and pinkish-gray in color, uncannily resembled the lowly intestines. It had the consistency of paste or cream cheese, making the actual brain encountered quite different from what one would expect after studying the solid-looking renditions in anatomy texts. The brain's walnut-shaped appearance held endless fascination for me as I kept on dissecting. Its landscape dipped and rose and turned in on itself—a topographical map of all the mountains on earth compressed into a tiny space. (Those folds increase the surface area thirty-fold.)

Red and blue lines crisscrossed the topography, and I breathed a prayer of thanks that I was practicing on a dead brain. A surgeon operating on a living patient spends much time avoiding those vital channels of blood and stanching the vessels severed by his scalpel. In addition, formaldehyde had strengthened the brain tissue and, though it was softer than any tissue I had yet encountered, I could prod it and move it with my hands without tearing it. A living brain laid on a flat surface would sag and perhaps rupture under its own weight.

I had hoped to trace sensory nerves to their ultimate sources, but the brain does not yield easily to map-making. Nerves there, ensconced in the ample armor of skull, have the doughy consistency of the rest of brain matter and will break at the slightest push or pull. Following a soft thread of white into a white mush devoid of surgical landmarks was like trying to track a river's confluence with the ocean: after a certain point, the river becomes the ocean. In only a few cases did I succeed in finding the final destination of nerves. In the others, I labeled the source from what I had seen in the textbooks, not from my own tedious exploration. The pathways of thought and sensation were unmarked by signposts and indiscernible by dissection, almost as if the frequent passage of a thought had left invisible footprints that only thoughts could follow.

Professor West took tutorial delight in my ambitious undertaking, insisting he had not seen a head dissected in quite that way before. He awarded the completed cadaver head a prize and ordered that it be pickled and put on display in the Welsh National School of Medicine Museum. As far as I know, a certain jar is still gathering dust there, its contents leering out at tourists with a naked, Cyclopean stare. I, of course, had schoolboy fantasies of becoming a pioneer brain surgeon. Years later, when of necessity I attempted a few hazardous ventures into neurosurgery, I thought with gratitude how wise I had been in *not* pursuing that enormously challenging field.

In some surgeries on living brains, the patient stays awake in order to cooperate with the exploring surgeon. As a result, the atmosphere in the operating room crackles with unspoken tensions. The patient's consciousness serves to edit the normal prattle of surgery, and any mild emergency is met with suppressed anxiety. Standing on the sidelines, watching such procedures, I notice the sounds. The faint electronic beeps of monitoring machines and the deep sighs of the respirator give a percussive accompaniment to the more interruptive sounds of medicine at work: the shrill whine of the drill, a popping sound from the electric cautery, and the clinking of instruments being passed around like dinnerware. The object of all this attention glistens in the bright lights, and if you look closely you can see it heaving gently. The brain is alive.

Brain surgeons face the relentless threat of uncontrolled bleeding. When other bodily tissues bleed, vessels can be clamped and tied off, but the brain is too soft to hold a clamp or to tie off. Even a slight tear can unleash enough blood to flood the site and make further probing impossible. A suction nozzle follows the surgeon's knife like a meticulous housekeeper, slurping up blood to clear the view.* Sometimes the surgeon will put forceps to the bead of blood and touch a cautery to that instrument. *Zzzt* — the blood coagulates and bleeding stops. Other times, an assistant will drop small squares of cotton lint called "pledglets" onto the bleeding vessel. A quick application of the suction nozzle will pull blood into the pledglet, encouraging clotting. After an hour of surgery, fifty or sixty of these used squares, attached to long black threads for easy removal, may dot the landscape of the brain.

Even the most experienced surgeon has difficulty with orientation in the brain, for everything appears soft and white, like a

---

*All suction must be regulated carefully; otherwise, pieces of brain tissue will disappear forever into the central garbage disposal. "Oops, there go the piano lessons!" a surgeon may joke if the patient is unconscious. Fortunately, the brain rarely notices a small loss.

blizzardy Arctic landscape. Brain surgery would still be in a primitive state were it not for one remarkable discovery of science. When a surgeon inserts a needle-like electrode into a portion of the brain and switches on the current, the brain responds, indicating what functions that area controls. The brain itself has no sensation of pain or touch, so the patient will say something like "I feel a tingling sensation in my left leg" if the surgeon lightly stimulates the surface of a particular lobe.

Wilder Penfield, a brain surgeon in Montreal, has recorded bizarre results from such stimulation. While trying to locate the source of epileptic seizures, he found that in certain portions of the brain he could electrically stimulate specific memories in sharp detail. One young South African patient began laughing, reliving second by second an incident on a farm in his native land. A woman recalled every note in a symphony concert she had heard long before. The memories surged up in such vivid detail for one patient on the operating table that she remembered sitting at a train crossing years before and could verbally describe each train car as it went by. Another counted aloud the number of teeth of a comb used in childhood. Often these memories from early childhood precede the patient's first conscious memory.

By drawing on such techniques and by studying stroke victims, anatomists have been able to develop a fairly reliable map of the brain. Most brain research centers on the top layer of the brain, the cerebral cortex, which is far more advanced in humans than in any animal. The thickness of the sole of a shoe, the cortex contains neurons that sift, sort, collate, and process the information we perceive as sight, sound, touch, conscious behavior, and the higher activities of learning and memory. The bulk of nerve cell population lives in that layer of gray matter, the fertile topsoil on the brain.

Eminent neurologist Sir Charles Sherrington neatly divided certain brain nerve cells into two groups: "the way in," or *afferent* cells which carry impulses from the organs of the body to the brain, and "the way out," *efferent* cells which carry instructions from the brain out to the extremities. In the entire brain, only one in one thousand cells reports in from the extremities: all visual images, all sounds, all touch and pain sensations, all smells, the monitors of blood pressure and chemical changes, the sensations of hunger, thirst and sex drives, muscular tension — all the "noise" from the entire body — occupy only one-tenth of one percent of the brain's cells. Each second those fibers bombard the brain with a hundred million messages. Of these, a few hundred at most are admitted above the brain stem.

Another two-tenths of one percent of cells control all motor activities: the motions involved in playing a piano concerto, speaking a language, dancing a ballet, typing a letter, or operating a video game. In between these two groups, The Way In and The Way Out, lie all the others: enormous numbers of cells cooperating in a vast network of intercommunication to allow the processes we know as thought and free will.

Brain biologist J. Z. Young likens the network to ten billion bureaucrats constantly phoning each other about plans and instructions for keeping a country running. Sir Charles Sherrington, more poetically, rhapsodizes about an "enchanted loom" with lights that flash on and off as messages weave their way through the brain.

Unlike a telephone switchboard that connects single subscribers indirectly through a central switching station, *each* nerve cell in the brain has up to ten thousand of its own private lines. All along its length dendrites reach out and form connections with other neurons, in effect linking each cell with wires from an entire city. It "listens in" for the patterns of impulses and their average rate of arrival and decides whether to continue the message by firing off chemicals along its thousands of other connections.

Physiologically, the whole mental process comes down to these ten billion cells spitting irritating chemicals at each other across the synapses or gaps. The web of nerve cells defies description or depiction. One cubic millimeter, the size of a pinpoint, contains one billion connections among cells; a mere gram of brain tissue may contain as many as four hundred billion synaptic junctions. As a result, each cell can communicate with every other cell at lightning speed — as if a population far larger than earth's were linked together so that all inhabitants could talk at once. The brain's total number of connections rivals the stars and galaxies of the universe.

Even in sleep the nerve cell community never stops chattering. The brain is a turbulent cloud of electrical potentials. During each second of life it performs about five trillion chemical operations. When we are awake, only a few reach our level of consciousness, and those so quickly we are hardly aware of the process. I decide to write the next sentence; in a flash my brain computes first the thoughts and then the words I will use, then the elaborate coordination of muscles, tendons, and bones required to type the words. Before I finish typing, my brain begins composing the sentence to follow.

━

Steven Levy recorded this reaction when he came across a jar containing Albert Einstein's brain: "I had risen up to look into the jar, but now I was sunk in my chair, speechless. My eyes were fixed upon that jar as I tried to comprehend that these pieces of gunk bobbing up and down had caused a revolution in physics and quite possibly changed the course of civilization. There it was."

I have a similar reaction to any human brain I have ever seen. Solzhenitsyn once referred to a man's eyes as "sky-blue circles with black holes in the center and behind them the whole astounding world of an individual human being." I will never forget the sensation that washed over me the first time I chipped through bone and exposed the cadaver brain in my laboratory room in medical school. Even with all the blood vessels, membranous linings, fluid-filled cavities, and billions of specialized nerve cells, the organ weighed barely three pounds. Yet that fragile, grayish jelly once contained a whole life.

In a biological sense a whole body had existed just to keep that brain nourished and protected for forty years. The brain had used up one-fourth of all the oxygen its owner had breathed in — its lack of oxygen for five minutes had caused his death.

One nerve had controlled all the subtle movements of his lips that made speech and eating and kissing possible. Another had brought in every nuance of color and light to form his visual construct of the world.

The brain contains imagination, morality, sensuality, mathematics, memory, humor, judgment, religion, as well as an incredible catalog of facts and theories and the common sense to assign them all priority and significance. In the human head, concludes Nobel laureate Roger Sperry, "there are forces within forces within forces, as in no other cubic half-foot of the universe that we know." There is nothing on the earth so wonderful.

And yet nothing on earth is so fragile. One bullet may destroy it, or one spill from a motorcycle. One dosage of a powerful drug can upset the delicate balance inside a brain forever.

I have been inside a human brain on maybe a half-dozen occasions. Each time I have felt humble and inadequate, a trespasser entering where no man was meant to. Who am I to invade the holy place where a person resides? Perhaps if I worked on brains daily I would grow more callous and unimpressed. But I think not — the brain surgeons I know still talk of their subject in hushed, almost worshipful tones.

In the analogy of the Body of Christ used in the Bible, Christ himself is said to take on the role of the Head. In the next chapters we will explore some parallels that do apply and also sense the limitations of that analogy, of any analogy, to convey the essence of God in the world.

If you have been inside a human brain, as I have, and held the quivering substance in your hand, if you have gazed through a microscope at a tiny section of the unimaginable network of nerve cells, if you have watched brain wave machines record a minute sampling of the communications between cells, if you have pondered the interwoven mysteries of brain and mind and human personality, then I think you should be prepared, if not for the concept of the analogy, at least for its emotional force. A whole person lies inside the bony box, locked in, protected, sealed away for the indispensable duties of managing one hundred trillion cells in a human body. The Head of the Body is the seat of mystery and wisdom and unity. He is the Source.

# Chapter 11

# CONFINEMENT

*That glorious form, that light unsufferable,*
*And that far-beaming blaze of majesty, ...*
*Forsook the courts of everlasting day,*
*And chose with us a darksome house of mortal clay.*
John Milton "On the Morning of Christ's Nativity"

Although it seems as if nothing much is happening when I sit in my cluttered office and gaze vacantly out the window, as we have seen, the apparent stillness deceives. My brain is humming and crackling, performing five trillion operations each second.

The common catalog of five senses — sight, hearing, touch, taste, and smell — hardly covers all that is taking place. Other vital senses inform me of muscle tension and the pressure on joints and tendons; I know instinctively the tilt of my head, the bend of my elbow, the position of my left foot. Different sensors inform me of lunchtime; my stomach "feels empty." Below the conscious level, automatic systems adjust the chemical components of blood, control air pressure in my lungs and blood pressure in my arteries, and monitor organ stretch receptors. My brain, isolated in its thick ivory box, receives all these signals in a kind of electrical Morse code.

It appears the brain needs this ceaseless turmoil. When a person reduces the number of sense impressions, for example by lying in a dark tank of warm water cut off from most sensations, before long the brain begins to hallucinate and fill the void with sensory content of its own devising. And during sleep billions of cells spark through the night, their level of activity barely diminishing from daytime levels.

Often the interplay between the sense organs and the brain's fund of memories is so subtle that the two cannot be easily distinguished. Consider, for example, a Beethoven piano sonata. In the totally deaf state of his later years, Beethoven never "heard" the music he composed — that is, the eardrum, three bones, and sound receptor cells never participated in the experience. Yet somehow by the extraordinary ability of his brain to reconstruct tone and harmony and rhythm, he did hear it. No molecules danced their tarantella; all took place in silence, cerebrally, in code.

Today, if my musically talented wife picks up a written score of Beethoven's *Sonata Pathetique*, she recognizes it almost at once. She can hum along as she reads, relying on her own mental file of sounds. She "hears" it in her mind. Or, if we merely sit at home and select a radio station, after hearing just a few measures we can recognize the sound as part of that same sonata.

How many billions of brain computations are required to recognize a piece of music? Yet how long does it take — two seconds? Or, what process of neuronal communication instantly convinces me that red globe hanging in a tree in my yard is not a balloon caught on a branch, but a star located 93,000,000 miles away? All these processes occur with blinding speed and little conscious effort.

When you read this page, you are not conscious of the individual letters forming each word. You do not spell them out one by one, reassemble them into a composite, and then scan a dictionary for the meaning of that composite — and yet in reality your mind does all that, subconsciously. It works so fast that when I speak, using letters, words, grammar, and punctuation, I can concentrate solely on the meaning of what I want to communicate. Neurons with stored knowledge freely supply the individual elements, and my central nervous system arranges the glottal puffs and slides to create intelligible sounds.

My brain presents the world to me not in data banks and reductionist blips, but wholly, conceptually, meaningfully. And herein is the great mystery. The mind that coordinates all this profound activity lies locked away. The brain itself never sees: if I opened one up to light, I would likely harm it irreparably. It never hears: the brain is so sheltered and cushioned that it feels only the most reverberant sensations. The brain does not experience touch: there are no touch or pain cells there. Its temperature varies no more than a few degrees; it has never felt hot or cold. It never sustains a mechanical force; upon meeting up with one, it would quickly lapse into unconsciousness.

Everything that forms me, Paul Brand, reduces down to a sequence of dots and dashes (-. — .-.. — ) reporting from millions of remote stations into a bony box that has never directly experienced those sensations. The taste of chocolate, the prick of a pin, the sound of a violin, a view of the Grand Canyon, the smell of vinegar — all these reach my consciousness via signals that are virtually identical. I perceive them because tiny, flower-shaped neurons have shot chemicals at each other.

The brain, floating in its ivory box in a pool of cerebrospinal fluid, contains the person I am. Every other cell in my body ages and is replaced at least every seven years. My skin, eyes, heart, even bones are entirely different today from those I carried around just one decade ago. In all respects but one I am now a different person — the exception being my long-lasting neurons or nerve cells. These maintain the continuity of selfhood that keeps the entity of Paul Brand alive.

From the darkness and loneliness of that bony box I reach out to reality with millions of living wires. They extend from my brain like tendrils of a plant, stretching desperately toward impulses of smell, sight, sound, and touch into the world of light and matter.

First through a glimpse at the sense organs, then through my dissection of a cadaver head, and now through the individual elements that conspire to give me a total experience, I have been pointing toward the summary function of the amazing lump of cells we carry around in our skulls. I have extended this biological survey in order to lay the groundwork for the analogy of Christ as Head of the church, a title the New Testament applies to him seven times. We customarily think of power and authority when we envision someone in the role of Head. The biblical metaphor applied to Christ expresses some of that meaning, surely, but the actual physiological working of the brain sheds light on the style in which Headship is exercised.

The analogy from the body hints at a fundamental choice God has made in interacting with this world. The parallel we will explore, in short, is this: God, a Spirit untrammeled by space and time, in an act of deep humility took on the confinement of matter and time. God became enfleshed. Later, Christ's body departed (or, more accurately, was transformed) and he withdrew into the position of the Head. Today, Christ's Body consists of millions of individual cells in his church. As the Head, he establishes his presence in the world through people like us. In a mysterious way he has chosen to make our prayers, our actions, our proclamation of truth and justice his chief means of communicating into the world of matter.

Why? Why would a God who is pure Spirit take on matter? And why, in fact, did Jesus choose to rely on ordinary human beings while he receded to the isolated "ivory box" role of Headship? God could, if desired, express himself again through the flash and smoke of Sinai. God's presence on earth could again ignite a bush or cause a terrifying glow of light, as it sometimes did in the Old Testament. Instead, God has chosen a self-limiting way.

Questions are often raised about God's style of involvement with the created world. For the agnostic, those questions take on a shrill tone of accusation: "If there is a God, let him prove it somehow! Let him step in and straighten out the royal mess of this world!" For me as a Christian, the issue is not so much Is God really there? as Why has God chosen such an indirect, hidden style of activity? Why not reveal himself more clearly?

The term "self-limiting" may help explain this world. If we can accept God limiting himself to the extent of relying mainly on human agents, then we understand dimly why God does not, and must not, brazenly interfere with what he has made. "God has, so to speak, imprisoned Himself in his own resolve," said Kierkegaard.

⚊

I gained some insight into the issues behind self-limitation when my one-year-old daughter Pauline discovered the electrical outlets in our Indian home. The outlet boxes, conveniently mounted six inches off the floor, carried a 220-volt current and were designed for metal plugs that were round rather than flat — exactly the shape and diameter of Pauline's tiniest fingers. Pauline had a habit of sucking her fingers two at a time. Like any normal infant of that age, she was inquisitive and loved to poke her fingers into things.

My wife and I were naturally alarmed by Pauline's interest in the enticing paired holes. We tried covering the outlets with adhesive tape, but Pauline quickly learned she could peel off the tape. She looked mischievously over her shoulder at us, removed her wet and slippery fingers from her mouth, and waited for us to leave the room.

What could we do as parents? We could tie her to her crib or attempt to control her every movement. Or, we could somehow convince her of the danger. But how?

"Pauline, now listen to me! Inside those holes, electrical terminals are producing a potential difference of 220 volts. You have wet fingers, which decreases the resistance of your skin to electric current. If you touch those terminals, the current will travel up your arms, destroying your nerves and denaturing the protein of your muscles. . . ." That explanation, albeit true, would have meant nothing to my gurgling daughter.

I grasped at something that had already entered Pauline's experience. "Pauline!" I began in my most threatening voice, "If you touch those holes, fire will come out! You will be burned!" She looked at me skeptically, certain I was merely denying her access to fun. But I sounded earnest. And she had learned one very painful lesson about burns from the floor-level fire our Indian cook had been using. Was it worth the risk?

"And, Pauline, if you touch those holes I will punish you." This warning struck home. She retreated. She knew that threat and had learned to fear it. The dark holes suddenly lost their intrigue.

Pauline has now graduated from college and could probably teach me about ohms and volts and resistance. When she reflects on that experience, if she ever does, I rather doubt that she questions her father's honesty or wisdom. She realizes now that in the most literal sense those dark holes contained no fire. But she also knows the ignorance then was in the child, not the father. To communicate with her, I had to use a language and concept she could understand.

In my work with various cultural groups, I have similarly had to accommodate my language. I explain an electron microscope to an eager student in the Tamil language by analogy, using approximations of concepts that he or she can understand. And if I someday learned that a nuclear device was about to explode in remote Somalia, I would warn the nomads there to dig for cover not by expounding the mutability of matter and principles of nuclear fission, but by saying something like "Fire in the sky!" or "Poison dust!" I must use words that mean something to the person who hears them.

Is this not the problem God faces in communicating with human beings? How can infinitude express itself to finite beings? The analogy of language is enlightening. A concept exists in the mind but has no reality until distilled into a thought, and has no communication potential unless it can be expressed in language. Only as the concept—mysterious, spirit-like—wraps itself in the clothing of language and enters the material world of vocal chords and puffs of air and pen scratchings, does it exist in a way anyone else can recognize.

Jesus, appropriately, was called the Word of God. Infinite, ineffable, inexpressible God became a man. God spoke in as articulate a way as humans could possibly bear: God became one of us and "tabernacled among us."

"It was much, that man was made like God before/ But, that God should be made like man, much more," said John Donne. For thirty-three years Jesus gave us an image; we can now look back upon it to perceive the true image of God. Through Christ, God softened language to his hearer's ears. One example: If you had said to Isaiah, "God is going to touch you today," he would have fled in terror. For him, touch was not a quality of communication between God and man. With Jesus, all that changed.

Yet the Incarnation, as great as it was, did not complete God's purposes on earth. Christ receded to the role of Head in order to create a new Body, this one composed not of living cells but of millions of men and women all cohering in him. "As you sent me into the world," Jesus said to his Father, "I have sent them into the world" (John 17:18). The profound change could hardly be expressed more succinctly.

In one sense Christ's departure was an ascension — it is called that on every church calendar — but in another sense it was a further condescension. Now God "tabernacles" neither in a Most Holy Place, nor in one perfect body, but in millions of ornery, frail, bodies — some short, some tall, some smart, some dull, some steady, some volatile. Christ withdrew into the ivory box.

God does not, it is true, "need" anything to be done by finite agents. He need not work indirectly, in the role of Head. Omnipotence could find a way to nourish bodies without food, to fuel the brain without red blood cells, to convert people without missionaries. But for some reason God has chosen the terrene stuff of soil and vegetables and chemistry and words and human will to carry out his plan on earth.

Today, we are God's medium, Christ's Body. When you look at me, you never see the whole Paul Brand; rather you see a thin layer of skin cells stretched across my frame. The real Paul Brand resides inside, especially centered in my brain, locked away from the outside world. The same is true with God. We cannot "see" God; we have no perceiving organs adequate for that. Rather, we see God in a comprehensible form in the shape of each other as members of his Body. God could not accommodate language to human ears and shape to human eyes more fully than by dwelling inside men and women.

—

Dorothy Sayers lists three great humiliations God has willfully undergone. In the first, the Incarnation, God stripped off the prerogatives of deity and stooped to become a man. In the second, the Crucifixion, God's Son became sin for us, suffering the ignominy of death. The third humiliation, she says, is the church. God humiliated himself by choosing to live within a Body comprising people like us.

From one standpoint, she is absolutely correct. The Head working through us involves a sort of shrinking, an abdication wherein God chooses to lay aside omnipotence and take on an invisible, behind-the-scenes role in human history. In so doing, God again self-limits, investing the divine reputation and name in imperfect human beings. Once a nation bore that name, and bore it to disgrace. We who are Christ's Body have similarly stained God's reputation by galloping off on bloody crusades, cracking bones and joints on torture racks, christening a slave ship *The Good Ship Jesus*, preaching racist doctrine. God in Christ, in human form, is one thing; God in us is quite another.

The church, Christ's Body, is indeed a humiliation. And yet, counterbalancing that humiliation, a kind of exaltation shines forth, a hint that perhaps from the very beginning God planned for his name to be carried by people exactly like us. For the deliberate shrinking of Omnipotence into the role of Head allows us as members of Christ's Body to participate in the restoration of the universe. "The whole creation," says Paul, "is on tiptoe to see the wonderful sight of the sons of God coming into their own. . . . And the hope is that in the end the whole of created life will be rescued from the tyranny of change and decay, and have its share in that magnificent liberty which can only belong to the children of God!" (Romans 8:19, 21 PHILLIPS).

A reward will come, to be sure. C. S. Lewis suggests it: "As mere biological entities, each with its own separate will to live and to expand, we are apparently of no account; we are crossfodder. But as organs in the Body of Christ, as stones and pillars in the temple, we are assured of our external self-identity and shall live to remember the galaxies as an old tale."

Because God has risked entrusting the kingdom to bumblers such as us, we gain by becoming the sons and daughters of God. The image of God is being restored. "Even angels long to look into these things" (1 Peter 1:12).

⟞

As a teacher, I have at times experienced the peculiar satisfaction of work done through others.

If I were to review my years in India and try to calculate the number of hands that I personally operated on, I might come up with a number around 10,000. In some ways that number seems overwhelmingly large to me, and it points up my advancing age with a rude jolt. But as I reflect further, I realize how negligible that number is. Millions of people in the world suffer from leprosy, a quarter of whom have hand damage. In a lifetime of surgery, putting in as many hours as I can muster, I have personally only been able to help a tiny fraction of the people with needs.

But again and again I have visited a tiny rural clinic in a place like Borneo and watched a young doctor perform procedures that derive from those we developed at Vellore. In Japan, Singapore, Hawaii, Ethiopia, or virtually anywhere a leprosy work thrives, you can find students who were trained at Vellore or Carville. Nothing — absolutely nothing — fills me with more joy than to see the seeds of ideas and disciplines I taught now sprouting in peoples' lives. It seems almost a miracle when I see it in action. My work done in a classroom can multiply a hundred times what I could possibly achieve on my own.

When I leave this world, the number of hand surgeries I have performed will not increase; no other patient will be helped by my own hands. But the students I have left behind will continue to multiply the original mission we adopted at Vellore. That realization gives me additional insight into God's way of working in the world.

A teacher extends his or her work through students left behind. A brain expresses itself through cells obedient to its command. And God expresses himself through a Body in which Christ serves as Head.

"He who listens to you listens to me; he who rejects you rejects me," Jesus once told his followers (Luke 10:16). The identification of the Body with its Head is that complete. A little later, on the night before he died, Christ explained his imminent death for the confused and somber disciples. "It is for your good that I am going away," he said (John 16:7). They did not know it at the time, but the era of Headship was about to begin.

Chapter 12

# THE WAY OUT

*In "The Happy Hypocrite" Max Beerbohm tells about a regency rake named Lord George Hell, debauched and profligate, who falls in love with a saintly girl, and, in order to win her love, covers his bloated features with the mask of a saint. The girl is deceived and becomes his bride, and they live together happily until a wicked lady from Lord George Hell's wicked past turns up to expose him for the scoundrel she knows him to be and challenges him to take off his mask. So sadly, having no choice, he takes it off, and lo and behold beneath the saint's mask is the face of the saint he has become by wearing it in love.*

Frederick Buechner

The television camera was merciless. It never blinked, not when the teenage girl's tongue lolled over to the side, not when her eyes rolled wildly, not when she drooled and sputtered and fought off gagging on her own saliva. For this science program devoted to cerebral palsy, the camera recorded every extreme manifestation of the disease.

Another person with cerebral palsy, a young man, entered the girl's room, brought there by the television program's producers. He had made astonishing progress in rehabilitation, and he demonstrated his skills for the bedridden girl. He spelled out words, one alphabet letter at a time, with wide scraping arcs of his feet, so fast that an accompanying "interpreter" had trouble keeping up. He also typed with his toe, using a metal connection to complete a circuit on the keys. He had even learned to use a machine that amplified his clicking, glottal speech enough to make it intelligible to a trained ear.

In contrast, the girl had received no rehabilitation therapy. An Ohio state agency, unable to care for her medically, had placed her in an insane asylum. The television program pointed out the stark irony: everything was wrong with this girl *except* her mind. Behind the wild expressions, the drooling, and the catalepsy was a beautiful and intelligent mind, imprisoned.

Workers at the hospital had drawn a large chart divided into eighty squares of key phrases such as "I want" or "I need." The girl communicated by looking at a square with the appropriate phrase, whenever she could make her eyes hold steady long enough. Someone asked her if she had any questions for her "progressive" cerebral palsy visitor. She twitched and shook, and her eyes darted and weaved and danced. A volunteer watched her eyes carefully for telltale clues. It took about five minutes for the girl to look at three squares coherently enough to ask a question: "Were ... you ... angry?"

⟿

For anyone who watched that television program, the lesson would last forever: a mind is not enough. To express itself and to communicate with others the mind needs a cooperative body.

People afflicted with diseases such as acute cerebral palsy face the constant frustration of disobedient cells. Some of the victims possess magnificent minds: Englishman Stephen Hawking, for example, one of the world's premier theoretical physicists, suffers from spasticity caused by ALS, or "Lou Gehrig's disease." And yet often these people are dismissed as ignorant or even retarded. They have an obvious dissension between mind and body.

A healthy body relies on proper channels from the brain to body parts, as well as a commitment from individual cells to do the will of the head. In a spastic disease or paralysis, somewhere, often in the descending fibers to the cells (The Way Out), communication breaks down. A paraplegic can lie in bed all day and plot how to move her toe, and then *will* to move it with her full mental energy, but if the connection is broken the toe will not move.

In the spiritual Body, The Way Out describes the descending aspect of the Head's channels to each cell. As we have access to God, so does God have access to us. There is a sense — a guarded, mysterious, ineffable sense that the next chapter will explore — in which God relies on bursts of messages from human "nerve fibers" in the world. But there is a blatant, life-preserving, absolute sense in which we individual cells must rely on the messages streaming down from the Head to each of us. One quality affects whether a cell will do its job effectively: a willingness to follow the messages from the Head. Only the Head can determine the needs of the whole Body. And obedience alone determines our individual usefulness in Christ's Body.

The Body of Christ, like the spastic patient's, can be judged by its disobedient body parts. When Dorothy Sayers made her comment about the church being God's third great humiliation, no doubt she was thinking of the soiled reputation we have given our Head in historical demonstrations of selfishness, greed, intolerance, and spiritual pride. The flaw is not in the Head, to be sure, but the humiliation is there.

God continues to work through blundering human agents. God does not interfere to correct impaired perception or overrule an awkward movement, but limits activity to such flawed representatives as David the murderer and adulterer, Jonah the insubordinate, Peter the traitor, Luther the Jew-baiter, Calvin the executioner. God has taken up people like them—and these five represent some of the best of the lot—into himself. God's Spirit incorporates us into Christ's Body, in which Christ himself remains content to serve as Head. If the Incarnation is a mystery, how much more this?

I have searched the four Gospels to observe how Jesus prepared for the new phase of Headship, and a trend does emerge: during his three years of ministry Jesus increasingly turned his work over to his disciples. At first he did all the healing, exorcising, ministering, and evangelizing. But as the time for his death neared, Jesus concentrated more on training those who would be left behind. A few key events stand out.

"I am sending you out like lambs among wolves," he warned one of the first groups of his followers to go forth on his behalf (see Luke 10:1–24). Thus he began to entrust sacred tasks to a ragtag group of six dozen novices. Despite the stern warnings, the seventy-two met with great success on their mission. "Lord, even the demons submit to us in your name," they reported exuberantly. Jesus responded with unparalleled enthusiasm—I know of no other scene that shows him so full of joy. He burst into prayer and then pronounced these ringing words, "For I tell you that many prophets and kings wanted to see what you see but did not see it, and to hear what you hear but did not hear it." The work of the kingdom had advanced, but this time while Jesus himself was serving in an indirect role. His exclamation underscored the significance of that step of progress.

Later, at the very end of his earthly life, Jesus took a further step: he turned over the entire mission. The transfer occurred in a gathering, The Last Supper, that has no equal in the New Testament for its emotional intensity. "I confer on you a kingdom, just as my Father conferred one on me," Jesus said that night (Luke 22:29). From that point on, he has mainly relied on The Way Out, the indirect way of working through human "cells."

Incredibly, God now depends on us to do his will in the world, allowing us to do awkwardly and sluggishly what could otherwise be done perfectly and instantaneously. In a manner full of mystery, Christ has put himself at our mercy; our lack of faith can paralyze his action.* Clearly, he seems to prefer delegating authority to his creatures.

Errors inevitably creep in — spastic movements, if you will. It cannot be easy for Omnipotence to endure the humiliation we bring on. (Is there a divine counterpart to the frustration a paraplegic feels?) But before we become too concerned about what the church has dragged God through, we should remember that the great, soaring Pauline words about the church — Body of Christ, Bride of Christ, Temple of God — were addressed to actual, visible, and decidedly sinful congregations. God welcomes sinful human beings as his children; likewise, Christ depends on flawed members to accomplish the work of his Body.

⊸

Even if the mind-body connection is severed completely, utterly eliminating The Way Out, death does not always follow. Surprisingly, animals can stay alive and function at some level with their

---

*"He could not do any miracles there, except lay his hands on a few sick people and heal them. And he was amazed at their lack of faith" (Mark 6:5–6).

higher brains removed. The lower cells, in this event, do not follow voluntary orders, but merely respond to localized instincts. Sir Charles Sherrington studied a brainless frog swimming easily across a pond. You can, he said, get the impression the injury is trivial until you examine the behavior closely and see that the frog is swimming randomly, with no purpose, just kicking its legs in reflexive patterns. There can be no "purpose" with a brain removed.

Higher animals are more affected by the removal of a brain. A decerebrated dog stands in a rigid, statuesque posture. Although it can be propped up on all fours, like a stuffed animal, it cannot adjust its stance to maintain balance and will topple over at the slightest touch.

Human beings also may experience an interruption in the links between brain and body. One test for damage to those channels is simple: a gentle tap on the knee with that ubiquitous rubber hammer. Normally that tap, as we all know, brings on a reflex response from the patellar tendon. When the hammer blow reaches the tendon, the reflex loop has the momentary impression that the knee is bending. In quick response, the *local* neurons (the message reaches the higher brain only later) tighten the muscle that straightens the knee. In normal life, that reflex keeps us from falling if we stumble.

However, if a spinal injury has destroyed the connection between a person's brain and leg, a tap with a hammer will produce a radically different reflex, and the doctor who taps the hammer will need fast reflexes of his own. The patient's muscles will jerk violently, his leg shooting forward with enormous force. It may then flail back and forth, the muscles in spasm.

Such leg muscles and tendons are healthy — they are exhibiting their power spectacularly — but have lost contact with higher orders from the head. The brain normally constrains involuntary reflexes (in Sherrington's words it "has a civilizing influence on primitive parts"). When this vital pathway is severed, the body part can still act, but autonomously, disconnectedly, irrationally, over-reacting to local parts of the body.

Analogies to the spiritual Body apply only partially, for dysfunction there never results from brain damage. But many nervous disorders — cerebral palsy, for example — occur when synaptic channels below the level of the brain somehow clog up. Poisons, such as cocaine, botulinus, and atropine, can also jam the chemical transmission across synapses.

We have a theological word for such poisons in the Body: sin. Sin steals into the intimate channel between Head and member, interrupting communication and separating the cell from the higher authority that directs and coordinates its actions. The usefulness of a single cell requires unimpeded communication from above and an obedient response from below.

The apostle Paul, master of metaphor, gives a precise description of a person suffering from a sort of disconnection, in his letter to the Colossians. The person he describes had erred by legalistically judging other members of the Body; he had focused on his neighboring cells rather than on receiving individual orders from the Head. "Such a person goes into great detail about what he has seen, and his unspiritual mind puffs him up with idle notions. He has lost connection with the Head, from whom the whole body, supported and held together by its ligaments and sinews, grows as God causes it to grow" (2:18–19). Once severed, new pathways linking the mind and body do not reestablish themselves easily.

⟶

The normal brain assigns a specific area to govern each finger, each toe, each significant body part. If, for instance, the assigned area represents my ring finger, that portion of the brain will contain all the associations of my finger. Can it play the guitar? Steady my hand in writing? Does it bear a scar from a prior injury? The brain stores these memories and abilities. If my finger is used prominently, as in playing the guitar, the brain will have an increasing richness of association with the finger.

As a surgeon, I sometimes get involved in disrupting these associative pathways and trying to establish new ones. For example, we give some leprosy patients new eyebrows (for cosmetic purposes) by cutting a swatch of hairy scalp and tunneling it under the forehead to the eyebrow area. It comes still attached to the scalp's original nerve and blood supply, and so the patient's new eyebrow still "feels like" part of his scalp. If a fly crawls across the transplanted eyebrow, the patient will likely respond by slapping his crown.

Or, in a tendon transfer procedure I may move a healthy tendon from the ring finger to replace a weak or useless one on the thumb. To the recuperating patient, orders from the brain still feel like the ring finger should respond. "Move your thumb," I will say, and nothing happens. The patient just stares at his hand. "Now move your ring finger," I say, and the thumb springs forward.

Over time, the patient must repattern his or her brain to interpret the sensation of ring finger motion as activity by the thumb. It can take months to reestablish smooth patterns, and many patients over the age of forty never fully adjust to the change.

The image of thumb cells struggling to receive a strange new set of orders from the head helps in visualizing Paul's injunction to be transformed "by the renewing of your mind." He urged fellow-members, cells in Christ's Body, to learn God's "good, pleasing and perfect will" (Romans 12:2).

Elsewhere, Paul drew specific applications of how God's will should express itself in our lives. He exhorted the Philippians to "Let this *mind* be in you which was also in Christ Jesus" (2:5 KJV), and then defined what the mind or attitude should be:

Who, being in very nature God,
> did not consider equality with God
>> something to be grasped,
but made himself nothing,
> taking the very nature of a servant,
> being made in human likeness.
And being found in appearance as a man,
> he humbled himself
> and became obedient to death —
>> even death on a cross! (vv. 6–8 NIV)

I envision this renewing process as the intensive effort to develop a smooth, steady stream of transmission between the cell and its Head, both on ascending and descending fibers. By examining the image or model set down by Christ, and by forming a relationship with him, I am, in fact, learning the mind of Christ. I have seen the biological process at work in hundreds of my patients, and the spiritual process in many committed Christians.

Some Christians are now rediscovering ancient disciplines of faith. In such acts as meditation, fasting, prayer, simple living, worship, and celebration, we can build proper communication between ourselves and the Head. Even the simple practice of repeating prayers from the Book of Common Prayer can help discipline the mind. In neurophysiology as well as spirituality, repeated acts of obedience strengthen the connections. A concert pianist does not consciously think through the motions involved for each finger to strike a note. Rather, a performer's mind dwells on mood and timing and interpretation; the fingers follow pathways laid down through hours of practice long before.

Just as musicians and athletes develop skill through the repeated exercise of the brain-to-cells pathways, members of Christ's Body can develop an ever-increasing richness of association between themselves and the Head. For the beginning Christian, the process of learning Christ's mind may seem mechanical and ungainly. The Christian "walk," as does the infant's walk, begins with hundreds of false starts and stumbles and missteps. (Paul alludes to "another law at work in the members of my body, waging war against the law of my mind" [Romans 7:23].) Gradually, though, those muscles and joints in knee and leg and foot learn to cooperate together so concertedly that the infant runs across the room without giving a single conscious thought to the process. Each attempt at a new skill or a sport will begin in a fumbling, error-prone way until movements become fluid and dependable. Daily, we adults take these motions for granted unless we are shocked into gratitude by someone afflicted with paraplegia or cerebral palsy.

⌐⌐.

On long walks outdoors, I have been watching a pair of orchard orioles build their nest. The birds are young, and this is undoubtedly their first nest. Just a few branches away hangs another nest, built last year by older orioles; it has survived a winter storm that tore branches from the tree. Yet these young birds never go over to inspect the old nest or study it for design innovations. They know exactly what to do. They neglect eating in the urgency of their task.

First they spend time selecting the best location. They need a branch with a well-spaced fork on which to weave the nest. The branch must be so thin as to droop a little from the mere weight of the leaves, in order to protect the nest from squirrels. Foliage must surround the site to conceal the young from hawks and other predators flying high above.

Once a prime location is agreed upon, the birds search for individual blades of grass, of one type only, that must conform to a certain length and consistency. One of the birds stands with a foot perched on each branch of the fork. It holds a blade of grass under one foot against the twig. Then, using only its beak, it ties a half-hitch knot around that twig, leaving a long end dangling. After flying away for another blade, it ties a half-hitch on the other twig, pulling the blades under its body. Then it plaits other hanging strands into a thick cable. The nest itself will swing between these cables. After several days of selecting, weaving, plaiting, and wattling, the two birds will have a neat, spherical home, strong enough to withstand gale-force winds.

Inside my house, at the same time, my wife is knitting a pullover sweater for me. I can see her through a window. She is a good knitter, and I will wear the sweater with pride. The wool demanded the skill and experience of shepherds and shearers and spinners and dyers. Margaret keeps glancing down at a printed pattern that combines the artistry and calculations of master knitters. Reading those instructions requires education, and following them employs a skill she has learned over the years. The sweater will finally emerge, a result of the shared intelligence of many brains over many years. Given a live sheep and told to create a sweater with no outside help, my wife would probably fail.

I know that I, even with full concentration and the manual dexterity developed in years of surgery, cannot weave strands of grass into a hollow globe that will cling to a branch in a storm. I tried it once, and the result fell apart, limp and useless. Yet I have ten fingers while an oriole has only a beak and feet.

Instinct is the key, of course.* A kindred species, the bunting, follows another imprinted code that guides it across the Gulf of Mexico to a new land five hundred miles away. I have watched migrating birds take off. They sit on a reed in the swamp and look out across an expanse of water that must appear endless. Fortunately the birds, unencumbered by reason, take off every time. Their wisdom predates the egg they came from.

I sometimes think of the bunting and the oriole as I struggle with spiritual decisions. Messages from God reach me along the pathways of The Way Out. With my reason, even as I contemplate what the Bible says, I can easily rationalize my way to other conclusions. The commands are hard; they require love and sacrifice and compassion and purity whereas I have excuses that make those seem unattainable for me at any moment.

At such times, as my own selfishness and pride surge up, I need a force more dependable than reason. Just such a force comes built into each of us: the conscience or subconscious, a law written in our hearts (see Romans 2:15). This instinctive sense of our responsibility to God can be encouraged and nurtured by the disciplines of faith. Hiding God's Word in my heart and meditating on it help to strengthen this force and thus to renew my mind.

---

*But how blithely we dismiss phenomena as "mere instinct"! A genetic code built that oriole's brain, cell by cell, directing neurons to line up with appropriate synapses so that the arrangement would inevitably, one day, direct its feet and beak to accomplish these intricate maneuvers. Even the wisdom of what grass to select and what site to choose was included in the instructions of the genetic code that preceded the brain. The oriole's brain is the product of the need for thought, but a prior thought anticipated the requirements of that brain and built in a genetic code that would instruct all the bird's cells to cooperate obediently, without debating the commands.

When the moment of critical choice arrives, there is often little chance for conscious reflection, and all that has gone before enters into the result. I think of those tiny birds, the oriole and the bunting, and ask that in renewing my mind God would imprint instructions into me as if they were put there genetically. I ask for an uninterrupted flow of messages and for an obedient response.

# Chapter 13

# THE WAY IN

*I was a stricken deer that left the herd*
*Long since; with many an arrow deep infixed*
*My panting side was charged, when I withdrew*
*To seek a tranquil death in distant shades.*
*There was I found by One Who had Himself*
*Been hurt by the archers. In His side He bore,*
*And in His hands and feet, the cruel scars.*
*With gentle force soliciting the darts,*
*He drew them forth, and healed, and bade me live.*

William Cowper, *The Task*

A t a precise time in each of our lives, normally around the age
of twelve months, a profound change takes place. A person's
perception of the world moves from a predominant reliance on
touch to a reliance on sight. Touch precedes and teaches sight, until
the sight cells gain dependable notions of shape and distance and
solidness. This learning process occurs in everyone — that is, everyone except the blind.

Sightless people never make the transition unless their sight
somehow is restored. And early in this century that dramatic event
occurred often, thanks to the just-perfected miracle of cataract

surgery. People blind from birth, who had always lived by a tactile conception of the world, suddenly could see. When their eyes opened, they encountered a world far different from what they had imagined. (In some cases of long-term blindness central vision had atrophied, but peripheral vision gave these patients a first look at the world).

One prescient author, Marius von Senden, sensed an unrepeatable opportunity to observe adults coming to terms with a perceptual revolution that most of us experience as inarticulate infants. He recorded what took place among sixty-six patients in his startling book *Space and Sight.*

Basic notions of space, motion, and shape are incomprehensible to the newly sighted, von Senden concluded. For example, sighted people have learned certain assumptions about spatial distance. A building "within sight" is nearby, within walking distance; a destination that requires a bus, train, or plane is obviously farther away. The sightless, in contrast, judge distance by its effect on their muscle tension. To them, reaching a building a mile away requires the taking of many steps, but a destination involving a train, bus, or plane ride seems nearby because getting there uses little muscle tension.

Once these patients could see, a bewildering world of size and perspective confronted them. Previously they had a firm conception of size: an orange was about the size of a cupped hand, a face two hand-widths. In a shocking reversal, after surgery none of these rules applied. "How big is your mother?" a researcher asked a sixteen-year-old girl. The girl held her index fingers a few inches apart, the same distance she had estimated for the size of a book. Her mother, standing across the room, took up about that much of her field of vision. And the sun? Obviously, it was about the size of a dime — who could believe the sun was larger than the earth?

Gradually, over a period of months these patients had to learn the meaning of space, distance, and perspective. Vertical distances remained unfathomable for a long time, for the newly sighted had no prior conception of space beyond what they could feel by touch. Skyscrapers and trees loomed high, but how could they gauge height over ten feet, the height reachable with a cane? One patient, observing some interesting activity on the street below, stepped off the balcony of a tall apartment building and was killed. A plane in the sky, or an elevator that moved them with no muscular effort were mysteries defying explanation.

The blind also had learned motion in terms of muscle changes and could not readily perceive it with their eyes alone. A doctor waved his hand in front of the face of an eight-year-old boy. "Can you see it is moving?" he asked. The boy, confused, stared intently straight ahead. He "saw" interludes of light and darkness, but his eyes made no attempt to follow the moving hand. "He was clearly trying to grasp the meaning of this phrase [moving] in relation to the gesture," reported the doctor, "but without success. His eye failed to follow the long swinging motions of the hand." Finally, allowed to touch the hand, the boy cried out joyfully, "It's moving!"

Even common shapes proved totally indecipherable to those who had known the world only through touch. A researcher arranged a row of fruit on a table before a woman patient; the row corresponded exactly to the row of six different fruits before him. "Pick this up," he said, selecting an apple from his row. The patient stared intently at the objects before her, trying her best to distinguish the six shapes visually. Finally, hesitantly, she reached down only to choose a plum — easily one-sixth the size of the apple. When allowed to touch the researcher's apple, she instantly succeeded in choosing an apple, but the strange world of different sizes, confusing colors, and blurry shapes was simply too much to take in visually.

An alert twenty-year-old-patient usually required four intensive weeks of training to learn to distinguish visually between round, square, and triangular shapes. One patient mistook an apple for a key, a loaf of bread for a hand. Another, grasping for some clue to please the teacher, seized on color. She learned a matchbox was yellow; from then on everything yellow she called a matchbox whether it was an apple, a banana, or a book jacket.

If it took weeks of trial and error to differentiate a circle from a square, imagine the obstacles to recognizing just one face. A newly sighted husband required four months of practice to distinguish his wife's face from anyone else's, unless she spoke or he could touch the tiniest patch of her cheek.

One young girl played with a pet cat for twenty-one days, four hours each day. Then, upon seeing a hen in a garden she squealed with delight, "My cat!" After all, the thing was small and somewhat gray and it moved. The same girl mistook a bookcase for a stove and called a fountain a tree "because it is big and round." The simplest sights provoked great alarm in her: a black coat on the floor looked like the mouth of a well, a column of smoke from the chimney appeared to crack the sky in two, and the spots on her dog Muffy seemed like holes through him.

"How is it that I now find myself less happy than before?" one distraught woman wailed in the midst of her training. "Everything that I see causes me a disagreeable emotion. Oh, I was much more at ease in my blindness!" She could not cope with a baffling world in which she was expected to distinguish between a knife, spoon, and fork without touching them. (Eventually, to her pleasure, she went blind again.) Virtually all patients muddled through such despondent periods for a time. They were being asked to relearn the world, like persons abruptly deposited on another planet where the laws of physics do not apply.

The newly sighted had even more difficulty mastering such advanced concepts as spatial wholeness, or two-dimensional depth perception (a quality that stumped artists until five centuries ago). After receiving sight a girl realized she had never conceived of her dog as a whole, made up of a head, ears, and legs joined together to make one animal. Like the proverbial blind men feeling an elephant, she had never touched all the parts at once and thus had not pictured the dog as a whole being.

In order to explain depth perception, the researchers led patients to heights. A landscape held no meaning for them at first. A band of green (forest) or a strip of blue (river) gave no clues to the newly sighted about actual identity. They had never touched anything so faraway; how could they comprehend it? It took even more months of effort to train such patients to recognize objects from paintings or photographs. The image of a face, hard enough to distinguish in flesh and blood, did not transfer well when pressed onto a two-dimensional square of light and shadow.

Eventually, of course, most of these people adjusted to the world of light and color and shape and size, and discovered levels of perception and beauty that previously had eluded them. But the process involved great anxiety in every case. For months, sometimes years, the patients shut their eyes for critical maneuvers, such as walking around a cluttered part of a house near a staircase. The new world had betrayed them; it was not at all what they had expected. Or, more accurately, their other senses had betrayed them by giving them an incomplete conception of what the world is like.*

---

* Brain researchers have further demonstrated that our picture of the world depends largely on all sensory input from the environment we are exposed to. Kittens raised in boxes painted with horizontal stripes do not even notice vertical stripes at first: their brain cells

━

Within the analogy of this book, von Senden's accounts illustrate how the brain, shut off in its ivory box from the actual stuff of matter, must interpret reality based on partial clues from the rest of the body. When a condition such as blindness restricts those clues, the entire body is affected.

I hasten to admit that the perception analogy cannot be pushed too far. The Mind or Head of this Body is not dependent on or limited by perceptions gained through the other members. God's knowledge encompasses all and does not need our frail fibers to increase in wisdom. Yet in another sense, because of the awesome fact of God's self-limitation, the analogy of the lonely mind does apply.

We have seen already that God self-limits activity (The Way Out) by relying primarily on bumbling human agents. In ways beyond our comprehension God also has chosen to make Christ's presence on earth dependent on The Way In, the communication from the members, or cells, of his Body.

Of all the marvelous aspects of the human body, I know of no greater wonder than that every one of the hundred trillion cells in my body has access to the brain. Many cells, such as those used in sight, have direct neuronal connections; others have channels immediately available to them to report in on their needs or current states. And in the Body of Christ, I know of no greater wonder than that each one of us has direct contact with Christ himself, the Head. Amazingly, Christ listens to our input, considers our requests, and

---

have not yet developed a category of "verticalness." And, bizarrely, kittens raised in a painted cylinder with constantly rotating sides can not readily cope when exposed to a nonmoving environment. They start spinning in circles to duplicate the effect of the cylinder!

quite literally uses that information to influence his direction of activities in the world. "The prayer of a righteous man is powerful and effective" (James 5:16).

Through us who serve as hands and ears and eyes and pain cells, God stays "in touch with" this world and the people in it. God's activity takes into account the communication we supply. There is also a "benefit" for God, so to speak. In varied and striking phrases, the Bible expresses the awesome truth that God takes pleasure in the church: we are "peculiar treasures," "a pleasing aroma," "gifts that he delights in." And more than thirty times the New Testament reminds us that we are Christ's Body, joined to him so fully that what happens to us happens to him as well. As astounding as it may seem, the conclusion is inescapable: God wants fellowship with us and longs for communication from the Body: The Way In. God created us in order to receive our love.

Do we somehow miss the revolution that has taken place in the universe? In ancient religions, the actions of the gods in the heavens above were believed to affect the earth below. Gods cavorting in the skies brought forth rain and earthquakes and thunderbolts. Like kids dropping rocks off highway bridges onto the cars below, they dropped judgment and cataclysm onto the earth. Now Christ reverses the ancient Hermetic formula: "As above, so below," becomes "As below, so above." Human action, such as prayer, affects heaven. The conversion of one sinner causes all of heaven to rejoice.

Prayer is the central channel, of course, a way for us to "participate in the dignity of causation," in Pascal's phrase. Prayer itself can be a full-time occupation; for centuries cloistered mystics have adopted it as that. Again and again, so often that writers unavoidably repeat the same words, the Bible reminds us in the strongest terms that God hears our prayers. Incredibly, it seems that God yearns for contact with the disparate members of the Body. The lack of such contact and the absence of human faith limit the spiritual Body as surely as the lack of a sense like sight limits the entire physical body.

⟵

The intimacy, or open channel, we now have with God traces back to the reconciliation won for us by Christ. In the Incarnation God took on a role like that of a "cell," stepping into creation. And throughout his time on earth Jesus felt the need to slip away and commune with the Father. God talking to God — the mystery of the Trinity. By his example the Son of God showed us the vital pattern of sending a ceaseless stream of communication to the Father.

In his reflections on the Incarnation, the author of Hebrews tied together in three stages the progression of intimacy between God and people: the Old Testament approach to God through a priest, Christ's personal visitation, and the more intimate Body that resulted. He concluded, "For we do not have a high priest who is unable to sympathize with our weaknesses, but we have one who has been tempted in every way, just as we are — yet was without sin. Let us then approach the throne of grace with confidence, so that we may receive mercy and find grace to help us in our time of need" (4:15–16).

Later, that same book hints at profound truths that we cannot fully understand: Jesus "learned obedience from what he suffered," Hebrews says (5:8). It is a disquieting concept, to say the least, that God, omniscient and self-complete, learned through suffering. And yet the Incarnation was a form of learning, a direct experience of confinement within matter. Jesus felt the joy of a wedding and the grief of a funeral; the love and then betrayal of close friends; and finally the lash of a whip and the sting of spittle.

Today, God's tendrils of activity in this world of matter mainly reach out through members of Christ's Body. And, most significantly, because of the Incarnation God hears our prayers in a new way, the Son having lived here and having prayed himself. We now have a high priest who is able to sympathize with our weakness ... let us then approach him with confidence.

The Body of Christ has a clear advantage over the physical body, for in it the Head remains totally accessible and receptive to the faintest communication from an extremity. The Head never needs to be awakened or enlightened. No lack of wisdom or power limits the activity of God on earth. Rather, the only limitation is the participation of member cells in relating to the Head. Individual Christians need only learn to refer every emotion, every action, every experience of their lives to God.

David is an example of a flawed human, a murderer and an adulterer. Nevertheless, he found favor with God, so much so that he was called "a man after God's own heart." Reading the poems attributed to him, I can see why David deserved that appellation. His poetry contains anger and despair, but also joy and praise; helplessness and sorrow, but also strength and confidence; pain and vengeance, but also humility and love. Blatantly contradictory moods butt up against each other. His emotions welter. David hid nothing from God, neither the bad nor the good. That, I think, is what God loved. The "cell" named David took God seriously. He gave a daily, sometimes minute-by-minute reporting of every situation in his life, and expected — sometimes demanded — that God respond to him.*

---

*Many of the Psalms by a variety of authors show this divergent quality. As an example, consider the full range of human response shown in just five psalms, 21–25.

The Way In and The Way Out: both are essential for a healthy body. The entire Body of Christ may be harmed if one part of the Body does not communicate with the Head. If a prophetic cell refuses to discern truly and to warn the rest of the Body, we may all stumble off course. Like von Senden's blind people, we may go through life unaware and uninformed. A silent intercessory cell will surely take its toll. And if one part of the Body becomes insensitive to pain in a finger or a limb, that part will gradually deteriorate.

Through The Way In the cells in the sense organs, extremities, and other vital parts send in a flood of data, informing the head about the condition of cells themselves and the sentient world outside. Likewise, brain cells coordinate a stream of ordered instructions along The Way Out. To walk, we need a "feedback loop" of muscle and joint cells reporting in tone and position and pressure and also receiving instructions on proper movement. Motion requires a dynamic equilibrium of the ascending and descending messages. If The Way In is accurate and complete, and the cells receiving messages along The Way Out are obedient and responsive, only then will the body work.

---

One scene more than any other symbolizes for me the role of the head in the human body, and of the Head in the spiritual Body. It involves a blind person, a patient I will call José.

José's body had suffered much damage from leprosy by the time he came from Puerto Rico to Carville for treatment. His insensitivity to touch was so great that, when blindfolded, he could not even detect whether someone had entered the room and held his hand. Touch cells and pain cells had fallen silent. As a result, scars and ulcers covered his hands, face, and feet, bearing mute witness to the unintentional abuse his body had endured without any sensation of pain. Mere stubs on his hands marked where fingers used to be.

Because pain cells in his eyes no longer alerted him when to blink, gradually José's eyes dried out. That condition, aggravated by severe cataracts and glaucoma, soon made him blind. My wife Margaret (who is an eye surgeon) told him surgery might correct the cataract problem and restore some vision, but she could not operate until inflammation of the iris went away. A terrible misfortune cut off José's last link with the outside world. In a desperate attempt to arrest the sulfone-resistant leprosy, doctors tried treating him with a new drug, and José had a rare allergic reaction. He lost his hearing.

Thus, at the age of forty-five José lost all contact with the world. He could not see, nor hear if a person spoke. Unlike Helen Keller, he could not even use tactile sign language — the leprosy had dulled his sense of touch. Even his sense of smell had disappeared as the leprosy had invaded the lining of his nose. All his inlets from the world, except taste, had been blocked off. Weeks passed and we watched the effect on José as his mind began to accept the reality that it had lost all meaningful contact with a world of flowers and rivers and islands and people.

José's body responded with a pathetic reflection of what was happening inside: his limbs pulled inward toward his trunk, and he began curling into a fetal position on the bed. He would wake up from sleep and forget where he was. He did not know whether it was day or night, and when he spoke, he did not know if anyone heard or answered. Sometimes he would speak anyway, bellowing because he could not hear the volume, pouring out the inexpressible loneliness of a mind condemned to solitary confinement.

In such a world, thoughts go in circles and spirals, stirring up fears and suspicions. Is not madness the loss of perception of the real world? José's body coiled tighter and tighter on the bed. He was preparing for death in the same posture as his birth. Those of us on the staff would pass his room, pause for a moment at the door, shake our heads, and continue walking. What could we do?

Margaret faithfully visited José. Unable to bear watching this otherwise healthy man self-destruct, she felt she must attempt some kind of radical treatment to restore at least part of his sight. She waited impatiently for the infection in his eye to improve enough to schedule surgery.

Trying to follow government rules, Margaret faced a nearly insurmountable problem. Naturally, she must obtain "informed consent" forms for the surgery. But who would sign for José? No one could penetrate through his isolation even to ask him for permission to help. After painstaking research, the hospital staff finally located a sister in Puerto Rico, and the police department there visited her with a surgery release form. The illiterate sister marked an X on a paper, and surgery was scheduled at last, with faint hopes for success.

José, of course, did not comprehend what was happening as he was moved to a stretcher and wheeled to the operating room. He lay passive throughout the eye surgery. After a two-hour procedure, he was bandaged and sent back to his room to wait.

Margaret removed the bandages a few days later, an experience she will never forget. Although José had sensed some gross movement, and had probably reasoned someone was trying to help him, nothing had prepared him for what actually did happen. He got use of one eye back and could see again. As his eye struggled against the bright light and slowly focused on the medical people gathered around the bed, the face that had not smiled in months cracked into a huge, toothless grin. Contact had been restored.

During that long period of isolation, José's brain had floated intact inside his skull, complete with memory, emotions, and instructions for directing his body. But it stayed useless because The Way In had been blocked.

I think of José when I think of what God endures by electing to serve as Head for a Body comprised of human beings. The most magnificent organ in the body can lie isolated and useless without the cooperation of informing senses and obedient cells. God chose that very position, working not despite or in opposition to us, but through us. That is the humiliation.

But there is also a triumph, and it comes to light when communication is restored. When José's sensory channels were reestablished, suddenly all that had been isolated and useless was free to express itself to the world outside. José made it known to us that he wanted his wheelchair parked at the door to his room all day long. He would sit there quietly, every few seconds glancing up and down the long corridors of the leprosarium. When he saw another person coming, his face would break into that irrepressible smile.

Today, José has contact with the world. He insists on coming to our small church every Sunday, even though he can hear nothing of the service. With stubby fingers, he can barely grasp the control knob of his electric wheelchair, and his narrow tunnel vision causes him to bump into objects up and down the long corridors. But still he comes, regardless of the weather outside. Other attenders have learned to greet him by stooping down, putting their faces directly in front of his, and waving. José's wonderful smile invariably breaks out, and sometimes his bellowing laugh. Although he cannot see well, and cannot hear or feel at all, somehow he can sense the fellowship of that church. It is enough for him.

José's mind is no longer isolated and alone, but united with the other cells in his body. All that is in his powerful brain now has an outlet to the rest of us outside. He can express the image that had been sealed inside.

# SPIRIT

# Chapter 14

# BREATH

*When a prospector first strikes oil there is often a violent erup-*
*tion of the oil which sometimes bursts into flames and burns for*
*many days before it is brought under control. Later on there will*
*be no room for such displays. The oil will all be pumped through*
*pipes and refineries to its destination, and a desire to go back to the*
*early fireworks will be rightly regarded as infantile. But the early*
*displays did at least prove something; they proved that oil was*
*there, and without this all the pipes and refineries in the world*
*are merely futile.*

Lesslie Newbigin

What tree rivals the banyan in extravagance? It drops roots not only from its trunk but also from its branches, dozens and soon hundreds of thewy stalks wending toward the ground to sprout root systems of their own. Uninterrupted, a banyan tree will grow forever, renewing itself in the radial extremities even as the inner core dies of old age. A single tree may cover acres of land, becoming a self-perpetuating forest spacious enough to shelter a full-scale bazaar (its name comes from the Hindi word *banian*: a caste of merchants).

You can see a majestic example of a banyan in Calcutta today, preserved in the Botanical Gardens. The Great Banyan Tree there covers ground 1,251 feet in circumference. It looks like a giant, bushy tent supported by colonnades of wooden poles. Somewhere in the middle of that velutinous thicket of trunks and branches the central trunk began growing two hundred years ago. After sustaining damage from a fungus and a cyclone the inner core was finally removed in 1925, but the outer tree grows on.

For a child who likes climbing and swinging from vines, the banyan tree provides endless amusement. As a six year old, I found myself free to explore one for several days when my parents camped under a banyan during a missionary venture. As they went about their medical and spiritual work, my sister and I played Swiss Family Robinson inside the great tree. The stalks that fell like stalactites from upper branches made for ideal climbing. Even better, some helpful people had looped and knotted various vines to form low swings and high swings and trapezes.

I was swinging on one such loop through a corridor within the tree, calling on my sister to push me higher and higher. As the height of my arc increased, I felt another loop of tendril brush against the back of my neck on my back-swing. I ducked to avoid it, but failed to duck again as the swing lurched into its downward descent. The high loop caught right under my chin and held me by the throat. The swing abruptly stopped. Fortunately, my main weight still rested on the seat, but my windpipe was totally clamped shut by the vine and I could not breathe or speak or scream. I hung suspended there like a puppet tangled in its wires. My sister, on the ground, made a few frantic efforts to pull me off, and then must have run for help.

I woke up sometime later with my mother stooping over my camp cot pleading with me to speak to her. When I said her name, she burst into tears. She had feared brain damage, and my first word came as a welcome relief to her.

Other than a sore neck and a slight skin abrasion resembling a rope burn, I carried no physical scars from the experience, but for many years I harbored a primitive terror of breathlessness. Anything that covered my mouth and nose, even immersion in water, brought back that terror, and I would fight as if for my life. I learned starkly that lack of breath does not feel like anesthesia or sleep; it is like death.

Since that afternoon in the banyan tree, I have seen many medical situations that confirm the terror I felt that day. Emergencies of all types produce panic: heart attack victims clutch their chests; people with brain damage may thrash violently; soldiers in war gape, unbelieving, at a severed limb. But I know of no human experience that produces such a spasm of uncontrolled panic as does breathlessness.

We have all seen film clips of the marathon runner staggering across the finish line with mouth agape, his ribs heaving, his head bobbing like a rooster's, his whole body jerking in a bellows motion until gradually the oxygen floods in and the emergency subsides. Yet the marathoner feels no panic, for he has planned to end the race in a critical oxygen debt. His gestures underplay those of a person who *must* have oxygen: eyes bulge, hands grasp frantically at empty air, and the heart races. Oxygen shortage kicks into motion a vicious cycle: the accelerated heartbeat, trying to distribute faster what oxygen is there, consumes energy itself and requires even more oxygen. The downward spiral begins.

We are, all of us, five minutes from death. Life depends on our ability to stay in contact with the vital element of oxygen around us. When deprived of air for any length of time, the patient actually turns blue, first around the fingernails, tongue, and lips, projecting the internal drama onto the visible screen of skin. High school biology students learn what causes the color shift: blue blood has not gotten the supply of oxygen from the lungs that normally turns it a rich scarlet. The animal kingdom lives in utter dependence on this one element, oxygen.

Some lower animals' devices for gathering oxygen are inexpressibly beautiful: the jewel-like fronds of marine worms, the fluted gills of tropical fish, the brilliant orange skirt of a flame scallop. Our own lungs come down on the side of function, not form, but they work well enough to make an engineer drool. The beginning medical student who first cuts into a corpse's torso gets graphic evidence of the lungs' importance. He has studied the vital heart and kidneys and pancreas. But the lungs!* They crowd all the rest, spilling into every crevice and cranny. When air is pumped in to simulate breathing, they seem to want to burst out of the chest cavity.

Bronchial tubes from the throat bisect, narrow down, divide again, and fan into a tree of tubes that culminate in three hundred million sacs called alveoli. The sacs, only one cell thick, are caught like dewdrops in a spider web of blood vessels that channel blood around the alveoli for the all-important oxygen transfer. The folds and convolutions of the lungs result in a surface area forty

---

*The medical student is in for another shock when he compares lungs of different patients. The lungs of a non-smoker from the country have a gorgeous pink sheen of health. Tiny blood vessels show clearly against their light background. In dramatic contrast, the lungs of a city-dwelling smoker are dull charcoal in color, almost as dark as those of a coal miner. Perhaps if the skin on our chest were transparent membrane like a tropical fish's so that every person could see for himself that contrast, as well as the fungoid ugliness of lung cancer, our society might undergo some major changes.

times larger than the skin's, an area large enough to carpet a small apartment.*

We need the space. On an average day our lungs move enough air in and out to fill a medium-size room or blow up several thousand party balloons. Each breath sucks in about a pint of air, and if we don't think about it we take around fifteen breaths a minute. Any slight change, such as going up stairs or running for a bus, can double the capacity of air per breath and also double the intake frequency. Receptor centers scattered around the body constantly take oxygen and carbon dioxide measurements to determine the ideal rate. The entire process continues uninterrupted during sleep, without conscious control, or we would die. And the utilitarian body makes us borrow the same air flow system for such acts as speaking, singing, laughing, sighing, and whistling.

My own love affair with breath began after my young body hung from the banyan tree. I breathed with even more gratitude after I studied the mechanisms involved. Since then, I have watched a whole series of patients live out the drama of breathing.

Shortly after arriving in India as a doctor, I received two telephone calls on the same day, one from Calcutta and one from London. Both concerned the medical predicament of a young polo player in Calcutta. He was British, the only son of a wealthy lord,

---

* We could, theoretically, carry around sufficient oxygen dissolved in blood plasma and avoid red cells entirely — one icefish in the Antarctic lies around in 34° F water with his huge mouth open gulping in oxygen for his blood plasma, with no red cells at all. But a human so outfitted would need seventy-five gallons of plasma and would likely resemble a jellyfish with four floppy limbs and a head attached. Even so, the dissolved oxygen would only suffice for two and a half seconds; a long sneeze would probably prove fatal. Fortunately, a complex molecule called hemoglobin permits twenty times as much oxygen to be ferried around in our blood. The chemical molecule looks like this, $C_{3032}$ $H_{4812}$ $N_{780}$ $Fe_4$ $O_{872}$ $S_{12}$, and gives blood its characteristic red color. In all, 9,508 atoms hook up in intricate formation around four crucial atoms of iron. Hemoglobin grabs passing oxygen atoms like a magnet, and the red cells' biconcave shape assures the maximum exposure to oxygen in the lungs. Each red cell carries 280,000,000 hemoglobin molecules.

and had come to Calcutta to learn and practice international banking on behalf of his father's global network of banks. The doctors in Calcutta and his relatives in England urged me to take the very next flight to Calcutta to examine him, because the day after a strenuous polo match he had become suddenly paralyzed with poliomyelitis.

Over the staticky phone line I shouted instructions for the hospital to prepare an iron lung and also to perform a tracheostomy, if he developed breathing difficulties, to prevent fluid buildup in his throat. Then I dashed to the Madras airport to catch the night flight. When I arrived in Calcutta, a car sped me to his hospital bedside.

I have a lasting impression of the figure I found inside that hospital room. A life of good nutrition and much leisure time on the rugby and polo fields had given the young man a superb physique. He was large in stature, and his arm and leg muscles bulged even in repose. All four limbs and trunk, however, were paralyzed. He had built up an enormous lung capacity, now virtually useless on its own, so useless he had been placed inside the iron lung. The machine worked on a bellows principle, pushing his chest in and out in order to force respiration.

The cruel irony of the scene struck me: that marvelous body shoved inside an ugly metal cylinder that noisily forced air in and out of his lungs. I thought briefly of a series of sculptures I had seen, *The Captives*, by Michelangelo. In these works magnificent bodies seem trapped in marble despite their efforts to free themselves. Now before me, this man's Herculean body lay locked in steel. Nurses told me he had felt symptoms of "influenza" on Friday, but had gone ahead with a polo match on Saturday in order not to disappoint his teammates. Exertion at the onset of polio can prove deadly.

To my dismay, I learned that the hospital had not performed the tracheostomy, so I immediately ordered up an anesthetist. I worried about the fluid that can collect when muscles for coughing or clearing the throat no longer operate. I explained to the young athlete what we planned to do. An aide who stood beside him assured me that money was no object and we should attempt whatever might help. The young man responded, just two sentences. He could only say one word per breath, and that with great effort. Every sound came in a clicking, wheezing, almost choking expulsion of air. "Give ... me ... breath ..." he said, and paused. I leaned closer to hear him over the rhythmic pumping of the iron lung. And then, "What ... is ... the ... use ... of ... money ... if ... you ... can't ... breathe?" I looked at his face with great sadness.

After reassuring him we would do all we could, I stationed a nurse with a throat suction by him and went downstairs for a cup of coffee and bite of breakfast. The anesthetist had not yet arrived and I, having missed a full night of sleep, sought a little nourishment to improve my concentration. I had not finished my coffee when a nurse came with the news that the patient had died. Evidently, he had regurgitated some fluid which obstructed the flow of oxygen. The suction device could not keep up. His breathing stopped, and with it his life.

⟋

In English we describe breathing as a succession of two acts: inspiration, expiration ... inspire, expire. "I have expired" means I have breathed out, or, in the ultimate sense, I am out of breath and therefore dead. "I have inspired" means I have breathed in; if changed slightly to "I am inspired" it could mean I am filled with an enlivening breath from the artistic muses or, in a religious context, filled with the Holy Spirit. The writers of the Bible claim to have been inspired, or in-breathed.

I have mentioned already the tendency of languages — Greek, Hebrew, German, Latin, and English among them — to fall back on words for "breath" or "wind" to express the mysterious mode of contact between God and man. Thus in the Bible the Greek or Hebrew word for spirit, even when referring to the Spirit of God, is exactly the same word used for biological breathing or even the wind gusts from a storm.

Linguists love to speculate on double meanings, guessing why the ancients borrowed *that* word to express *this* concept. The relationship between breath and spirit is obvious. Jesus referred to one parallel in his conversation with Nicodemus: "The wind blows wherever it pleases. You hear its sound, but you cannot tell where it comes from or where it is going. So it is with everyone born of the Spirit" (John 3:8). An invisible force from far away, whether wind or Spirit, has visible manifestations. A person of faith sitting alongside a dying person would likely notice another relationship. As a dying person breathes his or her very last breath and *expires*, life departs. Although the body remains intact, breath and spirit leave hand in hand.

Books have been written exploring each of these conceptual links, but I will limit my discussion to an aspect of breathing I deal with daily. I must stay close to the biological fact of breath that impressed me first as a six-year-old dangling limply from a tree, and then again as a doctor watching my patients' last few expulsions of life. For me, breath represents the fuel that sustains living matter. Any break in the fuel supply means instant death (the fastest poisons, such as curare and cyanide, work by interrupting the transport and use of oxygen).

Life depends on an organism's ability to relate to its environment. On the desk before me rests a bowl of nuts: walnuts, pecans, cashews, Brazil nuts. They serve as decoration and provide an occasional snack. Each nut has within it the potential to grow into an organism far larger and more impressive than I, but none will do so unless I place it in the environment of soil and water that will stimulate life. Kernels of corn trapped inside a glass jar in our kitchen will not sprout and yield without a similar process.

Animals depend on oxygen for life, but each animal also needs organs specifically adapted to obtain that oxygen from the right environment, either water or air. The earth offers an atmosphere we can relate to, and if our physical bodies leave earth we must somehow reproduce that atmosphere.

I labor the point somewhat because, analogously, our entire faith begins here. We are told in so many words that eternal life cannot consist of mere oxygen and soil and water and nutrients. For eternal life we need contact with a new environment where oxygen will not suffice. Jesus affirms, "I tell you the truth, unless a man is born of water and the Spirit, he cannot enter the kingdom of God. Flesh gives birth to flesh, but the *Spirit gives birth to spirit*" (John 3:5–6). In the alien atmosphere of earth, a person's spiritual nature resembles a clumsy astronaut on the moon who must rely on a link to another oxygen source for his very survival. The breathing process of spiritual life will fail unless we establish correspondence with a spirit like the wind, the Holy Spirit.

"Blessed are those who hunger and thirst for righteousness," said Jesus — a picture comes to my mind of a runner gasping for breath, or an athlete in an iron lung — "for they will be filled" (Matthew 5:6). An Old Testament psalmist used the image of a deer panting for streams of water; "So my soul pants for you, O God," he cried (Psalm 42:1). The Holy Spirit offers the only adequate solution to the "oxygen debt" hinted at in these phrases.

⟋

I must confess a hesitance to write even a paragraph on Spirit, let alone several chapters. I have sympathy for the apocryphal Japanese gentleman cited by Dorothy Sayers who said, "Honorable Father, very good; Honorable Son, very good; but Honorable Bird I do not understand at all." Has any doctrine of our faith become more muddled? The word Spirit itself, taken from a metaphor as common as the air outside, remains nebulous and imprecise. It tends to foster extremism of all kinds and a slide toward mystagogy. As one trained in scientific disciplines, I find it much easier to write of the material world that I can touch and see and experiment with. And yet there is no Christian faith without Spirit. Because God is Spirit, only Spirit can convey the image of God in the church, Christ's Body on earth.

He was there in the original act of creation, the Spirit of God hovering over the waters as matter came into existence. He inspired God's spokesmen through the spiritual droughts and famines of Old Testament history. He anointed Jesus at the beginning of his ministry and was transferred to the apostles when Jesus *breathed* on them (John 20:22). The Spirit is essential, said Jesus, for the new birth required of each one who wishes to enter the kingdom of God.

At Pentecost the Holy Spirit ("with a sound like the blowing of a violent *wind*") dramatically invaded and transformed a tiny band that was to become the church. This event more than anything forced the church leaders to formulate the doctrine of the Trinity and include the Spirit as a separate person within the

Godhead. They could not exclude the Spirit: evidence for him seemed as real and convincing as evidence for another Person whom they had seen and touched.

The Holy Spirit, then, allows the reality of God's own self to establish a presence inside each one of us. God is timeless, but the Spirit becomes for us the present-tense application of God's nature. He is the personalized God, the Go-Between God, in Bishop John Taylor's wonderful phrase. Correspondence with the Spirit keeps us alive in a spiritual environment.

God does not dwell in a temple or tabernacle, or off in the heavens, or even in a physical body in Nazareth, but rather inside us, as vital to our spiritual lives as breath is to our physical lives. In the Spirit we have the indwelling contact point between heaven and earth across which run connections with the sustainer of the universe.

Unfortunately, the breathing response in the spirit is not so instinctive and urgent as that in the physical body. We can get out of breath and yet not sense it. Breath may choke off slowly, unnoticed at first, until a constant state of energy shortage sets in. I saw the physical parallel to this spiritual process in a patient I treated in London.

She came to me—a middle-aged woman, a widow and a hard worker—complaining about her recently noticed tendency to drop things. "My hands tremble," she said, "and just this week two of my best china cups broke when they slipped out of my fingers."

"I must be getting old," she said with a deep sigh and a shaky voice. "I get so tired, and now I can't seem to control my hands or my nervous disposition." In strong terms I told her that fifty was certainly not old, and that I would do my best to locate physical causes for her condition. As she described a variety of symptoms of nervousness, I began to suspect thyrotoxicosis, a disease of the thyroid gland that can cause such problems.

First I checked manually for a thyroid swelling, but found none. When a chest X-ray showed a shadow behind the upper end of her breast bone, I examined her neck again, this time probing with my fingers down into the base of her neck while she swallowed. Indeed there was an obstruction — I felt a rounded lump rise up out of her chest and touch my fingers. It seemed also that her windpipe may have bent over to one side.

Another X-ray of her upper chest revealed that the rounded shadow had compressed her windpipe, constricting it severely. I asked, "Don't you have trouble breathing?"

"No, not at all," she replied to my surprise. "I just get tired."

I explained that I believed her problem stemmed from a lump that had grown in an unusual place in her thyroid gland, causing thyrotoxicosis. The lump had extended into her chest, and because of the danger of cancer we needed to remove it. If we did not, I emphasized, she might soon find it difficult to take a breath.

I assisted at the surgery conducted by my chief. We were prepared to saw through bone to open up her upper chest, but after some gentle pulling the lump popped into view. It was fibrous and well-nourished, the size of an orange. It had indeed bent the windpipe, constricting it from both sides. We removed the tumor and closed the wound.

I next saw the woman a few weeks later when she returned for a checkup. She rushed up to me, and even before I had time to greet her she almost shouted, "I can breathe!"

I was puzzled. "Were you afraid the operation would stop your breathing?" I asked.

"No, no, you don't understand," she said with great excitement. "Now I can *breathe* for the first time in years and years. I can run up stairs! I feel like a teenager again. I can breathe!"

Her story came out bit by bit. That lump must have been growing slowly for fifteen years or more, gradually compressing her trachea, like a boa constrictor tightening its grip. The woman had adapted even without thinking about it. She had learned to stop and catch her breath frequently. It bothered her at first, but having known old people who became breathless and unable to climb stairs, she assumed she too had an aging heart. She restricted herself to walking very slowly and taking steps one at a time. She had become, in her eyes, prematurely senile. The hand tremors corroborated this image of herself.

Now, however, she could take great gulps of air and run up steps. Over fifteen years she had forgotten how good it felt to breathe deeply and freely. Her breath had all come back, she reported enthusiastically.

Since treating that woman early in my career, I have observed similar reactions among asthma patients recovering from a brief spell of breathlessness or among smokers who have quit the habit and regained their breathing. But I will never forget the near-miraculous change in the posture, facial expression, and total attitude toward life of this woman with the retrosternal thyroid lump. Absolute ecstasy spread across her face as she swelled her chest and announced loudly, "I can breathe!"

Occasionally I try to savor the pleasure of God's good gifts, like breathing, by imagining for a moment that I have lost them. I hold my breath and pretend my trachea is blocked. I sense the rising panic spreading throughout my body. I envision my red corpuscles turning blue. I hear a drumming in my head. Then suddenly I open my mouth and suck in a gulp of air. I blow out carbon dioxide and vapor and then distend my chest and let the air rush in. I feel a short burst of the relief and ecstasy experienced by the woman with thyrotoxicosis.

The cells of my body need the breath of oxygen to survive. Herbert Spencer expressed the scientific principle: whatever amount of power an organism expends in any form equals the power that was taken into it from without. The same principle holds true in the spiritual world. Christ's Body needs breath, the inspiration of his Spirit. We need the stream of life that comes from God, and only the Spirit can provide that. "Do not put out the Spirit's fire," warned the apostle (1 Thessalonians 5:19).

Chapter 15

# BELONGING

*We cannot follow the movement of our own eyes in a mirror. We can, by turning our head, observe them in this position and in that position with respect to our body, but never in the act of moving themselves from one position to the other, and never in the act of gazing at anything but the mirror. Thus our idea of ourself is bound to be falsified, since what to others appears the most lively and mobile part of ourself, appears to us unnaturally fixed. The eye is the instrument by which we see everything, and for that reason it is the one thing we cannot see with truth. The same thing is true of our Power of response to a book, or to anything else . . . this is why books about the Holy Ghost are apt to be curiously difficult and unsatisfactory — we cannot really look at the movement of the Spirit, just because It is the Power by which we do the looking.*

Dorothy Sayers

T here are few hermits, in humanity or in nature. At the smallest observable levels cooperation prevails, and we could neither breathe nor eat without it. Producing the oxygen we live by requires colonies of bacteria to aid the photosynthesis process, and nutrition relies on similar colonies to help break down all that we ingest.

In the insect world species cooperate to such a degree that even the most prudent observers come away muttering strange phrases such as "a common mind." Listen to Lewis Thomas's description of a termite colony at work. "When three or four termites are collected together in a chamber they wander about aimlessly, but when more termites are added, they begin to build. It is the presence of other termites, in sufficient numbers at close quarters, that produces the work: they pick up each other's fecal pellets and stack them in neat columns, and when the columns are precisely the right height, the termites reach across and turn the perfect arches that form the foundation of the termitarium. No single termite knows how to do any of this, but as soon as there are enough termites gathered together they become flawless architects, sensing their distances from each other although blind, building an immensely complicated structure with its own air-conditioning and humidity control."

These termite structures, conical rococo castles of red dirt, decorate the deserts of India and Africa. In the towers you would look in vain for a mastermind, an architect with blueprints who semaphores orders with his front legs or antennae. The cooperation occurs at a deeper, more primeval level than simple hierarchy.

Wherever we look, it seems, community is the order of the day. Our earth is not the center of the universe, but rather a speck of dust in a boundless community of planets, stars, and galaxies, all of which interact with and affect each other. The tiny atom, once thought indivisible, now appears as a universe of its own, with whirring electrons and mesons and quarks and glimmers of reality that last a scant nanosecond.

Living matter ushers in new levels of unpredictability. The smallest living unit, the cell, comprises a nucleus jammed with chromosomes as well as an Irish stew of various organelles: mitochondria, sacs, tubules, cilia, all squirming around in near-chaotic freedom. And this book concerns a community of such cells, one hundred trillion in all, which must cooperate together to produce a functioning human body. In short, each system of reality yet disclosed — atom, cell, organism, universe — forms a subunit in a higher system. We can only understand any of them through a study of group behavior.

What makes the joint ventures possible? How do the termites or the electrons or the mitochondria communicate? What mysterious force unites the cells in my body so that they all act like Paul Brand (with a few rebellious exceptions)? No question of modern science provokes such a mixed response. Eminent scientists (Agar, Dobzhansky, Thorpe, and Heisenberg) see an "awareness" in the very primary particles of matter, whereas the sociobiologists don't even admit to freedom in human behavior. As Sir Arthur Eddington said some years ago, "We often think that when we have completed our study of *one*, we know all about *two*, because 'two' is 'one and one.' We forget that we have still to make a study of 'and.'"

The study of the Holy Spirit concerns that "and." In the role of Creator the Spirit seeks, in Paul's words, to liberate "from its bondage to decay" a creation that "has been groaning as in the pains of childbirth right up to the present time" (Romans 8:21–22). Perhaps the Spirit of God is personally at work at the molecular level as the dynamic force that reverses decay and holds together the fabric of existence. The Bible hints at such a role, but only briefly. It does, however, comment explicitly on another "and": the current of communication that runs between God and all cells in

Christ's Body. In 2 Corinthians 13:14, one of the few verses to name all members of the Trinity, Paul gives this benediction: "May the grace of the Lord Jesus Christ, and the love of God, and the fellowship of the Holy Spirit be with you all." In a neat summary of the essence of the triune God, he does not say "the power of the Holy Spirit" or "the wisdom of the Holy Spirit," or "the purity of the Holy Spirit," but rather "the fellowship," the communion, the in-betweenness.

In my body some remarkable systems orchestrate the hundred trillion cells, applying the will of the head to the multifarious parts below. Similarly, the Spirit applies the infinite God to his people on earth. We do not commune with the Spirit; rather, the Spirit *is* the communion between God and us.

We cannot imagine the invisible. We need a symbol, something thrown across from our world of sight and touch, and the human body provides that symbol. Breath fills in only one aspect of the role of the Spirit. Perhaps the characteristics of a healthy, coordinated body described in the next few chapters will take us further into the mystery of a Body controlled by the Spirit of God.

~

Cells that form the human body share one most basic feature: a near-infallible sense of belonging that links each cell to every other one. All cells in my body know, through their DNA, that they belong to Paul Brand, and the body maintains constant vigilance against intruders. Teams of transplant surgeons go to great lengths to thwart that early warning defense. They bombard transplant sites with X-rays and immunosuppressant drugs to lull the guards, hoping to sneak in a kidney or heart or skin graft from someone else. They know, painfully, that as soon as the body realizes it has been invaded, the foreign cells will be thrown out.

Occasionally children are born without an immune system. You see their photos in the newspaper: they spend their lives in a plastic tent, untouched by humans, breathing purified air. NASA rigged up a bulky space suit for one such child, the "bubble boy," and he tugged behind him a clicking golf-cart-size contraption that scrubbed the air of impurities. This unfortunate boy's cells lacked the sense of belonging. They welcomed invaders, even bacteria and viruses that would kill them.

At its most basic level, the image of the Body of Christ expresses this shared sense of belonging. We members take on Christ's name and identity, and he asks of us the same kind of loyalty and unity that my own body's cells give to me. The Holy Spirit acts as Christ's agent to accomplish that identity transfer. The Spirit lives in those, and only those, who belong to Christ's Body — the New Testament unmistakably assumes that fact (Acts 15:8; Romans 8:9; 1 John 3:24; 4:13). He provides the fundamental mark of belonging to Christ.

Drawing on a variety of figures of speech, Paul explores how the Spirit applies God himself to the lives of individual believers. It is the Spirit, he says in Romans 8:15–16, who gives us a sense of sonship so that we approach God not as cringing slaves, but freely, as God's children. "By him we cry, 'Abba, Father.' The Spirit himself testifies with our spirit that we are God's children." The Book of Ephesians uses the word "seal" or "deposit" to describe the Spirit as a down payment God has given us to guarantee the future redemption to come (1:13; 4:30). Do not undervalue that seal of God's presence, Paul warns, for the power behind it is the very same as that which raised Christ from the dead (1:19–20).

All these varied references to the work of the Spirit assume a unity among the scattered and diverse members of Christ's Body. It is a unity guaranteed by the Spirit's presence, and no artificial labels or doctrinal boundaries can alter the fact. Calls for "unity in the church" that get bruited about periodically have no meaning unless they begin with the fundamental sense of belonging determined by the Spirit of God. We *are* Christ's Body. Whether we accept the fact or act in a manner in keeping with the new identity is left up to us.

The term "Spirit" appears sporadically throughout the Old Testament, but Paul's letters make clear that something new occurred with Pentecost. God now establishes a presence on earth by knitting together the members of Christ's Body by the Spirit. Bishop John Taylor noted this historic change by counting only 126 references to the Spirit from Genesis through Luke, but 196 from that point onward. "In other words, it is only in the epistles and the gospel of John that the Spirit appears in that fullness in which the Christian church has always known Him.... In a disturbing flash of insight the Gospel of John says with reference to the death and resurrection of Jesus: 'the Spirit had not yet been given, because Jesus had not yet been glorified,' which R. P. C. Hanson suggests might be better rendered: 'it was not yet Spirit,' as one might say, 'it was not yet spring.' That is exactly how it must have appeared to anyone looking back from the end of that prodigious first century. There had never been anything like it before, and it had all stemmed from Jesus."

As the Incarnation gives way to Pentecost, the departure of God in the flesh opens the way for the presence of God in Spirit to live inside many bodies. "It is for your good that I am going away. Unless I go away the Counselor will not come to you," Jesus said. The Holy Spirit brings that quality of communion or in-betweenness that defines Christ's Body as decisively as DNA defines my own body by imprinting itself in each of my many cells.

⟶

In the human body, the sense of belonging extends two ways: every cell attunes to orders from one brain, and every cell recognizes an inherent bond with every other cell in that body. So too, in Christ's Body, the Spirit establishes a connection not only between each cell and the Head but also among all the cells of the Body. The very word "church" in Greek means *called-out ones* and in the church God calls us into an organic community. The Spirit does not approach me in the solitude of my own soul, for that would leave me alone and unreconciled to my neighbor. Rather, the Spirit calls me to join a Body that binds me in love with a community of diverse cells. Each individual cell awakens to the conscious reality of the larger whole.

In human society, we approach such unity only rarely. Families achieve it sometimes — it is the tug of loyalty that binds me to my children scattered around the world. In a crisis, a town or even an entire nation may join together spiritedly in common cause.

Jesus prayed for an even richer experience of unity in his Body. He asked "that all of them may be one, Father, just as you are in me and I am in you. May they also be in us so that the world may believe that you have sent me" (John 17:21). Do we catch a glimmer of the wonder of that unity in the church, a unity based not on social class or interest group or kinship or race, but on common belonging in Jesus Christ? I have seen it, rarely, in small outposts of Christ's Body. Those few scenes give me a lasting vision of the image of God at work in the world. I will mention only one example.

John Karmegan came to me in Vellore, India, as a leprosy patient in an advanced state of the disease. We could do little for him surgically since his feet and hands had already been damaged irreparably. We could, however, offer him a place to stay and employment in the New Life Center.

Because of one-sided facial paralysis, John could not smile normally. When he tried, the uneven distortion of his features would draw attention to his paralysis. People often responded with a gasp or a gesture of fear, and so he learned not to smile. Margaret, my wife, had stitched his eyelids partly closed to protect his sight. John grew more and more paranoid about what others thought of him.

He caused terrible problems socially, perhaps in reaction to his marred appearance. He expressed his anger at the world by acting the part of a troublemaker, and I remember many tense scenes in which we had to confront John with some evidence of stealing or dishonesty. He treated fellow-patients cruelly, and resisted all authority, going so far as to organize hunger strikes against us. By almost anyone's reckoning, he was beyond rehabilitation.

Perhaps John's very irredeemability attracted my mother to him, for she often latched onto the least desirable specimens of humanity. She took to John, spent time with him, and eventually led him into the Christian faith. He was baptized in a cement tank on the grounds of the leprosarium.

Conversion, however, did not temper John's high dudgeon against the world. He gained some friends among fellow-patients, but a lifetime of rejection and mistreatment had permanently embittered him against all non-patients. One day, almost defiantly, he asked me what would happen if he visited the local Tamil church in Vellore.

I went to the leaders of the church, described John, and assured them that despite obvious deformities, he had entered a safe phase of the arrested disease and would not endanger the congregation. They agreed he could visit. "Can he take communion?" I asked, knowing that the church used a common cup. They looked at each other, thought for a moment, and agreed he could also take communion.

Shortly thereafter I took John to the church, which met in a plain, whitewashed brick building with a corrugated iron roof. It was a tense moment for him. Those of us on the outside can hardly imagine the trauma and paranoia inside a leprosy patient who attempts for the first time to enter that kind of setting. I stood with him at the back of the church. His paralyzed face showed no reaction, but a trembling betrayed his inner turmoil. I prayed silently that no church member would show the slightest hint of rejection.

As we entered during the singing of the first hymn, an Indian man toward the back half-turned and saw us. We must have made an odd couple: a white person standing next to a leprosy patient with patches of his skin in garish disarray. I held my breath.

And then it happened. The man put down his hymnal, smiled broadly, and patted the chair next to him, inviting John to join him. John could not have been more startled. Haltingly, he made shuffling half-steps to the row and took his seat. I breathed a prayer of thanks.

That one incident proved to be the turning point of John's life. Years later I visited Vellore and made a side trip to a factory that had been set up to employ disabled people. The manager wanted to show me a machine that produced tiny screws for typewriter parts. As we walked through the noisy plant, he shouted at me that he would introduce me to his prize employee, a man who had just won the parent corporation's all-India prize for the highest quality work with fewest rejects. As we arrived at his work station, the employee turned to greet us, and I saw the unmistakable crooked face of John Karmegan. He wiped the grease off his stumpy hand

and grinned with the ugliest, the loveliest, most radiant smile I had ever seen. He held out for my inspection a palmful of the small precision screws that had won him the prize.

A simple gesture of acceptance may not seem like much, but for John Karmegan it proved decisive. After a lifetime of being judged on his own physical image, he had finally been welcomed on the basis of another Image. I had seen a replay of Christ's own reconciliation. His Spirit had prompted the Body on earth to adopt a new member, and at last John knew he belonged.

# Chapter 16

# Go-Between

*If a man carry treasure in bullion, or in a wedge of gold, and have none coined into current money, his treasure will not defray him as he travels. Tribulation is treasure in the nature of it, but it is not current money in the use of it, except we get nearer and nearer our home, heaven, by it. Another man may be sick too, and sick to death, and this affliction may lie in his bowels, as gold in a mine, and be of no use to him; but this bell, that tells me of his affliction, digs out and applies that gold to me, if by this consideration of another's danger I take mine own into contemplation, and so secure myself, by making my recourse to my God, who is our only security.*

John Donne

It is a familiar route, Interstate 10 linking New Orleans and Baton Rouge. I have just flown in from another city and reclaimed my car at the airport. I concentrate more intently than usual because a heavy downpour has spread a sheet of water across the macadam, and the headlights and line markers tend to play tricks on the eyes. Without warning, a small dark shape scurries out onto the road — probably an armadillo or opossum. But before

I can even think that thought, my foot has instinctively tapped the brake pedal.

I can feel the sickening, out-of-control sensation of a skid coming on as the rear of the car planes off to the right. My hands grip the steering wheel more tightly. In response to a few quick jerks of my wrist, the car fishtails and finally straightens out. Once I have steering back under control, I breathe deeply and slow down until my anxiety subsides.

The entire incident has lasted maybe three seconds. When I arrive home, I will recount to my wife what happened: an animal crossed a rain-covered highway and I arrested a dangerous skid just in time. Those are the external events, simple and matter-of-fact. But the rest of the way home, still keyed up from the adrenaline pumping through my body, I think back on a few of the internal events.

It all started in the brain. When the sight of the animal reached my visual cortex, a trained reflex response directed my foot onto the brake pedal. After that, my hypothalamus ordered up chemicals to launch with lightning speed a series of reactions designed to put me in prime condition to cope with the alarm.

Few parts of my body went untouched by the crisis. First, my vision intensified as my pupils dilated. All my muscles went on alert. Stress hormones affected my entire circulatory system. My heart beat faster, contracting more forcefully, and even in the extremities vascular muscles relaxed in order to allow blood vessels to widen and carry a greater blood flow. Blood components themselves changed: more blood sugars surged in, providing emergency reserves for working muscles, and clotting materials multiplied in preparation for wound repair. Bronchial tubes flared open to allow faster oxygenation of the blood.

On my largest organ, the skin, blood vessels contracted, bringing on a pale complexion ("white as a ghost") but lowering the danger of surface bleeding in case of injury. A reduced volume of circulation in skin also freed up more blood for the muscles' urgent need. The electrical resistance of skin changed as a protective mechanism against potential bacterial invaders. "Goose-pimples" bulged up all over my body, holding erect millions of hair shafts. Sweat glands poured out assistance to increase the traction of my palms on the steering wheel.

Meanwhile, nonessential functions slowed down. Digestion nearly came to a halt — blood assigned to that and to kidney filtration was redeployed for more urgent needs.

In an external sense, not much happened. I avoided the animal, corrected the skid, and drove on with a racing heart, dilated pupils, and a slight tremor in my muscles. Yet inside my body a full-scale battle was fought and won to equip me for the classic alternatives of "fight or flight." A single unifying chemical messenger, adrenaline, managed to coordinate an entire galaxy of select cells.

We experience the effects of adrenaline every day: we are startled by a loud noise, we hear a bit of shocking news, we drive through a dangerous neighborhood, we stumble and nearly fall. Adrenal reactions occur so smoothly and synchronously that we rarely, if ever, stop to reflect on all the elements involved. And yet adrenaline is just one of many hormones at work in my body coaxing a cooperative response from diverse cells.

The incident on the highway offers a clear illustration of two types of communication that unite the body. My first response, applying my foot to the brake, resulted from a direct command of the nervous system. Long ago, when I first learned to drive, my brain sorted out the sequence of nerve firings required for me to lift my foot and slide it to the left, and to turn the steering wheel with short, jerky motions. Unlike a novice, I did not have to think, "Where's the brake pedal?" In a moment of stress, my brain relied on a memory bank of programmed responses and sent high speed orders along nerve pathways. The orders were, so to speak, "foot-specific" and "wrist-specific."

However, the other complex reactions — the heart rate, skin changes, respiratory adjustments — occurred because of the hormonal system. My brain initiated an order to a gland, in this case the adrenal, to secrete a chemical messenger into the bloodstream. The hormone does not deliver a message as immediate, precise, and definite as the nerve's, but in a few seconds it can reach every cell in my body.

Fear, relief, heightened awareness — I felt all these sensations, and for the next twenty miles they made me a much better driver. All my muscles, not just my foot and wrists, were poised for action. I saw better and concentrated more on the hazardous driving conditions.

These two types of communication, the nervous and hormonal systems, have a parallel in the spiritual Body also. At times we may have a direct "hotline" from the Head, a clear directive for a specific action. In my experience, those times occur infrequently. More commonly, I sense a certain prompting to respond, a heightened awareness, or a pang of conscience about some command of Christ's I have failed to follow.

Christian literature has devoted much attention to the "gifts of the Spirit." Could such gifts follow alternate types of communication systems within the Body? Some are chosen to be pastors and teachers and prophets and administrators. By ability and by calling, these represent a sort of central nervous system, a direct line of communication from the Head. We cells rely on them to teach and interpret and to direct us in our various functions within the Body.

But in addition the Spirit moves as a go-between force among all cells, gently bringing to mind the will of the Head and thus permeating and mobilizing the entire Body.

Until recently anatomists believed that glands such as the adrenal and pituitary sent out their hormonal instructions independently. New discoveries point to reliance on the brain at virtually every point. Instructions on growth, on deployment of resources, on how to meet a crisis all originate in the head, which senses the needs of the entire body. The glands and enzymes and prostaglandins act as agents for the will of the head, carrying the message to each independent cell. And so in the spiritual Body, "We will in all things grow up into him who is the Head, that is, Christ. From him the whole body, joined and held together by every supporting ligament, grows and builds itself up in love, as each part does its work" (Ephesians 4:15–16).

⟵

Besides the communication from the head through nerves and hormones, a third system of communication operates in the body. To me it is the most impressive of all. It determines the needs of individual cells and informs the rest of the body. In my adrenaline response to the skidding car, messages went from my head to cells, quickly arousing each cell in my body. Intracellular communication reverses the flow: an alarm sounding in individual cells works its way to neighboring cells and outward until finally the message reaches the brain itself.

Medicine has coined a wonderful word to describe the state that results from such cooperative behavior: homeostasis. A noble physician and fine writer, Dr. Walter Cannon, introduced the term in his classic study *The Wisdom of the Body*. He viewed the body as a community that consciously seeks out the most favorable conditions for itself. It corrects imbalances in fluids and salts, mobilizes to heal itself, and deploys resources on demand, all in order to maintain a dependable *milieu interieur*, as the French like to say.

Even the most common acts rely on elaborate confederacies. Already I have referred to the monitors that measure oxygen intake and regulate breathing. Oxygen requirements also trigger changes in the heart rate, and the chain of cells serving as the pacemaker of my heart is far better attuned to the needs of the body than any electronic wizardry inserted to replace it. The natural pacemaker listens to instructions from the vagus nerve, factors in readings of oxygen requirements, and also takes note of any special conditions that might call for increased heartbeat as indicated by the presence of adrenaline. (Walter Cannon found in a series of experiments that the pacemaker of a cat could detect the presence of 1 part of adrenaline in 1,400,000,000 parts of blood. A quantity that minute would make the cat's heart beat faster.)

You can see evidence of homeostasis on vivid display in modern hospitals where constant digital readouts report a patient's pulse and other vital functions. I visit a woman patient who suffers from high blood pressure. When I enter the room, the red numerals glow a steady 82, her resting pulse. She notices my presence and greets me; the flurry of emotional responses shoots her pulse up to 91. She reaches over to shake my hand; the rate surges past 100. During my thirty-minute visit, the numbers rise and fall in concert with her moods and actions. A sneeze causes the most violent reaction of all, a pulse of 110. That kind of ceaseless monitoring and adjustment goes on in all our bodies each moment in order to keep oxygen supplies in balance.

Similarly, cells communicate other needs. From the viewpoint of the body, taste and appetite are mere techniques to compel us to provide nourishment. Inside our bodies, sophisticated chemical sensors measure which minerals and salts are lacking and, in an utterly mystifying way, communicate a desire for them to our appetite. A mountain goat travels five miles to lick a block of salt; a pregnant woman feels strange cravings for the taste of certain foods that just happen to contain the specific vitamins and minerals she needs.

The body's relentless search for homeostasis never stops. The delicate kidneys increase or decrease the level of fluid that goes out based on the body's need for reserves. They may halt the excretion of sodium while unloading a surfeit of potassium. If the person has exerted himself or herself to an unusual degree, kidneys may stop excretion altogether to prevent dehydration. Thus a marathon runner may not urinate for twenty-four hours after a race.

Sweat. I could write an entire chapter on that remarkable aspect of homeostasis. What a lizard wouldn't give for warm blood and sweat glands! In the morning that reptile must somehow wriggle over to the sunlight and warm up before it can start climbing trees and catching flies. If the lizard overheats, it frantically scuttles toward shade. In humans, however, an efficient cooling system uses sweat to cool our bodies to a constant internal temperature so that sensitive organs can maintain a *milieu interieur.* (Muscle contractions, or shivering, correspondingly warm the body.) Were it not so, we could hardly function in a climate where temperatures exceed 80° F.

Japanese physiologist Yas Kuno spent thirty years studying sweat, and in 1956 published the authoritative 416-page book

*Human Perspiration.* He found human nervous and hormonal systems to be so sensitive that a change of one-twentieth of a degree Celsius may trigger the mechanisms that heat or cool the body. Humans have the finest cooling system of all mammals; most animals will run fevers on a hot day. (Animals compensate variously. A dog or tiger pants, creating its own internal fan. An elephant finds a refreshing-looking waterhole and wades in for a hose-down.)

Over a hundred years ago a meticulous German counted 2,381,248 sweat glands on a human body — he needn't have bothered, since the total varies from person to person. Regardless, we all have enough to get the job done. A marathon runner may shed three to five quarts of fluid in a three-hour race, but inside his temperature will hardly waver.

⸺

All these operations — heart rate, fluid control, perspiration — adapt every second as the body seeks the very best environment for its vital functions.* We are barely beginning to understand how cells communicate with each other. Two Swedes and an Englishman earned the 1982 Nobel Prize in Medicine for discovering some of the substances that control these homeostatic activities. They identified substances called prostaglandins (so named because the first was erroneously traced to the prostate gland), and now thirty prostaglandins have been isolated. One lowers blood pressure,

---

*Occasionally, something more violent is needed to maintain homeostasis. When an intruder gets in, something irritating or toxic, the body calls on spectacular forces of expulsion. A sneeze produces hurricane-force winds in the nasal passages and sends the heart rate soaring. Coughing or vomiting solicits the combined forces of scores of muscles in the chest cavity and diaphragm, with such vigor it can leave us sore. When homeostasis is threatened, the body does not take chances. Without our conscious cooperation, whether during a pianissimo concert or on a business flight, it protects at all costs.

while another raises it. One widens bronchial tubes, a second constricts them. One initiates inflammation; another inhibits it. Prostaglandins aid in such processes as clotting, regulating gastric acid, and controlling uterine contractions. These messenger fluids travel constantly from cell to cell, visiting nearly every tissue of the body, linking isolated cells and organs into units of a coordinated response.

This type of cell-to-cell communication has a parallel in Christ's Body on earth. Here, too, the Spirit serves as the Go-Between God who unites each of the members of that Body to each other and to God. It is the Spirit who expresses the needs of the Body to the Head and who brings a sense of commonality to individual members.

In several places the New Testament refers to the Spirit's role in conveying and even formulating words of intercession to God. "The Spirit helps us in our weakness," says Paul. "We do not know what we ought to pray for, but the Spirit himself intercedes for us with groans that words cannot express" (Romans 8:26). In a play on words that must have been intentional, Paul uses that word "groan" two other places in the same chapter: once to express the pains of a fallen creation that groans, "as in the pain of childbirth," for restoration, and again to express the Christian's longing for a fully redeemed body. The Spirit senses those inexpressible, primeval groans of fallenness, separation, and incompleteness and presents them to God on our behalf. "And he who searches our hearts knows the mind of the Spirit, because the Spirit intercedes for the saints in accordance with God's will" (8:27).

Because we are a Body, it is only natural that God rely on other "cells" to meet individual needs. A local area in my physical body responds quickly to a call for help; in Christ's Body the Spirit achieves homeostasis by calling on neighboring parts. The Spirit awakens us to human need in our neighbors and prompts us to shift resources from a section of plenty to a section of want.

Charles Williams uses the phrase "co-inherence" to describe the mystical way in which all of us cells join together in that Body. Co-inherence sounds ethereal, but in reality the responsive actions can take on such mundane forms as sharing food, sitting with a grieving person, or cleaning a bedpan. A short time after the exuberance in the Spirit at Pentecost, the early church found itself needing guidance on the practical matters of poverty and the distribution of relief supplies.

The word *another* signifies a kind of cell-to-cell cooperation, and we cannot escape the word in the New Testament. It appears as a relentless leitmotif. "Accept one another," we are told. "Serve one another" by "washing one another's feet." We are to confess our sins to one another, pray for one another, forgive one another, teach and admonish one another, comfort one another, bear one another's burdens. And, of course, Jesus left us the most inclusive command of all: "Love one another as I have loved you." Our obedient response and our openness to one another are the points of contact where the Spirit of God works in us. That intracellular communication is the very sign of God's presence. Christ is forming his Body in the world, his Presence, through a Spirit that draws all of us together.

As a surgeon, I have opportunity each day to see cells serving one another in perhaps the body's most beautiful display of working toward homeostasis: healing. In the human body, cells cry out to their neighbors when injured — the chemistry of the wound attracts healing cells — and the body responds on a local level. The process does not depend on instructions from the head, but goes on even if the head has not been informed. My leprosy patients prove that: if one cuts a finger, healing will start even if there is no pain system to inform the head. Healing seems a part of the DNA program built into each cell and takes place at the cell-to-cell level.

In *Fearfully and Wonderfully Made* I described the thrilling experience of sitting at a microscope and watching what happens at an injury site. Fibroblasts weave their delicate clotting web, white cells rush in to battle infection, blood vessels magically self-repair, inflammation sets in to assist the whole process.

In my medical career I have never felt more helpless and despairing than at one time in India when I treated a patient who lacked the basic mechanism of healing. A young missionary couple brought in their infant daughter who had been vomiting and showing signs of a blocked intestine. I operated immediately, removing the section of impacted and gangrenous bowel. It was a routine surgery and baby Anne came through well. The parents left delighted and grateful, taking Anne home for post-operative care.

A few days later, the couple returned with their daughter. The mother had noticed the dressings were wet. As I unwrapped the bandages, I could detect the unmistakable odor of intestinal fluid, and indeed I could see it seeping out of the wound. Feeling embarrassed, I took the baby back to the operating room and reopened the incision. Strangely, as I cut through the surface stitches, the wound fell loosely apart. It showed no sign of healing. Similarly, inside the abdominal cavity I found the intestine leaking and unhealed. It did not look diseased or infected, just porous. This time I cut away the edges and made a most meticulous closure using many very fine stitches.

A series of operations followed. It soon became clear that the little girl lacked the unifying healing processes that coordinate various cells. Her body failed at achieving homeostasis in its most crucial form. Sewing her intestine was like sewing a rubber balloon: it would always leak, because nothing summoned new living cells to seal up the puncture marks. Repairs lasted a few days, until the stitches ripped through the tissue.

We prayed over Anne's tiny body. I did research on her condition. We gave her nourishment and blood transfusions through her veins, and I even tried wrapping the intestinal junction with the filmy omentum that the body uses to heal accidental wounds. But nothing ever healed. The skin flaps refused to adhere, the muscles gaped apart, and intestinal juices sooner or later trickled out between the stitches.

Little Anne would lie there with a sweet and trusting smile as we surveyed the damage, and her face would tear at my heart. She grew thinner and thinner. I don't think Anne experienced much pain; she just quietly faded away.

When her tiny, wasted body was wrapped for burial, I cried in grief and helplessness. Even now as I write these words the little smile in her wrinkled face comes back with a stab of pain.

Anne's body lacked the go-between, the mechanism that responds to a wound by healing it. She had plenty of fibroblasts and new cells — her body was using them for growth all over, weaving fiber for tendons and tissue. Nothing, however, informed them that her body was wounded and that they must rush to the site of injury. No alarms went off alerting one part of the body to another's need.

Fortunately, in medicine we encounter very few patients like Anne; otherwise our entire profession would disappear. Physicians and nurses do not heal; we merely coax the body to heal itself. Without its help, our own efforts prove futile.

The same is true in the spiritual Body composed of diverse members representing different races and statuses and income levels and intelligences and cultures. When we allow the Spirit of God to move in, hovering in between the differences and disproportions and varied hurts and needs, he can direct the process needed for healing and for growth. Sometimes orders come directly through the central nervous system, sometimes indirectly through hormones, and sometimes through simple cell-to-cell contact. But without that Spirit, regardless of all our methodology, institutions, or techniques, we will all be as helpless as poor Anne.

# Chapter 17

# LISTENING

*To insure the greatest efficiency in the dart, the harpooners of this world must start to their feet out of idleness and not out of toil.*

Herman Melville, *Moby Dick*

One-half the human population comes equipped with the potential for a major internal upheaval. If the event happens, it will absorb the body's full attention for a long time, usually nine months. I speak, of course, of pregnancy.

Each month certain cells in a woman routinely conspire in a cycle of activity intended to anticipate pregnancy. They strip away the old lining of the uterus if no conception occurs and reline it for the next month. Then one day a fertilized egg settles on the receptive cells of a freshly lined uterus and new life begins. Everything changes.

At first local fluids nourish the fertilized egg, but very quickly the lining cells recognize they have at last encountered what they have been created for. A most remarkable organ, belonging neither to the mother nor the child, begins to develop: the placenta. People who see the placenta only after it has completed its function and been expelled dismiss it with the ignominious name "afterbirth."

In reality it is one of the most active and discriminating organs in nature. It forges a supreme bond of symbiotic intimacy.

Burrowing deep into the tissues of the mother, the placenta interlaces a web of vessels through membranes so fine that all the chemicals in the mother's blood can diffuse into the child's, and all the wastes from the child can be eliminated through the mother. Yet no open passage joins one to the other, no cells cross the membrane, and the mother remains wholly mother and the child wholly child. (Often, their respective blood types differ, so that any blending of blood might prove fatal.)

The placenta is an organ full of mysteries. It develops soon after fertilization, and from the mother's immunological standpoint its tissue is foreign matter — yet her body welcomes it for nine months. Furthermore, its nucleate cells fuse together to form what is in effect a single cell, the largest single cell in all of human anatomy.

In addition to nourishing the fetus, the placenta plays a major role in directing the intricate proceedings of pregnancy. From it, as well as from the ovary and the brain, come hormones to organize and induce each stage of response. Very little distinguishes these messengers from a host of similar hormones that maunder through the bloodstream, and only an expert chemist can differentiate them. Even when the chemical formulas are written out, one must look carefully to notice the placement of a few atoms that distinguish, for example, between the hormone that makes a male from that which makes a female.

Chemists may have problems discriminating, but not the cells themselves. Chemicals that previously have never provoked more than a mild reaction suddenly, after conception, foment revolution. Cells seem to listen to hormonal messages with a new alertness and receptivity. The hormone progesterone, for example, visits the uterus regularly in small concentrations, sometimes irritating the lining and indirectly causing the noxious reaction of menstrual cramps. But after the onset of pregnancy, it and estrogen launch a series of ventures that galvanize millions of cells in remote sites.

Inside the uterus, those hormones prompt uterine cells to begin a massive fortifications project, thickening the walls of that organ to prepare for the child it will soon shelter and protect. Cells pile on top of cells, layering, stretching, dividing, crowding each other. Eventually the uterine wall grows to one hundred times its resting size.

The mother's blood likewise increases in volume, by as much as 50 percent during pregnancy. The surplus safeguards against potential heavy loss during delivery itself. Blood also automatically adjusts its clotting properties to prepare for probable vessel breakage. Thus, although the same hormone contacts many kinds of cells, each group interprets the specific message very differently.

These same hormones excite a contrary response in certain joints and ligaments. As the chemical messengers wash through pelvic joints, they leave their imprint on fibroblasts and osteoblasts and osteoclasts, the building blocks of cartilage and bone. Rather than increasing in quantity or strengthening, these cells begin to reverse their normal construction procedures and slacken up. Fibroblasts, which lay down cells to make ligaments joining bone to bone, lengthen their fibers. Ligaments that have always kept the skeleton taut and stable and strong now defy their heritage. They must: the pelvic bones need to stretch apart enough for a baby's head to pass through. The loosening of connective tissue brings on backaches and a waddling gait that Shakespeare called "the proud walk of pregnancy."

Fortunately, not all ligament cells follow these orders. Fibroblasts in other joints, while receiving the same chemical message, recognize that it does not apply to them, and thus pregnant women are spared the problem of a wobbly head, loose knees, and elbows that dislocate easily.

Skin also expands to accommodate enlarging breasts and abdomen (a fact that causes some women consternation if their bodies later retain the stretch marks). Similarly, smooth muscle cells throughout the body slacken, and the pregnant woman notices lessened precision in her urination and digestion. As the smooth muscles relax and the body devotes fewer resources to the production of digestive enzymes like pepsin, nausea may result. More and more, the woman's body reorders its priorities toward creating a new life, not just preserving a familiar one.

Finally, in the fullness of time, the woman's body prepares for parturition. A complex interaction of enzymes and hormones between mother and child convinces the mother's body that the fetus is ready. For months uterine muscles have been gently contracting in waves, practicing for the extreme act they were engineered to perform but, in the case of a first birth, have never accomplished.

During birth, everything speeds up violently. Hormones direct a frenzy of sudden contractions and relaxations as dramatic as anything the body will ever know.

━

A child is born. Even so, those same hormones keep flooding the body, in many cases causing the opposite reactions from those in effect just minutes before. The uterus no longer enlarges, but contracts. (It is the only organ programmed to grow and then shrink.) Blood vessels torn from the placenta seal up. The placenta itself, masterful orchestrator of much of this activity, exits anticlimactically shortly thereafter and is discarded without a whisper of

438 ——. IN HIS IMAGE

thanks. The umbilical cord stops pulsing and begins to shrivel. New priorities take over: healing, restoration, and a new bonding between two separate individuals.

The drama of independent life is underway. Air rushes into lungs previously unused but in perfect working order. The entire congregation of bronchial passageways, diaphragm muscles, and all the other components of breathing must simultaneously coordinate. Oxygen filters into blood cells through the lungs now, not through the placenta.

Even the infant's heart must make renovations. Before birth, only one-third of the fetus's blood — the amount needed to nourish developing lung tissue — traveled to the lungs. A separate artery, the *ductus arteriosus*, channeled off two-thirds of the volume into the aortic arch for direct passage to the rest of the body. But from the moment of birth all the blood must pass through the lungs for oxygenation. To accomplish this change, an amazing event occurs. In response to a chemical signal, a flap suddenly descends like a curtain, deflecting the blood flow, and a muscle constricts the *ductus arteriosus*. That muscle had developed, like all other muscles, through an elaborate process of cell division and growth in the embryo. But it is needed only for this solitary act. Once the extra channel is shut off, the heart permanently seals it and the body gradually absorbs the *ductus arteriosus*.

The fetus is now a baby, free and independent but still incapable of supporting its own life. Happily, the woman's body has been readying itself for just this situation since about age eleven. Younger boys and girls have nearly identical cells on the upper parts of their trunk, including similar nipples. Beneath the skin, specific cells related to fat and milk-production rest in a primitive and sedentary state. But at puberty, a certain hormone present only in females begins to secrete at a gentle level. Ninety percent of the body's cells ignore the chemical; breast cells, among others, listen. They irrupt spectacularly and shape the perfect symmetry of a mature breast. Once a certain size is reached, they simply stop multiplying. For more years, they wait, quiescent. Breast cells grow old, die, and are replaced each year, without ever making the milk they were designed to produce.

During pregnancy progesterone and estrogen, the same hormones that loosen ligaments and firm up uterine walls and indirectly cause nausea, visit the breasts. Cells that have lived in the relaxed contentment of reserve duty receive a summons to active service. Other hormones have floated past these breast cells each day for years, with no effect. They are screened in an indifferent, mildly curious way, much as one might scan a vacationing neighbor's mail. But today, the message applies to the tranquil breast cell.

It would be wrong to call what follows pandemonium, because the activity proceeds in a spirit of orderliness. But in nine months a complete factory must take shape, constructed on the foundations laid during puberty. First, each summoned cell gains reinforcements by breeding. It divides and divides again until finally enough cells exist to arrange themselves into a tube. Then the tube begins to ramify and these buds and branches burrow into the surrounding fat of the breast tissue.

Neighboring fat cells read a different interpretation into the identical hormone message. For them the message says, "Prepare to decrease. You must give up your fat and your space to make room for new ducts and milk factory cells. Release your substance to be recycled." Paradoxically, these same hormones also inhibit the production of milk until the proper time.

At the same signal, blood vessels in the breast elongate, skin grows to accommodate a larger shape, and pectoral muscles strengthen to support the new weight. Far away, the cells responsible for appetite and taste respond to the same message by concocting strange and unfamiliar cravings and some revulsions that the body may not understand, but will do well to obey.

After several months new hormones from the departing placenta travel to the breast and circulate among the host of cells that now congregate in the place previously occupied by a lone duct cell. These hormones announce that the time has arrived, and the new factory churns into motion. Cells that line the ducts open up their cell walls to allow secretions to ooze out into the hollow of the tubes. The tubes themselves, having never carried anything before, may clog with material too viscous to flow easily. If so, the mother will feel a soreness that tells her of the distention, and her nurse or perhaps her mother may show her how to milk it out a little.

Into this crisis comes the new living creature. The baby has no experience — it has never been a baby before. It has never seen a breast and may, in fact, have never opened its eyes. But a baby knows what to do upon contact with a woman's breast.

An observing engineer, knowing that fluid flows from an area of high pressure to an area of low pressure, might marvel at the mechanics of suction employed. The baby creates low pressure in the pharynx by closing its mouth over an area of compliant skin and then contracting its superior pharyngeal muscles, while not forgetting to close off the glottis so as to maintain the low pressure vacuum and also avoid drowning in the fluid. A nutritionist would surely marvel at the remarkable broth of vitamins, nutrients, antibodies, and macrophages that comprise mother's milk. The baby thinks of none of these, but he knows when and how to suck.

In a beautiful symbiotic feature of nursing, now the mother needs the baby just as the baby needs the mother. The blocked duct and engorged tubes of the breast have no easy alternative to rid themselves of congestion and pain. The breast is designed to serve the baby. The placenta's final messages before expulsion, a sucking force, and even the baby's cry all combine to stimulate the flow of milk.

—

One can hardly avoid words like "miracle" when speaking of childbirth. Yet the phenomenon occurs so commonly that more than six billion proofs of its effectiveness exist on this planet today. Relatively few messengers direct the process, and they elicit utterly different responses from cells in the breast, pelvis, uterus, and blood. Today, in the body of every young woman, millions of cells lie in wait, carefully perusing the molecular structure of every chemical that happens by, searching for the precise signal that will prompt them into action.

As impressive as pregnancy is, the real miracle of cooperation unfolds within the growing infant, whose hormones regulate the development of one hundred trillion cells. What handicaps would result if the kneecap grew 10 percent faster than the tendons, ligaments, and muscles surrounding it, or if the right leg grew slightly longer than the left? (Sometimes, as a result of a genetic defect, one of the two parallel bones in an arm may grow faster than its partner, contorting the angle of the wrist into an odd and almost useless position.) Some body parts double in size, some triple, and some enlarge to hundreds of times their original length. Yet with few exceptions each body part grows in proportion to supporting structures and is well-supplied with blood at each stage of growth. The entire body works together.

I like to imagine myself as one cell in such a body, for analogously that is the position of every Christian in the Body of Christ.

I must admit, I sometimes chafe at being one cell. I might prefer being a whole body, or another kind of cell with a more significant role in Christ's Body. But gradually I have learned to view myself as a very minor part of a great enterprise that will only work if directed by the Spirit of God, not by me or any other conjunction of human leaders.

In that Body, I come in contact with diverse messages, similar to the chemical messengers that course through my physical body. Some of them come mediated through human agents: spiritual leaders, my loved ones, the community of faith around me. Some come directly through God's Word in the Bible. Still others, though few, come through the direct contact every cell has with the Head. The messages arrive in code, and I must examine them to determine how they relate to me. They may seem confusing or even contradictory at first. What is my role in such a Body? How do I discern the time for action? Is this specific message for me or someone else?

In the Body of Christ, the Holy Spirit performs the function of prompter. He must coordinate all its members to assure that the work of God continues according to the Father's will. A sensitive member of the Body will hear many stirring calls to action. Some will describe the desperate needs, physical and spiritual, of people in other lands. Some will point to neighbors close by. Others will give emphasis to the contemplative life, or to reform of the justice system, or to the need for high personal ethics. All these calls have merit, are supported by Scripture, and apply in some degree to each of us. But the Holy Spirit will instruct us in our *specific* response, and it is to the Spirit that we must listen.

My own response has included spending time in another culture, India, where physical needs are great. Every sensitive Christian should feel stirred by the human and spiritual needs of such countries. We should all respond, but the form of our response will vary. Praying, writing letters to missionaries, lobbying for humanitarian aid, taking a short-term assignment, supporting Christian work financially — all of these constitute appropriate responses, as diverse as the responses of my body's cells to a hormone, but equally valid if the Spirit has given clear instructions.

One chemical messenger instructs uterine cells to contract but cervical cells to relax during childbirth. Likewise, even messages from the Bible may seem at first to contradict. If you read the book of Galatians and then 1 Corinthians consecutively, you may question whether the same author could have written both. But Paul wisely knew that parts of the Body need different messages at different times. The legalistic Galatians needed the fresh, cool breeze of God's gracious acceptance, whereas the pagan, lawless Corinthians needed a prod toward obedience and righteousness.

I have learned that the first and perhaps most essential requirement of a loyal cell is learning to listen to the code. I must wait, scrutinize the messages, tune in. The Spirit will employ various means to speak to me and instruct me in the way I should go, but only if I hear his voice.

I can hardly think of a more difficult task than listening for the voice of God. We want to leap into action, to exercise our faith in dramatic ways. Regardless of our motives, unless such actions are prompted by the Spirit, they will not help the growth of the Body, just as a kneecap spurting in growth disproportionately may demonstrate its own strength but will handicap the rest of the body.

Think back to the resurrection of Jesus Christ. In that event, all of history converged. It was, in J. R. R. Tolkien's phrase, a "eucatastrophe," an event of unimaginable goodness. The disciples and followers of Jesus could hardly contain themselves with the news that their faith in the Messiah had proved right despite the ugly fact of his crucifixion. Yet even in light of that eucatastrophic news Jesus told them to stay in Jerusalem and wait. They sat still for forty days. Something else was needed: the baptism of the Holy Spirit. Counselor, he is called, and elsewhere Comforter. He is the Guide, the Prompter of what activity is required of each cell.

The great saints and mystics have left us guidebooks on aligning ourselves with "the mind of God," and some have devoted their lives to the discipline and commitment involved in finding his message for them. Bishop John Taylor refers to two kinds of prayers: the prayer of movement, in which the mind moves from topic to topic, bringing each to God's attention; and the prayer of stillness. The latter is a profound concentration on hearing God's Word for one individual cell. I think of Elijah despondent in the cave: the voice of God he heard came not in the mighty wind, nor in the earthquake, nor in the fire, but in the gentle whisper, the still, small voice. Or I think of Jesus, the Son of God. Even he confessed the need for direct contact with the Father through prayer and fasting.

Mahatma Gandhi, one of the busiest and most famous men in the world, used to set aside Monday as a Day of Silence. He needed the stillness, he said, in order to rest his vocal cords and to promote an inner harmony in his soul amid the turmoil of life around him. I wonder what power would be released if all Christians devoted one day a week to listening to the voice of God to discern the coded message for our lives. The Counselor can only lead us if we receive his voice.

I have vivid memories of the person who best demonstrated for me this skill of listening to God: my grandmother. Grandma Harris was eighty when I first knew her, and lived to age ninety-four. I never saw her walk unassisted; her health confined her either to bed or to "Grandma's chair" in her quaint room with its lace curtains and dark Victorian furniture. My sister and I would visit that room for about an hour or so each day. Of Huguenot descent, Grandma had us read the French Bible to her so that we could practice our French while also learning the Bible and hearing her talk about the passage we had read.*

Grandma was bent and wrinkled, and she suffered severe headaches. She rarely laughed and could never comprehend our jokes, but her quiet joy and peace somehow reached even us play-minded children. We never resented our daily visits to her room. She radiated love.

When Grandma had trouble sleeping, she sometimes lay awake half the night quietly reciting chapters from her storehouse of memorized Scripture and praying for her eleven children and scores of grandchildren. My aunts took turns sleeping in her room. Quite often, in the middle of the night Grandma would suddenly call for paper and pen and someone to write down her thoughts. She would say, "I sense that Pastor Smith in Ipswich is in need of help just now. Please write to him like this. . . ." She would then dictate a letter and ask my aunt to enclose a check.

Days later, when the mail brought a letter of reply, Grandma would beam with joy. Invariably, the letter expressed astonishment

---

*Grandma was not above using extrinsic motivation on her grandchildren. Knowing that whatever we committed to memory in childhood would last a lifetime, she rewarded our word perfect memorization of a chapter of Scripture with a bright, freshly minted silver coin. Those half-crowns and shillings were like a fortune to us. To this day, almost all the full chapters of the Bible preserved in my memory are those I was paid for by Grandma Harris.

that she should have known the precise timing and amount of a need. She would laugh with a pure sense of innocent delight. We children marveled at the conspiracy of intimacy between the Holy Spirit and Grandma.

In the Body of Christ, I picture her as a nerve in the sympathetic nervous system, a sensor that God entrusted with the moment-by-moment responsibility of sensing his will. Pastor Smith had sent cries for help to the Head. My grandmother "heard" the transmitted impulse from the Head and supplied whatever resources were needed. Grandma had prepared all her life for that role. In her youth she had physical energy and beauty. During those busy years of rearing eleven new lives, despite constant demands on her schedule, she had taken the time to know God. She had saturated her mind with the Word of God, storing away whole books of the New Testament, as well as all of the Psalms, in her memory. Later, when her body grew old and withered, she became a clear channel for the grace of God.

Today, more than fifty years later, much of my own love for the Bible derives from her. She could do little but listen to the Prompter, but her faithfulness is still bearing fruit.

In the human body, a minute quantity of the proper hormone can launch a complex upheaval; the still, small voice of God, if responded to, can change a person, a community, and perhaps a world.

# Chapter 18

# THE PROMPTER

*The computer makes us fantastically more able to calculate and analyse; it does not help us to meditate. We have instruments to enable us to see everything from the nebulae to the neutron — everything, except ourselves. We have immeasurably extended our gift of sight, but not of insight. For that we have the same equipment as the eighth-century prophets. Potentially the same, but actually far poorer, for while we have been so busy extending one aspect of the knowing and telling self, we have allowed other aspects to atrophy. We have built ourselves up into powerful transmitting stations, but as receiving sets we are feeble.*

John V. Taylor

When I first returned to India as a doctor, in 1946, I traveled by ship. I had learned navigation several years before, when I spent a summer as one of a crew of five sailing a schooner along the coasts of Great Britain and France. On the schooner we had used direct navigation based on sighting lighthouses and buoys and calculating progress from one to another. But on the passenger ship, in the boundless, open sea, we had no landmarks against which to check calculations. How did the captain know our location with any certainty?

Ships had no radar equipment in those days. The instruments used — sextant, compass, and chronometer — differed little from those used by Columbus and Magellan. I went to the bridge and asked the captain if I could observe his methods of navigation. He kindly agreed and loaned me a sextant, which I already knew how to use. I looked forward to comparing my own readings with those of the experts.

A sextant consists of two tubes resembling telescopes, joined at a hinge. To measure the height of a mountain, for example, you sight the summit precisely in one tube and line up the second one along sea level. When the images converge in the eyepiece, you read the exact angle off the sextant. Using a little geometry, you can then arrive at the measurement of height. All this works easily on or near land, but the open sea is a different matter. There, you have no fixed point to guide you, only the clear line of the horizon. You also need the stars.

I quickly learned the most important secret of celestial navigation: the timing of the measurements. We needed a clear sighting of both a star and the horizon to determine an angle, and only two times of day, dawn and dusk, offered such conditions. Those were by far the most dramatic times on the bridge of the ship. Each day I awoke early and made my way to the bridge, sextant in hand. I asked which bright star to sight on (it had to be listed in our astronomical tables) and fixed one tube of the sextant on it. With one eye cocked on that star through the sextant, I searched for the horizon with the other eye.

At first the stars shone bright and well-defined and the horizon line was dark and hazy. But as the edge of horizon gradually sharpened against the brightening dawn, the stars faded away and rapidly became invisible. There was just one moment, and we awaited it anxiously, when the horizon stood out distinctly and the stars still shone faintly. At that critical moment I locked my sextant on the precise angle between the star and the earth.

At its surface the earth spins nearly one thousand miles per hour, changing our ship's position and angle of reference to that star constantly. For this reason, the instant I had my reading I dashed over to the chronometer and noted the time, correct to a fraction of a second. Now I could fix the position and direction of the ship, because at only one place on earth could that angle to the star be measured at that particular instant in time. I had no second chance; if I missed the first reading and returned to the sextant, the star would have vanished.

Dusk reversed the order of sighting. I stood on the bridge with the crew watching the clear horizon, as sharp and fine as a ruler's edge, and waiting for the first star to appear. On that journey we usually looked for Alpha Orion and Betelgeuse. Suddenly someone would shout "There it is!" and we all swung our sextants. We focused one tube on the star and one on the horizon, flipped down the mirror that converged the images, and locked the sextants. Then, again, came the scramble to the chronometer.

Those two times of day — dusk and dawn — bracketed the passing of time on the ship. All day we could see the sea and all night observe the stars, but in order to navigate we had to bring heaven and earth together. Other sophisticated instruments on board for measuring drift, propeller velocity, and tidal forces gave us an approximate location, and these were especially useful on cloudy days. But they ran the danger of compounding the previous days' errors. For accuracy, we needed the alignment of fixed points on earth and in the heavens.

⟵

A word in the English language reminds me somewhat of my experiences with celestial navigation. It takes on several forms: orient, orientation, or the modern sport of "orienteering." At its most basic level it means finding the East (the Orient), and the connotation actually derives from an ancient religious practice.

In Jewish and early Christian faith, churches and synagogues had to face east, toward Jerusalem—that was the only acceptable "orientation" for the worship of God. This practice stemmed from a prayer articulated by Solomon at the dedication of the temple, when he asked God to hear any call for help prayed toward the temple in Jerusalem. Later, syncretism with sun worshipers further settled the practice of facing east. Jesus discounted the notion that location mattered in worship (see his dialogue with a Samaritan woman in John 4), but the tradition lived on and in some places still does.

The practice has a sort of symbolic significance that brings to my mind the principles I learned in celestial navigation. It captures the concept of planting my feet firmly on earth while sighting along a line of spiritual direction. I need a time of day to orient myself, to bring heaven and earth together. In the midst of the clamor and tumult of this material world, I must find a place of quietness to listen to the still, small voice for guidance of my life.

The Old Testament gives one striking example of spiritual orientation, as performed by a Jewish executive in the worldly government of Babylon. For Daniel, orienting toward Jerusalem meant an act of civil disobedience punishable by imprisonment in a den of lions. Regardless of the king's edict, three times a day Daniel flung open his window and turned toward Jerusalem for his prayers. Surely when he did so, the reality of Babylon—the aroma of spices and produce from the bazaar, the strange jumble of urban architecture, the alien language and traffic noise—overwhelmed his sense organs. Yet as Daniel faced Jerusalem, his body language aligned him with the God Jerusalem represented. In a foreign, polluted culture, he fell back in dependence on Jehovah God.

Orientation, aligning heaven and earth, has become for me a metaphor of my reliance on the Spirit as I live in an alien, material culture. I no longer face a city for my prayers — God does not dwell in an earthly structure — but the symbolism of prayer has changed little. To survive, I must pause to breathe in the power of the living God and consciously direct my mind to him.

At times I find myself nearly overwhelmed by the physical realities that press in from all sides. My appointment book fills up with the names of patients who need personal attention. The hospital and government bureaucracies churn out new projects and memos and reporting procedures. I know that in a few days I will leave on an overseas trip. I have speeches to prepare, books to review, a manuscript to edit. At such moments, I am strongly tempted to shunt aside my normal time with God.

Over the years I have learned, with difficulty, that those moments amid intense earthly pressures are precisely the times when I need most to rely on the Spirit for guidance. In the morning and in the evening, I look for a time when the Spirit can bring heaven and earth together. I commit my day's clutter to God, asking to see the details of my life in the light of his will.

Spiritually, I cannot survive the alien atmosphere of earth without live contact through the Spirit. Daniel looked out over the streets of Babylon, but his mind and soul were in Jerusalem. The astronauts walked in the cold, forbidding atmosphere of the moon only by carrying with them resources from another world that would keep them alive. I need just that kind of reliance on the Spirit of God.

⟿

A practical matter arises. What does this reliance consist of? Does the Spirit actually help with the specific pressures and choices confronting me each day? How, in fact, does God guide us?

I confess that on very few occasions have I felt clear, unmistakable guidance from the Spirit. I explain my dilemmas and pour out my needs, but God does not respond by telling me what to do. And the Bible itself contains little advice on techniques of guidance. (The often cited instances of Gideon's fleece and the Macedonian call are notable because of their exceptional nature; they hardly offer a practical model for guidance.)

The Bible does, however, have much to say about maintaining a love relationship with God. He wants a conscious and willing acceptance of his presence whenever I make a decision. There is no shortcut, no magic, only the possibility of a lifetime search for intimacy with a God who sometimes seems close by and sometimes far away. Normally, I believe, God guides in subtle ways: feeding ideas into my mind, speaking through a nagging sensation of dissatisfaction, inspiring me to choose better than I otherwise would have done, bringing to the surface hidden dangers of temptation. The Prompter supplies real help, but in ways that will not overwhelm my freedom.

If someone asked me to trace the guidance of God on my life I could do it fairly easily, I think. Looking back, the circumstances of my life do fit together with an order and design that seem purposeful. And yet, at individual points along the way, exactly the opposite seemed true.

In my childhood and teenage years I wanted to be a missionary. My parents had impressed me with a value system that ranked their own work of helping people in India as among the highest ends a person could seek.

Due partially to the influence of my father, a builder, I decided to pursue a career in building. My father had built schools, hospitals, and homes, and I knew that such skills would prove useful in India. If I could learn that trade, then surely I would find a place as a missionary builder. As I have recounted, I stubbornly resisted an uncle's generous offer to pay my way through medical school and began to study masonry, carpentry, and principles of engineering. Many of my close friends thought the whole scheme was a waste of time. They proposed to me dozens of alternative careers, but for four years I persisted.

After my full apprenticeship I spent one year at Livingstone College taking a medical course designed to help missionaries with first aid and basic treatment. There for the first time I felt a pull toward medicine (mainly because of the experience at Connaught Hospital mentioned earlier in this book). I wondered whether I had made a mistake by choosing against a career in medicine. But after finishing the course I put these thoughts behind me and went with great eagerness to call on the director of my parents' mission.

With some pride, I announced to him my willingness to serve in India. A small booklet of Scripture texts had fortified my determination. I had prayed for guidance and opened the booklet to the first text, and this is what I had found: "I have chosen you for my kingdom and glory." It all seemed clear to me: a second generation of Brands would carry on the work of Jesse Brand, who had died in the Lord's service.

But J. B. Collin, the president of the mission, did not see matters in quite the same light. He asked numerous questions about my motives and preparation and then cordially said, "No." He did not dispute my direction, but rather judged me unready for the kind of work the mission required. He suggested more preparation and then a fresh application if I still felt the same. I was crushed. God's will had seemed so clear to me, and now this key person was standing in the way.

I slipped into medicine by apparent accident. I signed up for a course at the Missionary Training Colony, a Bible school that also taught how to prepare for the rigors of life in remote settings. I learned to mend boots, make my own clothes, and live off the land. There too I took a brief course in medicine, and the inner voice inside me got louder and louder. I felt inescapably drawn to the field of medicine. So intense was the feeling that I withdrew from the two-year missionary course and enrolled in medical school.

When I finally did sign up for medical school, the four years in construction loomed over me as a wasteful diversion. Despite the late start, I did well in school and finished my general training as a doctor.

Once again I presented myself to a mission board, now trained in two separate fields, building and medicine. Again I was turned down! This time the interference came from the Central Medical War Committee of Great Britain. They rejected my application to work in a mission hospital on the border of Nepal and instead ordered me into the bomb-casualty clearing services in London. Impatiently biding my time during the forced delay, I studied for higher qualifications in the field of surgery.

Twice my good plans had been stymied, once by a wise and godly mission administrator and once by a secular committee of bureaucrats. Each time I felt shaken and confused. Had I somehow misread God's will for my life?

Now, as I look back, I can see that God's hand was directing me at every step. Eventually Dr. Bob Cochrane in India convinced the same Central Medical War Committee to assign me to a new medical college in Vellore, India, and it was he who challenged me to apply the principles of orthopedics to leprosy patients. One intense moment (the story is told in *Fearfully and Wonderfully Made*), while shaking the powerful but insensitive hand of a leprosy patient, I experienced a stirring, unforgettable call from God. Ever since, I have devoted my life to leprosy work.

Decades later, I now look back with profound gratitude on the time I spent in construction and engineering. Hardly a day goes by that I do not use some of those principles in trying to perfect a rehabilitation device, or form a better pair of shoes, or apply engineering mechanics to surgery techniques, or set up stress experiments. And I am equally grateful for the decision that forced me into surgery.

I have stood under the thatched roof of our New Life Center in India and reflected on God's pattern in all those years. Watching the patients do carpentry in the workshop I established, I have a momentary sense of being back in my London carpentry shop; the smells of the wood shavings and rhythmic sounds of the tools come rushing back. I am among colleagues, my fellow-apprentices. But I quickly awake from my reverie and see the differences. These are all Indians with reconstructed hands and tools adapted to protect them. God has permitted me the honor of serving these patients on several levels: as a doctor treating their disease, as a surgeon remaking their hands, and as a carpentry foreman helping to fashion new lives for them.

Only the zigzag course of guidance allowed me to interact with them on all these levels. At any point — if I had gone to India earlier or had bypassed those years in construction, for example — I could easily have strayed slightly out of line and thus have proven less useful. In hindsight, I have a wonderful sense of how God planned ahead and ordered the details of my life.

⟶

The summer I sailed the coasts of Britain and France, I was responsible for guiding the boat into the treacherous harbor of St. Malo, notorious for centuries as a pirates' cove. Jagged rocks hidden just beneath the surface of the water make the harbor unnavigable, except through one narrow route. To follow that route, I had to rely on two sets of leading lights to the harbor. I would fix our course by lining up the first pair, sailing southeast until the next two lights lined up. Immediately I would turn sharply starboard and keep the second set of leading lights in line. Our boat rarely headed in the ultimate direction of the harbor, but zigzagged through a pattern required to avoid unseen obstacles. I concentrated solely on the lights before me, putting my trust in the one who knew the harbor well enough to mark off that route.

Similarly, God does not ask that we figure out the reason for each change in our direction, or look on apparent obstacles with frustration. Rather, God wants us to accept the circumstances in our lives and respond in obedience and trust even when they appear confusing and contradictory. Events not under my control, such as the war and the slamming of doors by the bureaucracy, served to guide me by blocking my way. These, in turn, sent me back to the Holy Spirit for help in facing a new set of circumstances requiring new evaluation and new strategies.

I take great comfort in the promise of Romans 8: "Moreover we know that to those who love God, who are called according to his plan, everything that happens fits into a pattern for good" (v. 28 PHILLIPS). God does not promise only good things will happen; nor does the verse say all that happens is sent by God. I seek God's wisdom primarily to guide me through and around circumstances that happen to appear, moving always toward the fulfillment of his will. And I have confidence that the end result of all things will show a pattern for good. Obedience to the Spirit at every point ensures fulfillment of that promise.

I am, after all, a mere cell in Christ's Body. It is the role of the Head to direct the other members and coordinate the actions for the whole church. What God asks of me is simple loyalty, a commitment to follow the messages of the Spirit in whatever form they come, in a way that builds up the whole Body.

# PAIN

# Chapter 19

# PROTECTION

*"How much reverence can you have for a Supreme Being who finds it necessary to include tooth decay in His divine system of creation? Why in the world did He ever create pain?"*

*"Pain?" Lieutenant Shiesskopf's wife pounced upon the word victoriously. "Pain is a useful symptom. Pain is a warning to us of bodily dangers."*

*"And who created the dangers?" Yossarian demanded. "Why couldn't He have used a doorbell to notify us, or one of His celestial choirs? Or a system of blue-and-red neon tubes right in the middle of each person's forehead?"*

*"People would certainly look silly walking around with red neon tubes in the middle of their foreheads."*

*"They certainly look beautiful now writhing in agony, don't they?"*

Joseph Heller

In a lithography by Honoré Victorin Daumier, a distinguished gentleman in a white waistcoat is sitting on a high-backed Victorian sofa — no, not sitting, contorting. His legs are jerked up under him spectacularly and his back arches downward, nearly forming a fetal position. He is doubled up with pain. Four sets of leering little devils perch mischievously at each corner of the sofa, half of them playing tug-of-war with cables looped around the gentleman's midsection and half gleefully brandishing a huge, jagged-tooth saw that is sundering his abdomen. His face is frozen in an expression of utter agony. Daumier added a simple title: *La colique* — the pain of colic.

Virtually everyone who views Daumier's print responds with a wince, a mirroring of the figure's anguish. We have all felt at least a twinge from a muscular spasm caused by intestinal blockage or distention. Pain is the hallmark of mortality.

We plunge into the world through the stretched and bloody tissues of a grimacing woman. "My mother groaned, my father wept. Into the dangerous world I leapt," wrote William Blake. Our own first reaction is a loud cry of fear, or grief, or both. Years later we exit the world through suffering, sometimes in one last paroxysm of pain. Between those two events, we live out our days with pain always lurking at the door.

Large industries exist to loosen the cables and dull the saw-blades of pain. A parade of modern mountebanks fills television talk show slots, promising relief through a new method of foot or ear massage, or acupuncture, or a new electronic marvel sewn beneath the skin. Pain is the tainted sensation: the word itself derives from *poena*, Latin for "punishment," hinting that the demons manning the saw are not imaginary.

Ironically, I have spent half my life among people whose faces bear the same disfigurement of punishment and torment, but for the opposite reason. Leprosy patients suffer because they feel no pain; they yearn for the demons who would alert them to impending danger.

My love/hate relationship with pain began, I suppose, in my childhood. Wherever we went in the mountains of South India, my parents would take along a few pairs of dental forceps, for they knew that toothache was one of the most persistent and overwhelming pains. Their reputation for pulling teeth preceded them even in the most remote mountain hamlets.

Hundreds of times I interrupted my play to stand by, with wide eyes and a wildly thumping heart, as my mother or father extracted patients' teeth — without anesthetic. I would watch my tiny mother wriggle her pointed forceps up between the gum and tooth, seeking a firm grip so the crown of the tooth would not break off when she yanked. When dealing with a very large patient, she hung on fiercely to those forceps while the patient's own thrashing motions worked the tooth loose. The patients cried out, danced around uncontrollably, and spit up blood. Yet, even after seeing those reactions, onlookers lined up for treatment. Ridding themselves of toothache was worth any cost.

Occasionally in villages on the plains we would also see the impressive *fakirs*, religious men who demonstrated their conquest over pain. Some would push a thin stiletto-type blade through their cheek, tongue, and out the other cheek, then withdraw the blade without bleeding. Others strung themselves high in the air by pulling on ropes that passed through a metal ring at the top of a pole and ended in meat-hooks stuck into the flesh of their backs. Passively, showing no signs of pain, they dangled like spiders above an admiring crowd. Still others garishly decorated themselves with scores of oranges attached to large safety pins which they jabbed into their skins. They laughed and merrily danced down the streets on stilts, jiggling the oranges in time with music.

Later, as a medical student in England I had the rare privilege of working as a house physician under Sir Thomas Lewis, one of the great pioneers in the exploration of pain. I remember those days well because Sir Thomas gained much of his knowledge of pain by using his students as guinea pigs. One gets an unforgettable perspective on pain by recording sensations while being pinched, pricked, or bound by a tourniquet. Lewis collected his findings into a book, *Pain*, that became a classic, a model of beautiful language as well as medical research.

Then, returning to India I immediately encountered the full spectrum of human misery: vast numbers of victims of poliomyelitis, osteomyelitis, joint tuberculosis, spinal tuberculosis, paraplegia, and other crippling disorders. These all came to our hospital at the Christian Medical College in Vellore.

Unaccountably, I found myself drawn to those who never came, the pitiful deformed people who lined the entrances to temples, railway stations, and most public buildings, begging for alms. They had clawed hands with missing fingers, ulcerated feet, paralyzed thumbs, and every other conceivable kind of orthopedic defect, yet no orthopedist had ever treated them or their fifteen million fellow-sufferers worldwide. Because they had leprosy, few hospitals would admit them.

Eventually, of course, I decided to spend my life among leprosy patients and concentrate on their orthopedic problems. I have been studying pain ever since, because leprosy destroys pain nerves, making the body devastatingly vulnerable to injury. Those creatures snapping their cables like bullwhips in Daumier's lithograph — are they truly demons? Without their torments, would the gentleman attend to his colic? A lifetime among suffering people has planted such questions in my mind.

⟿

A career devoted to any sensation will inevitably distort one's perspective so that the specialist considers his or her sensation to be the richest and most wonderful. Thus a gourmet will pay thousands of dollars to visit France for the sole purpose of scraping particles of food across taste buds, or an oenophile will trade a month's salary for a bottle of vintage Bordeaux. The nuances of taste and smell have come to mean that much. Over the years, paradoxically, I have developed an appreciation for the pain system that approaches their fanaticism. To be sure, I do not seek out personal experiences of pain, but my study of its design features has overwhelmed me with awe.

The mechanics of pain resemble those of other sensations: like taste or sight or sound, pain is detected by the nerve endings of receptor cells, translated into a chemical and electrical code, and conveyed to the brain where a meaning or interpretation is assigned. One portion of my brain is receiving impulses that it recognizes as the typewriter in my office while another area alerts me that a phone is ringing. Similarly, steadily firing nerve cells remind my brain that my strained back needs attention.

Pain, however, functions with such brutal efficiency that its message can preoccupy the brain and drown out all pleasurable signals. It travels along a hotline, insisting on priority. Moreover, its impact can spread out from the brain and ultimately involve the entire body. At the muscular level, my body responds to back pain by contracting or tensing. Unchecked, this response can initiate a vicious cycle in which the tension causes even more pain as it squeezes nerves.

My blood flow changes: blood pressure reacts to pain just as it reacts to anxiety and fear. I may even go pale or flush or, in the event of vascular collapse, I may faint.

Pain may upset my digestion by causing a spasm of my gut or even nausea and vomiting. My endocrine system responds to pain by secreting chemicals like adrenaline. And finally the pain may come to dominate me on the psychological level. I may complain to my colleagues and family. Perhaps I'll cancel an overseas trip to give my back extra rest. But that too may lead to complications: guilt from letting people down, depression about my inability to work.

Amazingly, this sensation of pain, which provokes such a powerful response in every part of my body and mind, soon fades away into oblivion. Think back to your worst experience of pain and try to remember what it felt like. You cannot. You can summon up an accurate recollection of a visual scene, like a face or a childhood home; or a sound, such as a few bars of music; or even a memory of taste or smell piquant enough to provoke salivation. But the sense of tyrannical pain has somehow vanished. You have forgotten.

Dominating, subjective, ephemeral — pain offers a target for research as elusive as the quark. What is pain? When is it really there — and where? The answers must begin with a study of individual nerve cells that first trigger pain. My old teacher in London (along with Bishop, in America, and von Frey before them) laboriously mapped out the subtleties and complexities of the nervous system devoted to pain. Having studied under Sir Thomas Lewis, I know well the real heroes who sacrificed to produce our knowledge: medical students whose potential careers depended upon their voluntary cooperation in a series of tests that might daunt the Marquis de Sade. Many professors insisted on subjecting themselves to the same tests; otherwise they would find it difficult interpreting their students' reports of pain.

Research subjects allowed blood pressure cuffs to be inflated around a metal grater that pressed into their arms, endured drippings of hot sealing wax, and dutifully performed isometric exercises while a tourniquet cut off their blood supply. Von Frey's

pressure tests with boar bristles and sharp pins attached to miniature scales soon gave way to a new generation of laboratory
devices: supersonic oscillators of high frequency sound waves,
ultraviolet lights, super-cooled copper wires, radiant heat devices,
metal rods dropped from heights onto the skin, 1000-watt bulbs
intensified with mirrors. Electricity offered a creative medium for
torture machines, including many repetitive spark producers and
one maleficent contraption that shot voltage through the fillings of
a tooth.

Today's sophisticated breed of experimental subjects have
potassium sprinkled onto open blisters, balloons inserted in their
stomachs, irritating chemicals applied to their nasal mucosa, and
corrosive mixtures such as diluted hydrochloric acid swabbed on
their skin. They submerse their hands in ice water, then hot water.
They have cheeks and hands pricked simultaneously to determine
which pain "extinguishes" the other. They hear bells rung and stories read aloud and must repeat sequences of numbers in forward
and reverse order, all the while being assaulted by one of the torture machines.

These exhaustive methods yield a few basic measurements. At
what point does it start hurting (pain threshold)? Do you ever
grow accustomed to the heat or pressure (adaptation to pain)?
Where does it hurt (distribution of pain)? At what point can't you
endure it anymore (tolerance of pain)? Subjects may also describe
each pain verbally and try to distinguish degrees of pain (as many
as twenty-one have been reported).

The students come away with slight lesions, blisters, and pin-
pricks, and a diploma that exempts them from being victimized
again. The professors come away with graphs mapping out sensitivities on every square centimeter of the body. Such experiments
have proceeded unabated for a hundred years for one reason: the

nervous system is incredibly complex. Each tiny swatch of the body has a different perception of pain.

I need not reproduce the charts here; everyone knows, albeit subconsciously, the principles of distribution of pain. A single speck of dust (or, worse, an eyelash) flies into your eye. You respond immediately: your eye tears, you squint it shut and dab at the eyelid with your finger to remove the speck. Such a speck can immobilize even a superbly conditioned athlete like a baseball pitcher; the pain is so great he cannot continue pitching until the speck is removed. Yet the same speck on the pitcher's arm goes wholly unnoticed. Undoubtedly, thousands of dirt particles will accumulate there in the course of the game. Why the disparity in sensitivity?

The eye has certain rigid requirements of structure. Unlike its sensitive neighbor the ear, it must lie exposed on the surface, in a straight line with light waves. An eye must be transparent for obvious reasons, which severely limits a blood supply (blood vessels would make the eye opaque, blocking vision). Any intrusion causes serious danger, since the blood-starved eye cannot easily repair itself. Therefore a well-designed pain system makes the eye extraordinarily sensitive to the slightest pressure or pain.

Every part of our bodies has a unique sensitivity to both pain and pressure, depending on function. The face, especially in the area of the lips and nose, is acutely sensitive to both. Feet, subject to a day's stomping, are better protected by tough skin and mercifully insensitive. The abdomen is moderately sensitive, the back less so. Fingertips present an unusual case: their constant use requires them to be sensitive to pressure and temperature but relatively pain-resistant. Where limbs join the trunk, protecting vital organs becomes the main concern; there, cells are four times more alert to pain than to pressure. A light tap on the foot goes unnoticed, on the groin is felt as painful, and on the eye causes anguish.

As I study pain throughout the human body I gain deep respect for the Creator's wisdom. Sometimes I could wish that the lining of the trachea were even more sensitive to irritants, causing more pain and coughing and so making lung-destroying tobacco smoke intolerable. But could humans even survive with a hypersensitive trachea in a dust storm or in the smoke of our modern polluted environment?

Or I think again of the eye. Some wearers of contact lenses might wish for less sensitivity in the eye, but the sensitivity benefits the great majority of people and their need to preserve vision. The eye has a split-second response to danger — intense pain, a blinking reflex, and an effusion of tears — that occurs numerous times each day, often below our level of consciousness.

Each part of the body responds to the appropriate danger that might interfere with it and thus affect the whole body.

⟵

Pain contributes daily to a normal person's quality of life, even in such a common activity as walking. A leprosy patient, with perfectly normal skin tissue on the soles of his feet, can take a daily five-mile walk and return with foot ulcers. A healthy person who undergoes the same stress will return without ulcers. Why? A file cabinet in my office contains a box of photographic slides that illustrate the reason.

The slides of color-coded feet show that the way a healthy person puts feet to the ground changes radically from the first mile to the fifth mile. If at the beginning your great toe is doing most of the work, by the end of the run your lateral toes and the lateral border of your foot will take over. Later the toe and heel will come down together. When you begin a really long hike, you will start off heel-toe, heel-toe. But when you return you'll be lifting your foot and setting it down as one unit — all adjustments having been made subconsciously. The photographic evidence of these changes is quite astounding.

Muscular fatigue does not cause the shifts. Rather, pain cells in your toes, heels, arches, and lateral bones are intermittently informing your brain, "Ease up a little. I need some rest." You jog along oblivious, since your brain assigns these functions to a sub-liminal control, but every spot on your body is constantly talking to you. Even as I sit and write this, the pain cells in my hips and legs are frequently asking me to shift my weight around, and I reflex-ively obey.

Pain employs a tonal range of conversation. It whispers to us in the early stages of damage: subconsciously, we feel a slight dis-comfort and toss and turn in bed. It speaks to us as danger increases: a hand grows tender and sore after a long stint at raking leaves. And pain shouts at us when the danger becomes severe: blis-ters, ulcers, and tissue damage break out, forcing us to change behavior.

A leprosy patient, having lost this incessant hum of intercellular conversation, will walk five miles without changing gait or shifting weight. The same pressure strikes the same cells with unrelenting force, and ulcers open up.

A limp graphically demonstrates in exaggerated form the body's adjustments to pain. Out of orthopedic habit, I suppose, I have always stared impolitely at people who limp. I learn a lot from them. What they may view as an embarrassing malfunction, I view as a wonderful adaptation. A limper's body is compensating for damage to one leg by redirecting weight and pressure to the other, healthy leg. Every normal person limps occasionally. Sadly, leprosy patients do not limp. Their injured legs never get the rest needed for healing.

In an extreme form, this inability to "hear" pain can cause permanent damage because the body's careful response to danger will break down. For example, a healthy person nearly always falls when beginning to sprain an ankle. Perhaps you step on a loose stone or curb. As your ankle begins to twist, the lateral ligaments of the ankle endure a terrific strain. Nerve cells detecting the strain categorically order the body to take all weight off the damaged leg immediately. The thigh and calf muscles will become momentarily flaccid. But if your other, undamaged leg is off the ground taking a step, you will now have no support and will lurch to the ground. (A step, says the anatomist, is a stumble caught in time.) Your body prefers falling to forcing the ankle to take weight in its twisted position. You get up feeling a fool and hoping no one was watching, but in reality you have just achieved a beautifully coordinated maneuver that saved you from a sprained ankle or worse.

However, I recall watching a leprosy victim sprain his ankle without falling. He stepped on a loose stone, turned his ankle *completely* over so that the sole of his foot pointed inward, and walked on without a limp. He did not even glance at the foot he had just irreparably damaged by rupturing the left lateral ligament! He lacked the protection of pain. Afterward, without the support of the ligament he had ruptured, he turned his ankle again and again until eventually, due to more complications, he had to have that leg amputated.

# Chapter 20

# LINKING

*Compassion is the chief law of human existence.*

Fyodor Dostoyevsky

—

I admit, a professional career devoted to people with leprosy, whose main defect is an absence of pain, has biased me on the subject. And yet numbness too is a form of suffering. In the case of leprosy patients it can lead to a life of acute suffering.

When I reflect on pain I prefer not to think in a detached way of a hypothetical sum of the world's suffering; instead I focus on one individual with a face and body. At such moments my mind often flashes back to the refined, upper-caste features of my friend Sadagopan, whom we called Sadan. Readers of *Fearfully and Wonderfully Made* know him as the forbearing subject of my early experiments with proper footwear for leprosy patients.

When Sadan first came to Vellore, his feet had shrunk to half their normal length and his fingers were shortened and paralyzed. It took us nearly two years of unflagging effort to stop the pattern of destruction in his feet. Meanwhile we began reconstructing his hands, a finger at a time, attaching the most useful tendons to the most useful digits and retraining his mind to control the new set of connections. In all, Sadan spent four years with me in rehabilitation. He personified the soft-spoken, gentle Indian spirit. Together, we wept at our failures and rejoiced at the gradual successes. I came to love Sadan as a dear friend.

At last Sadan decided he should return home to his family in Madras for a trial weekend. He had come to us with badly ulcerated hands and feet. Now his hands were more flexible, and with a specially designed rocker-type shoe he could walk without damage. "I want to go back to where I was rejected before," he said proudly, referring to the cafés that had turned him away and the buses that had denied him service. "Now that I am not so deformed I want to try my way in the great city of Madras."

Before Sadan left, we reviewed together all the dangers he might encounter. Since he had no warning system of pain, any sharp or hot object could harm him. Having learned to care for himself in our hospital and workshop, he felt confident. He boarded a train to Madras.

On Saturday night, after an exuberant reunion dinner with his family, Sadan went to his old room where he had not slept for four years. He lay down on the woven pallet on the floor and drifted off to sleep in great peace and contentment. At last he was home, fully accepted once again.

The next morning when Sadan awoke and examined himself, as he had been trained to do at the hospital, he recoiled in horror. Part of the back of his left index finger was mangled. He knew the culprit because he had seen many such injuries on other patients. Evidence was clear: telltale drops of blood, marks in the dust, and, of course, the decimated clump of tendon and flesh that had been so carefully reconstructed some months before. A rat had visited him during the night and gnawed his finger.*

---

*To prevent such tragedies, we later tried to maintain a rule at the hospital: all released patients must take a cat home to protect them from rats during the night.

Immediately he thought, *What will Dr. Brand say?* All that day he agonized. He considered coming back to Vellore early, but finally decided he must keep his promise to stay the weekend. He looked in vain for a rat trap to protect him that last night at home—the shops were closed for a festival. He concluded he must stay awake to guard against further injury.

All Sunday night Sadan sat cross-legged on his pallet, his back against the wall, studying an accounting book by the light of a kerosene lantern. About four o'clock in the morning the subject grew dull and his eyes felt heavy and he could no longer fight off sleep. The book fell forward onto his knees and his hand slid over to one side against the hot glass of the hurricane lamp.

When Sadan awoke the next morning he saw instantly that a large patch of skin had burned off the back of his right hand. He sat trembling in bed, despair growing like a tumor inside him, and stared at his two hands—one gnawed by a rat, the other melted down to the tendons. He had learned the dangers and difficulties of leprosy, in fact had taught them to others. Now he was devastated by the sight of his two damaged hands. Again he thought, *How can I face Dr. Brand, who worked so hard on these hands?*

Sadan returned to Vellore that day with both hands swathed in bandages. When he met me and I began to unroll the bandages, he wept. I must confess that I wept with him. As he poured out his misery to me, he said, "I feel as if I've lost all my freedom." And then, a question that has stayed with me, "How can I be free without pain?"

⟤

Sadan represents millions of people who suffer from leprosy and other numbing diseases; taken together they offer a powerful negative lesson about the true message of pain. At its most basic level pain serves as a signal that something is wrong, like a smoke alarm that goes off with a loud noise whenever the danger of fire reaches a certain level. Sadan nearly lost his hands because he lacked such a signal.

Besides this warning aspect, pain offers a related contribution that often gets overlooked: it unifies the body. In truth, Sadan suffered because the rest of his body had lost contact with his hands. No jolt of pain informed his brain a terrible thing was happening at the extremities.

A body only possesses unity to the degree that it possesses pain. An infected toenail proves to me the toe is important; it is mine, it needs attention. Hair — yes, that matters, but we see it as a decoration. It can be bleached, shaped, ironed, and even cut off without pain. But what is indispensably mine is defined by pain.

Nothing arouses more distress in me than watching my patients in the Carville hospital "lose touch" with their own hands and feet. When pain fades away they start viewing their own limbs as stuck-on appendages. You and I speak metaphorically of a hand or foot going "dead" when we have slept on it in an awkward position. The leprosy patients seem to regard their hands and feet as truly dead.

The most common injury at Carville, "kissing wound," occurs when a cigarette burns unnoticed down to the nub and brands matching scars into the skin between the two fingers. The patients think of their hands as impersonal accessories, not unlike a plastic cigarette holder. One such patient, who was gradually destroying his hands, said to me, "You know, my hands are not really hands — they're things, just like wooden attachments. And I always have the feeling they can be replaced because they are not me."

As rehabilitation director of the hospital, I strive to remind the patients of parts of their bodies they might "forget about" in the absence of pain. I have spent much of my life repairing the damage that results when patients lower their guard. I would give anything to awaken in such people a sense of their body's unity, but overcoming this peculiar sense of detachment seems impossible without the sensation of pain. Just as pain unifies the body, its loss irreversibly destroys that unity.

In India I had one group of teenage patients nicknamed "the naughty boys" because they tested the limits of our medical longsuffering. These rapscallions competed to appall others with their displays of painlessness. They would thrust a thorn all the way through a finger or palm, pulling it out the other side like a sewing needle. They juggled hot coals or passed their hands over a flame. In addition, they often injured themselves by doing things other boys could do without damage and then proceeded to hide the wounds from us. When quizzed about a wound on hands or feet, they grinned mischievously and said, "Oh, it must have come by itself."

Eventually, after taxing all our skill in psychology and motivational therapy, most of the "naughty boys" acquired a respect for their bodies and learned to transfer their ingenuity to the task of preserving their hands and feet. Throughout their rehabilitation process I felt as if I was introducing the boys to their limbs, forcing them to welcome these parts of their bodies.

Years later when I began working with laboratory animals, I learned to my dismay that they felt even more estrangement from deadened parts of their bodies. If I denervated rats or mice for an experiment, I had to keep them well fed; otherwise, the next morning I would find animals with shortened feet and legs. I am told that a wolf or coyote, losing sensation through frostbite or a trap injury, will gnaw through its leg, severing it, and limp away unperturbed. That single scene captures for me the worst curse of painlessness: the painless person, or animal, loses all normal sense of self-unity.

⊷

An amoeba, one-celled, automatically perceives any threat as a danger to the whole organism, and the whole organism responds. But organisms consisting of many cells need something more. Pain provides the crucial link that keeps a multicelled organism informed. The head must feel the needs of the tail.

Anatomically, the method of linking is quite astonishing. In the circulatory system cells are joined by blood vessels composed of millions of intermediate cells. But in the nervous system, a single cell reaches out in unbelievable disproportion from one end of the body to the other. One thin nerve cell joining toe and spinal column may span four feet — no other body cell approaches that length.

As I turn from the network of pain in biology to its analogy in the Body of Christ, comprising all believers, again I am struck by the importance of such a communication system. Pain serves a vital role in protecting and uniting that corporate membership as it does in guarding the cells of my own body.

There are great differences between the unity attainable in a physical body of linked cells and in a Body composed of autonomous members. No tangible axons stretch from person to person in the church. Nevertheless, the Body of Christ offers a primary channel through which to share pain with others. In biology, individual cells must suffer with one another for multicelled organisms to survive. When living tissues are wounded, they cry out and the whole body hears the cry. And we in Christ's Body — loving our neighbors as ourselves — are called to an even higher level of identification: "If one part suffers, every part suffers with it," says Paul (1 Corinthians 12:26).

Deep emotional connections link human beings as certainly as dendrites link cells in our bodies, evident even in such relative trivialities as sporting events. Watch the face of a wife sitting in the stands at Wimbledon as her husband plays in the championship tennis match. Strands of concern and affection unite them so intensely that every on-court success or failure can be read on the wife's face. She winces at every missed shot and smiles at each minor triumph. What affects him affects her.

Or, visit a Jewish household in Miami, San Francisco, or Chicago around election time in Israel. Many Jews know more about the campaign ten thousand miles away than about their local elections. An invisible web, a plexus of human connections, links them with a tiny nation of strangers far away.

Or, recall the effect on a nation when a great leader dies. I experienced the unifying effect of pain most profoundly in 1963 when I came to the United States to address the student chapel at Stanford University. As it happened, the chapel service occurred just two days after the assassination of President John Kennedy. I spoke on pain that day, for I could read nothing but pain on the faces of hundreds of students jammed into that building. I described for them scenes from around the world, where I knew clusters of people would be gathering together in prayer and mourning to share the pain of a grieving nation. I have never felt such unity of spirit in a worship service.

Something like those sympathetic connections should link us to members of Christ's Body all over the globe. When an oppressive government jails courageous Christians, when Central American death squads torture nuns, when Muslims drive a person from town for the crime of converting, when my neighbors lose their jobs, a part of my Body suffers and I should sense the loss. Pain can come to our attention in whispered signals of loneliness, despair, discrimination, physical suffering, self-hatred.

"How can a man who is warm understand one who is cold?" asked Alexander Solzhenitsyn as he tried to fathom the apathy toward millions of Gulag inmates. In response, he devoted his life to perform the work of a "nerve cell," alerting us to pain we may have overlooked. In a Body composed of millions of cells, the comfortable ones must consciously attend to the messages of pain. We must develop a lower threshold of pain by listening, truly listening, to those who suffer. The word compassion itself comes from Latin words *cum* and *pati*, together meaning "to suffer with."

Today our world has shrunk, and as a Body we live in awareness of many cells: persecuted Chinese believers, starving Africans, oppressed Indo-Chinese and Central Americans ... the litany fills our newspapers. Do we fully attend? Do we hear their cries as unmistakably as our brains hear the complaints of a strained back or broken arm? Or do we instead turn down the volume, filtering out annoying sounds of distress?

And closer, within the confines of our own local gathering of Christ's Body — how do we respond? Tragically, the divorced, the alcoholics, the introverted, the rebellious, the unemployed often report that the church is the last group to show them compassion. Like a person who takes aspirin at the first sign of headache, we want to silence them, to "cure" them without addressing the underlying causes.

Someone once asked John Wesley's mother, "Which one of your eleven children do you love the most?" Her answer was as wise as the question foolish: "I love the one who's sick until he's well, and the one who's away until he comes home." That, I believe, is God's attitude toward our suffering planet. He feels the pain of those who suffer. Do we?

God gave this succinct summary of the life of King Josiah, "He defended the cause of the poor and needy, and so all went well." And then this disturbing postscript: "Is that not what it means to know me?" (Jeremiah 22:16).

⟿

I hear many cries for unity in the church today; a watching world sees divisiveness as our greatest failure. Calls go out exhorting one denomination to merge with another, or for many denominations to join hands in a national or worldwide campaign. Out of my experience with the nervous system in the human body I would propose another kind of unity: one based on pain.

I can read the health of a physical body by noting how well it "listens" to pain — most of the diagnostic tools we use, after all (fever, pulse, blood cell count), measure the body's healing response. Analogously, the corporate Body's health depends on how the stronger parts attend to the weaker.

Some cries of pain in the Body come to us loudly and persistently. We cannot help but acknowledge them. Distant outposts of pain cause me more concern, the extremities of limb in Christ's Body that we have somehow silenced. I have performed many amputations in my life, most of them because the hand or foot has gone silent and no longer reports pain. There are members of Christ's Body too, whose pain we never sense, for we have denervated or cut whatever link would carry an awareness of them to us. They suffer, but silently, unnoticed by the rest of the Body.

I think of my Palestinian friends, for example. In places like Bethlehem, children have grown up knowing nothing but war.

They play, not in parks, but in crumbling buildings pockmarked by rifle fire and explosives. Palestinian Christians feel utterly abandoned by the church in the West, which focuses so much attention on Israel and assumes all non-Israelis in the Middle East to be Arab and Moslem. Spokesmen for Palestinian Christians and others in places like Lebanon and Syria plead for some token of understanding by their brothers and sisters in the West, but we act as though the neuronal connections have been cut, the synapses blocked. Few hear their pain and respond with Christian love.

Or I think of the homosexual population scattered throughout our churches and colleges. Surveys show that 10 to 20 percent of students in Christian colleges struggle with homosexual tendencies. Yet some college administrations simply pretend the problem does not exist. Those affected are left to flounder, cut off from the balance and diversity of the larger Body and the compassion that might help them.

Or I think of the elderly, often put away out of sight behind institutional walls that hold in all sounds of loneliness and mourning. Or of battered children who grow up troubled, unwelcomed into foster homes. Or of races who feel cut off from participation in the Body.* Or of prisoners sealed off behind tall fences. Or of foreign students who live tucked away in cheap lodging, isolated and afraid. Even those within the church judged for some minor doctrinal disagreement can feel shut off, severed.

In modern society we tend to isolate these problems by forming organizations and appointing social workers to deal with them.

---

*A terrible example of exclusion from the Body occurred in South Africa, when a young spiritual searcher named Mohandas Gandhi tried to hear the missionary C. F. Andrews. Gandhi was not allowed in the meeting because of his brown skin color. Soon afterward he rejected Christianity and went on to lead 400,000,000 people as a Hindu. Concluded E. Stanley Jones, "Racialism has many sins to bear, but perhaps its worst sin was the obscuring of Christ in an hour when one of the greatest souls born of a woman was making his decision."

If we are not careful, a form of institutionalized charity will grow up that effectively isolates hurting members from close personal contact with healthy ones. In such an event, both groups atrophy: the charity recipients who are cut off from human touch and compassion and the charity donors who think of love as a kind of material transaction.

In the human body, when an area loses sensory contact with the rest of the body, even when its nourishment system remains intact, that part begins to wither and atrophy. In the vast majority of cases — 95 of 100 insensitive hands I have examined — severe injury or deformation results. The body poorly protects what it does not feel. And in the spiritual Body also, loss of feeling inevitably leads to atrophy and inner deterioration. So much of the sorrow in the world is due to the selfishness of one living organism that simply does not care when another suffers. In Christ's Body we suffer because we do not suffer enough.

I must also mention one further service that members of Christ's Body perform by embracing others' suffering. I say this carefully: we can show love when God seems not to.

The great accounts of Christians who have suffered, beginning with the book of Job and the Psalms and continuing through the writings of and about the saints, speak of a "dark night of the soul" when God seems strangely absent. When we need God most, he is most inaccessible. At this moment of apparent abandonment, the Body can rise to perhaps its highest calling; we become in fact Christ's Body, the enfleshment of his reality in the world.

When God seems unreal, we can demonstrate that reality to others by revealing Christ's love and character. Some may see this as God's failure to respond to our deepest needs: "My God, why have you forsaken me?" I see it as a calling for the rest of the Body to push through loneliness and isolation and to embody the love of God.

Praise be to the God and Father of our Lord Jesus Christ, the Father of compassion and the God of all comfort, who comforts us in all our troubles, so that we can comfort those in any trouble with the comfort we ourselves have received from God. For just as the sufferings of Christ flow over into our lives, so also through Christ our comfort overflows. If we are distressed, it is for your comfort and salvation; if we are comforted, it is for your comfort, which produces in you patient endurance of the same suffering we suffer. And our hope for you is firm, because we know that just as you share in our sufferings, so also you share in our comfort. (2 Corinthians 1:3–7)

One of my favorite patients at Carville, a man named Pedro, taught me about developing greater sensitivity to pain. For fifteen years he had lived without sensation of pain on his left hand, yet somehow the hand had suffered no damage. Of all the patients we monitored, only Pedro showed no signs of scarring or loss of fingertip.

My associate went over Pedro's hand with great care and came up with a surprise. One tiny spot on the edge of his palm still had normal sensitivity so that he could feel the lightest touch of a pin, even a stiff hair. Elsewhere on the hand he could feel nothing. We also found on a thermograph that the sensitive spot was at least six degrees hotter than the rest of Pedro's hand (which supported our theory, still being formulated, that warm areas of the body resist nerve damage from leprosy).

Pedro's hand became for us an object of great curiosity, and he graciously obliged without protest as we conducted tests and observed his activities. We noticed that he approached things with the edge of his hand, much as a dog approaches an object with a searching nose. He picked up a cup of coffee only after testing its temperature with his feeling spot.

Finally Pedro tired of our endless fascination with his hand. He said, "You know, I was born with a birthmark on my hand. The doctors said it was a hemangioma and froze it with dry ice. But they never fully got rid of it, because I can still feel it pulsing." Somewhat embarrassed that we had not considered the option, we verified that the blood vessels in his hand were indeed abnormal. A tangle of arteries brought an extra amount of blood and short-circuited some of it straight back to the veins without sending it through all the fine capillaries. As a result, the blood flowed very swiftly through that part of his hand, keeping its temperature close to that of the heart, too warm for the leprosy bacilli to flourish.

A single warm spot, the size of a nickel, which Pedro had previously viewed as a defect, had become a wonderful advantage to him when he contracted leprosy. The one remaining patch of sensitivity protected his entire hand.

In a church that has grown large and institutional, I pray for similar small patches of sensitivity. We must look to prophets, whether in speech, sermon, or art form, who will call attention to the needy by eloquently voicing their pain.

"Since my people are crushed, I am crushed," cried Jeremiah (8:21). And elsewhere, "Oh, my anguish, my anguish! I writhe in pain. Oh, the agony of my heart! My heart pounds within me, I cannot keep silent" (4:19).

Micah, too, wrote of his grief at Israel's condition:

Because of this I will weep and wail;
    I will go about barefoot and naked.

> I will howl like a jackal and moan like an owl.
>
> > For her wound is incurable. (1:8–9)

These prophets stand in great contrast to insensitive Jonah, who cared more about his comfort than about an entire city's destruction. The prophets of Israel tried to warn an entire nation of social and spiritual numbness. We need to encourage modern Jeremiahs and Micahs and to value these compassionate, pain-sensitive members as much as Pedro valued his tiny spot of sensitivity.

By shutting off pain, we risk forfeiting the wonderful privileges of being part of a Body. And a living organism is only as strong as its weakest part.

# Chapter 21

# ADAPTATIONS

*Although I still did not know that I had cancer, I hit intu-*
*itively on the correct diagnosis as regarding the tumor as an accu-*
*mulation of "swallowed tears." What this phrase suggested to me*
*was that all the tears I had not wept and had not wanted to weep*
*in my lifetime had gathered in my neck and formed this tumor*
*because they had not been able to fulfill their true function, which*
*was to be wept. In strictly medical terms, of course, this poetic-*
*sounding diagnosis is beside the point. But, seen in terms of the*
*whole person it expresses the truth. All the suffering I had swal-*
*lowed and dammed up could no longer be compressed inside me.*
*The pressure became too great, and the resulting explosion*
*destroyed the body containing all that compressed pain.*

Fritz Zorn

It is a typical Louisiana summer day. Moisture hangs so heavy in
the atmosphere it feels as if each breath is filling my lungs with
water droplets. In the few minutes required to climb a three-story
steel fire escape outside the hospital building, I become soaked
with perspiration. Fortunately, the animal research room is air-
conditioned.

I glance briefly at the orderly cages lining both sides of the aisle. Rats, mice, rabbits, armadillos — not exactly species you would choose for companionship, but each animal here has contributed to the cause of leprosy research. In one large cage at the end of the aisle I can hear Clarence shuffling around. Clarence, a monkey, compensates for what the other animals lack in relational skills, and I greet him warmly.

I have developed a certain fondness for Clarence, partly because of sentimental memories of pet monkeys in India and partly because of his fun-loving disposition. We care for him well and are circumspect in our experimentation, causing as little pain as possible. He, in turn, has served us well.

After playing a bit with Clarence on a table, I take his right arm and begin unwrapping the bandages covering it. His fingers are pink and wrinkled, like a human baby's, but a shock of dark hair sprouts from the knuckles. Only the fingertips interest me. I notice a slight swelling on two of them, and the first signs of a water blister on a third. With a magnifying glass I study them more closely, looking especially for significant differences between the first two fingers and the second two. I find none.

Clarence jumps a little when I touch two of the fingers. Externally, they seem no more swollen than the others, but they are clearly more tender. When I first obtained Clarence, I surgically opened up his hand and cut the nerves of sensation to those two fingers. Ever since, he has had two normal monkey fingers and two with no feeling of pain. My research attention focuses on his partially numb hand, which I keep swathed in a protective splint so he will not injure his two painless fingers.

Experiments with Clarence — he is anesthetized for most of them — have revealed much about the body's responses to pain stimuli. Mainly, he has shown that insensitive fingers absorb no greater damage than normal ones when subjected to equal stresses. All four of his fingers are equally vulnerable. Thus I can prove to my leprosy patients that damage is not inevitable and that they can, with care, prevent serious damage even without pain.

Scar tissue in Clarence's painless fingers shows that his body mobilized healing processes even when the message of pain never reached his central nervous system. My scalpel long before severed the nerves that would have carried pain to Clarence's brain; thus he felt nothing. The body's healing response to pain — the swelling, extra blood supply, scar tissue — occurred *on the local level.*

~⌐~

In the previous chapter we looked at pain as a valuable unifier of individual cells and, analogously, of a Body. As a member of Christ's Body, I should attend to the pain of a suffering member nearby. But then what? How should I respond? The physical adaptations to pain in my own body teach me much about the appropriate responses of neighboring cells.

To better understand the mechanisms of response to pain, I have subjected my own fingers to the mechanical devices we use on Clarence: machines that press a metal rod against fingertips with measured force and frequency. If I put my hand under the tiny mechanical hammer delivering a force of exactly one pound over one-twentieth of a square inch (twenty pounds per square inch), I find it not painful at all. It feels rather pleasant, like a vibro-massage. But if I let the machine run on for several hundred beats, my finger turns slightly red and feels uncomfortable. After 1,500 beats I must pull my finger out, for I can no longer endure the pain. My finger, now sore to the touch, is distinctly warmer than its neighboring fingers. When I return to the machine the next day I can only tolerate a couple of hundred beats before yanking my finger away. In a mysterious and complex process, my body evaluates pain not only by the mechanical forces but also by how the cells are "feeling" when the stress begins.

My body's protective response shows visibly in inflammation, as blood surges to the affected area and the body cushions the point of stress with extra fluids. In regard to the pain system, inflammation brings on a condition called hypersensitivity. My finger that has endured hundreds of tiny hammer blows becomes hypersensitive to hammer blows, because in its inflamed condition just a few more stresses could lead to a blister or ulcer.

Similarly, a finger that has been burned becomes hypersensitive to heat, because even a little heat would harm the mildly inflamed tissues. I have more than once put my hands in a basin only to discover, to my surprise, that my hands are sending mixed signals. My left hand tells me the water is hot; my right hand says warm. Then I remember an incident from breakfast: a drop of hot bacon grease popped out of the pan and landed in my left hand. I had not noticed it at the time, but pain nerve endings at that spot lowered their threshold and are now reporting warm water as hot.

Who has not felt the irritation of a sore finger, from an infected hangnail perhaps, always seeming "in the way." It gets bumped every few minutes no matter how careful you are. That sensation has a sound physiological basis: your pain cells have suddenly become ten times more sensitive to pain. My finger becomes hypersensitive so that I won't foolishly subject it to more hot grease or hammer blows. Pain cells in effect "turn up the volume." In these remarkable ways, hypersensitivity builds up a shield of pain to protect unusually vulnerable parts.

All of us experience a psychological parallel to the reaction of hypersensitivity. When we are under severe strain, maybe resulting from an accumulation of small stresses — bills, work pressures, irritating habits of family members — suddenly every minor frustration hits like a blow. We have become hypersensitive, and our minds are telling us we need a respite as surely as neuronal hypersensitivity warns our bodies of a need for relief.

Following the example of cells in the human body, we members of the Body of Christ would do well to learn the place of hypersensitivity and how to respond. Cells in my fingers, although uninjured themselves, take up the cry for relief from a nearby injured cell and report it to the head. There is a place for "intercessory pain" in the Body of Christ.

In addition, the body makes certain allowances for its hurting cells. Pain works precisely because it is loud and insistent. People in pain, physical or mental, while in a hypersensitive state may lash out against those who try to befriend them. They require from more healthy members a forgiving acceptance that sees past surface reactions to the hidden needs.

The Christian church, said one noted pastor, "is the only outfit I know of that shoots its wounded." He referred to a common tendency to harshly judge a person who is already in emotional or spiritual pain. In contrast, a healthy body will make far-reaching adaptations to announce the pain and make sure it is heeded. Healing agents are summoned by the area of local need, as my study of the monkey's denervated fingertips clearly confirmed.

Real love protects and defends areas of special vulnerability. We may be called on to bolster bruised egos, gently confront an insensitive person, or take upon ourselves some of the minor stresses that have accumulated. As a former missionary, I cannot overstate the life-sustaining role of people back home who invested themselves in me by praying and writing letters. These specially sensitive cells sought out my pain and nourished me in time of need. Such dedicated people make the difference between a missionary who serves twenty years and one who breaks down after a short time.

━

Once I had the experience of serving as medical officer at a professional boxing match. I was assigned to treat the injuries that occurred during the match. (I only accepted the assignment once — the sight of two men pounding living cells to destruction offended all my medical sensibilities.) One vivid scene stays with me. The trainer of one of these heavyweight boxers ran up to his man, in the corner where I was standing, after a particularly furious round. "The left eyebrow!" he yelled excitedly, pointing to his own wildly dilated eye for emphasis. "Pound him on the left eye! You've landed some good ones — it's already swelling. A couple more jabs and you'll bust it open!"

The boxer followed his instructions, bearing down relentlessly on the inflamed, hypersensitive lump above his opponent's eye. I had to sew up the remains of skin and eyebrow after the fight. The pummeling had taken its toll.

That scene has come to my mind periodically, in very different circumstances, such as at a dinner party at a friend's home. Everyone is eating and conversing amiably until the husband says something to his wife that seems slightly charged. By itself, the comment is harmless. Yet the wife flushes with obvious embarrassment, and the husband appears a bit smug. Without comprehending details, I realize a blow, genteel but deadly, has landed. Dinner proceeds with some awkwardness after the comment.

When I intercept that kind of interchange, or hear a remark slightly veiled in humor about housecleaning, some past disagreement, a personal habit, sexual performance, or in-laws, I hear replayed, "Hit him again — the left eyebrow!" Each partner knows well the other's vulnerable points. Intimacy increases the vulnerability of the person who loves and makes us naked to ridicule. At such moments I wish the Body of Christ would show the consistency of my physical body in its healing responsiveness to other cells. Love requires it.

—⸺

The human body is not so defenseless that it merely shouts a warning, swells red with injury, and abandons the struggle. If I had to summarize the grand design of pain in one phrase it would be this: pain is directional. It hurts not in order to cause discomfort, but to demand a change in response to danger.* And hypersensitivity occurs not as part of a cruel scheme to introduce even more suffering into the body, but as a quick adaptation to force the rest of the body to devote more attention to the vulnerable part.

Once a suffering member has gained the body's attention, either by firing messages through the central nervous system or by alerting surrounding cells via enzymes, a healthy body reacts immediately. After hypersensitivity, it relies on the second level of response: distribution of stress.

I dig in my garden. Again and again I thrust the spade into the hard soil, with my hand absorbing the back-thrust on its handle. For a while the action causes no pain, but gradually the cells under the skin call out for more blood and the skin reddens (inflammation and

---

*I believe this principle applies to all pain, not just physical. Emotional and spiritual pains are likewise directional signs. Guilt "hurts" so that the person will repent and find forgiveness. Depression points to the need to resolve certain tensions. Marital conflict merely expresses the deeper underlying discord that must be worked out. In short, emotional and spiritual pain are, like physical pain, symptoms and not diseases. Normally, a symptom will not disappear until the disease is treated.

hypersensitivity). As my hand grows more tender, without thinking about it I distribute stress by changing my grip on the spade so that a different patch of skin will take the pressure and I can continue digging.

I go through a similar process whenever I buy new shoes. Although the loafers felt comfortable during my test paces in the store, when I return home and walk a mile, a spot on my foot begins to call for help. An area of friction or pressure that I had not noticed before demands attention. If I must go on walking, my body adapts with a massive redistribution of stress out of proportion to the hypersensitive spot: I limp. The new gait, though awkward and unnatural, minimizes stress on the tender area.

I was called on once to treat the star basketball player of Louisiana State University. He was leading all scorers on the LSU team and ignited each game with incredible displays of his speed and leaping ability. But he could never complete a game. Invariably, in the second half a large tender spot would develop on his forefoot that would blister and ultimately break open and force him from the game. Our remedy for him was simple and proved an instantaneous cure: we carefully shaped a paste of cork dust and rubber latex into the exact shape of his forefoot, taking into account the stress points. By distributing the stress over a wider area, we freed him to pivot, jump, and run all over the court for the entire game.

Without the adaptation of stress distribution, all of our daily activities would be fraught with danger. I know, because I have treated scores of leprosy patients who will never walk again because a defective pain system failed to warn the central nervous system to redistribute the stresses being applied to just one spot on their feet. The force of walking itself should not cause damage—

feet are designed so that the foot of an elephant, a rat, and a human all absorb the same comfortable pressure per square inch. But unrelieved, repeated pressure on the same spot will cause damage.

There is no escape from danger. An act of seemingly total rest — sleeping — can destroy. The most gentle pressures can keep blood from an area and ultimately silence the pain cells there. If the body heard a cry of pain, it would turn a bit, distributing the stress to other cells. But with no pain, purulent bedsores may result. I thank God for the millions of sensors embedded in my skin that tell me when to shift weight in my buttocks, or reposition my legs or back, or change my step when walking.*

When I turn from my physical body to the Body of Christ, I see the need for a similar adaptation. Just as a healthy body wisely senses the frictions and stresses on each individual cell and adjusts its role accordingly, so a spiritual Body, under direction from the Head, must constantly evaluate which cells need special attention or perhaps even redeployment. Outer front-line cells will require qualities of resistance and firmness. Other, inner cells need to be protected and sequestered to lead lives of quiet contemplation.

From my own observation, the church tends to fail at this principle of redistributing stress in two crucial areas. First, when we put leaders on the front line — pastors, priests, missionaries, other public representatives — we demand too much. We exert extraordinary pressures on them to fit into our preconceptions of spirituality. When they fall short, instead of gracious acceptance and forgiveness, we respond with rejection. We give them no chance to "limp." I caution such leaders to surround themselves

---

*Inventors have tried to correct the problems that lead to ulcers and bedsores on insensitive or paralyzed people who do not redistribute stress. They have designed wheelchairs and beds featuring rollers that look like those on warehouse conveyor belts and are constantly on the move to distribute pressure more evenly. Viscoelastic foam (like the brand Tempurpedic) helps in a similar way.

with hypersensitive friends and associates who can detect signals of damaging stress and bring about whatever changes are necessary to redistribute those pressures.

Too easily we overlook the cumulative effect of minor, inconsequential mechanical stresses. To my great surprise, my research proved that the subtle, less dramatic forces of *repetitive* stress hold greater peril for my patients than the obvious hazards of laceration or burning. Similarly, we must not overlook the cumulative effect of hundreds of everyday stresses in the lives of pastors: incessant phone calls, a fractious board, financial pressures, the burdens of counseling, loneliness, the vulnerability of public speaking, social ostracism. These represent far greater dangers than spectacular crises in the church.

The church could learn a second major lesson from the human body: certain members need protection during specific periods of their lives, especially in spiritual infancy. I have seen a consistent pattern of elevating new converts such as athletes, politicians, actors, beauty queens. Often, these enthusiastic new recruits captivate the attention of the media for a short time. After trying to project the image expected of them — an image not yet real — they abandon their faith in bitterness and disgust. When this happens, I cannot help thinking of a disease of the skin, psoriasis.

Severe psoriasis can change a person's appearance far worse than leprosy. In bad cases, red patches of scurfy, flaky skin may spread across the body. The disease has one cause: skin cells that normally take three weeks to migrate to the surface force their way up in a few days. Those callow cells arrive unprepared for the stresses of light, ultraviolet rays, temperature, and atmosphere on the surface. They die quick, ugly deaths, scarifying their miserable victims. Is there not a lesson here for the Christian world that insists on forcing newly converted celebrities toward the glare of the surface before any spiritual maturity has taken place? Distribution of stress includes the need to protect those unprepared for any stress.

Sometimes I have seen the Body of Christ react with extraordinary speed and wisdom in redistributing painful stress. In such cases, fellow members can mean the difference between collapse and survival. I think of a divorced woman I know in a small church. After her husband left her for another woman, she struggled to hold her life together. Haunted by feelings of guilt and rejection over his leaving, she also had to face four children, an empty bank account, and a house in poor repair. For that woman, the local church became the only means to health. People responded in loving and practical ways: by babysitting, painting the house, repairing the car, inviting her to special events. Her condition did not go away; today, five years later, she still "limps" and relies on the church to help her cope. I am convinced that local church saved her from personal ruin. She is healthy today because they, like cells in a body, surrounded her with their strength and relieved the pressures that would have destroyed her.

⌒

Sometimes, even after repeated cries of alarm, individual cells still face the percussive repetition of damaging force. The affected area has one last strategy for relief, and a remarkable process springs into motion.

I push a spade into dirt two hundred times. I feel some soreness, but the garden soil must be turned, so I politely ignore the warning signs. Finally, without my willful cooperation, my body makes a radical architectural change on the surface of my thumb. The top layer of epidermis separates from the layers underneath it and mushrooms up to form a perfect dome supported by the sudden influx of a cushioning liquid. A blister.

My dermis, formerly mashed flat and vulnerable, now has soothing relief from stress as the forces of my spade are gently absorbed by this new structure. Such an adaptation can easily go unappreciated or, worse, be viewed with irritation. But it is a startling phenomenon, requiring the coordination of millions of cells.

A blister is a dramatic, temporary response. It cools the area, cushions shock, disperses stresses — in short, gets me through the day.* Human beings have bad habits, though: we tend to repeat, over and over, the very stresses that bring on inflammation, hypersensitivity, and blisters. A tennis player will work through five consecutive blisters before he convinces his body of the need to develop alternative, more permanent adaptations. Bones thicken and grow dense and muscles expand in the presence of continued stress; the skin alters blister into callus.

I can look at the feet of a runner and get a fair idea of how far he or she runs in a week. For the serious runner, calluses fill in crevices, build up weak spots, form-fit the borders to running shoes, and generally add layers of protection against the merciless forces of long-distance running. If the stress continues long enough, a *bursa* develops in the body: a pocket of fluid buried deep in the tissue under the thickened piece of skin. These localized adaptations occur so regularly among certain occupations that we have informal medical categories for them: "housemaid's knee," "coal-heaver's back," "tailor's bunion," and my favorite, "Episcopal knee" (from the prayer rail).

---

*In a somewhat related process, the body responds to deeper pressures by rushing fluid to the scene to cushion the blow. Experienced handball players know the importance of smacking a few balls in a warm-up before the match. This causes a condition of edema: a cushioning layer of fluid under the skin.

Bodies adapt quickly but grudgingly, and rarely without a sense of loss. As I have mentioned, during one summer of medical school in England I joined the crew of an eighty-foot sailing schooner. At first the friction of ropes burned and chafed my hands and fingers until my fingertips were raw and bleeding. Finally, after two or three weeks, my skin added on thick layers of callus. But, to my chagrin, when I returned to school I found I had completely lost my knack for dissecting. Previously, I could feel any slight resistance of the scalpel as I cut; now I felt only gross pressure. I panicked—surely those thick pads of dead callus had forever destroyed my career as a surgeon. In time, however, when the body sensed I had no need for the extra protection, it shed the layers as gladly as an insect sheds its skin. I regained sensitivity.

Friction in human affairs can likewise cause calluses. Just to survive, a person in a stressful environment will grow extra padding to protect his own psyche from being too easily abraded. I compare my field trips out into Indian villages, where hundreds of patients lined up for treatment, to the situation at Carville where we have as many staff members as patients. The slower pace at Carville allows me time to think about problems in depth and to know each individual patient. On the Indian field trips, I had to sacrifice that personal sensitivity for the greater demands of efficient medical procedures. I could not possibly have gotten personally involved with each of the hundreds of patients.

Similarly, nurses, social workers, and counselors who live among clamorous human needs must sometimes develop a protective callus. They dare not let each instance of child abuse, horrible as it is, incapacitate them. Young nurses and doctors sometimes ask my advice on how to cope with overwhelming human need without developing the hardness and cynicism they see in some of their older colleagues. They walk a thin line. Surely they cannot involve themselves with the intimate details of suffering in every patient, and yet they must not shut off personal concern. I have found it an important discipline to pray daily, asking God to identify one or two selective patients with special needs. I cannot be equally sensitive to everyone, and I must not grow insensitive to all. Rather, I depend on the Spirit to help me catch a sense of those who need more than strictly medical care.

Those of us in support roles in the Body must accept the responsibility of carefully monitoring our representatives on the front lines. We cannot expose them to infinite human sorrow. A new phrase, "burnout," describes a familiar pattern of self-extinguishment. These people rely on us for a balanced perspective to help convince them to pull back and rest or to shift their load to someone else. Warning signs come in the form of hypersensitivity, fatigue, or emotional trauma. Too much sensitivity or too little can immobilize either a physical body or a corporate one.

⟼

I have never seen a clearer example of poorly handled repetitive stress than that which occurred among a trio of brilliant surgeons at a major hospital in the Midwest. When I first visited there in 1952, an esteemed old man, renowned as a hand surgeon, was training two assistants to take his place. The old man had passed retirement age, and his assistants, Morris and Bates, were in their forties, already possessing impressive skills and experience. Both Morris and Bates were well-known all over the country; one edited a leading medical magazine. But the old man couldn't bear to relinquish control over any patient. He leaned over his assistants' shoulders, correcting, advising, and scolding like a parent. To Morris, a superb surgeon, he would say, "No, don't make that incision quite so long!"

The two gritted their teeth and determined to hang on until his impending retirement. When I met with them, I could sense the venom that had been building up inside them and could see blood pressure rise as they talked about the splenetic old man.

Ten years later I went back to that hospital. Both Morris and Bates were dead. One had had a stroke and was totally paralyzed, unable to speak, for several months before he died. The other died of apoplexy, a hemorrhage. Both had been in perfect health before working for the chief surgeon. The old man? He was still there, well into his seventies, training younger doctors.

No one comment from the old surgeon, taken alone, had caused the injury. Rather, the steady, repeated application of irritating force had gradually worn down healthy psyches, as surely as my repetitive stress machine had destroyed living tissue in Clarence the monkey and in my own finger. This same elderly surgeon was a model of Christian gentleness toward his wife, who had Parkinson's disease, and yet showed insensitivity to the feelings of those who worked with him so closely.

I think of all the people who would have been helped had those two brilliant surgeons lived. What went wrong? Had others around them failed to notice the problem and respond with hypersensitivity? Should the management of the hospital have stepped in to redistribute the stresses? Should Morris and Bates have developed a layer of callus strong enough for them to confront the old man? Or sought divine resources of the cleansing power of forgiveness? Apparently, none of these responses occurred. The two simply absorbed the harmful stresses, and their bodies responded with steadily mounting blood pressure.

I have seen that pattern of destruction occur often in Christ's Body too: a captious church gossips about its minister, an employer mercilessly harasses a well-meaning employee, parents or siblings needle a clumsy child. Where is the grace that forgives and the love that accommodates to weakness? Where the power of reconciliation? All of us could take a lesson from the human body's adaptations to pain. "Carry each other's burdens," said Paul, "and in this way you will fulfill the law of Christ."

# CHRONIC PAIN

*One wonders what will become of a society in which cer-*
*tain forms of suffering are avoided gratuitously, in keeping with*
*middle-class ideals. I have in mind a society in which a marriage*
*that is perceived as unbearable quickly and smoothly ends in*
*divorce; after divorce no scars remain; relations between gener-*
*ations are dissolved as quickly as possible, without a struggle,*
*without a trace; periods of mourning are "sensibly" short; with*
*haste the handicapped and sick are removed from the house and*
*the dead from the mind. If changing marriage partners happens*
*as readily as trading in an old car on a new one, then the expe-*
*riences that one had in the unsuccessful relationships remain*
*unproductive. From such suffering nothing is learned and noth-*
*ing is to be learned.*

Dorothy Soelle, *Suffering*

O n rare occasions I have met a pain that defies understanding. Although it seems to serve no purpose, it dominates a life so that the patient can think of little else. This was the case with Rajamma. I had been in India only a year or two when she came to me for treatment. In my training in London, whenever I encountered a problem case that belonged in another specialty I promptly referred the patient to someone more experienced. In South India I had no such luxury.

Rajamma crept into my office with an expression of fear on her face. As if scouting for an enemy, she peered suspiciously around the room before lowering herself into a chair. She had many enemies: anything capable of startling her or creating a sudden noise, or even a gust of wind that might blow on her face. Her cheeks were sunken; she was thin to the point of emaciation. Burn marks of a peculiar circular pattern scarred her face; I recognized them as treatments by the traditional medicine man. She had scratched and burned the skin so often that it had taken on a tough, leathery texture like that of an animal.

Rajamma had the condition of *tic doloureux*, neuralgia of the face, in its most severe form. The pain usually attacks spasmodically, in an overwhelming shot of agony to one side of the face. It causes a sudden grimace, or it may seem to be caused by a grimace, thus the name "tic" suggesting a twitch of the facial muscles. Sometimes the condition begins with no apparent cause and sometimes it starts from a real source of infection, such as a septic molar tooth. Even though Rajamma could not remember any tooth problems, various doctors had extracted all the teeth on one side of her face in hopes of locating and removing the source of pain.

As she told me her story, speaking slowly, she held her mouth open and moved her lips carefully to avoid sudden movements of her cheeks. Rajamma lived in a tiny earthen hut with her husband and four children. Her children never played in or near the house anymore, she said. They tiptoed around and would not laugh or even tell a joke for fear of triggering one of their mother's attacks. Chickens (which usually have the run of village houses) were kept penned so that none would fly up or startle her by cackling. Rajamma's obvious weight loss had resulted from her fear of eating. She dared not chew, so she lived on fluids, making sure they were neither too hot nor too cold.

Despite all these precautions Rajamma lived at the mercy of excruciating pain. Jolts of pain hit her many times every day and totally incapacitated her. Sometimes in desperation she or the Indian village "doctors" would heat a metal tube in the fire and burn blisters onto her face in an attempt to quell the pain. Her mental health had deteriorated badly. Her husband tried valiantly to understand a pain with no apparent cause, but the family anxiety was clearly beginning to reach a state of critical mass, just before an explosion.

I made every effort to locate a cause, but failed. Twice I tried to deaden the trigger area which seemed to lie just in front of her right cheek bone. The first time, the sight of the needle approaching her face touched off one of her most savage attacks. My second attempt, under anesthesia, did not succeed.

Reluctantly I concluded there was only one sure way to stop this incurable pain: I must open her skull and divide the nerves supplying that part of her face. I put off this decision, because I had not been trained for neurosurgery and indeed had never even observed such a procedure. But I had little recourse. Fortunately, in my anatomy course in Wales years before I had dissected the cranial nerves and knew just where to find the Gasserian ganglion within the bony coverings of the brain.

I explained the procedure to Rajamma and her husband, emphasizing two dangers. I might fail because of my inexperience. Perhaps worse, I might cut more of the nerves than should be cut. In that event, her eyeball as well as her cheek might become insensitive, which could eventuate in blindness. I painted a bleak picture of potential consequences.

Nothing I said to the couple, however, caused the slightest flicker of hesitation. The effects of her suffering were so great that even if I had told them she would definitely lose an eye in the operation, they would have readily consented.

Over the next week I studied all the books I could find and planned a strategy with our anesthesiologist Dr. Gwenda Lewis. Because I wanted to communicate with the patient during surgery, we chose an anesthetic that would keep her alert enough to respond to questions. The day for surgery arrived.

We arranged Rajamma in a sitting position to minimize pressure on the veins in her head, and after the anesthetic had taken hold I began to cut. The Gasserian ganglion lies at the junction of the fifth cranial nerve, in a venous sinus surrounded by bone. Inside this cavity, veins and nerves crisscross in a skein of tangled threads, making it impossible to keep the site free of blood. I chipped away the overlying bone and entered the cavity, picking through the layers of tissue one by one. At last I could see the base of the cavity. A plexus of nerve tissue, an inch across and half an inch deep, lay glimmering under my light like a crescent moon. From under it, fine white nerve fibers fanned out, like tributaries of a river, toward the face.

One of the nerves was a motor nerve, and any damage to it would partially paralyze her jaw. I took special care to identify that one. But the other fibers all looked the same, and lay bundled so close that I could not be confident which was which. I electrically stimulated one tiny fiber and asked Rajamma what she could feel. "You are touching my eye," she said. Beads of sweat popped out on my forehead as I dropped that thin nerve back into place.

In most of the body, a tough sheath that tolerates a certain amount of pulling enwraps each nerve. But in the bony skull, nerves are not designed to be touched or stretched. They have no sheath, and the smallest tremor of my hand would tear a nerve irreparably.

I stared into the spreading pool of blood, pale and watery from the anemia caused by Rajamma's malnutrition. (At that time we had no blood bank to enrich her blood before surgery.) Finally I separated two tiny white nerve fibers and lifted them away from the blood. These two fibers seemed the most likely carriers of the pain impulses that were making her life a misery. All I had to do was cut them and I would be through.

I lifted the two fibers with my probe, and an unexpected, awful sensation broke over me like a wave. I was transfixed by the significance of the tiny act I was about to perform. We surgeons are trained to maintain a certain distance from patients so that personal feelings will not impair our judgment — we are warned not to operate on our own wives or children for this reason. At that moment, I had a vision of Rajamma's family gathered around me in a circle, staring, waiting to know what I would do with her life.

As I looked at those trembling strands of soft white matter, as thin in diameter as cotton sewing threads, I found it hard to believe they held such significance. Were these two the faulty nerves? So little is known about the physiology of nerves that I could not possibly spot a visual defect. Yet these nerves, containing hundreds of axons serving thousands of nerve endings, were tyrannizing a woman's life. Nerves just like them were steadying my hands and letting me know exactly how much force to use on my instruments.

With a start I came to myself. My reverie lasted only five or ten seconds, but I have never forgotten the vision brought on by a tiny, shimmering nerve. I could not be sure which of the two carried the pain; I had to sacrifice both. So I cut them with two snips. Quickly we got the bleeding under control and closed the wound.

Back in the ward, after Rajamma awoke fully, we mapped out the area on her cheek that no longer had sensation. My knots of tension relaxed when we learned the insensitivity did not include her eye. Haltingly, Rajamma began to try the things that previously had triggered her spasms of pain. She tried a slight smile, her first intentional smile in years. Her husband beamed at her. With a quizzical look, she scratched her cheek, knowing that she would never feel anything there again.

Little by little after that, Rajamma's world fell into place. She became the gentle, sweet person she used to be. Her husband's anxiety began to lessen. Back home, chickens were welcomed into the house again. The children began to play and then to jump and skip, even when they were near their mother. In ever-widening circles, life returned to normal for that family.

In my entire career in surgery I have encountered a mere handful of patients who, like Rajamma, suffer from fierce, unyielding pain that is apparently untraceable to a physical cause. And only a few times have I been called upon to silence pain surgically by cutting a nerve. All of medicine views such a procedure as a radical one of last resort. It carries with it grave risks—the possibility of denervating the wrong areas, danger to the body parts made insensitive—and, most mysteriously, the chance that even after nerves are cut the pain may persist.

In view of the debilitating effect of Rajamma's pain on her health and family, I reluctantly concluded I had no other option but the risky surgery. The physical cause of her condition had eluded my search, and I had to go counter to all medical instinct by treating her pain itself as the problem, not as a valuable symptom. That change in perspective is the peculiar peril of chronic pain: pain is no longer a directional signal that points to something else; it is a demon that dominates and immobilizes. Sufferers of chronic pain care only about how to turn it off.

Most commonly, chronic pain occurs in the back, neck, or joints, although victims of diseases such as cancer can experience such pain anywhere. Whereas painless people like my leprosy patients yearn for the warning signal of pain, chronic pain sufferers hear a blaring, ceaseless alarm. A flurry of pioneering research has focused on the problems of people plagued by chronic pain, and about five hundred pain clinics in the U.S. now specialize in their treatment.

Yet, despite the obsessive nature of chronic pain, the preferred methods of treatment are moving away from the older surgical techniques. A new term, "pain management," is entering the vocabulary of specialists. The director of one of America's largest chronic pain clinics has said we may need to apply a different model to chronic pain than medicine's normal surgical removal approach. Perhaps, he observes, we should view chronic pain as we view such diseases as diabetes and collagen disorders, teaching patients to live comfortably *despite* the disease.

I could fill a good-sized room with exercise machines and electronic gadgets that are sold as panaceas for chronic pain. Newspapers and magazines regularly feature other alternatives: techniques of acupuncture, foot or earlobe massage, biofeedback, self-hypnosis. And a catalog of such exotica as transcutaneous nerve stimulators offers a more technological (and expensive) approach. Most of these techniques of pain management depend on overloading the brain circuits with diversionary stimuli and thus suppressing incoming pain signals.

(I prefer simpler methods to accomplish the same purpose. For example, I often prescribe a stiff-bristle hairbrush for a person with arm or leg pain. The effect of briskly stroking the skin will excite touch and pressure sensors and often relieve pain. Or, when my chronic pains intensify I go for a barefoot walk on the rough shell-and-gravel sidewalks near my home.)

I cannot in this book, of course, attempt to speak directly to those people who suffer from chronic pain. Rather, I will focus on its analogies within the Body of Christ. That Body, too, has chronic pains that will not go away, and in the church we need to learn much about pain management.

In our age the specters of poverty, famine, and violence never leave some areas of the world. Consider the impulses from the church in a region like Africa. We cannot ignore the signs of chronic suffering. They fill our mailboxes, our television screens and radio speakers with a daily recitation of gloom. Jesus acknowledged the chronic nature of this type of human suffering when he observed (in a statement that is often grossly distorted), "The poor you will always have with you" (Mark 14:7).

Because I lived in a country where suffering is an oppressive daily reality, I know well the terrible dilemmas raised by chronic pain on a massive scale. I have stared at long rows of patients, knowing I must decline treatment for all but a handful, and knowing thousands more await attention in remote areas. Even in affluent America, pockets of human misery exist, though on a different scale.

We tend to view the worst suffering indirectly, via television documentaries, and thus pain forces a choice upon us. We can choose to extend our aid and food and wealth to help ease human misery, or we can simply numb the chronic pain by switching the channel, averting our gaze from the problems, or by dispensing token gifts without a true personal commitment.

The Bible makes clear that we in the Body have a responsibility to the suffering of those outside the church also. Overseas relief aid administered by Christian agencies has mushroomed in recent years, indicating that we are healthfully listening to the short-term, crisis pains of the world. Christians helped spearhead emergency responses to various crises in Indochina, Central America, and Africa. Hundreds of millions of dollars poured in to support such efforts. We who are strong helped the weak. But in handling chronic, long-term pain, the church still seems in its infancy.

The head of one large Christian relief agency confessed, "I must restrain myself from global ambulance-chasing. When a major disaster occurs that captures media attention, our donors respond with incredible generosity. All the agencies collect millions of dollars, and move in with a kind of overkill. When the crisis is 'hot news,' we have no difficulty raising support. Six months later, the desperate problems are still there, but the camera crews have gone elsewhere, and no one cares about the long-term suffering."

Intense suffering provokes a sudden outpouring of aid, but people soon tire of hearing about depressing conditions. Instead of increasing sensitivity, as a human body does in response to injury, we decrease it. Our focus on the pain turns from "How do I deal with the cause of the pain?" to "How can I silence it?" No longer a motivator and stimulus for action, the pain becomes a dull, ineffective throb. It has worn us down.

The field of health services symbolizes the conundrum of relief work. People eagerly donate for hospitals, drugs, and medical supplies.* Yet, according to the World Health Organization, the great majority of health problems — more than half of all diseases — derive from polluted water supplies and inadequate sewage systems. Parisian sewers had more impact on that city's health than a hundred hospitals. But development programs for sanitation and hygiene simply don't have the drawing power of more flamboyant approaches to health.

Of course, chronic pain occurs much closer to home than Somalia or the Sahel. During hard economic times the United States and Europe also hear the plaintive cries of people who cannot provide for their own basic necessities. That sound, too, can become a dull throb, easier to tune out than attend to.

In the early 1980s as the impact of budget cuts in social programs began to affect individuals in the large cities, churches found themselves facing overwhelming human need. The poor began coming to the church, not a government office, for aid. The mayor of New York City, alarmed about the sudden increase of homeless people roaming the streets, made a radical proposal to church leaders. Thirty-six thousand people wander New York streets without shelter, he said; if each of the city's 3,500 churches and synagogues would take in ten of them, the problem of the homeless would be solved. The mayor brought to urgent attention a chronic pain that had long plagued a large city.

The churches responded defensively. One Protestant leader seemed offended that he had first read of the proposal in the newspaper. "It is a very complex situation and the remedy will be complex," said another. "There are many problems of implementation."

---

*An example: after Albert Schweitzer's death, his friends and supporters launched a campaign to build a simple, village-oriented hospital on the scale Schweitzer preferred. The fund raising hopelessly bogged down until a professional agency convinced the committee to build instead a massive, Western-style hospital with state-of-the-art technology. Only then did donors respond and funds pour in.

Most asked for time to evaluate the proposal. They claimed their houses of worship were ill-equipped to shelter the homeless. Only seven congregations responded affirmatively.

Although the mayor's proposal did have a complex dimension, its simple appeal to charity stands in direct line with the message of the Old Testament prophets, Jesus, and the apostles. "Share your bread with the hungry and bring the homeless poor into your house," said Isaiah. And Jesus urged disciples to "give to everyone who begs from you." In the early church, members routinely brought vegetables, fruit, milk, and honey to distribute to widows, prisoners, and the sick. Fortunately, since that time churches have taken the lead in operating soup kitchens and homeless shelters, and have performed so effectively that the U.S. government sponsored "charitable choice" legislation to aid their efforts.

In no way do I mean to imply that chronic pain will gradually fade away. No one who has worked in a country such as India could easily come to that conclusion. I think of a lonely woman, abandoned by her husband, left alone to raise children with insufficient resources; and of Christians under persecution in some Moslem countries; and of monumental problems of health in Third World countries. Neither governments nor the church will relieve all their suffering. More important measures are the attitude and energy with which we face these pains. Do we soon grow numb and insensitive? Do we react with a quick burst of enthusiastic support that wanes if dramatic results are not obvious?

I retain a clear memory from my childhood of the monthly charity of my Aunt Eunice. She would keep a little book from the Aged Pilgrims Friend Society and visit women from that list every month without fail. Often I would accompany her as she took money or food or clothing or Christmas packages to those elderly women. In her own quiet, unglamorous way, Aunt Eunice taught me how to turn impersonal, chronic pain into a personal experience of sharing. She insisted on visiting the women, not mailing them packages, and she kept up her simple ministrations faithfully for years.

People with chronic pain, such as quadriplegics or the parents of retarded children, describe a common pattern: friends and church members respond initially with sympathy and compassion, but over time they lose interest. Most people find an ordeal with no end in sight unsettling, and can even come to resent the person who is suffering. A similar deadening of sensitivity can occur with regard to problems of a national or global scale.

A body's health can be measured in large part by its instinctive reaction to nagging, chronic pain. Management of pain requires a delicate balance between proper sensitivity, to determine its cause and mobilize a response, and enough inner strength to keep the pain from dominating the whole person. For the Body of Christ, the balance is every bit as delicate and as imperative.

# Chapter 23

# Pain of God

*"I see everything," he cried, "everything that there is. Why does each thing on the earth war against each other thing? Why does each small thing in the world have to fight against the world itself? Why does a fly have to fight the whole universe? For the same reason that I had to be alone in the dreadful Council of the Days. So that each thing that obeys law may have the glory and isolation of the anarchist.... So that the real lie of Satan may be flung back in the face of this blasphemer, so that by tears and torture we may earn the right to say to this man, 'You lie!' No agonies can be too great to buy the right to say to this accuser, 'We also have suffered.'..."*

*He had turned his eyes so as to see suddenly the great face of Sunday, which wore a strange smile.*

*"Have you," he cried in a dreadful voice, "have you ever suffered?"*

*As he gazed, the great face grew to an awful size, grew larger than the colossal mask of Memnon, which had made him scream as a child. It grew larger and larger, filling the whole sky; then everything went black. Only in the blackness before it entirely destroyed his brain he seemed to hear a distant voice saying a commonplace text that he had heard somewhere, "Can ye drink of the cup that I drink of?"*

G. K. Chesterton, *The Man Who Was Thursday*

━

At the age of fifteen an imprisoned Jewish boy named Elie Wiesel endured unspeakable horrors at the Buna and Auschwitz concentration camps. One lives forever in his memory: an incident not of mass murder or torture but of punishment applied to a single child. The victim, maybe twelve years old, had been caught helping a Dutchman hoard arms inside the camp. He was sentenced to death.

The boy had a refined and beautiful face, so different from the gaunt, disfigured faces of most prisoners — the face, said Wiesel, of a sad angel. To execute such a child publicly before thousands of prisoners was no easy thing, even for the SS. The camp stoolies refused to assist this time, so the SS had to perform the deed themselves. They erected three gallows, one for the child and two more for other condemned prisoners.

The three victims mounted chairs and the SS placed their necks in nooses. "Long live liberty!" cried the two adults. The child said nothing.

But from the rows of anguished spectators, a cry came up. "Where is God? Where is He?"

The chairs were tipped over and the bodies jerked, then dangled limply from the ropes. Guards ordered all the prisoners to march past the three victims. It was a terrible sight. The two adults were dead, their tongues hanging out, already swollen and blue-tinged. But the third rope was still twitching lightly. The child, being so light, was still alive.

In all it took the boy perhaps half an hour to die. The prisoners had to file past, looking him full in the face as his life fluttered away.

"Behind me," says Wiesel, "I heard the same man asking, 'Where is God now?'

"And I heard a voice within me answer him: Where is He? Here He is — He is hanging here on this gallows. . . .

"That night the soup tasted of corpses."*

That question, "Where is God?" has haunted Wiesel and thousands of other survivors who cried out in their human hells and heard no answer. Wiesel intended his conclusion to be understood in its most literal, atheistic meaning: God's silence proved he was on a gallows, dead, helpless, unresponsive, undependable. Others would use the same words, but with a different meaning: God had suffered alongside the young child, as he grieves and suffers with every pain of his children on earth. But if God was there, hanging on the gallows, watching the thousands — no, millions — of innocents march to the ovens, why did he not intervene? And why did they not sense God's presence? Never had God seemed more distant.

⟶

In a medical career that has spanned four decades, I have never stopped thinking of pain. I have seen its beauty and brilliant design as I have studied physiology and observed the effects of painlessness on my leprosy patients. I have seen its cruelty as I have watched patients die in agony and have listened to families traumatized by the mutilating injury of a child. In my reflections on theology, no matter where I begin, my mind circles back to this enigmatic topic of pain.

For this reason, I cannot end a section on pain and a book on the Body of Christ without raising the issue of God's concern for human suffering.

*Elie Wiesel, *Night* (New York: Discuss/Avon Books, 1969), 75–76.

If the message of pain is directional, a call for us to link up compassionately with those who suffer, how then does the Head of the Body relate to such suffering? How does God "feel" about those who are abused or divorced or alcoholic or unemployed or homosexual, about the needy in Africa and Central America and everywhere? The scope of this book does not permit me to address the "why" questions of causation. But at least I must consider how God views the suffering of creatures. Does it affect God?

A common theme has surfaced throughout this book: that God has undergone a series of self-humiliations — in the Creation, the covenants, the failed monarchy, the Exile, the Incarnation, the Crucifixion, and finally as Head of a very human church. And, I have said, in the role of Head Christ can truly — not just figuratively or analogously — feel our pain. Yet, having made that assertion, I cannot ignore certain important questions about the nature of infinite God. Perhaps they have lurked uncomfortably in your mind as you have read about God's self-limitations. Is not God changeless, eternal? Can our pain truly affect an essentially changeless God? Can God hurt? Did God in any sympathetic way share the gallows with the child in Buna? These are good questions, inescapable questions.

Such careful documents as the Anglican Communion and Westminster Confession declare that God is "without body, parts or passions." Can a God without passions feel our pain? Admittedly, theologians over the centuries have largely concluded that God does not feel passion or suffering.* Early Christian theology, thrashed out in a Greek intellectual environment, held that such qualities as movement, change, and suffering distinguish humans from gods. God is *apathos*, or apathetic, with no disturbing emotions whatever.

---

*Clement, for example, urged people to strive toward freedom from passion, becoming like an impassable God. Purge yourselves of courage, fear, cheerfulness, anger, envy, and love for creatures, he said. A similar prejudice against passion and emotions continued through philosophy and theology up until the Romantic movement. Spinoza called emotions "confused ideas," and Kant urged "duty for duty's sake."

Bible passages describing God as angry or grieved or rejoicing were dismissed as anthropomorphic or metaphorical.

Yet, here is a strange thing: if someone with no background in philosophy and theology simply picked up the Bible and started reading it, he or she would find a startlingly different picture. The Bible gives overwhelming emphasis to God's passionate involvement with creation. It is virtually a catalog of God's emotions in relating to humanity. From creation onward, God places himself in the position of an anxious Father whose children run free.

Each key event in the Old Testament tells of God sharing the pain (or, less frequently, triumph) of his people. He heard the cry of the captives in Egypt. For thirty-eight years God pitched his tent among the shifting tents in Sinai, joining Israelites in their punishment by tabernacling among them. "In all their distress he too was distressed," concludes the prophet Isaiah (63:9).

The prophets seem to compete in describing the depth of God's emotional attachment to his people. The books of Jeremiah and Hosea swell with the cry of a wounded God. "Is not Ephraim my dear son, the child in whom I delight?" God asks (Jeremiah 31:20). "Though I often speak against him, I still remember him. Therefore, my heart yearns for him; I have great compassion for him." (Luther translates that penultimate phrase, "My heart is broken.")

In Hosea God declares, "My heart is changed within me; all my compassion is aroused" (11:8). "Why did you forsake me?" God asks often. "My people have forgotten me," he laments. In Isaiah the boldest figure of speech used by any prophet compares God to a woman undergoing labor:

> "For a long time I have kept silent,
>     I have been quiet and held myself back.

But now, like a woman in childbirth,
>    I cry out, I gasp and pant." (42:14)

Clearly, events arouse in God either joy or sorrow, pleasure or wrath. The Old Testament portrays a God who is not "wholly other" or remote, but One involved with creation. God goes with his people into exile, into captivity, into the fiery furnace, into the grave.

A phrase like "My heart is broken" is metaphorical, to be sure — when applied to God or to a human being. But a writer employs metaphor to point to a truth, not to its opposite. Abraham Heschel, a Jewish theologian, concludes, "The statements about pathos are not a compromise — ways of accommodating higher meanings to the lower level of human understanding. They are rather the accommodations of words to higher meanings."

Could it be that the church fathers, so intent on protecting God from any deficiency of being, missed an obvious possibility: that God voluntarily put himself in the position of being affected by creation? Love involves giving, and God, self-complete, has only himself to give. God surely does not suffer out of some deficiency of being, as his creatures do, but from the love that overflows from being. That is, in fact, how the Gospels define love: "For God so loved the world *that* he gave his one and only Son."

The pictorial Chinese language combines the two concepts of love and pain in eloquent symbolism. In the character that expresses the highest kind of love, symbols for love and for pain are brushed on top of each other to form a word like "pain-love." Thus a mother "pain-loves" her child. She pours out her whole being on the child's behalf. In essence God showed pain-love to creation by emptying himself and joining us in the Incarnation.

Any Christian discussion of what effect human suffering has on God must center on the Incarnation, when God lived among us. In the gospel accounts, Jesus opposed illness and suffering without exception. At the beginning of his ministry Jesus announced healing the sick as one of his chief goals (Luke 4:18) and used it as a proof of his messianic identity when questioned by John the Baptist (7:22). The Gospels record no instances of Jesus declining to heal when asked, or of advising a sufferer, "Be happy with your illness!" or "Simply bear the pain of your son's death." When his friend Lazarus died, Jesus wept. God, as revealed in Christ, takes no pleasure in the suffering of his children; rather, God is grieved.

When Jesus himself faced suffering, he did not show the tightlipped resignation of martyrdom. In Gethsemane he accepted pain almost as a last resort. Three times he prayed, "If it is possible, may this cup be taken from me." And on the cross Jesus bore pain not with silence, but with the forlorn cry of abandonment, "My God! Why have you forsaken me?" Deliverance from the cross was the one miracle of healing he refused to perform.

"What can I say that others have not said already ... told many times over and drawn again and again? ... What can these places say to you, if in your mind's eye you do not see ... the fearful day of the death on the cross within the walls of Jerusalem?" I share those sentiments of Nikolai Gogol whenever I attempt to speak about the cross. What more could be said? Yet I cannot explore the pain of God without pausing before that most poignant moment, for it was then that God took on himself the groaning and travailing of all creation.

What is so unique, after all, about that death in Jerusalem? Why is it called the "day that shook the world" and "the greatest event in history"? How did it mutate the symbol of the cross from one of execution to one of religious adoration?* The fact of Jesus' physical suffering does not account for the impact; it differed little from Stephen's or Peter's or even Socrates's. Nor could it be the unfair punishment inflicted on a person innocent of a crime; Socrates, too, was innocent, as well as Solzhenitsyn and the Jews described by Elie Wiesel. Not even the manner of execution was that momentous; *Foxe's Book of Martyrs*, for instance, chronicles tortures even more horrible than crucifixion.

How can one obscure man, executed like other common men in an outpost of the empire and virtually ignored by contemporary secular historians, claim to occupy the center of history and affect what goes on before and after him? Scoffers call it "the scandal of particularity," and the question looms before our faith. The answer, of course, is nonsense but for the acceptance of one belief — that the man executed was God in the incognito of history. The cross expresses the suffering of God, who joined humanity by stepping into the historical plane and letting us experience him in shame and nakedness and pain.

At this point, the doctrine of the Trinity becomes so mystifying that other religions shrink away. Did Almighty God simply allow the Son to suffer for us, or did God suffer in Christ on our behalf? Moslems believe that God, unable to go through with the execution of the prophet Jesus, substituted another victim at the last moment. One Jewish Rabbinic argument against Christ's Sonship goes like this: "If God could not bear to see Abraham's son

---

*Charles Williams writes, "When St. Paul preached in Athens, the world was thronged with crosses, rooted outside cities, bearing all of them the bodies of slowly dying men. When Augustine preached in Carthage, the world was also thronged with crosses, but now in the very center of cities, often in processions and above altars, decorated and jewelled, and bearing all of them the image of the identity of dying Man." Even the Colosseum, the imposing site for so many bloody spectacles, was ultimately crowned with a Christian cross and the single word "Benedictus."

slain, surely he would not let his own Son die." Could the thrust of the gospel be missed more widely? In Christian belief, God gave up his own son precisely because God could not, in love, bear to see those such as Isaac suffer. *"He who did not spare his own Son, but gave him up for us all — how will he not also, along with him, graciously give us all things?"* (Romans 8:32).

And still today we miss the point. American television personality Phil Donahue, explaining why he became disillusioned with Christianity, asks, "How could an all-knowing, all-loving God allow His Son to be murdered on a cross in order to redeem my sins? If God the Father is so 'all-loving,' why didn't He come down and go to Calvary?" The answer, of course, is that in some incomprehensible way it *was* God who came to earth and died. "God was in Christ reconciling the world to Himself" (2 Corinthians 5:19 NASB).

When I contemplate the pain of God in the suffering of Christ on Calvary, invariably I turn back to the passage by Isaiah, that most eloquent of prophets. He captures the pain of God in the description of the Suffering Servant in Isaiah 53, a passage the New Testament authors apply to Christ.*

> He was despised, the lowest of men:
>> a man of pains, familiar with disease,
> One from whom men avert their gaze —
>> despised, and we reckoned him as nothing.
>
> But it was our diseases that he bore,
>> our pains that he carried,

---

*Jewish interpreters often apply the symbol of the Suffering Servant to themselves as a race. Could this be the reason, asks Japanese theologian Kazoh Kitamori, that Judaism has attracted so few converts in the world? No race has suffered more than the Jews. But human pain, no matter how great, is meaningless and barren unless it can become a symbol of God's pain sharing in it — unless God really is on the gallows with the boy at Buna.

While we counted him as one stricken,
    touched by God with affliction.

He was wounded for our rebellions,
    crushed for our transgressions;
The chastisement that reconciled us fell upon him,
    and we were healed by his bruises.

All of us strayed like sheep,
    each man turned to his own way;
And Yahweh brought the transgressions of all of us
    to meet upon him.

Oppressed he was, and afflicted,
    but he did not open his mouth;
He was led like a sheep to slaughter;
    and as a ewe is speechless before her shearers,
    he did not open his mouth.

By a perverted judgment he was taken away;
    and who was concerned with his case?
For he was cut off from the land of life;
    for our rebellions he was struck dead.

He was given a tomb with the wicked,
    with the evildoers his sepulcher,
Although he had done no violence,
    and there was no deceit in his mouth.
(ANCHOR)

The Incarnation made possible one further aspect of the pain of God, one that has direct bearing on our analogy of the human body. I think of my futile attempts to develop an artificial pain system. All my patients intellectually understood pain, acknowledged its value as a warning signal, and abhorred the injuries and wounds on their painless hands and feet. Yet until they "felt" pain for themselves, inside their own brains, they had not suffered.

It seems inappropriate to think of a "developing awareness" within God, but something like a progression did occur as implied in the mysterious phrase in Hebrews 2:10, "made perfect through suffering." Imagining pain is one thing — God as designer had surely understood its physiological values and limitations. Grieving in response to pain, feeling with his people, suffering with humanity — all these, too, link God and man. Still, something was missing.

Until God took on the soft tissue of flesh along with its pain cells just as accurate and subject to abuse as ours, God had not truly experienced pain. By sending the Son to earth, God learned to feel pain in the same way we feel pain. Our prayers and cries of suffering take on greater meaning because we now know them to be understood by God. Instinctively, we want a God who not only knows about pain, but shares in it and is affected by our own. By looking at Jesus, we realize we have such a God. He took on the limitations of time and space and family and pain and sorrow.*

Christ has now ascended, and in the new role of Head receives messages of pain reporting in from all over his Body. My brain does not feel pain inflicted on its own cells — protected in a skull of bone, it needs no such warning cells. Yet it desperately feels the

---

*It would have been far easier and more pleasant for God simply to abolish pain rather than to share it. Pain exists not as a proof of God's lack of concern, but because it has a place in creation significant enough that it cannot be removed without great loss. I, of course, see the effects of that loss every day in my leprosy patients. For this reason, if I held in my hand the ability to eliminate human pain, I would not exercise the right. Pain's value is too great. Rather, I lend my energies to doing all I can to help when that pain turns into suffering.

pain of other cells in the body. In that sense, Jesus has now placed himself at the receiving end of our pain, with actual consciousness of the pain we endure.

⸺

Christ did not, however, stop at identification and shared experience. I have focused on the cross, but in the resurrection that followed he transformed the nature of pain. He overthrew the powers of this world by first allowing sin to do its worst, then transmuting that act into his best. The most meaningless of all acts, his own innocent death, became the most meaningful.

The apostle Paul explored this change in a hymn at the end of Romans 8. No one can condemn us, he says, because of Christ Jesus who died and was raised to life and now is present with the Father. Now, nothing can separate us from the love of Christ, not the pains of trouble or hardship or persecution or famine or nakedness or danger or sword. No, he concludes, we are all more than conquerors through him who loved us. And then this summing-up: "For I am convinced that neither death nor life, neither angels nor demons, neither the present nor the future [time], nor any powers, neither height nor depth [space], nor anything else in all creation, will be able to separate us from the love of God that is in Christ Jesus our Lord."

This, then, is the conclusion of pain. God takes the Great Pain of the Son's death and uses it to blot up into himself all the minor pains of our own confinement on earth. Meaningless pain is absorbed.

Jesus had told his followers to "take up a cross" and follow him and to "drink of the cup" that he drinks. Paul went even further, alluding to "the fellowship of his sufferings" and to a process of filling up what is lacking in Christ's afflictions (Philippians 3:10; Colossians 1:24). He seldom missed a chance to refer to such terms as crucifixion with Christ, union with his death, sharing in his sufferings. In one passage he said explicitly, "We always carry around in our body the death of Jesus, so that the life of Jesus my also be revealed in our body" (2 Corinthians 4:10). All these fragments of mystery speak to me of the miracle that has taken place. God absorbs our own pain so that what we endure becomes a part of what he suffered and will become a part of what is resurrected in triumph and transformed into good. Following a similar train of thought, the apostle Peter concludes buoyantly, "Even angels long to look into these things" (1 Peter 1:12).

In two profoundly suggestive passages, Christ identifies with suffering people so completely that he fills their place and bears their pain. Matthew 25:35–40 shows him accepting ministry to the hungry, the thirsty, the sick, the naked, the vagrants, the prisoners, as though it were done unto him. In Acts 9:4, during Saul's blinding epiphany en route to Damascus, Jesus asks, "Saul, why do you persecute *me*?" The whips and stones directed against persecuted Christians had fallen on Jesus himself. In these cases, at least, it seems inappropriate to ask, "Why does God allow their suffering?" "Why does God allow himself to suffer?" would be closer. God's identification with our pain is that complete.

Elie Wiesel was right: in a way, God did hang on the gallows with the lightly twitching body of the young boy. God hangs on our private gallows in our own private pains. Jesus has been here in person, serving a sentence for a crime he did not commit; he is here still, receiving every sensation and making it his own.

⌐

The portion of human anatomy I have specialized in is that marvelous creation the hand. To my mind, nothing in all of nature rivals the hand's combination of strength and agility, tolerance and sensitivity. Our most wonderful activities — art, music, writing, healing, touching — are performed by hands. It is natural, then, that when I think of the Incarnation and the pain of God, I visualize the hands of Jesus Christ.

I can hardly conceive of God taking on the form of an infant, but he once had the tiny, jerky hands of a newborn, with miniature fingernails and wrinkles around the knuckles and soft skin that had never known abrasion or roughness. "The hands that had made the sun and stars," says Chesterton, "were too small to reach the huge heads of the cattle." And too small to change his own clothes or put food in his mouth. God, too, experienced infant helplessness.

Since I have worked as a carpenter, I can easily imagine the hands of the young Jesus as he learned the trade in his father's shop. His skin must have developed calluses and rough spots and tender spots. He felt pain gratefully, I am sure. (Carpentry is a precarious profession for my leprosy patients who lack the warning of pain that allows them to use tools with sharp edges and rough handles.)

And then there were the hands of Christ the physician. The Bible tells us strength flowed out of them when he healed people. He chose not to perform miracles *en masse*, but rather one by one, touching each person he healed. He touched eyes that had long since dried out, and suddenly they admitted light and color. He touched a woman with a hemorrhage, knowing that by Jewish law she would make him unclean. He touched people with leprosy — people no one else would touch in those days. As he did so, people could feel something of the divine spirit coming through. In small and personal ways, Jesus' hands were setting right what had been disrupted in his beloved creation.

The most important scene in Jesus' life also involved his hands. Then, those hands that had done so much good were taken, one at a time, and pierced through with a thick spike. My mind balks at visualizing it.

I have spent my life cutting into hands, delicately, with scalpel blades that slice through one layer of tissue at a time, to expose the marvelous complex of nerves and blood vessels and tiny bones and tendons and muscles inside. I have been on treasure hunts inside opened hands, searching for healthy tendons to reattach in order to free up fingers that have been useless for twenty years. I know what crucifixion must do to a human hand.

Executioners of that day drove their spikes through the wrist, right through the carpal tunnel that houses finger-controlling tendons and the median nerve. It is impossible to force a spike there without crippling the hand into a claw shape. Jesus had no anesthetic. He allowed those hands to be marred and crippled and destroyed.

Later, his weight hung from them, tearing more tissue, releasing more blood. There could be no more helpless image than that of a God hanging paralyzed from a tree. "Heal yourself!" the crowd jeered. He had saved others — why not himself? The disciples, who had hoped he was the Messiah, cowered in the darkness or drifted away. Surely they had been mistaken — this figure could not be God.

Finally, in one last paroxysm of humanness, Jesus said simply, "Father, into your hands I commit my spirit." The humiliation of the Incarnation ended. The sentence was served.

But that is not the last glimpse we have of Jesus' hands in the biblical record. He appears again, in a closed room, where Thomas is still doubting the unlikely story he thinks his friends have concocted. People do not rise from the dead, he scoffs. It must have been a ghost, or an illusion. At that moment, Jesus holds up those unmistakable hands his disciples had seen perform miracles. The scars give proof that they belong to him, the One who had died on the cross. The body has changed — it can pass through walls and locked doors to join them. But the scars remain. Jesus invites Thomas to come and trace them with his own fingers.

Thomas responds simply, "My Lord and my God!" It is the first recorded time that one of Jesus' disciples calls him God directly. Significantly, the assertion comes in response to Jesus' wounds.

Why did Christ keep his scars? He could have had a perfect body, or no body, when he returned to splendor in heaven. Instead he carried with him remembrances of his visit to earth. For a reminder of his time here, he chose scars. That is why I say God hears and understands our pain, and even absorbs it into himself — because he kept those scars as a lasting image of wounded humanity. God has been here and has borne the sentence. The pain of humanity has become the pain of God.

# A LITANY OF
# THANKSGIVING

BY PAUL BRAND, EDITED BY PHILIP YANCEY

# DR. BRAND'S "LITANY OF THANKSGIVING"

⌐⟋

G ratitude was the one quality that most impressed me about Paul Brand. For him, the universe was God's own work of art, and the human body God's masterpiece. Long after we had published our books together, Dr. Brand kept making notes on scattered computer files: "A Litany of Thanksgiving," he called them. He meant these prayers to express more formally the spirit of gratitude and thanksgiving he felt every waking day. Dr. Brand never finished his litanies, but here in incomplete form are his final musings on the human body he knew so well. Read after his death, some seem eerily prophetic; taken together, all sum up the spirit of a man who accepted the world as a marvelous gift, to which the proper response is gratitude.

*Philip Yancey*

# Heart

I thank you, Lord, for my heart.

It has served me without resting or failing for all my years. Moment by moment and day after day my heart has pumped blood to every limb and organ of my body, supplying the nutrients that give life and energy while simultaneously cleansing my tissues of the harmful residue of their daily work. In all those years it has needed no maintenance or spare parts, no special fuel or lubrication. It has surged with power when I needed help for high exertion. It has quietly sustained me during sleep.

Grant me, O God, the grace of self-control. I must not eat so much that I accumulate unnecessary fat, increasing the work required of my heart to keep me alive and fresh enough to climb the mountains of high endeavor and the stairs of every day. Help me avoid the seduction of rich foods that narrow my arteries until my muscles cry for lack of blood. Neither let me neglect to maintain my strength, by lazily relying on cars and machines when I could as readily use my legs and arms.

Save me, Lord, from ambition that gives high place to wealth and power and prestige, that builds stress into my waking hours and robs me of restful sleep at night. Control me with your Spirit who teaches me to forgive when anger builds up, to seek forgiveness when I'm oppressed by guilt, and who bears in me the fruit of love and peace. Then shall my heart beat with the rhythm of contentment, and my whole body will know harmony and quiet joy.

When in the fullness of time the beat of my heart must falter and fail, give me this grace, dear Lord: that my response shall not be petulance that it does not last forever, but gratitude that it has served me long and well.

# SIGHT

⚊

I thank you, Lord, for the gift of sight.

Not content that I should see light and shade, you have blessed me with the ecstasy of color. A thousand beauties surround me. I think of the millions of cells lining the back of my eye, each calibrated to its own wavelength of color, each shielded from blinding light by watchful guardians that adjust the pupil size in response to changing light and shade. You designed living lenses, crystal-clear, flexible, and guided by tiny muscles that allow instant and precise focusing. I praise you for tears that cleanse, and for eyelids poised to blink down protection in a split-second reflex.

Lord God, I marvel that, though light never enters my brain, thousands of the finest nerves, each responsive to just one light-perceptive cell, convey images of reality into my mind, which stores them away for future retrieval. At this moment I carry around a memory bank of friends and children and grandchildren; I close my eyes and my mind re-creates the images those nerves once ushered in.

I know many people who can no longer see. If I live beyond the life span of the cells in me that sense the light, or if cataracts cloud the shining globe that gives me sight, I too shall live in shadows and depend on the eyes of those who see. Help me, dear Lord, to use these days of sight in a way that honors the gift of light. Help me to gaze at each sunset as if it were my last, to look upon scenes and friends with an artist's eye, compiling a memory bank of beauty and love. If I someday lose your gift of sight, these same images may return and beautify my inner life when all outside falls dark.

And while I see, may my guiding hand be quick to help the one who falters because his world is dark, to share with others the benefits of the gift of sight.

# HEARING

I thank you, Lord, for the sense of hearing.

Deep in the dense bone of the base of my skull, protected from vibration and from heat, you have placed rows of tiny hairs that bend to the movement of the fluid that bathes them. Each hair vibrates to the frequency of just one wavelength of sound. Too fragile to be exposed to the hurly-burly of the outside world, they feel vibrations filtered through canals and mediated by tiny guardian instruments of bone.

Music and voices come to me without effort, awakening without my conscious thought memories of sounds and of speech. I hear an echo of a concert from long ago, or recollect a person long forgotten whose face suddenly springs to mind, roused by a tone of voice or a lilt of laughter that calls up a remembrance stored in the web of nerves that will live as long as I shall live. The design that makes such wonder come to life lies beyond the fathoming of science, but God forbid that I should revel in the ecstasy of music and the joy of sound without giving thanks to you, my Lord.

A capacity to hear sufficient to warn me of danger and protect my life is all I might have asked, dear Lord, but I have joy far beyond that need. For the sound of rushing water, singing birds, and the quiet whisper of a friend, I thank you now. Grant me the wisdom to guard this gift well and to be content with sound enough to hear and yet not to blast my eardrums and shatter the finest hairs with sound amplified beyond nature. Teach me to love the silence of open spaces, the distant cry of the loon, and the soft sounds of falling night that lull me to sleep, knowing that my hearing never sleeps but remains alert to awaken me to danger or to the chorus of the dawning day.

You have given, too, an extra gift beyond that of my sense of hearing: the ability to listen. My open ears have no way to shut out sound that comes their way. But at the level of my mind I can and do shut out noise and talk, and even calls for help, that I do not want to hear. Grant, oh Lord, that I may tune my hearing mind to detect the human voice that needs a listening ear.

To listen is my gift to give. To a soul who has lost hope, whose way ahead is dark, whose sense of worth has fallen and is too weak to rise, I have a way to bring back hope. I can let them know that someone cares. The simple statement of their fear may be all they need, because now it has been shared, and they are not alone. Help me, Lord God, to listen to your lonely child and so express my thanks to you for ears to hear.

# MIND

⌐

I thank you, Lord, for my mind.

In the darkness and silence within my skull rests a soft, white substance that appears to have neither form nor structure. It floats, gently pulsating, in a fluid that serves to cushion it from vibration and any jarring movement of my head. A surgeon, probing this tissue, finds no resistance to his knife. A fingertip may crush the fragile texture and break the thin walled vessels that keep the blood flowing to this realm of thought.

Yet I know that when my brain is viewed with clear and magnified perception, its tiny cells stand out. Then a whole new universe appears, one that staggers all imagination. In numbers like the stars, the living cells within my brain link to each and every other cell along lively wires that crisscross the interspace in what may seem a hopeless tangle. To me however, to the "I" that lives inside that bony box, that tangle of wires carries the hum of harmonious messages that all have meaning and that are distinct and clear.

Every cell in my body has a place and function all its own, and each belongs to a limb or organ represented in my head. The mind keeps track of every action, every stress, and every pain. When I am hiking, with my senses tuned to guide my limbs along a narrow path, or when all my conscious thought is directed toward one decision, even then a billion sequestered cells quietly keep track of how often my eyelids blink and when my bladder needs to void. So in my brain my mosaic body comes together and every part knows that it is not alone.

My brain gets energy and lives by nourishment that has been selected by the eyes, gathered by the hands, eaten by the mouth, then dissolved, transformed, and carried to the brain by a multitude of organs, the process ending when a blood cell meets a twig of nerve. In gratitude, the eyes and hands, the mouth and heart are served and are governed by the cells within the brain that make the human body truly one, and whole.

But my mind, oh Lord, is so much more than the sum of all its parts. I only have to stop and think. When my eyes are closed and all my limbs are still, when in the silence of the dawn my mind runs free, the mists of time can rise and blow away. Then my thoughts take me back in time and I become a child again, playing and laughing again with children now long dead and building sand castles on a beach that has been washed by tides of ages past. Unlimited by space, my mind can speed and visit loved ones far away, and in a way I cannot understand, can sometimes feel their need or sorrow while I pray.

And sometimes my mind takes wing and flies to times ahead. I dream and see new vistas that have never been. I have ideas and know what I should do, to overcome a problem or to build anew some project that, for lack of vision, has languished until now.

My mind, oh Lord, is the true meeting place between the human and divine. Within my skull and in between my thinking cells stands the threshold of the temple of my God. There also lies the battleground between the good I desire to do and the evil that I need deny. I must struggle to prevent the daily interaction of my wondrous neurons from becoming the total substance of my conscious life; I dare not live and die with no thought that rises higher than my flesh. Fill me, Lord, with thoughts of truth that you inspire. May my mind dwell on things of beauty and of good report; lift me above those that will debase; make me daily aware that I am made for your glory, and that in the seeking of that fulfillment lies real ecstasy of body, mind, and spirit.

# PAIN

I thank you, Lord, for pain.

For most of every day, Father, I live in total unawareness of thy gift of pain. It does not burden me or weigh me down. And yet sensors stand alert in every limb and organ that I have, ready to interrupt or change my course when they perceive some threat or harm. Pain in my stomach informs me when I've eaten wrong; my bladder speaks when I have waited too long to empty it.

Pain sometimes interrupts what I want to do. When my eye demands attention to a speck of grit, all the while blinking and weeping tears to wash away the invader, all my plans must wait until my eye feels safe and pain, receding, tells me I am free again. I dare not resent those minutes stolen from my day; rather, I should be grateful for my clear and fragile eyes, preserved for all my life by a pain system that knows tiny wounds or scratches may lead to blindness.

Pain allows me to exert myself, to tense my muscles within a pound of breaking stress as joyfully I leap from rock to rock across a mountain stream. Then pain restrains me with a warning cry that tells me to slow down or risk some harm. And when I sleep and rest my body, compressing portions of my skin twixt bone and bed, pain sensors stay awake to whisper to my brain, "It's time you turned." I need not wake or lose my sleep, but shift my limbs so all members contentedly take turn.

For most of every day pain whispers its advice. And when with thoughtless zeal I move in danger zones, or when a wounded limb needs rest so it can heal, then pain in sharp crescendo screams an agonizing plea that dominates all action and all thought. Give me grace, oh Lord, not only to obey the shrill command but even to be thankful for the hurt that keeps me whole, for the fetters which allow me to be free.

Even as I sense the need of my own body parts, and slow my pace to give them healing rest, so too may I reach out to feel the needs of others: visitors in my home, my office staff, patients in their pain. May my nerves of sensitivity extend beyond the boundaries of my own skin so that I feel their pain as well. Then I will know that my wondrous nervous system is designed as part of wider consciousness, and never knows fulfillment until it opens wide to human need around and to inspiration from above.

So I give thanks, Creator Lord,
For pain I once despised.
I've learned to listen, gratefully,
most times my body speaks to me.
It speaks in phrases you prepared, inscribed in DNA,
and follows rules that make for health if only I obey.
While I rejoice at all the good my senses do for me,
I pray for those whose pain defense has broken under stress.
When injury or creeping ills yield pain beyond control;
Then, Lord, reach out your loving hands,
scarred with pain you suffered willingly,
Lift them now and bear them up in fellowship with Thee.
Though mortal flesh may be in strife,
Your peace may fill their conscious life,
from suffering set free.

# Immune System

⌐

I thank you, Lord, for my immune system.

I am surrounded. All about me lurk myriad forms of life, most too small to see but many all too willing to invade my body, there to multiply and feed upon me until I can no longer live. With every breath I carry scores of them into my lungs. My mouth is an open gate which, though I try to eat clean food, admits more of these parasites that would prey upon me.

But, Lord, you made me for this perilous world. You knew the hazards of our life on earth, and even risked your Son to live in human flesh and encounter these germs. The insects that bite me bit you too; mosquitoes sucked your blood, and no doubt left behind the deadly invaders. That Jesus Christ survived these germs was due, not to special intervention from on high, but to the wonder of the warrior cells you prepared to fight for all mankind.

Great God of Providence, I contemplate the gift of cells who live and sacrifice and die for me, patrolling every part of every limb, both day and night. Marching through my fingertips, rushing through my heart, watching over the air that sweeps through my lungs — they stand where they are needed, my devoted ones, billions of my living cells each one pledged to me.

Each cell knows its special skill, and knows its enemy. They do battle everywhere, before I know my need of them. Most of my sicknesses, they cure before I feel them. Sometimes I feel a tender spot. I look and see a swelling, and then I know that under that reddened skin, battle lines are forming. I feel grateful for the throbbing pain, for the inflammation that causes it assures me I'm being defended.

I wait until a bead of pus tells me the battle has ended. I cannot wipe that pus away without recognizing it is made of my own cells that sacrificed, for me, their lives. In dying they took with them millions of germs set on destroying me. I live because they died. Now thousands more take up the task, closing ranks behind them, new cells born in my bone marrow that have the same loyalty as the old cells as well as extra skill learned from their ancestors' battles.

Part of the wonder of my defenses is that they work without my conscious direction or help. But the system God has made for human health works best if we pursue the path of discipline that he designed for full enjoyment of our human frames. Keep me faithful, Lord, in the way that I live, so I may expect harmony of my own cells within my body.

There are those today who suffer and who die because they have lost their immune cells, destroyed by the virus associated with AIDS. Grant me the grace of love and compassion for them. Let not either fear or a judgmental spirit hinder me from recognizing their need of help and their need of Thee.

One day I shall experience a sickness that is unto death. I shall sense my mortal frame has no more strength to fight and that my pathway is leading into the valley of the shadow. Let me not feel the despair of one who is losing a battle, or that a triumph of evil is ahead. Focus within me, oh Lord, the light of your eternal Spirit. Show me again that my body, for all its wonder, is but the mantle of a greater wonder, my spirit and my soul.

Hold me, Lord, in such awareness of your presence and your love that my parting from my body shall be but the opening of a more vivid intimacy and union with the spirit of my Savior. May my last thought be not of regret that I have no more time, but of gratitude that I have had so long to enjoy such a wonderful life. Then he who has been the inspiration of my stumbling body shall be the very light and substance of my soul.

# PAUL WILSON BRAND
# TIMELINE

1914: On July 17, Paul is born to Jesse Mann Brand and Evelyn Harris Brand in Ootacamund, South India.

1916: On December 19, sister Connie is born in Sendamangalan, South India.

1920: Ruth is adopted into family; the senior Brands see first conversions in hill tribes.

1923: Paul, nine, and Connie, six, begin schooling in England.

1929: Jesse Mann Brand dies due to blackwater fever, a complication of malaria.

1930–1935: Paul works in England as a building apprentice.

1935: Takes course at Livingstone Medical School as part of missionary training.

1936: Prepares for missionary service at Missionary Training Colony.

1937–1943: Attends University College, London, and University College Medical School.

1943: Graduates with MD equivalent. On May 29, marries Margaret Elizabeth Berry.

1944: Son Christopher is born.

1946: Daughter Jean is born. In December, Paul arrives in India ("for one year").

1947: Paul spends one day a week in Chingleput learning about leprosy at Dr. Cochrane's hospital. Persuades Christian Medical College Hospital in Vellore to set aside a few beds for leprosy patients; works on their hands. Founds New Life Center to teach leprosy patients a trade. In June, Margaret, Christopher, and Jean join Paul in India.

1948: Daughter Mary is born.

1950: Daughter Estelle is born. International study tour sponsored by Rockefeller Foundation Fellowship.

1952: Paul delivers Hunterian Lecture before Royal College of Surgeons on "The Reconstruction of the Hand in Leprosy."

1953: Schieffelin Leprosy Research and Training Centre opens about fourteen miles from Vellore.

1954: Daughter Patricia is born. Margaret specializes in eye work, via eye camps studies leprosy patients with eye problems.

1957: Daughter Pauline is born. The Brands begin final five year term in India.

1960: Paul receives Albert Lasker Award for outstanding leadership and service in the field of rehabilitation.

1961: Appointed Principal of Christian Medical College.

1962: Queen Elizabeth awards Paul Commander of the British Empire.

1963: The Brands move to United Kingdom. Margaret makes presentation on eye problems in leprosy at the International Leprosy Association meeting in Rio de Janeiro.

1964: Paul delivers second Hunterian Lecture, "The Reconstruction of the Foot."

1965: Helps establish ALERT (the All Africa Leprosy and Rehabilitation Training Center) near Addis Ababa, Ethiopia.

1966: The Brands move to Carville, Louisiana, to serve U.S. Public Health Service.

1974: Evelyn Harris Brand ("Granny Brand") dies.

1977: Receives the Damian-Dutton Award for outstanding contributions in prevention of disabilities due to leprosy. Awarded U.S. Surgeon General's Medallion for contributions to rehabilitation.

1981: The United States Department of Health and Human Services awards Paul its "Distinguished Service Award."

1986: The United States Department of Health and Human Services awards Paul its "Surgeon General's Medallion."

1986: Paul elected president at the 8th ICMDA Congress, Cancun, Mexico.

1987: Paul, seventy-two, retires from medicine to write, preach, and teach. Margaret, sixty-eight, retires from active medical work. The Brands move to Seattle in November.

1993–1999: Paul becomes president of Leprosy Mission International.

2001: The Brands become U.S. citizens.

2003: The Brands celebrate their sixtieth wedding anniversary. On July 8, Paul dies of brain hemorrhaging after a fall.

# ACKNOWLEDGMENTS

In the process of writing *Fearfully and Wonderfully Made*, some twenty people gave us valuable editorial comments and suggestions, for which we are profoundly grateful. Three in particular — Harold Fickett, Elizabeth Sherrill, and Tim Stafford — offered constructive comments which led to a major restructuring of the entire manuscript. We offer special thanks to them and to our perceptive and faithful editor, Judith Markham.

For the sequel, *In His Image*, doctors Christopher Fung and Kenneth Phillips checked over medical details, and John Skillen, Tim Stafford, and Harold Fickett each made enormously helpful editorial suggestions. Typist Harriet Long imposed order on hopelessly scrawled-up drafts of the book.

# A Skeptic's Guide to Faith

*Philip Yancey,*
New York Times *Bestselling Author*

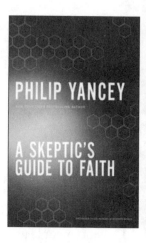

What on earth are you missing?

Philip Yancey writes: "I am where you are … an ordinary person trying to figure things out. I love, I experience beauty and pain, my friends die, I weep, I live. And as I live I try to figure out if there is a God, and what difference would that make.… This book comes out of my own search and is written on behalf of those who live outside of belief — that borderlands region between belief and unbelief."

How many times have you heard someone say, "I'm spiritual but not religious?" Or perhaps you've had that thought yourself. For some people, religious faith seems to come easily, but for others it comes in a swirl of doubts and questions.

In *A Skeptic's Guide to Faith*, Philip Yancey confronts the questions head-on, from the stance of a skeptic. He asks, "Is the visible world around us all there is?" and then examines the apparent contradictions. If this is God's world, why doesn't it look more like it? Finally, the book considers how two worlds — the visible and invisible — might affect our daily lives. Does faith really make a difference day to day?

*A Skeptic's Guide to Faith* reads like a conversation, inviting those skeptical of religion and turned off by the church to consider the possibility of an unseen world coexisting with our visible world.

According to Yancey, "A thin membrane of belief separates the natural from the supernatural."

What makes it so hard for some of us to cross that membrane?

Look inside to find out.

Softcover: 978-0-310-32502-4

*Pick up a copy today at your favorite bookstore!*

# What's So Amazing about Grace?

*Philip Yancey, Author of*
The Jesus I Never Knew

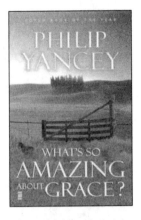

In 1987, an IRA bomb buried Gordon Wilson and his twenty-year-old daughter beneath five feet of rubble. Gordon alone survived. And forgave. He said of the bombers, "I have lost my daughter, but I bear no grudge.... I shall pray, tonight and every night, that God will forgive them."

His words caught the media's ear — and out of one man's grief, the world got a glimpse of grace.

Grace is the church's great distinctive. It's the one thing the world cannot duplicate, and the one thing it craves above all else — for only grace can bring hope and transformation to a jaded world.

In *What's So Amazing about Grace?* award-winning author Philip Yancey explores grace at street level. If grace is God's love for the undeserving, he asks, then what does it look like in action? And if Christians are its sole dispensers, then how are we doing at lavishing grace on a world that knows far more of cruelty and unforgiveness than it does of mercy?

Yancey sets grace in the midst of life's stark images, tests its mettle against horrific "ungrace."

In his most personal and provocative book ever, Yancey offers compelling, true portraits of grace's life-changing power. He searches for its presence in his own life and in the church. He asks, How can Christians contend graciously with moral issues that threaten all they hold dear?

And he challenges us to become living answers to a world that desperately wants to know, What's So Amazing about Grace?

Softcover, Gatefold: 978-0-310-24565-0

# Reaching for the Invisible God

## What Can We Expect to find?

*Philip Yancey*

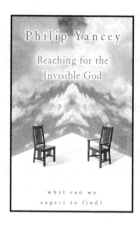

Life with God doesn't always work like we thought. High expectations slam against the reality of personal weaknesses and unwelcome surprises. And the God who we've been told longs for our company may seem remote, emotionally unavailable.

*Reaching for the Invisible God* offers deep, satisfying insights that affirm and dignify the questions we're sometimes afraid to ask. Honest and deeply personal, here is straight talk on Christian living for the man or woman who wants more than pat answers to life's imponderables. Ultimately, Yancey shifts the focus from our questions to the One who offers himself in answer. The God who invites us to reach for him—and find.

> "I love Philip Yancey's work. He is a brilliant, graceful writer."
>
> —Anne Lamott, Author, *Traveling Mercies*

> "This passionate book, unflinching in its honesty, will build your faith by helping you wrestle authentically with your doubts."
>
> —Lee Strobel, Author, *The Case for Faith*

Softcover: 978-0-310-24730-2
Study Guide: 978-0-310-24057-0

*Pick up a copy today at your favorite bookstore!*

**ZONDERVAN®**
.com

# The Jesus I Never Knew

*Philip Yancey, Author of*
What's So Amazing about Grace?

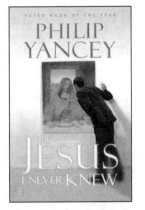

*"There is no writer in the evangelical world
that I admire and appreciate more."*
— BILLY GRAHAM

Philip Yancey helps reveal what two thousand
years of history covered up.

What happens when a respected Christian journalist decides to
put his preconceptions aside and take a long look at the Jesus described in the Gospels? How does the Jesus of the New Testament
compare to the "new, rediscovered" Jesus — or even the Jesus we
think we know so well?

Philip Yancey offers a new and different perspective on the life of
Christ and his work — his teachings, his miracles, his death and resurrection — and ultimately, who he was and why he came. From the
manger in Bethlehem to the cross in Jerusalem, Yancey presents a
complex character who generates questions as well as answers; a disturbing and exhilarating Jesus who wants to radically transform your
life and stretch your faith.

*The Jesus I Never Knew* uncovers a Jesus who is brilliant, creative,
challenging, fearless, compassionate, unpredictable, and ultimately
satisfying. "No one who meets Jesus ever stays the same," says
Yancey. "Jesus has rocked my own preconceptions and has made me
ask hard questions about why those of us who bear his name don't do
a better job of following him."

Softcover: 978-0-310-21923-1

*Pick up a copy today at your favorite bookstore!*

# The Bible Jesus Read

*Philip Yancey*

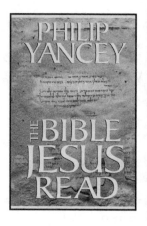

With his candid, signature style, Yancey interacts with the Old Testament from the perspective of his own deeply personal journey. From Moses, the amazing prince of Egypt, to the psalmists' turbulent emotions and the prophets' oddball rantings, Yancey paints a picture of Israel's God—and ours— that fills in the blanks of a solely New Testament vision of the Almighty.

Probing some carefully selected Old Testament books—Job, Deuteronomy, Psalms, Ecclesiastes, and the Prophets—Yancey reveals how the Old Testament deals in astonishing depths and detail with the issues that trouble us most. The Old Testament, in fact, tackles what the New Testament often only skirts. But that shouldn't surprise us. It is, after all, the Bible Jesus read.

Join Philip Yancey as he explores these sometimes shocking, often cryptic, divine writings. You will come to know God more intimately, anticipate Jesus more fervently, and find a wonderful, wise companion for your faith journey.

Softcover: 978-0-310-24566-7
Leader's Guide: 978-0-310-24184-3
Participant's Guide: 978-0-310-24185-0

*Pick up a copy today at your favorite bookstore!*

# Where Is God When It Hurts?

*Philip Yancey*

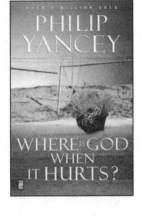

If there is a loving God, then why is it that ...?

You've heard that question, perhaps asked it yourself. No matter how you complete it, at its root lies the issue of pain.

Does God order our suffering? Does he decree an abusive childhood, orchestrate a jet crash, steer a tornado through a community? Or did he simply wind up the world's mainspring and now is watching from a distance?

In this Gold Medallion Award–winning book, Philip Yancey reveals a God who is neither capricious nor unconcerned. Using examples from the Bible and from his own experiences, Yancey looks at pain — physical, emotional, and spiritual — and helps us understand why we suffer. *Where Is God When It Hurts?* will speak to those for whom life sometimes just doesn't make sense. And it will help equip anyone who wants to reach out to someone in pain but just doesn't know what to say.

Softcover: 978-0-310-24572-8

*Pick up a copy today at your favorite bookstore!*

# Disappointment with God

## Three Questions
## No One Asks Aloud

*Philip Yancey*

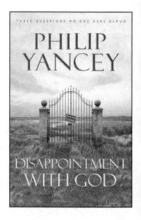

Philip Yancey has a gift for articulating the knotty issues of faith. *In Disappointment with God*, he poses three questions that Christians wonder but seldom ask aloud: Is God unfair? Is he silent? Is he hidden? This insightful and deeply personal book points to the odd disparity between our concept of God and the realities of life. Why, if God is so hungry for relationship with us, does he seem so distant? Why, if he cares for us, do bad things happen? What can we expect from him after all? Yancey answers these questions with clarity, richness, and biblical assurance. He takes us beyond the things that make for disillusionment to a deeper faith, a certitude of God's love, and a thirst to reach not just for what God gives, but for who he is.

Gatefold Softcover: 978-0-310-51781-8

*Pick up a copy today at your favorite bookstore!*